Advances in the Practice of Public Investment Management

Narayan Bulusu • Joachim Coche
Alejandro Reveiz • Francisco Rivadeneyra
Vahe Sahakyan • Ghislain Yanou
Editors

Advances in the Practice of Public Investment Management

Portfolio Modelling, Performance Attribution and Governance

palgrave
macmillan

Editors
Narayan Bulusu
Bank of Canada
Ottawa, ON, Canada

Joachim Coche
Bank for International Settlements (BIS)
Basel, Switzerland

Alejandro Reveiz
Finance Department
Inter-American Development Bank
Washington, DC, USA

Francisco Rivadeneyra
Bank of Canada
Ottawa, ON, Canada

Vahe Sahakyan
Bank for International Settlements (BIS)
Basel, Switzerland

Ghislain Yanou
World Bank
Washington, DC, USA

ISBN 978-3-030-07972-7 ISBN 978-3-319-90245-6 (eBook)
https://doi.org/10.1007/978-3-319-90245-6

Cover illustration: Andrew Paterson / Alamy Stock Photo

Printed on acid-free paper

This Palgrave Macmillan imprint is published by the registered company Springer Nature Switzerland AG
The registered company address is: Gewerbestrasse 11, 6330 Cham, Switzerland

Preface

The great financial crisis has left a large imprint on investment management. The combination of (1) a fragile recovery in the major economies and its spillover effects on global growth, (2) increased pressures on established patterns of global trade, and (3) uncertainty about the effect of an eventual unwinding of accommodative monetary policies intended to provide support to the financial system has created new challenges for investment managers, from divergent policy responses across countries to shifts in the joint dynamics of asset prices across geographies. In this environment, asset managers are challenging their commonly-accepted investment paradigms.

In particular, public investment managers are navigating the challenges posed while taking into account their unique investment rationales, risk preferences, and governance structures. For example, public investors have been called upon to re-evaluate their investment universe and the benefits of active trading strategies to be able to achieve the returns that would help meet their obligations. Further, they are also rethinking their governance structures as well as their human and technical resources to keep pace with changing management practices.

This book covers some of the latest advances in the practice of public investment management, which were presented at the 6th Public Investors Conference, jointly organised by the Bank for International Settlements, the World Bank, and the Bank of Canada. The papers presented in this edition of the premier biennial conference for public investment management, hosted at the headquarters of the World Bank in Washington, DC, contain some of the most up-to-date developments in the research and implementation of public asset management.

This book is relevant to four categories of readers: (1) practitioners of public investment management, (2) investment consultants advising public managers, (3) academics/researchers, and (4) regulatory and oversight bodies of public investors. By familiarising readers with both the state-of-the-art research dealing with, and policies adopted by, public investors, this book aims to provide the context to current public investment practice.

The book is organised into four parts, each covering one of the four major topics of interest to public investment managers. In part one, four chapters deal with the implementation, performance, and governance of foreign reserves. The first two chapters address fundamental questions of whether (and how) foreign reserves should be managed to hedge liabilities and whether a mix of active or passive investing is optimal. This is a perennial question for foreign reserves and sovereign wealth funds alike. The next two chapters deal with the governance of public investors, including a unique measure to help benchmark fund managers' performance.

The second part of the book proposes quantitative tools to tackle uncertainty in the interest-rate and credit-risk environment. The first two chapters propose frameworks to actively manage sovereign bond portfolios of (1) one country using macro variables for predicting zero-coupon yield curves and (2) multiple countries based on their exposure to interest-rate differentials across countries. The next two chapters analyse the short-term and long-term drivers of credit risk.

Part three discusses portfolio construction paradigms. The first chapter shows a method to conditionally optimise portfolios based on the prevailing macroeconomic regime. The next two chapters discuss the relative merits of the well-established paradigms of benchmark-relative, absolute-return, factor-based, and industry-based portfolio construction.

The final part of the book dives deeper, emphasising the dynamics of the major asset classes in which public investors have a significant presence. Two chapters demonstrate the effect of benchmark investors and investor clienteles on asset flows and prices, and a third analyses sources of possible diversification in asset markets that are increasingly correlated.

Taken together, we believe that the advances in the practice and theory of public investment management highlighted in this volume could not just serve as a reference to readers but could also prove to be a launchpad for future advances in the field.

This book would not have been possible without the contribution of, first and foremost, the presenters at the 6th Public Investors Conference. We are grateful for their permission to publish their original work in this volume. The editors wish to acknowledge the hospitality of the World Bank and the funding provided by the Bank for International Settlements, the World Bank, and the Bank of Canada, for making the conference possible. We thank Shengting Pan and María Margarita Sánchez, of the World Bank, for their unflinching support in organising the conference. We also thank the many participants and referees from multiple institutions, whose insightful comments greatly benefitted the authors and editors in preparing the chapters included in this book: Reena Aggarwal, Laura Alfaro, Jacob Bjorheim, Pierre Cardon, Ludwig Chincarini, Aimee Dibbens, Kevin Dunn, John Gandolfo, Scott Hendry, Jianjian Jin, Sylvain Leduc, Jorge Cruz López, Philippe Muller, Ruth Noble, Ken Nyholm, Arunma Oteh, Tommaso Perez, and Oreste Tristani. Finally, we are indebted to Tula Weiss, our Editor at Palgrave Macmillan, whose perseverance, negotiation abilities, and sage advice were essential to the publication of this book.

Ottawa, ON, Canada	Narayan Bulusu
Basel, Switzerland	Joachim Coche
Washington, DC	Alejandro Reveiz
Ottawa, ON, Canada	Francisco Rivadeneyra
Basel, Switzerland	Vahe Sahakyan
Washington, DC	Ghislain Yanou

Contents

Notes on Contributors

Santiago Alberico received his BA in Economics from Instituto Tecnológico Autónomo de México (ITAM) and his master's in Mathematical Finance from the University of Toronto in 2011. He has worked in different departments of the Markets Division at the Central Bank of Mexico, ranging from the liquidity forecasting office, domestic FX trading, G10 FX and commodities trading, and heading the asset allocation department. He is now working at the Bank of France in an exchange programme (the first of its kind) as a Fixed Income Portfolio Manager.

Jacob Bjorheim is a lecturer at the Faculty of Business and Economics at the University of Basel. He is also a Visiting Fellow with the Department of Philosophy, Logic and Scientific Method at the London School of Economics (LSE). Between 2007 and 2017, Jacob was Head of Asset Management with the Bank for International Settlements (BIS). He holds an MSc from the University of St. Gallen (Switzerland) and an MSc and a PhD from the LSE.

Marie Brière PhD, is head of the Investor Research Center at Amundi, France. She is also an affiliate professor at Paris Dauphine University and an associate researcher at the Centre Emile Bernheim at Solvay Brussels School of Economics and Management, Université Libre de Bruxelles. Her scientific articles have been published in international academic journals including the *Financial Analyst Journal*, *Journal of Banking and Finance*, *Journal of International Money and Finance*, *World Development*, and so on. She received the Markowitz Award for her article with Zvi Bodie on "Sovereign Wealth and Risk Management," published in the *Journal of Investment Management.*

Joachim Coche is Head of Financial Analysis at the BIS. This unit provides services to the BIS Banking Department and its customers in the form of analytical, technical, and advisory support, as well as information on the business activity of the department. He joined the BIS in 2007 as an Asset Management Specialist supporting central bank clients in strategic asset allocation, asset liability management, and outsourcing. Before joining the BIS, he worked for the World Bank Treasury and the European Central Bank (ECB). He has a master's and a doctorate in economics from the University of Osnabrück, Germany.

Daniel E. Diaz is an Analyst of the Research and Analysis Group at the International Investment Department of Banco de la República, the central bank of Colombia. His duties encompass research, development, and the creation of quantitative tools to support the management of Colombia's foreign reserves and sovereign wealth funds. Among the team's most relevant responsibilities is the development of quantitative tools for the asset allocation of the portfolios. He holds a BSc in Physics from Universidad Nacional de Colombia in Bogotá and is finishing an undergraduate degree in Economics and an MSc in Physics from this university.

Julián David García-Pulgarín is Professor of Financial Engineering at the Universidad Autónoma de Bucaramanga UNAB (Colombia). Prior to UNAB, he was a Senior Analyst of the Research and Analysis Group at the International Investment Department of Banco de la República, the central bank of Colombia, where his duties encompassed research, development, and the creation of quantitative tools to support the management of Colombia's foreign reserves and sovereign funds. He holds a BA in Industrial Engineering from Universidad de Antioquia (Colombia) and an MSc in Applied Mathematics with a focus on stochastic processes from EAFIT University (Colombia).

Erik Hennink is a Senior Quantitative Financial Analyst at the Scenario Modelling and Research Department of Ortec Finance, where he specializes in time series modeling for external clients. The aim of Ortec Finance is to improve financial decision-making using a combination of mathematical models, IT, and market knowledge for public investors (e.g. pension funds). Before joining Ortec Finance, Erik used to work in Rabobank International as a Quantitative Risk Analyst for the Derivatives Modelling and Research Department. He holds a master's in quantitative finance from the Erasmus University of Rotterdam.

Jianjian Jin is a Senior Analyst in the Research Division of the Funds Management and Banking Department at the Bank of Canada. His primary research interests are the impact of macroeconomy and unconventional central bank policy on returns in financial markets and investors' asset allocation. He has also worked on topics such as stochastic volatility consumption-based asset pricing models, variance risk premium puzzles and so on. Jin received his PhD in Economics from Northwestern University.

Alex Joia is Head of Portfolio Management at the Banking Department of the BIS. Prior to joining the BIS in August 2000, Alex worked at Kleinwort Benson in London. Alex graduated in physics at the University of Bristol and gained his PhD at the Department of Applied Mathematics and Theoretical Physics at Cambridge University. Alex has worked in the Basel and Hong Kong offices of the BIS and has had both client- and market-facing responsibilities.

Mark Knezevic is a Senior Asset Management Specialist at the Representative Office for Asia and the Pacific of the BIS, Hong Kong. Prior to joining the BIS in 2015, Knezevic spent ten years in the financial market areas at the Reserve Bank of Australia (RBA), which included roles in reserves management and the RBA's pension fund, and over two years at the New York representative office managing the USD and CAD components of Australia's official foreign reserves. Knezevic has a master's in Applied Finance from Macquarie University and a Professional Risk Manager (PRM) designation.

Michael G. Papaioannou is a Deputy Division Chief in the Debt and Capital Markets Instruments, Monetary and Capital Markets Department of the International Monetary Fund (IMF). While at the IMF, he served as a Special Adviser to the Governing Board of the Bank of Greece and has led numerous IMF missions on designing and implementing sovereign asset and liability management frameworks, establishing and managing sovereign wealth funds (SWFs), and developing economic and financial policies for developed and emerging economies. Prior to joining the IMF, he was a Senior Vice President for International Financial Services and Director of the Foreign Exchange Service at the WEFA Group (Wharton Econometrics Forecasting Associates) and served as Chief Economist of the Council of Economic Advisors of Greece.

He has also taught as Adjunct Associate Professor of Finance at Temple's FOX School of Business and was a Principal Research Fellow at the University of Pennsylvania, Department of Economics, LINK Central. He holds a PhD in Economics from the University of Pennsylvania and an MA in Economics from Georgetown University. He has authored or coauthored numerous books and articles in the areas of international finance and applied econometrics.

Gabriel Petre is responsible for developing asset allocation strategies for the World Bank's staff retirement fund. As part of his work, he has also been involved in advising central banks of developing countries on reserves management issues, governments from developing countries on investment policy issues related to public pension funds, and official institutions of commodity-rich countries in setting up sovereign wealth funds. He joined the World Bank Treasury in July 2006. Before, he worked for three years at the National Bank of Romania, as part of the team in charge of the foreign reserves portfolio. He has an MBA from Georgetown McDonough School of Business and is a CFA charterholder.

Cristian Porras is an Economist of the Research and Analysis Group at the International Investment Department of Banco de la República, the central bank of Colombia. His duties encompass research, development, and the creation of quantitative tools for assessing the adequacy level of foreign reserves and its currency composition. He is an Economist and a candidate for master's degree in Economics from the Universidad Externado de Colombia.

Francesco Potente has a degree in Economics and is a CFA charterholder. He has worked as a market analyst in the Investment Management Division at the Bank of Italy where, inter alia, he has contributed to studies on various portfolio management and derivative pricing issues, as well as to the development of tools for supporting the investment decision process. He has also participated in Eurosystem working groups. He has direct experience in foreign exchange market trading and portfolio management. He is an Advisor in the General Financial Supervision and Regulation Directorate.

Claudio Raddatz is the Chief of the Global Financial Stability Analysis Division in the International Monetary Fund's (IMF) Monetary and Capital Markets Department. Previously, he was the Director of Financial Policy (2014–2017) and Head of Economic Research (2011–2014) at the

Central Bank of Chile, Senior Economist at the World Bank Development Economics Research Group (2008– 2011), and Economist at the same institution (2003–2008). Mr. Raddatz has numerous academic publications in macro-financial issues. He holds a BSc and an MSc from the University of Chile and a PhD in Economics from the Massachusetts Institute of Technology (2003).

Bayasgalan Rentsendorj is a Senior Membership Manager at the International Forum of Sovereign Wealth Funds (IFSWF), based in London, England. Prior to joining IFSWF, he was a Senior Research Officer at the International Monetary Fund in Washington, DC, where he published research on SWF strategic asset allocations and managed a knowledge-sharing platform for IFSWF member SWFs. He has also worked with the Asian Development Bank and the Bank of Mongolia (The Central Bank). He received his MBA with distinction from the University of Oxford and is a graduate of Williams College in Massachusetts, where he earned an MA in Policy Economics.

Francisco Rivadeneyra is a Research Advisor in the Funds Management and Banking Department at the Bank of Canada. His research overlaps payments and financial economics. His payments research focuses on the implications of recent technological innovations for central bank mandates and the development of computational tools to measure risk and efficiency of payments systems. His financial economics work focuses on tools for the management of domestic debt and foreign reserves portfolios. He holds a PhD in Economics from the University of Chicago.

Marco Ruíz is the Head of foreign reserves at Banco de la República, the central bank of Colombia. In this position, he is responsible for the investment of the country's foreign reserves and sovereign wealth funds. Before becoming the Head of the department, he worked in the portfolio management team, first as a Senior Portfolio Manager and later as the Deputy Head of portfolio management. Mr. Ruiz holds a BA in Economics from Universidad de los Andes in Bogotá and an MBA from New York University's Stern School of Business. Marco is a CFA charterholder.

Vahe Sahakyan joined the BIS in 2008 as an Asset Management Specialist supporting BIS internal committees and central bank clients in strategic and tactical asset allocation, asset liability management, and outsourcing. Before joining the BIS, he worked for the World Bank and the Central

Bank of Armenia and taught econometrics and financial market microstructure at the Universitat Pompeu Fabra. Vahe holds several titles: PhD in Mathematical Methods (Yerevan State University), PhD candidate in Quantitative Finance (University of Zurich), MA in Economics (Central European University), and MSc in Finance (Universitat Pompeu Fabra).

Antonio Scalia PhD, is Deputy Head of the Market Operations Directorate at the Bank of Italy and a member of the Market Operations Committee of the ECB. Previously, he has been Head of the Risk Management Division at the Bank of Italy, a consultant in technical assistance missions of the World Bank-IMF in Central Europe, and an expert in working groups of the BIS. His scientific articles have been published in international academic journals including *Journal of International Money and Finance*, *Review of Finance*, *Journal of Empirical Finance*, and *Journal of Fixed Income*.

Sergio L. Schmukler is the Lead Economist at the World Bank's Development Research Group. His research area is international finance and international financial markets and institutions. He obtained his PhD in Economics from the University of California at Berkeley in 1997. He is a member of the Money and Finance Research Group and Treasurer of the Latin America and Caribbean Economic Association. He has visited several central banks and institutions, taught at the of University of Maryland, worked at the IMF Research Department, worked as Associate Editor of the Journal of Development Economics, and has participated in several other editorial boards.

Robert Scott has been with the Official Institutions team at Schroders since 2008 responsible for training, advisory, research, and relationship management with official institutions around the world. Previously he spent ten years at the Bank for International Settlements (BIS), as Head of Portfolio Management, having earlier served in the Monetary and Economics Department and Portfolio Management of the BIS. He started his investment career in 1994 at Bank Credit Analyst Research Group as Quantitative Analyst and later as Editor of the BCA Fixed-Income Strategist. Education—CFA designation in 2003; BComm (Finance), BA (Philosophy) Dalhousie University, Canada; MSc. Finance Concordia University, Canada.

Jesús Sierra is Director at the Emerging Risks and Data Analytics Department at the Canada Deposit Insurance Corporation (CDIC), where he oversees the stresstesting of small and medium-sized banks. His current research focuses on Exchange Traded Funds' performance from a risk-management point of view. His previous research studied the impact of international capital flows on bond risk premia, the macroeconomic determinants of flows into mutual funds and the drivers of time variation in active risk exposures of fixed-income portfolios. He was previously Principal Researcher at CDIC and a Senior Analyst at the Bank of Canada. He holds a PhD from the University of Southern California.

Olga Sulla is a Senior Finance Officer with QSA Department at the World Bank Treasury. She performs strategic asset allocation, leads analysis on fixed income and equity for internal and external clients, and develops diversification strategies for portfolios of central banks' FX reserves. Prior to this, Olga worked extensively on private sector and financial markets development in East Asia, Europe, Africa, and Latin America, as well as at the IMF's Western Hemisphere Department as a Senior Economist. Olga started her career at the Bank of Israel's monetary policy and capital markets department and published in economics and finance, including in macroeconomics modeling.

Ariane Szafarz is a professor of finance at Université libre de Bruxelles (ULB), Belgium, and a co-director of the Centre for European Research in Microfinance (CERMi). She holds a PhD in Mathematics and currently works on financial markets and banking. She published articles in, for example, *European Economic Review*, *Journal of Banking and Finance*, *Journal of Business Ethics*, *Journal of Empirical Finance*, *Journal of International Money and Finance*, and *Review of Finance*. Her co-authored article "Selectivity and Transparency in Social Banking: Evidence from Europe" received the 2016 Warren Samuels Prize awarded at the ASSA Meetings by the Association for Social Economics.

Marcelo Yoshio Takami has worked at the Banco Central do Brasil (BCB) since 2003 and is currently responsible for the credit risk management of the BCB. He was formerly a visiting fellow at the Bank for International Settlements (BIS). Dr. Takami graduated in Computer Engineering and holds a PhD in Economics from the University of Sao Paolo. He has published a number of articles about financial risk and financial stability.

Daniel Vela Barón is a Financial Officer at the Quantitative Solutions, Strategic Asset Allocation, and Analytics Department (QSA) in the World Bank Treasury, where he specializes in risk modeling and strategic asset allocation for internal and external clients. Before joining the World Bank, Daniel used to work in Banco de la República (Central Bank of Colombia) as a Senior Quantitative Analyst for the International Investments Department. He holds a Master of Finance from MIT, an MS in Engineering, and a BS in Industrial Engineering from Universidad de Los Andes. He is an FRM and CFA® charterholder.

Tomás Williams is Assistant Professor of International Finance at George Washington University in Washington, DC. His main fields of research are International Finance, Financial Economics, and Empirical Banking. He has a special interest in financial intermediaries and how they affect international capital flows and economic activity. More specifically, he has been working on how the use of well-known benchmark indexes by financial intermediaries affects both financial markets and real economic activity.

Omar Zulaica is Asset Management Specialist at the BIS. His responsibilities include providing reserve management advisory to central banks and supporting the Bank's asset management activities, such as the enhancement of the investment process and strategic asset allocation—all with special focus on the quantitative framework. He was formerly Head of Strategic Asset Allocation at the Central Bank of Mexico and before that Head of Tactical Asset Allocation. His academic credentials are a BSc in Actuarial Science from Instituto Tecnológico Autónomo de México (ITAM)—where he worked as part-time professor—and an MSc in Financial Economics from the University of Oxford in the United Kingdom; he graduated from both with awards.

List of Figures

List of Tables

PART I

Foreign Reserves Management Strategies: Implementation, Performance and Governance

CHAPTER 1

Hedging Potential Liabilities of Foreign Reserves Through Asset Allocation

Daniel E. Diaz, Julián David García-Pulgarín, Cristian Porras, and Marco Ruíz

1.1 Introduction

The purpose of this chapter is to explore further the topic of asset-liability management (ALM) for foreign reserves. Although several central banks use ALM to determine the asset allocation of the foreign reserves, mostly they do so in order to cover defined liabilities such as government or central bank debt. However, most countries hold foreign reserves as a buffer for a substantial shock to the balance of payments, which includes private and public sector flows. For instance, foreign reserves may help reduce the impact of large, potentially disruptive portfolio outflows from the equity and bond market on the rest of the economy. Therefore, in our opinion, ALM for foreign reserves should take into consideration all of the relevant macroeconomic vulnerabilities that might affect the balance of payments.

This chapter proposes an approach to quantify and to hedge those liabilities, using data from Colombia as an illustration. The chapter seeks to contribute to the ALM discussion by defining the liabilities of foreign

D. E. Diaz • J. D. García-Pulgarín • C. Porras • M. Ruíz (✉)
Banco de la República, Bogotá, Colombia
e-mail: mruizgil@banrep.gov.co

N. Bulusu et al. (eds.), *Advances in the Practice of Public Investment Management*, https://doi.org/10.1007/978-3-319-90245-6_1

reserves and their volatility, not only to determine the size of the liquidity tranche but also to find the portfolio that most appropriately hedges those liabilities. As a result, both the currency composition and the allocation of the portfolio across different asset classes depend on their ability to hedge the unique liabilities of each country. In the same fashion as Bonza et al. (2010) and Alhumaidah (2015), this chapter proposes a two-tranche approach. For the asset-liability tranche, a country-specific reserve adequacy measure is used to proxy for the liabilities of reserves, and the objective of portfolio construction is to hedge those liabilities. Hence, the size of the asset-liability tranche should be roughly the same as that of the liabilities. For the long-term investment tranche, whose size is determined by the excess of total reserves over liabilities, a traditional asset-only approach aims for wealth maximization, given that the likelihood of liquidating this tranche in the short term is theoretically low.

The next section summarizes relevant literature on ALM for international reserves portfolios. The third section reviews the work on reserve optimality and reserve adequacy and explains in detail the measure chosen to quantify the liabilities of foreign reserves. The fourth section explains the methodology and the fifth section describes the data and the sources. The sixth section shows the results. The seventh section concludes.

1.2 Asset-Liability Management in International Reserves Portfolios

The last two decades have seen a growing trend in international reserve accumulation in most countries around the world (Berkelaar et al. 2010), which has caused a great interest in strategic asset allocation (SAA) for international reserve portfolios, considering that SAA is the main source of return and risk for any kind of portfolio (Brinson et al. 1986).

There are two widely-used approaches to asset allocation: asset-only optimization (AO) and ALM. In the former, the purpose is to obtain the highest possible return for an acceptable level of risk, regardless of the liabilities (outflows of future money, both expected and unexpected, if they exist). By contrast, the ALM approach explicitly takes into account future cash flows or obligations and constructs portfolios that reduce the volatility of the difference between the present value of the liabilities and that of the assets.

Cash flow matching is the most traditional and conservative ALM methodology (Fabozzi 2007). It attempts to match liability cash flows with coupon and principal payments of fixed income assets in the portfolio. Risk matching or immunization is the other traditional ALM methodology. Its objective is to match the interest rate and liquidity risks of liabilities with those of the assets. Immunization outperforms cash flow matching when it is not possible to find assets in the financial market that pay cash flows identical to those of the liabilities.

The ALM approach is extensively used in defined-benefit pension plans, whose objective is to cover future pension cash flows through contributions and returns from the pension portfolio and to maximize the surplus once the projected liabilities are funded. Banks also apply ALM to construct a portfolio that replicates the duration of their liabilities.

In the case of foreign reserves management, the choice between AO and ALM depends on the specific objective of the central bank. When a central bank has a broad mandate such as reducing the probability of occurrence of balance of payments crises or when the liabilities are difficult to estimate, the AO approach is preferred. On the other hand, when the central bank has well-defined liabilities that it wants to hedge, for instance, government or central bank debt, the preferred approach is ALM.

In recent years, there have been a number of studies applying ALM to the construction of foreign reserve benchmarks and an increasing number of countries have adopted this approach. In the case of Canada (Rivadeneyra et al. 2013), international reserves are managed using an ALM framework that requires currency and duration matching of international reserves and foreign currency liabilities issued. The model jointly optimizes the mix of assets and liabilities across currencies, instruments, and tenors that maximize the return of the portfolio subject to duration and currency matching. Canada's foreign exchange reserves are financed by the federal government. Further, the primary objective of foreign reserves in Canada is to help to promote orderly conditions for the Canadian dollar in currency exchange markets and provide foreign currency liquidity to the government. Thus, the appropriate liability is defined by the debt instruments issued to finance the reserves account. As a result, applicability of the ALM approach is straightforward.

According to Bhattacharya et al. (2010), the Reserve Bank of India incorporates an ALM model that consists of a balance sheet for each currency separately, allowing for currency transfers and incorporating transaction costs. The market prices of the assets come from a dynamic stochastic optimization model with a tree-based uncertainty structure, where the central bank can hold or sell the assets in any future rebalancing period. The model also incorporates the liabilities and risk preferences of the central bank as Conditional Value-at-Risk (CVaR) constraints. The liabilities are factored into the optimization problem by including (1) a lower limit on the size of reserves, (2) a lower limit on the ratio of Net Foreign Assets (NFA) to the sum of NFA and Net Domestic Assets (NDA), (3) an upper limit on the percentage fall in value of reserves in any period, (4) a lower bound on the expected mark-to-market value of reserves, (5) an upper limit on the Liquidity at Risk[1] of the assets, (6) a constraint that foreign currency assets should exceed the amortization of external debt over the next 12 months (Greenspan-Guidotti rule), and (7) a constraint that the ratio of short-term external debt to reserves should not exceed a pre-set level.

For the Latin American case, Bonza et al. (2010) approach SAA by balancing short-term liquidity needs and real capital preservation for central banks, considering robust optimization techniques. A contingent claim analysis is used to estimate short-term liquidity needs. They also estimate a distance-to-liquidity-crisis indicator. The SAA attempts to preserve real capital, assuming that reserve requirements will grow at the same rate as real GDP. Under this proposal, the investment objective of excess liquidity reserves is to obtain a real return equal to the growth rate of real GDP, considering that the estimated probability of a liquidity event is quite low.

Alhumaidah (2015) proposes the standard two-tranche approach for reserve management for the Saudi Central Bank, which separates the portfolio into liquidity and investment tranches. He defines the level of the liquidity tranche as the equivalent of predicted reserve outflows, exogenously derived from a forecasting equation. The proposal allocates excess reserves to an investment tranche, which is managed with the objective of maximizing a utility function that incorporates the amount and likelihood of stochastic outflows as a liability, while also allowing for variable trade sizes by specifying that liquidation costs grow in a non-linear way. Although this chapter takes into account the liability by including the liquidation costs in the investment tranche's utility function, its aim is not directly to hedge potential outflows through asset allocation.

1.3 Measuring Reserve Adequacy

The liquidity required during periods of balance of payments crises represents the potential liabilities of foreign reserves. Academic approaches on the liquidity needs of central banks have had two methodological perspectives: the optimal level of reserves and the indicators of reserve adequacy.

Calculating an optimal level of reserves requires a cost-benefit analysis. Among the benefits of maintaining international reserves is the reduction in the probability of an external crisis, which is costly due to foregone production or consumption. In this sense, an optimal level of reserves makes the economy more stable and less vulnerable to external crises (Gerencia Técnica 2012). On the other hand, there is an opportunity cost of holding foreign reserves, which comes from the fact that they are invested in low-risk liquid assets which have a lower expected return than other alternatives such as developing local infrastructure or, in the case of emerging markets, paying down external debt. The models used to determine the optimal level of international reserves have followed this sort of analysis since the pioneering work of Heller (1966). Ben-Bassat and Gottlieb (1992) formulated a model where international reserves reduce the probability of a balance of payments or a currency crisis. In this framework, the level of international reserves is optimal when the accumulation of additional foreign currency reduces the expected cost to a lesser extent than the opportunity cost incurred to hold them. Jeanne (2007) and Calvo et al. (2013) have proposed the most recent methodologies on optimal levels of reserves. Jeanne proposes a model for a small open economy, where a sudden stop prevents access to international financing to meet payments on foreign debt. International reserves mitigate the negative impact on output and stabilize the consumption pattern of households. Meanwhile, Calvo et al. (2013) propose a similar model to that of Ben-Bassat and Gottlieb (1992), including the possibility that reserves can reduce both the likelihood of a foreign crisis and its cost.

Despite their enormous contribution to the academic literature, the application of optimal reserves models has several limitations (García-Pulgarín et al. 2015). The most obvious are the sensitivity of the results to small changes in the parameters and the assumption of constant external liabilities. These limitations undermine the utility of optimal reserves models to guide policymaking (Gerencia Técnica 2012).

Unlike the optimal reserves approach, reserve adequacy measures seek to determine an appropriate level of reserves, using several macroeconomic variables that might explain the outflows of the balance of payments during a crisis. The International Monetary Fund (IMF) was the first to conduct a study on reserve adequacy (International Monetary Fund 1953). The IMF staff argued that reserve adequacy was not a matter of a simple arithmetical relationship but rather that it depended on the efficiency of the international credit system, the realism of the existing pattern of exchange rates, the appropriateness of monetary and fiscal policies, the policy objectives, and the stage of development of countries. Five years later, the IMF (1958) proposed a less qualitative approach, arguing that reserves should be compared with a country's trade figures, as foreign trade was the largest item in the balance of payments. The data analysis showed that countries in general appeared to achieve annual reserve-to-imports ratios between 30 and 50%. This ratio was a preliminary indicator of adequacy. Triffin (1961) criticized this minimum benchmark (30% or 4 months of imports), arguing that it would be too low given the specific economic circumstances of countries. Triffin found that the ratio of monetary gold to imports in 1957 was the same as it was in 1913 and 1928 but, at 35–36%, this ratio was low relative to historical standards. From an examination of the distribution of the ratio between reserves and imports across countries and over time, Triffin (1961) concluded that a 40% reserve-to-import ratio could be deemed adequate for the stability of the balance of payments.

In a similar way, Greenspan (1999) cites the proposal of Pablo Guidotti, the then-Deputy Finance Minister of Argentina, who suggested that countries should manage their external assets and liabilities in such a way that they are always able to live without new foreign borrowing for up to one year. That is, usable foreign exchange reserves should exceed scheduled amortizations of foreign currency debts during the following year. This is the famous Guidotti-Greenspan rule, which states that a country's reserves should equal short-term external debt, implying a ratio of reserves to short-term debt (STD) of one. The rationale is that countries should have enough reserves to resist a massive withdrawal of short-term foreign capital.

Since these measures of reserve adequacy are unaffected by a set of strong assumptions, they become a reliable and robust indicator (García-Pulgarín et al. 2015) and therefore they are preferred by central banks for the design of economic policy (Gerencia Técnica 2012). Despite their advantages, the most important challenge raised by standard reserve adequacy measures is that an adequate level of reserves depends on rules of thumb (e.g., one in the Guidotti-Greenspan measure) and not necessarily on the particular characteristics and vulnerabilities of each country.

The IMF (2011), aware of the limitations of optimality models and the issues that arise when considering isolated indicators of reserves based on individual metrics (e.g., GDP or M2), proposed a methodology that identified four sources of vulnerability for the balance of payments. First, exports could diminish severely due to an unexpected drop in foreign demand or due to a negative terms-of-trade shock. Second, a reduction in external financing may hinder debt roll over. Third, foreign investors might retreat from domestic capital markets. Finally, there might be unforeseen domestic capital outflows from residents.

Having determined the sources of risk and vulnerability of the balance of payments, the IMF takes four variables to quantify each of those risks: exports, STD, portfolio liabilities (net international investment position minus foreign direct investment and STD), and money supply. The IMF (2015a, b) estimates a formula that takes into account all of these variables and their relative importance. To this end, they calculate the distributions of changes in each variable in periods of stress in the foreign exchange market. To identify these periods, the IMF used the methodology proposed by Eichengreen et al. (1996). The adequate level of reserves is the sum of the tenth-percentile drop in each variable over periods of stress. The IMF estimates two standard formulas whose application depends on the exchange rate regime of each country (fixed or flexible).

Gomez-Restrepo and Rojas-Bohorquez (2013) acknowledge the merits of the IMF methodology but argue that using standard weights for all countries may not accurately capture the importance of each variable for any specific country. For instance, countries that depend heavily on foreign trade and have a relatively closed capital account may need to place a higher weight on exports than on portfolio liabilities. The authors estimate the weights of the specific variables using Colombian data and find that the optimal weights for Colombia are different from those under the standard IMF formula.

García-Pulgarín et al. (2015) improve the country-specific approached proposed by Gomez-Restrepo and Rojas-Bohorquez (2013), taking into account the correlations between the variables in the formula. They incorporate the calculation of implied correlations among the variables considered, which typically results in a less conservative measure, since the worst-case scenario of each variable does not materialize simultaneously in a period of pressure in the foreign exchange market. In addition, García-Pulgarín et al. (2015) discuss some changes that could enhance the calculation of the metric. First, they replace M2 by M3, since it is a broader monetary aggregate that includes information that M2 might not capture, such as increase the risk of a bank run. Second, the authors include foreign direct investment as an additional variable because those inflows might suffer in the middle of an external crisis. Finally, they consider the dependence on remittances of some Latin American economies and include this variable to improve the calculation of the metric for the Colombian case. This methodology is explained below in more detail.

The first step is to calculate the index of pressures in the foreign exchange market according to the methodology proposed by Eichengreen et al. (1996). Accordingly, the changes of the following variables during periods of pressure in the foreign exchange market are calculated: STD, other portfolio liabilities (OPL), M3, exports (X), foreign direct investment (FDI), and remittances. The percentage of each variable that could be needed during periods of stress is estimated according to the following equation:

$$\omega_t = \left[\rho_{jt}\right] * \frac{1}{\sum_{j=1}^{6} \rho_{jt}} \tag{1.1}$$

where ω_t is the vector with the percentage of each variable that could be needed in times of crisis at time t, where ρ_{jt} is the value of each variable j. $j = 1$ corresponds to STD, $j = 2$ to OPL, $j = 3$ to X, $j = 4$ to M3, $j = 5$ to FDI and $j = 6$ to remittances.

With this, a product of the associated vectors to the percentage of each variable and the percentage changes in each variable during periods of market pressure ($M\,P$) is computed (this is done for each period considering the same sample periods of pressure), as shown below:

$$\%NARI_t = M\,P * \omega_t^T \tag{1.2}$$

$\%NARI_t$ is the ratio of adequate international reserves to total reserves for period t. After this, the percentiles for each period (of the resulting set product vectors) are calculated, and then multiplied by the aggregate level of the variables for each period:

$$NARI_t = P_{(10,5,1)}\{\%NARI_t\} * \sum_{j=1}^{6} \rho_{jt} \tag{1.3}$$

$NARI_t$ represents the adequate level of reserves. This methodology takes into account the implicit correlations between the variables in periods of pressure, making it less conservative compared to the IMF methodology (which is of linear combination of the value of each variable needed in times of stress).

In this chapter, the contingent liabilities of foreign reserves are defined through the reserve adequacy measure, proposed by García-Pulgarín et al. (2015). This measure defines the liquidity that a central bank should hold against possible shocks that affect the outflows of the balance of payments. Additionally, based on historical information, it is possible to estimate the past behavior of this measure and, more importantly for the purpose of this chapter, its volatility.

It is worthwhile to notice that the required level of foreign reserves changes over time. Factors such as financial development, greater access to capital markets, a greater degree of openness of the capital account, and growth of world trade have resulted in higher reserve requirements, reaching annual growth rates above 12%. From an ALM perspective, it is not possible to construct a portfolio that achieves that level of return consistently. As shown in Fig. 1.1, most traditional asset classes have returns lower than 12% in the long term. Consequently, the asset-liability exercise in this chapter focuses on the variability of the potential liabilities and not

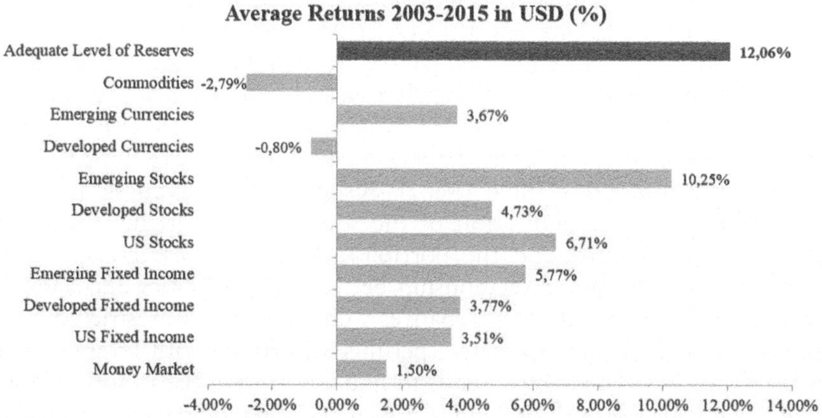

Fig. 1.1 Average annual growth of adequate level of reserves and returns of various asset classes

on their absolute level. When SAA is not sufficient to cope with increases in the level of the liabilities, it is necessary to accumulate foreign reserves, for example, by intervening in the domestic foreign exchange market, or by liquidating part of the long-term investment tranche. Building an optimal intervention rule that is consistent with the asset allocation of the portfolio is beyond the scope of this chapter.

1.4 Methodology

In order to determine the asset allocation that is most appropriate to hedge the liabilities of foreign reserves, it is important to understand what explains the behavior of the liability. Therefore, the first step in this process is to use a multi-factor risk model in order to identify the systematic factors that explain the liability. Although it is possible to work directly with asset classes in order to find the asset allocation that approximates most closely the behavior of the liability, the use of a multi-factor risk model allows the identification of the most important themes or macro variables that need to be considered when building a portfolio under this approach.

The multi-factor risk model used for fixed income is Wilshire's Axiom. This model provides historical factor returns for yield curve movements, sector allocations, inflation, and currency, among others, in the most important fixed income markets. The Appendix shows the list of factors from Axiom used in this analysis. For equity and commodity, some widely used indices are included. Through cross-sectional regression, it is possible to identify the factors with the best explanatory power.

Once the most relevant market factors are identified, the asset classes to construct the portfolio are chosen. For factors with positive coefficients, the related asset classes are included. Conversely, for factors with negative or non-significant coefficients, the related asset classes are excluded.

With the choice of eligible asset classes, portfolio construction is possible through the minimization of the squared error of the difference between the liabilities and the portfolio. Thus, portfolio construction attempts to find a linear relationship between the liabilities and various asset classes. Two portfolio alternatives were evaluated, unrestricted, and restricted. The former alternative permits a portfolio with leverage and short exposures. The latter intends to find a portfolio that is both investible and liquid. For both of them, a n asset and T periods system was used.

Year-on-year changes of liabilities and annual returns were used. The problem to solve is to find a coefficient vector w, such that:

$$\min \sum_{t=12}^{T} \left(r_t^L - \sum_{i=1}^{n} w_i r_t^i \right)^2 \tag{1.4}$$

Subject to:

$$\sum_{i=1}^{n} w_i = 1 \quad i = 1, \ldots, n \tag{1.5}$$

where r_t^L refers to annual factor returns at period *t*. The solution to this problem is a coefficient vector *w*. Under this approach, each coefficient w_i represents the weight for asset class *i* in the portfolio. Equation 1.5 ensures that the entire portfolio is fully invested.

Without additional restrictions, the solutions to the problem are able to take any value in $\mathbb{R}$. A value above one for one asset class in vector *w* requires leverage either through derivatives or short exposures in other asset classes. By contrast, a negative value for a specific allocation implies a short position either through derivatives or by borrowing and selling the securities. Although both leverage and short positions can in theory contribute to replicate better the volatility of the liabilities, it may be infeasible to do so, because of either the non-existence of certain derivatives or the unwillingness of counterparties to trade in the amounts required, particularly considering the average size of international reserves portfolios. Moreover, it is important to note that some asset classes might be relatively illiquid for large allocations, which requires the inclusion of a liquidity constraint in order to make the portfolio investible. Thus, the second portfolio alternative evaluated includes the following restrictions, where c_j is the maximum allocation to currency *j*:

$$0 \leq w_i \leq 1 \qquad \forall i \in [1, n] \tag{1.6}$$

$$\sum_{k=1}^{n_j} w_k^j \leq c_j \qquad \forall j \in [1, m] \tag{1.7}$$

Here, n_j represents the number of assets in currency *j* included in the exercise, superscript *j* in the coefficient characterizes each currency, and *m* denotes the number currencies included. Equation 1.7 is the liquidity constraint, which imposes an upper limit on the participation of the portfolio in the government fixed income assets of currency *j*. For this chapter, the maximum participation allowed in the government fixed income market of any given currency is 3%, since it may be difficult to liquidate a larger allocation in a short period. The government fixed income market was used to proxy for total liquidity in a given currency, considering that it is the largest asset class available in most cases.

For the long-term investment tranche, which represents the tranche of the portfolio that aims to maximize returns, asset-only optimization is a convenient choice. The optimization allows for a broader range of asset classes and a longer investment horizon. García-Pulgarín et al. (2015) developed a methodology to create the benchmark of the long-term investment tranche. The methodological approach follows the Black and Litterman (1991) framework with enhancements in the estimation of the covariance matrix.

The main purpose of the optimization of the long-term tranche is to maximize a utility function that considers the first two moments of each portfolio return distribution, as well as the specific risk aversion of the investor. García-Pulgarín et al. (2015) allow a broad asset space, representing most of the market, which provides a good estimate of Black-Litterman equilibrium returns. Besides, they define a non-linear constraint, which restricts the portfolios within the efficient frontier to those that do not result in losses with a 95% confidence level in a time horizon of ten years, which corresponds to the approximate period in which a crisis event happens, assuming a time homogeneous Poisson process and a sudden stop probability of 10%.

1.5 Data Description

As described in Sect. 1.2, the variables used to estimate the liquidity needs of international reserves are M3, exports, STD, OPL, FDI, and remittances. The goes back to December 2003. Data periodicity is monthly and the variables are denominated in US dollars. The data source for the chosen Colombian macroeconomic variables is Banco de la Republica.

The source of factor returns for fixed income and currency is Axiom (Wilshire Associates). For equity and commodity indices, the source is Bloomberg.

The assets classes evaluated for portfolio construction were:

1. Government bonds from one to ten years from the United States, Germany, the United Kingdom, Switzerland, Sweden, Canada, Japan, Australia, New Zealand, and Norway. A bond index of other developed countries is also included.

2. Inflation-linked government bonds from one to ten years from the United States, Germany, and the United Kingdom.
3. Corporate bonds from one to ten years in the United States and Europe.
4. Supranational bonds of developed markets from one to ten years.
5. US mortgage-backed securities.
6. Equities from the United States, from developed countries excluding the United States, and from emerging markets.
7. The following currencies: Euro, British Pound, Swiss Franc, Swedish Krona, Canadian Dollar, Japanese Yen, Australian Dollar, and New Zealand Dollar.

The returns of fixed income assets are obtained from the Intercontinental Exchange (ICE) Data Indices. Data on the returns of stocks and currencies are obtained from Bloomberg. All of the series start in December 2003 and end in December 2015, since all the data necessary to estimate the liabilities are only available from the last month of 2003 onwards. Price and return data of the selected assets are denominated in US dollars, because the liability is also denominated in that currency as intervention from central bank of Colombia is always made in US dollars.

1.6 Estimation and Results

Figure 1.2 shows the set of factors from Axiom's multi-factor model that best explains the liabilities of Colombia's foreign reserves.

The factors with the highest positive coefficients are European corporate and duration in Australia and in the United States. It is important to remember that, since we are dealing with factors and not with asset classes, in the case of the European corporate factor, it is necessary to hold exposure to this type of debt isolated from European duration, which it may be difficult to implement in practice. In the case of the exposure to United States duration, it shows that interest rates in the United States move in the opposite direction of the liabilities. One possible explanation of this observation is that increases in interest rates in the United States cause outflows from emerging markets, which could cause decreases in monetary aggregates such as M3 or OPL, thus decreasing the reserve adequacy measure used in this chapter. This finding is consistent with the high participation of US Treasuries in foreign reserves portfolios.

Additionally, in order to hedge the liability better, it would be necessary to take short positions in duration in Japan and Switzerland and in inflation

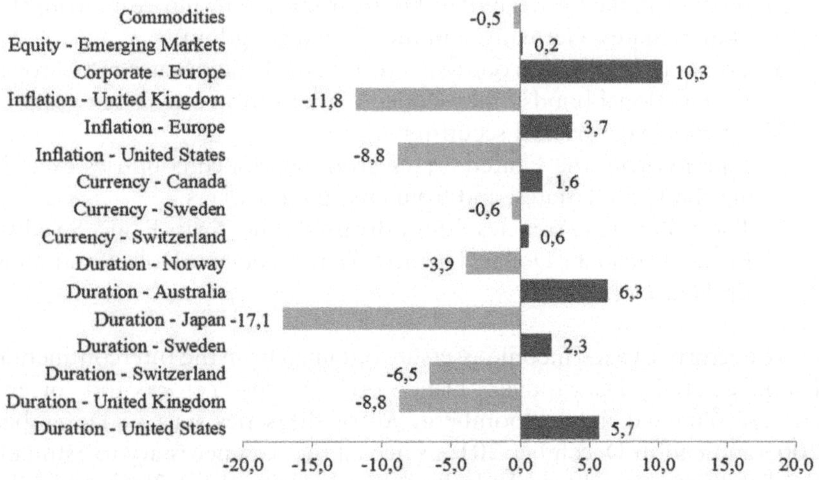

Fig. 1.2 Explanatory factors for the liability (reserve adequacy measure)

in the United Kingdom and in the United States. Although it may be difficult to implement short positions in those markets, particularly in the case of the inflation factors, the results indicate that certain traditional reserve assets may not be the best choice for the investment of foreign reserves of certain countries, once its correlation with the liabilities is considered.

One limitation of the current approach is that it is not possible to understand all of the reasons that explain the positive and negative relationships between the liabilities and the market factors, which should be the subject of further study. Notwithstanding, the factor analysis of the liabilities allows the identification of asset classes that are related to foreign reserves from an ALM perspective.

Figure 1.3 shows a comparison between the liabilities (reserve adequacy measure) and the combination of factors shown in Fig. 1.2. Both series have a similar behavior, with a 68% coefficient of determination.

Although the information on the most relevant market factors helps in portfolio construction, it is difficult to come up with an investible portfolio that has exposures to the factors matching those in presented in Fig. 1.2. Nonetheless, the information obtained from the exposure to factors is useful to narrow the universe of eligible assets to those that best explain the behavior of the appropriate level of reserves.

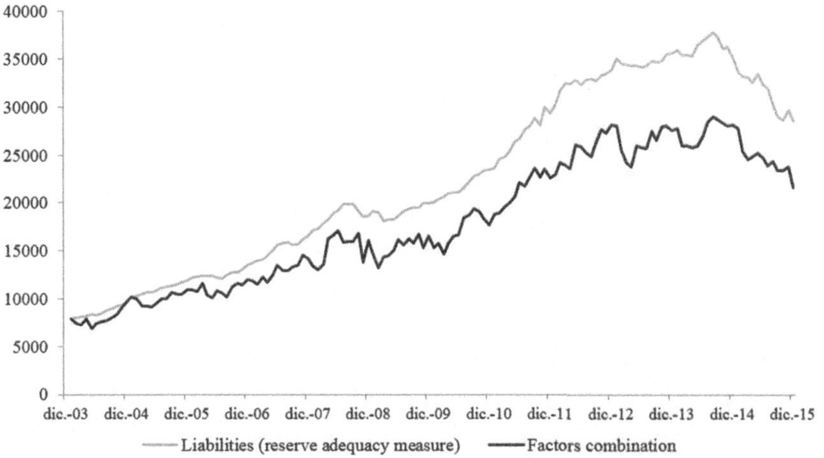

Fig. 1.3 Liabilities (reserve adequacy measure) and combination of factors with highest explanatory power (in US dollars million)

Figure 1.4 shows the unrestricted portfolio that minimizes the squared error of the difference between the liability and the portfolio; in other words, it is the solution to Eqs. 1.4 and 1.5. Ten asset classes are significant in the model with a 72% R^2. The asset with largest allocation in the portfolio is US mortgage-backed securities with 242% of the portfolio invested and the asset with the most negative allocation is US corporate bonds, with −391%.

There are five asset classes with an allocation over 100% in this portfolio and there are six asset classes with negative allocations. Figure 1.5 shows the currency allocation of the unrestricted portfolio. The largest allocation (271%) is to the US dollar and the most negative allocation is to the Australian dollar (−87%). This unrestricted portfolio has such large requirements in terms of leverage and short exposures that it is infeasible for a foreign reserve portfolio worth billions of dollars.

In order to obtain an investible portfolio, the restrictions in Eqs. 1.6 and 1.7 maintain the allocation to any asset class in a range from 0% to 100% and avoid concentrations in relatively illiquid currencies. Figure 1.6 presents the asset allocation of the investable portfolio, which invests mostly in government bonds of the United States, Canada, and Australia. Nonetheless, it is a portfolio with a high level of diversification, considering that there are various instruments and countries in the rest of the portfolio.

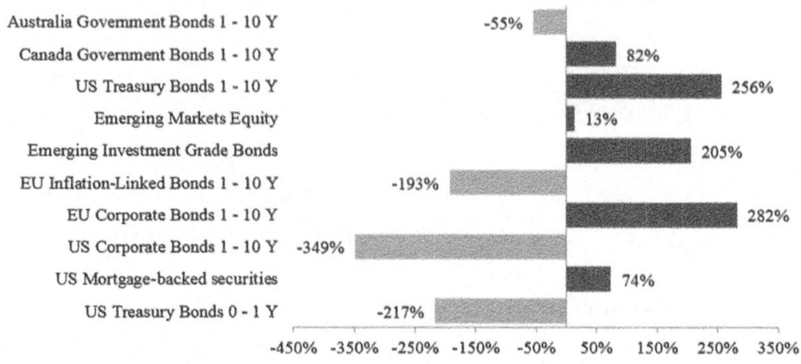

Fig. 1.4 Unrestricted portfolio

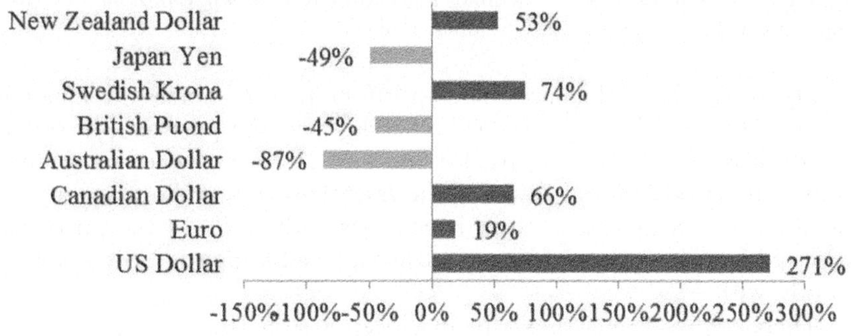

Fig. 1.5 Currency composition of unrestricted portfolio

Figure 1.7 shows the currency composition and the sector allocation of the investable portfolio. This portfolio includes 11 asset classes in three different sectors, denominated in seven different currencies. Despite this, the portfolio has high concentration in government fixed income securities, which results in low market risk (Fig. 1.7b). Finally, the portfolio achieves the objectives set out, as shown by the fact that the correlation between the investible portfolio and the liabilities is 0.73.

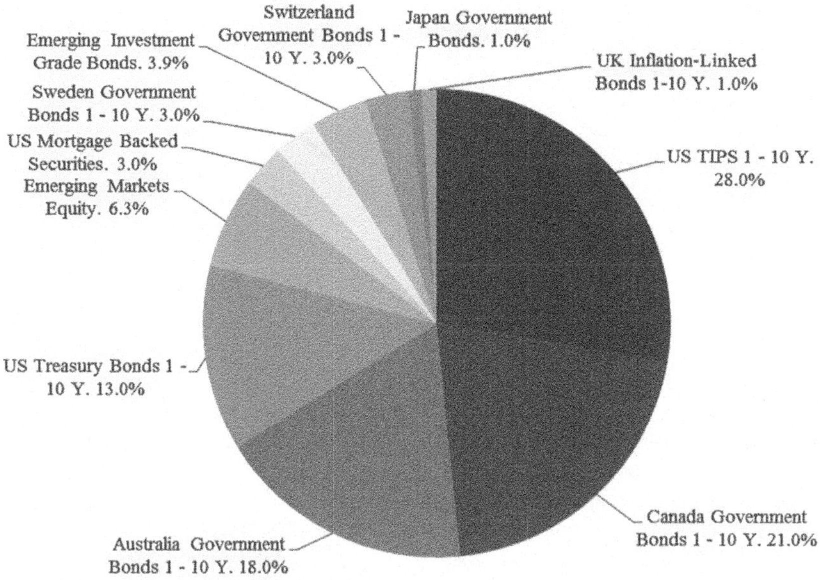

Fig. 1.6 Investable portfolio asset allocation

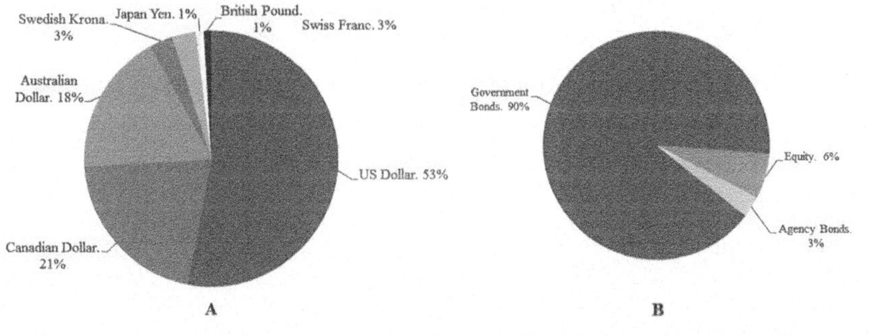

Fig. 1.7 Investable portfolio currency composition (a) and sector allocation (b)

Figure 1.8 shows the portfolio's risk and return in the mean-variance space in comparison with the efficient frontier obtained from an asset-only optimization using the same asset classes. As shown in Fig. 1.8, the ALM asset allocation is not risk-efficient from an AO perspective since the portfolio

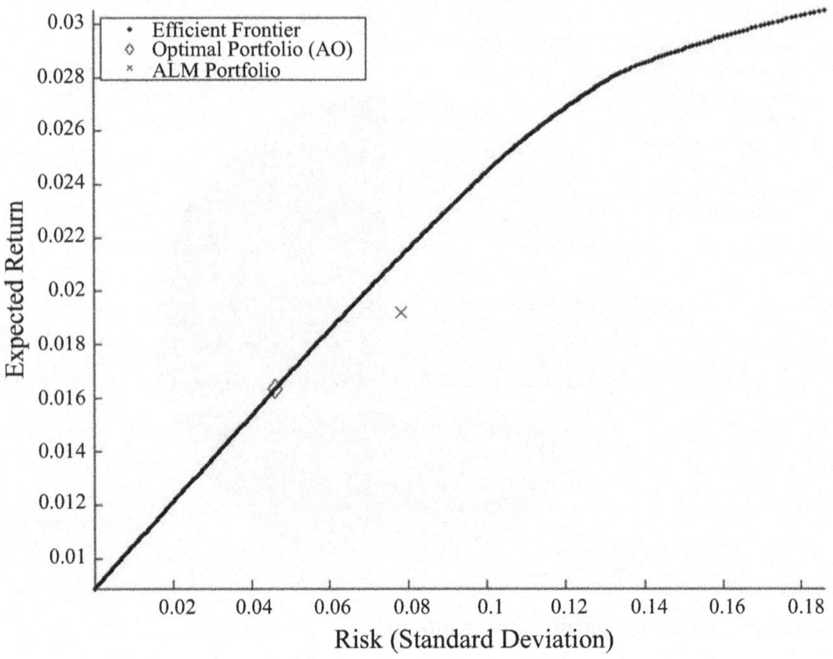

Fig. 1.8 ALM portfolio versus asset-only efficient frontier

Table 1.1 Descriptive statistics of the deviations of each portfolio returns from the adequacy level of reserves

	ALM portfolio	*Optimal portfolio (AO)*
Mean	0.43%	0.58%
Standard deviation	1.80%	2.50%
Maximum	5.21%	9.36%

Source: Authors' estimates

is located under the efficient frontier. This sub-optimality may be interpreted as the cost of meeting the objective of holding foreign reserves. As the statistics in Table 1.1 show, the ALM portfolio's annual returns deviate less from the annual variation of the liability (adequacy level of international reserves) than those obtained from the asset-only optimal portfolio.

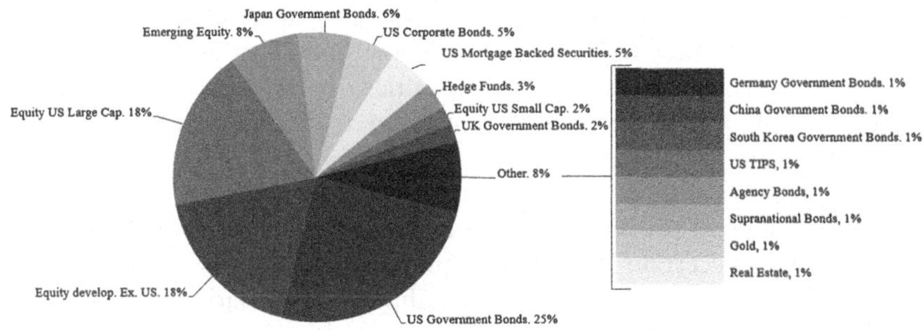

Fig. 1.9 Long-term investment tranche asset allocation

Figure 1.9 presents the asset allocation of the long-term investment tranche constructed with the García-Pulgarín et al. (2015) methodology. The portfolio is allocated mostly to US Treasuries and global equity. The portfolio has high diversification, considering its allocation in different instruments and countries, and it is more diversified in terms of sector allocation than the asset-liability tranche.

The portfolio in Fig. 1.9 does not have significant restrictions in terms of asset classes. For an implementation phase, a central bank should consider its operational, legal, risk aversion, and knowledge constraints before deciding what kind of assets and particular constraints are included in the portfolio construction.

1.7 Concluding Remarks

This document presents a methodology for the SAA of foreign reserves that takes into account the liabilities of each country. Since foreign reserves are a buffer for the entire economy and not only for the government or the central bank, the definition of liabilities is broad in order to encompass the possible sources of reserve requirements facing a balance of payments crisis.

A reserve adequacy measure proposed in García-Pulgarín et al. (2015) was used to estimate the liabilities. Unlike most standard reserve adequacy measures that are based on rules of thumb, the metric used takes into account all of the possible vulnerabilities of the balance of payments and the specific characteristics of each country.

After estimating the liabilities, a multi-factor analysis allows a better understanding of how to build an ALM portfolio. That analysis identifies which asset classes are the most appropriate to replicate the liabilities. Further restrictions were included, in order to obtain an investible and liquid portfolio.

This chapter presents a preliminary approach to enhance the role of foreign reserves to prevent and to confront external crisis, and therefore does not address certain issues that require further analysis. First, it would be desirable to have a better understanding of the relationship between liabilities, risk factors, and asset classes. Although the methodology achieves the goal of building a portfolio whose return hews closely to that of the liabilities, adjusting this portfolio over time requires an understanding of the relationships between all of the vulnerabilities of the balance of payments and each of the asset classes that are either excluded from (or included in) the final portfolio. Second, considering that certain relationships might change over time, it would be interesting to include a dynamic approach that allows for varying correlations and take into account the time-varying probability of interventions. Third, it is desirable to build larger samples of the macroeconomic variables used in the reserve adequacy measure so that it is possible to estimate a more robust indicator and include forward-looking estimations of assets and liabilities. Finally, it would be interesting to find out whether there are non-linear relationships between the liabilities and the asset classes or whether it is possible to use non-parametric estimators that are insensitive to outliers, in order to find portfolios with a better fit.

Additionally, there also remain challenges from an institutional perspective. Asset-only portfolio construction and ALM with a clearly defined set of liabilities, such as government debt, are more straightforward for policy makers from an accountability perspective. When a central bank considers a broader definition of liabilities, it may be more difficult to explain whether it has met the investment objectives. Moreover, ALM is easier to implement when assets and liabilities are in the same balance sheet. With the approach proposed here, the assets remain in the central bank balance sheet but the liabilities do not. Therefore, a central bank reports accounting losses where there is an absolute decrease in both assets and liabilities. As a result, this approach requires that policy makers take full ownership of the objectives and disclose them sufficiently.

Appendix: Selected Factors from Wilshire's Axiom Used to Explain Reserves Liabilities

Factor	*Country*
Duration	United States
	Europe
	United Kingdom
	Switzerland
	Sweden
	Canada
	Japan
	Australia
	New Zealand
	Norway
	Emerging Markets Investment Grade
Currency	Europe
	United Kingdom
	Switzerland
	Sweden
	Canada
	Japan
	Australia
	New Zealand
	Norway
Inflation	United States
	Europe
	United Kingdom
Corporate	United States
	Europe
Mortgages	United States
Supranational	All the World
Equity	United States
	Developed excluding United States
	Emerging Markets
Commodities	All the World

Note

1. A Liquidity at Risk rule takes into account the foreseeable risks that a country can face. This approach requires that a country's foreign exchange liquidity requirement can be calculated under a range of possible outcomes for relevant financial variables such as exchange rates, commodity prices, credit spreads.

References

Alhumaidah, F. (2015). Asset-liability management for reserves under liquidity constraints: The case of Saudi Arabia. *Procedia Economics and Finance, 29*, 17–40.

Ben-Bassat, A., & Gottlieb, D. (1992). Optimal international reserves and sovereign risk. *Journal of International Economics, 33*(3–4), 345–362.

Berkelaar, A., Coche, J., & Nyholm, K. (2010). *Central Bank reserves and sovereign wealth management.* Basingstoke: Palgrave Macmillan.

Bhattacharya, H., Kreuser, J., & Sivakumar, S. (2010). A sovereign asset-liability framework with multiple risk factors for external reserves management—Reserve Bank of India. In J. Coche, K. Nyholm, & G. Petre (Eds.), *Portfolio and risk Management for Central Banks and Sovereign Wealth Funds.* New York: Palgrave Macmillan.

Black, F., & Litterman, R. (1991). Asset allocation: Combining investor views with market equilibrium. *Journal of Fixed Income, 1*(2), 7–18.

Bonza, J., Gómez, N., & Pabón, R. (2010). Strategic asset allocation: Balancing short-term liquidity needs and real capital preservation for central banks. In A. Berkelaar, J. Coche, & K. Nyholm (Eds.), *Central Bank reserves and sovereign wealth management* (pp. 73–102). London: Palgrave Macmillan.

Brinson, G., Hood, L., & Beebower, G. (1986). Determinants of portfolio performance. *Financial Analysts Journal, 42*(4), 39–44.

Calvo, G., Izquierdo, A., & Loo-Kung, R. (2013). Optimal holdings of international reserves: Self-insurance against sudden stop. *Monetaria, 1*(1), 1–35.

Eichengreen, B., Rose, A., & Wyplosz, C. (1996). Contagious currency crises: First tests. *The Scandinavian Journal of Economics, 98*(4), 463–484.

Fabozzi, F. (2007). *Fixed income analysis* (2nd ed.). Hoboken, NJ: John Wiley & Sons, Inc.

García-Pulgarín, J., Gómez-Restrepo, J., & Vela-Barón, D. (2015). An asset allocation framework with tranches for foreign reserves. *Borradores de Economía* No. 899.

Gerencia, T. (2012). Nivel óptimo y adecuado de reservas internacionales. *Borradores de Economía* No. 727.

Gomez-Restrepo, J., & Rojas-Bohorquez, J. S. (2013). Assessing reserve adequacy: The Colombian case. *Borradores de Economía* No. 781.

Greenspan, A. (1999). Currency reserves and debt. *Remarks before the World Bank Conference on Recent Trends in Reserves Management.* Washington, DC. http://www.federalreserve.gov/boardDocs/speeches/1999/19990429.htm.

Heller, H. R. (1966). Optimal international reserves. *The Economic Journal, 76*(302), 296–311.

IMF. (1953). The adequacy of monetary reserves. *IMF Staff Papers, 111*(2), 181–227.

IMF. (1958). *International Reserves and Liquidity: A Study by the Staff of the International Monetary Fund*. Washington, DC.

IMF. (2011). *Assessing reserve adequacy*. Washington, DC: International Monetary Fund.

IMF. (2015a). *Assessing reserve adequacy*. Washington, DC: International Monetary Fund.

IMF. (2015b). *Assessing reserve adequacy—Specific proposals*. Washington, DC: International Monetary Fund.

Jeanne, O. (2007). International reserves in emerging market countries: Too much of a good thing? *Brookings Papers on Economic Activity, 2007*(1), 1–55.

Rivadeneyra, F., Jin, J., Bulusu, N., & Pomorski, L. (2013). Modelling the asset-allocation and liability strategy for Canada's foreign exchange reserves. *Bank of Canada Review, 2013*(Spring), 29–37.

Triffin, R. (1961). Gold and the dollar crisis: The future of convertibility. *Economic Journal, 71*(281), 142–144.

CHAPTER 2

Setting the Appropriate Mix Between Active and Passive Management in the Investment Tranche of a Foreign Reserves Portfolio

Daniel Vela Barón

2.1 Introduction

In their evaluation of central bank practices, Morahan and Mulder (2013) find that 56 of 67 foreign reserves managers report having deviation limits around the benchmark, 86% of which are with the purpose of active management. This indicates that central banks believe that there are opportunities to earn "alpha" that can be captured through active management strategies, either with external managers or with an internal active management program. Central banks see in active management a tool by which they can react

Comments from the participants of the Sixth Public Investors Conference Bank of International Settlements—World Bank—Bank of Canada are highly appreciated. The opinions and statements are the sole responsibility of the author and do not necessarily represent the World Bank.

D. Vela Barón (✉)
World Bank Treasury, Washington, DC, USA
e-mail: dvelabaron@worldbank.org

N. Bulusu et al. (eds.), *Advances in the Practice of Public Investment Management*, https://doi.org/10.1007/978-3-319-90245-6_2

to potential financial market inefficiencies to enhance returns, which is often the least important objective of foreign reserves managers.[1] Furthermore, some central banks set an active management framework in order to gather market intelligence. As shown by Jeffery et al. (2016), one of the main reasons central banks conduct gathering of market intelligence is to improve the information they can use for foreign exchange reserves management operations. Particularly, they seek information related to money markets, sovereign rates, currencies, and commodities, among others.

Many institutional investors, including central banks, believe that alpha is achievable on a sustainable and scalable basis, as mentioned in Berk and van Binsbergen (2016). However, there also exists a vast literature arguing for the efficiency of financial markets and the difficulty of finding and exploiting arbitrage opportunities leading to sustainable and scalable active management returns, as shown in Fama and French (2010). Merton (2014) introduces three sources of alpha (financial services, dimensional, and traditional alpha), partly explaining the contradiction between the empirical and the theoretical research, and describes which of them are sustainable and scalable and which are not. In this chapter, his analysis is viewed through the perspective of a central bank in order to identify the availability and the sources of alpha opportunities.

If a central bank identifies its competence to assess any of the sources of alpha, then it has to determine the proper amount it will invest in these strategies. The approach taken in this chapter for traditional alpha is contrary to the usual mean-variance approximation which is regularly used in the definition of strategic asset allocation. The suggested approach follows the Kelly criterion, which maximizes terminal wealth through a maximization of the portfolio's geometric mean return.

The intuition behind using the Kelly criterion for setting the appropriate mix between active risk and benchmark risk relies on the positive features of the methodology, as risk of ruin is eliminated and the final wealth of the seemingly sustainable and scalable alpha is maximized. Given that it is almost certain that the wealth generated with this approach is higher than the wealth generated with a risk-adjusted return approach in a long-time horizon, the Kelly criterion approach is suitable for a tranche invested for a long-term horizon and whose main objective is to maximize returns. For central banks, this is the case for an investment tranche, where excess foreign reserves are invested once all the main liquidity and safety goals have already been accomplished (as shown in García Pulgarín et al. 2015).

It was Daniel Bernoulli in the eighteenth century who first used a logarithmic utility function to solve the St. Petersburg paradox.[2] Later, Kelly (1956) reviewed its properties to define an optimal fraction that a gambler should bet when she or he has noisy private information and is betting for a substantial amount of time. Among the properties that Kelly discovered were that under this technique the gambler never risks ruin, and that the terminal wealth is very likely to be the highest among all strategies. The strategy may have high volatility, and betting more (less) than the optimal fraction increases (decreases) the growth of capital. Subsequently, as mentioned in Thorp (2006), both Claude Shannon and Edward Thorp used the Kelly fraction to obtain the series of blackjack bets that maximizes the expected value of the logarithm of wealth for a gambler with a probability of success higher than one half. Afterwards, they used the Kelly fraction in order to find the appropriate percentages invested in different market stocks.

Furthermore, Thorp (2006) links the fundamental problem of a gambler and an investor. For him, the former seeks positive expectation in betting opportunities and the latter tries to find investments with excess risk-adjusted expected rates of return. Both assess the probabilities of accessing the favorable opportunities and decide how much capital to bet in those strategies. The analogy can also be made with a portfolio manager seeking to set the amount of capital to be invested in a traditional alpha strategy.

This chapter is structured in five sections. The first one is this introduction. The second section overviews Merton's definitions of the sources of alpha and analyzes whether they are available to central bank foreign reserves managers. Afterwards, the third section describes and discusses the Kelly criterion. The subsequent section shows a simulation that compares the Kelly criterion methodology to a traditional risk-return perspective to set the optimal mix between active and passive management, as suggested by Violi (2010) following the Treynor and Black model. Finally, the fifth section gives some concluding remarks.

2.2 Sources of Alpha

Merton (2014) defines the super-efficient maximum Sharpe ratio portfolio of risky assets as the combination of the passive benchmark market portfolio, which holds an efficient diversification, and the active management strategies that can be incorporated in the portfolio, given the alpha resulting from the failure of the standard Capital Asset Pricing Model

(CAPM) to fit the data. The active components encompass bottom-up strategies, top-down strategies, and efficient market timing. Given this structure, Merton (2014) considers the possibility of higher Sharpe ratios over the passive benchmark as a consequence of the failure of CAPM.

He defines three distinct sources of alpha, two which he outlines as sustainable and scalable, and one that is not. The sustainable and scalable options are the financial services alpha and the dimensional alpha. The former is the result of market frictions arising from regulations and the interaction between financial intermediaries and the market. The latter is a result of risk premiums available from dimensions of risk different from market beta, considering the fact that the CAPM fails as not all investors hold the same portion of risky assets and the market portfolio is not mean-variance efficient. The neither-sustainable-nor-scalable source of outperformance is the traditional alpha earned by asset managers who are faster, smarter, or with better models or inputs.

The financial services alpha is a result of market participants that can take advantage of the setbacks and constraints of other more regulated and controlled market participants. The impediments and restrictions include (1) leverage inefficiencies or borrowing constraints; (2) short-sale restrictions; (3) institutional rigidities from regulation restrictions or requirements; and (4) taxes and accounting rules. A class of investors with the ability to take advantage of this type of alpha are hedge funds with lighter regulations and that can identify rigidities that are binding. Other institutions can also take advantage of this type of alpha, particularly if they have (1) a strong credit standing, (2) a long investment horizon, (3) flexible liquidity needs, (4) a large pool of assets, or (5) significant reputational capital. Such financial intermediaries can follow trading strategies that ease the impact of market frictions that affect other institutions, thereby earning outsized returns. However, earning this alpha requires first identifying securities that are impacted by the market rigidities discussed above.

A central bank has very limited access to financial services alpha since it is not a financial intermediary and its usual risk constraints prevent it from investing in institutions that gain from light regulations. Although central banks in developed countries may have long investment horizons, larger pool of assets, and flexible liquidity needs, they may still be curtailed in accessing financial services alpha to safeguard their reputational capital and abide by their risk aversion standards. In the case of most central banks in emerging and frontier countries, the risk aversion constraints demand high amounts of liquidity that are usually invested under a short-time horizon. Nonetheless, some central banks could have access to this type of alpha if they took advantage of their large pool of assets, although this is more often perceived as a disadvantage as they invest most of the times in very liquid markets. Another source of this type of alpha for central banks can be through asset substitution, where liquid on-the-run US treasury bonds are replicated with less liquid off-the-run US treasuries or agency bonds, to take advantage of liquidity premiums.

Dimensional alpha[3] exists as a result of uncertainty about the future investment opportunity set, uncertainty about liquidity, uncertainty about inflation and consumption goods in the future, and the hedging roles for securities in addition to diversification. Merton (2014) indicates that the existence of this type of alpha is consistent with an efficient financial market, since this type of alpha is earned from exposure to risks that investors are willing to pay to avoid. Thus, institutions can earn this alpha if their valuation of exposure to the additional dimensions of risk (other than the market risk factor) differs from the market price of such risks. Typically, institutions that can do this are hedge funds, long-term investment funds, and private equity firms.

According to Merton (2014), the following conditions should be met for identifying a dimension of risk with a premium: (1) there is a priori reasoning supported by economic theory; (2) it is persistent through time; (3) it is pervasive across different geopolitical borders; (4) it is monotonously increasing in the exposure of the security to the risk factor; (5) the exposure to the risk factor is not sensitive to precise parameter estimates; and (6) the exposure can be scalable in a cost-effective way. Some examples of recognizable dimensions different from the market that are scalable are the size of the company, the ratio of book to market value, the ratio of profits to market value, and liquidity (see Fama and French 1996; Pastor and Stambaugh 2003).

Limitations on the asset space of foreign reserves of central banks place a constraint on central banks' ability to gain dimensional alpha. According to Morahan and Mulder (2013), from a sample of 64 central banks, only two report investing in real estate investment trusts (REITs), both of them advanced countries, while only nine report investing in equities. Most central banks invest exclusively in traditional foreign reserves asset classes (government bonds, credit-related fixed-income securities, and gold). Nonetheless, there are a few empirical dimensions of risks with additional risk premiums, which a central bank can take advantage of, particularly if the central bank has enough foreign reserves to set an investment tranche, with a longer time horizon and with the objective of maximizing returns. One of the dimensions that can be considered under this scenario is liquidity.

Finally, the last source of alpha, the traditional alpha, is the only one described by Merton (2014) as neither sustainable nor scalable. Some conditions that allow for the existence of this alpha are market participants with access to non-public information or the ability to time the market. Like many academic studies, Merton (2014) stresses the unavailability of this type of alpha. Fama and French (2010) indicate that active investment is a zero-sum game; therefore, if some active investors have positive alpha before costs, it is at the expense of other active investors. They also point out that most active management returns do not compensate for the fees charged by such managers. French (2008) elaborates on the negative net returns of active management, and estimates that the typical investor would increase her or his average annual return by 67 basis points from 1980 to 2006 if she or he switched to a passive market portfolio. Furthermore, Bernile et al. (2014) present an argument for the lack of sustainability of the traditional alpha by showing that institutions on average are not skilled and their superior intra-quarter performance reflects only possible opportunistic access to short-term local information. Given this evidence, Foster and Warren (2013) explain the puzzling prevalence of active management as reflecting investors' beliefs in their ability to dynamically manage their allocations to external managers based on their investment performance. They provide evidence that investors believe that they have an above-average ability to select good managers, and they also believe in their ability to pursue an efficient dynamic strategy to replace bad-performing asset managers. They also show that some retail investors are impaired by behavioral biases, and use available information rather poorly.

It is important to point out, however, that there exists a contrarian strand of opinion about the ability of active management to generate traditional alpha. Andonov et al. (2012) note that institutional investors add value through active management, although some alpha may be attributable to momentum. Berk and van Binsbergen (2016) find sustainability of traditional alpha for as long as ten years into the future; additionally, investors seem to be able to identify and reward these skillful asset managers, given that better-performing funds collect higher aggregate fees. Likewise, in the fixed-income space, Aglietta et al. (2012) show that active management accounts for a substantial portion of performance, when aggregated with two other sources of return (market return and return from the asset allocation policy).

Therefore, there is no consensus on whether traditional alpha is achievable in a sustainable and scalable basis. The large number of central banks with an active management program seems to indicate belief in their ability to find highly skilled asset managers. We believe that the lack of academic consensus on the benefits of active management may suggest that central banks may find it more profitable to pursue sustainable and scalable sources of outperformance.

2.3 Adding the Sources of Alpha to the Market Portfolio

Whether a central bank has access to financial services or dimensional alpha, or supports the premise of traditional alpha, selecting the risk allocation of these strategies should not be a subjective matter.

Financial services alpha should be added to the maximum allowed by the portfolio constraints, as this type of alpha is a result of market regulations and intrinsic advantages that should be maximized by any investor.

The easiest way to add dimensional alpha to the mix of the super-efficient maximum Sharpe ratio portfolio of risky assets is through a mean-variance framework that allows the inclusion of new beta sources. A central bank with a long investment horizon that has the ability to access dimensional alpha linked to liquidity strategies can follow Lo et al. (2003), and optimize over the mean-variance-liquidity frontier to account for the liquidity factor. They construct liquidity indices of each asset from five dimensions of liquidity, viz., trading volume, logarithm of trading volume, turnover, percentage bid-ask spread, and Loeb price impact function. A linear form of the aggregated liquidity metric—that depends on the portfolio weights—is then additively introduced into the mean-variance objective function.

Lastly, one possible approach to add traditional alpha is by setting an optimal fraction of allocation to alpha-generating strategies by maximizing the expected value of the logarithm wealth, as done with the Kelly fraction by gamblers and investors.[4] Contrary to the usual maximization of risk-adjusted returns, measured by the Sharpe ratio, the Kelly criterion relies on the maximization of the terminal wealth. More concretely, the criterion maximizes the portfolio's geometric mean return. Generally, this optimized portfolio is not the same one that maximizes the risk-adjusted returns. Although the Kelly criterion may result in the maximum exponential growth rate of wealth, the solution is not the most efficient in terms of minimizing short-term risk. Given this caveat, when is it relevant to use this metric to select the appropriate mix between active and benchmark strategies?

The logic behind implementing the Kelly criterion for setting the appropriate mix between active risk and benchmark risk relies on the fact that the investment tranche is managed with the return-maximization perspective. The manager of this tranche is unaffected by short-term risks and seeks to maximize long-term returns. Such a manager seeks active investment strategies under the assumption that she or he has additional information that increases the odds of a positive alpha, following the constraint of avoiding financial ruin (the size of the investment tranche reducing to zero).[5]

The optimal Kelly fraction, which avoids ruin, can be estimated as follows. Assuming an investor (gambler) with N investments (bets) to place at each time invests (gambles) a fixed portion k of available capital. If there are n successful investments and $N - n$ losses, then the capital is:

$$V_{N,n} = \left(1 + kR_w\right)^n \left(1 + kR_L\right)^{N-n} V_0 \tag{2.1}$$

where R_w is the reward when the investment is successful and R_L is the loss when the investment is unsuccessful. The growth rate is given by:

$$G = \frac{1}{N}\log\left(V_{N,n}/V_0\right) = p\log\left(1 + kR_w\right) + q\log\left(1 - kR_L\right) \tag{2.2}$$

where p stands for the probability of a successful outcome and q for the probability of an unsuccessful one. When this log wealth is maximized, the resulting optimal Kelly fraction is:

$$k^* = \frac{pR_w - qR_L}{R_w R_L} \tag{2.3}$$

Under these conditions, as shown by Thorp (2006), the log wealth is maximized with a unique number k^*. Values lower than that level result in a positive expected growth coefficient, where the expected final wealth will be higher than the initial wealth. However, values above the optimal Kelly fraction start showing a decrease in the expected growth coefficient, even at one point making the coefficient negative (see Fig. 2.1).

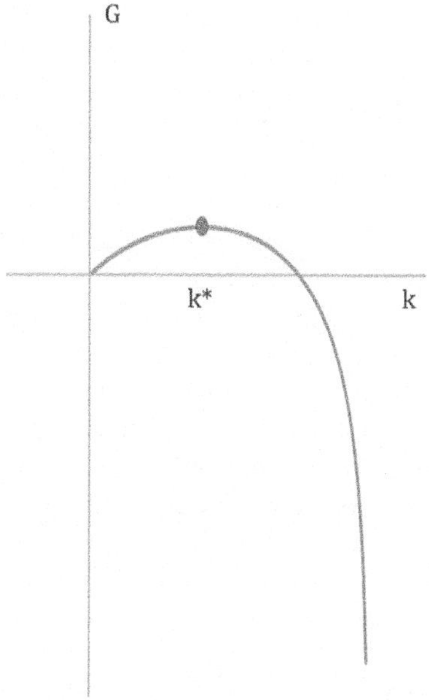

Fig. 2.1 Expected growth coefficient versus the Kelly fraction

The previous solution assumes a very simple scenario, where the investments behave as a flip of a biased coin with uneven payments. It follows a discrete probability distribution. However, the solution can be generalized to continuous outcomes and non-linear payoffs by estimating the numerical solution of:

$$V_N = V_0 \prod_{n=1}^{N} \left(1 + kR_n\right) \tag{2.4}$$

For selecting the appropriate mix between active and passive management with a single asset manager or when taking into account the whole amount of the active management program, Eq. 2.4 is solved assuming a stochastic distribution. Once the problem is expanded to more investment sources or bets, more optimal Kelly fractions are estimated. The growth rate for a discrete problem with two bets with uneven payments is given by:

$$\begin{aligned} G = {} & p_1 p_2 \log\left(1 + k_1 R_{w1} + k_2 R_{w2}\right) + p_1 q_2 \log\left(1 + k_1 R_{w1} - k_2 R_{L2}\right) \\ & + q_1 p_2 \log\left(1 - k_1 R_{L1} + k_2 R_{w2}\right) + q_1 q_2 \log\left(1 - k_1 R_{L1} - k_2 R_{L2}\right) \end{aligned} \tag{2.5}$$

When the problem of selecting the appropriate mix between active and passive management is extended to a set of asset managers, the problem is expanded to various optimal fractions. The following section describes a simulation that models different types of asset managers and compares the Kelly criterion results with the ones obtained with the Treynor and Black (1973) model.

The solution of the Kelly criterion is simple and intuitive. Moreover, in terms of leverage, the Kelly fraction depends on the product kR. Additionally, the risk of ruin is null and terminal wealth is maximized, properties that align with the objectives of an investment tranche. Furthermore, short-term volatility is not a pertinent issue when the problem is limited to defining only one fraction, the percentage allocated to the overall active management program. As no diversification benefits are considered, the difference with a Sharpe ratio-based model should not be substantial. An additional and possibly more important caveat is that the stability of profitability depends on knowing the correct parameters, which, in the context of this chapter, are the expected return distributions of asset managers.

2.4 Simulation

This section evaluates three distinct methodologies for setting the appropriate mix between active asset managers and a passive portfolio in the investment tranche of a foreign reserves portfolio. The passive portfolio is assumed to be composed by US Treasuries with a maturity between one and three years. The three methodologies to be considered are (1) Kelly criterion, maximization of the portfolio's geometric mean return; (2) the Treynor-Black model, mean-variance optimization; and (3) the alternative C, the option that assigns an arbitrary constant value of 90% to the strategy to the active asset managers. Alternative C is included in order to examine the outcomes when a significant portion is assigned to an active management strategy, without taking any leverage, constant values around 90% are expected to deliver similar results.

Violi (2010) describes the Treynor and Black (1973) model as a solution that allows an investor to set the mix of active and passive portfolio by maximizing the active Sharpe ratio. He treats the active and passive portions as two separate assets to then set a security selection framework. Hence, the problem is set with a quadratic utility function that considers the first two moments of the excess return distributions.

The simulation first considers three different asset managers, with the same expected alpha, but with distinct return distributions. The three are tested independently with the methodologies mentioned above to find the proper amount to be invested when they are mixed with the passive portfolio. In other words, we find the optimal allocation to the active portfolio separately for each of the asset managers following the three mentioned methodologies. Then, the Kelly criterion framework is tested for a portfolio that includes the three asset managers in the same portfolio. Thus, the weights are assigned considering the interaction between the three managers.

In order to set the distributions of the excess returns of the asset managers, this chapter follows Berk and van Binsbergen (2016). They use a sample of 5974 funds, gathered from the Center for Research in Security Prices survivorship bias-free database. The distribution of active returns has a positive mean value added, the percentage with less than zero is 57% and the distribution is positively skewed. In this chapter, this type of asset manager is represented with a gamma function, as shown in Fig. 2.2, identified as asset manager 1. Asset manager 2 is assumed to have the same expected value as asset manager 1, but its distribution is given by a t-student

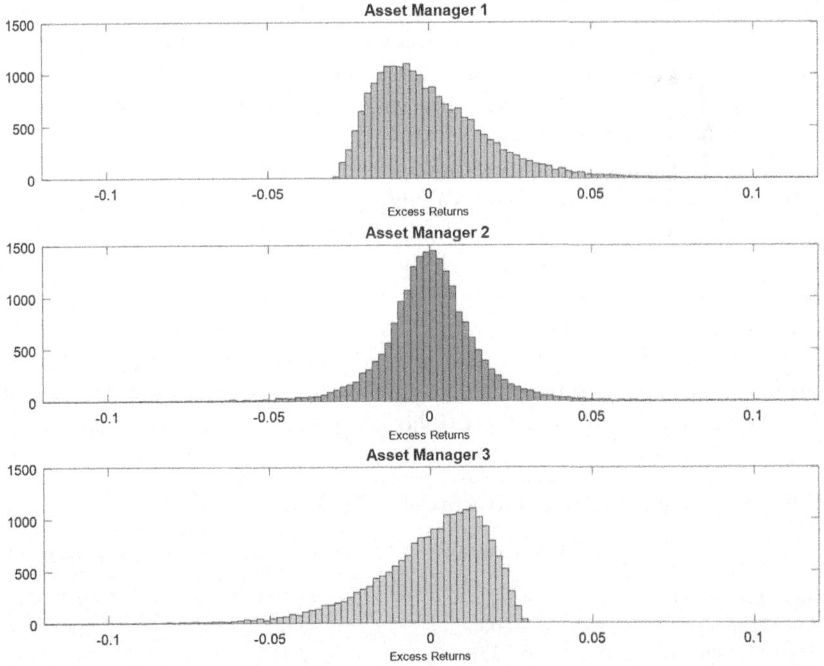

Fig. 2.2 Asset managers' excess returns distributions. The units of the Y-axis are number of funds

distribution. Finally, asset manager 3 is assumed to have the inverse marginal density function of asset manager 1, and therefore, it is negatively skewed, but the expected value is the same as the other distributions.

Table 2.1 shows the optimal fractions estimated independently under the three different methodologies for the various managers. The return distributions do not affect the amount allocated in the mean-variance model, as the methodology analyzes only the first two moments of the distributions (mean and variance). The amounts allocated with the Kelly criterion are large, but are somewhat limited by the risk of loss included in the distributions of the excess returns of the asset managers.

Figure 2.3 depicts the distributions of the terminal portfolio value when selecting the Kelly criterion as the methodology to set the mix between active and passive management. In a short-[6] and long-time horizon,[7] it can be seen that the methodology eliminates the probability of ruin. Nonetheless, the volatility and the probability of loss are high.

Table 2.2 summarizes the statistical analysis of the results of the three methodologies for the three asset managers—estimated separately. The Treynor and Black (1973) model shows a lower standard deviation; this is expected as the variance is one of the considerations within this framework. In the short-term horizon, the average cumulative excess returns are maximized with alternative C, which invests more in the asset managers compared to the other two options.

However, this option shows the highest volatility, the highest probability of loss and has a probability of ruin higher than zero for all the asset managers. The option that uses the Kelly criterion gives the highest average cumulative excess returns in a long-term horizon. This option and also the Treynor-Black optimization show a probability of ruin equal to zero and their probability of loss is very close.

As mentioned in the previous section, the methodology of the Kelly criterion can be expanded to include more than one asset manager. Figure 2.4 depicts the allocation of the portfolio once the three asset managers are

Table 2.1 Amount allocated to active asset managers

	Kelly criterion	*Treynor-Black*	*Alternative C*
Asset Manager 1	42.52%	33.24%	90%
Asset Manager 2	50.03%	32.50%	90%
Asset Manager 3	57.53%	33.13%	90%

Source: Author's calculations

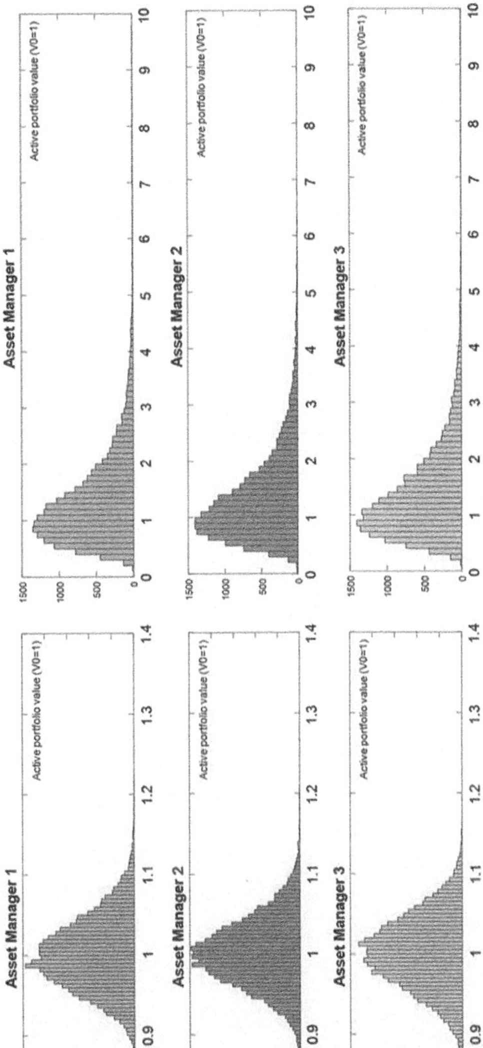

Fig. 2.3 Terminal portfolio value applying the Kelly criterion: **a**) Short-time horizon (graphs at the left), **b**) Long-time horizon (graphs at the right)

Table 2.2 Results for allocation for the overall active management program

	Standard deviation (excess returns)	*Average cumulative excess returns (long term)*	*Average cumulative excess returns (short term)*	*Probability of ruin*	*Probability of loss*
Kelly criterion					
Asset Manager 1	0.74%	53.02%	0.17%	0.00%	41.16%
Asset Manager 2	0.86%	63.69%	0.19%	0.00%	40.94%
Asset Manager 3	1.00%	76.21%	0.17%	0.00%	40.90%
Treynor-Black					
Asset Manager 1	0.58%	39.43%	0.15%	0.00%	38.21%
Asset Manager 2	0.56%	37.54%	0.14%	0.00%	38.70%
Asset Manager 3	0.57%	38.70%	0.18%	0.00%	38.59%
Alternative C					
Asset Manager 1	1.56%	45.27%	0.19%	0.65%	57.77%
Asset Manager 2	1.55%	47.69%	0.22%	0.79%	58.40%
Asset Manager 3	1.56%	43.18%	0.31%	0.98%	58.50%

Source: Author's calculations

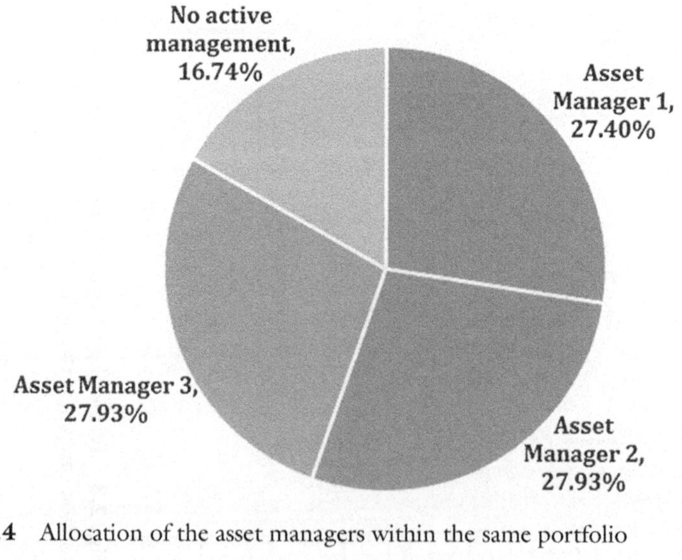

Fig. 2.4 Allocation of the asset managers within the same portfolio

Table 2.3 Results for allocation of the asset managers within the same portfolio

Standard deviation (excess returns)	0.83%
Average cumulative excess returns (long term)	126.52%
Average cumulative excess returns (short term)	0.37%
Probability of ruin	0.00%
Probability of loss	27.91%

Source: Author's calculations

considered for the same portfolio. In this case, the portion with no active management is reduced to 17%, while the rest is distributed almost equally among the three asset managers.

Table 2.3 shows the summary of the statistical analysis of the previous portfolio. The average cumulative excess returns increase both in the short-term and long-term horizons when compared with the options that considered every asset manager individually. The probability of loss decreases as in this case the negative outcomes of some active asset managers can be compensated with positive outcomes of the other active asset managers. The probability of ruin remains zero. However, the standard deviation increases compared to the options when the asset managers were considered individually.

2.5 Conclusion

This chapter reviews the three sources of alpha (dimensional, financial services, and traditional alpha) that are available for different types of investors, according to Merton (2014). The ability to access to each particular alpha relies on each investor's intrinsic characteristics; such is the case of central banks, which should consider their reputational capital and their risk aversion in order to gain exposure to them. The literature review shows contradictory conclusions as to whether a sustainable and scalable traditional alpha is feasible. Thus, to take advantage of traditional alpha strategies, a thorough analysis should be performed.

If a central bank believes that the traditional alpha is achievable, this chapter suggests setting the appropriate mix between active and passive management in the investment tranche of a foreign reserves portfolio with the Kelly criterion. The latter, considering that the behavior of an active investor resembles that of a gambler, who assumes an intrinsic advantage that gives higher probabilities of success and occasional uneven payments with higher rewards for successful outcomes and lower potential losses for unsuccessful events. Additionally, the characteristics of the Kelly criterion match those of an investment tranche of foreign reserves; more emphasis is on long-term returns than on short-term volatility.

Nonetheless, if short-term volatility is a crucial concern, the Kelly criterion can at least be considered to set an appropriate range in which the portion assigned to the active management program will fluctuate. As lower values of the Kelly fraction will still provide a positive expected growth coefficient, higher values might result in a positive probability of ruin, as shown in the empirical simulation done in this chapter. MacLean et al. (2010) show that security can be traded for lower growth by using a negative power utility function of applying a fractional Kelly strategy. Additional, it is important to note that the Kelly criterion can be extended to an active management program with various asset managers or sources of alpha.

Besides these benefits, it is important to highlight several shortcomings of the Kelly criterion. This strategy maximizes exclusively the expected logarithmic utility and ignores other possible utility functions. Furthermore, stability of the results relies on a priori knowledge of the excess return distributions of the asset managers. Moreover, despite the long-run growth properties of the strategy, it can be subject to low return outcomes and high impacts of short-term volatility.

Notes

1. The investment objectives of the foreign reserves of central banks are safety, liquidity, and return. Some central banks consider either safety or liquidity the first priority. Return is often given less importance than the other two objectives.
2. As explained by Hayden and Platt (2009), in the St. Petersburg paradox, the house offers to flip a coin until it comes up heads. The house pays $1 if heads appears on the first trial, otherwise the payoff doubles each time tails appears. The game stops, as well as the compounding, when the coin results in the first heads and the payment is given. By definition, the St. Petersburg gamble has an infinite expected value. However, most people share the intuition that no more than a few dollars should be offer to play.
3. It is feasible to link the dimensional alpha with Lo's (2012) Adaptive Markets Hypothesis (AMH). Lo suggests that the following assumptions of the relationship of risk and return are not likely under the current market conditions: (1) there is a linear relationship; (2) the relationship is constant

through time; (3) the relationship can be estimated with robust parameters; (4) all investors have rational expectations; (5) returns are stationary; and (6) markets are efficient. He recognizes that human behavior is not guided only by logical reasoning, and therefore, AMH seeks to explain how behavior is affected by the changing market conditions. One of the implications of AMH is that market efficiency is a function of the degree to which market participants have adapted to the market environment. Thus, the alpha converge to the beta as the degree of adaptability increases; investors that take advantage of this transition are investing in dimensional alpha.

4. The use of the Kelly criterion can be expanded to the other two sources of alpha; however, the scope of this chapter is to the scenario when the central banks believe to have additional information or timing abilities than the average market investor.
5. Another crucial point of the discussion is also the ability of the central bank to set an investment tranche; a rigorous analysis of the main liquidity needs should be done before going forward and setting this tranche.
6. The short time horizon is exemplified with a one-year horizon.
7. The long time horizon is considerably large, in order to represent the benefits of the Kelly criterion.

References

Aglietta, M., Brière, M., Rigot, S., & Signori, O. (2012). Rehabilitating the role of active management for pension funds. *Journal of Banking & Finance, 36*(9), 2565–2574.

Andonov, A., Bauer, R., & Cremers, M. (2012). *Can large pension funds beat the market? Asset allocation, market timing, security selection, and the limits of liquidity*. Netspar Discussion Paper No. 10/2012-062.

Berk, J. B., & van Binsbergen, J. H. (2016). Active managers are skilled: On average, they add more than $3 million per year. *Journal of Portfolio Management, 3*(4), 131–139.

Bernile, G., Kumar, A., Sulaeman, J., & Wang, Q. (2014). *Are institutional investors truly skilled or merely opportunistic?* Working Paper—Singapore Management University.

Fama, E. F., & French, K. R. (1996). Multifactor explanations of asset pricing anomalies. *The Journal of Finance, 51*(1), 55–84.

Fama, E. F., & French, K. R. (2010). Luck versus skill in the cross-section of mutual fund returns. *Journal of Finance, 65*(5), 1915–1947.

Foster, D., & Warren, G. (2013). Why might investors choose active management? *Journal of Behavioral Finance, 16*(1), 20–39.

French, K. R. (2008). The cost of active investing. *Journal of Finance, 63*(4), 1537–1573.

García Pulgarín, J. D., Gómez Restrepo, J., & Vela Barón, D. (2015). An asset allocation framework for excess reserves. *Exchange rate policy: Limits to flexibility, capital controls and reserve management* (pp. 133–140). Geneva: Graduate Institute Geneva.

Hayden, B. Y., & Platt, M. L. (2009). The mean, the median, and the St. Petersburg paradox. *Judgment and Decision making, 4*(4), 256–272.

Jeffrey, R., Neuhaus, H., Raskin, M., Schrimpf, A., Teo, A., & Vallence, C. (2016). Market intelligence gathering at central banks. *Markets Committee Bank for International Settlements.*

Kelly, J. L. (1956). A new interpretation of information rate. *Bell System Technical Journal, 35*, 917–926.

Lo, A. (2012). Adaptive markets and the new world order. *Financial Analysts Journal, 68*(2), 18–29.

Lo, A., Petrov, C., & Wierzbicki, M. (2003). It's 11 pm—Do you know where your liquidity is? The mean-variance-liquidity frontier. *Journal of Investment Management, 1*(1), 55–93.

MacLean, L. C., Thorp, E. O., & Ziemba, W. T. (2010). Good and bad properties of the Kelly criterion. *Quantitative Finance, 10*(2), 681–687.

Merton, R. C. (2014). Foundations of asset management goal-based investing the next trend. *MIT Finance Forum*. Cambridge: MIT Sloan.

Morahan, A., & Mulder, C. (2013). *Survey of reserve managers: Lessons from the crisis.* IMF Working Paper No. 1399.

Pastor, L., & Stambaugh, R. F. (2003). Liquidity risk and expected stock returns. *The Journal of Political Economy, 111*(3), 642–685.

Thorp, E. O. (2006). The Kelly criterion in blackjack, sports betting and the stock. In S. A. Zenios & W. T. Ziemba (Eds.), *Handbook of asset and liability management* (pp. 385–428). North Holland: Elsevier.

Treynor, J. L., & Black, F. (1973). How to use security analysis to improve portfolio selection. *Journal of Business, 46*(1), 66–86.

Violi, R. (2010). Optimal active portfolio management and relative performance drivers: Theory and evidence. *Portfolio and Risk Management for Central Banks and Sovereign Wealth Funds* (pp. 187–209). Basel: BIS, ECB, World Bank.

CHAPTER 3

A New Fixed-Income Fund Performance Attribution Model: An Application to ECB Reserve Management

Francesco Potente and Antonio Scalia

3.1 Introduction[1]

Portfolio managers' results can be analyzed from different perspectives. The first approach is used by empirical studies that aim to detect the market-timing ability of portfolio managers when granular data on portfolio composition, benchmark composition, and risk factors are not available. While in principle portfolio holdings would be best suited to infer the (ex-ante) managers' bets, given the data limitations, researchers generally resort to (ex-post) return-based tests, where assumptions have to be made about the relevant benchmark index.

The views expressed in the article are those of the authors and do not involve the responsibility of the Bank.

F. Potente
DG Financial Supervision and Regulation, Bank of Italy, Rome, Italy

A. Scalia (✉)
DG Markets and Payment Systems, Bank of Italy, Rome, Italy
e-mail: antonio.scalia@bancaditalia.it

N. Bulusu et al. (eds.), *Advances in the Practice of Public Investment Management*, https://doi.org/10.1007/978-3-319-90245-6_3

According to the literature on fixed-income portfolio management: (1) on average bond fund managers exhibit negative or neutral timing ability (Blake et al. 1993; Elton et al. 1995; Boney et al. 2009); (2) conditional performance adjusted for risk is slightly negative (Lam 1999; Ferson et al. 2006); (3) adjusting for non-linear effects, there is no evidence of positive performance after costs (Chen et al. 2010). The studies that employ measures of bond portfolio holdings show a similar picture with some nuances. In particular, Moneta (2015) finds that, on average, portfolio managers display neutral timing ability, with only a subgroup of funds exhibiting successful timing ability; Cici and Gibson (2012) show that conditional performance adjusted for risk is slightly negative; Huang and Wang (2014) find that fund managers specializing in Treasury securities show better market-timing ability in comparison with managers investing in portfolios including mortgage-backed and agency securities—however, after controlling for public information, ability becomes neutral.

A second approach, more oriented toward practitioners, includes performance attribution studies that seek to identify sources of outperformance based on granular data on the composition and risk exposure of portfolios. Compared with return-based tests, performance attribution models allow for pinpointing the skills of portfolio managers by linking return decomposition to specific portfolio strategies. For example, a manager's ability in terms of duration management could be offset by the lack of skill in spread management, or vice versa. In such cases, the econometric estimate of market-timing ability would be the result of two opposite forces, which might cancel each other in statistical terms. Performance attribution models overcome this problem.

Two main families of performance attribution models have been developed in the literature and in the financial industry: sector-based models and factor-based models. The first group tries to identify the contribution of each strategy via a comparison between the portfolio sector weights and returns, and the benchmark sector weights and returns. These models are usually applied to equity funds and identify three sources of performance variation from the benchmark (see e.g. Brinson et al. 1986): asset allocation, stock selection, and interaction. It is inappropriate to adapt this approach to fixed-income portfolios in order to identify the contributions of typical fixed-income portfolio strategies (e.g. Campisi 2011).

In factor models, the return on each asset is viewed as a function of specific risk factors (duration, convexity, carry, spread component, etc.). As a first step, the exposure to each risk factor is computed for each asset included in the portfolio. By aggregating individual asset exposure to each risk factor, it is possible to build the overall portfolio exposure to each factor vis-à-vis the benchmark. The specific risk factor's contribution to the extra performance is obtained as the interaction between the exposure to a specific risk factor and the measured change in that risk factor. In general, each risk factor can be considered as the constituent of a specific strategy. For instance, the contribution to extra returns coming from portfolio manager exposure to the risk factor 'parallel shift' can be viewed as the contribution of duration positions. These models provide a richer description of the performance contribution than sector models. However, the quality of the results of factor models may be affected by the presence of a non-negligible residual term as a component of the return.

This chapter presents a new performance attribution model to identify the main performance drivers of fixed-income portfolio managers. We develop an alternative approach that tries to preserve the richness of factor models without incurring in the drawback of a large residual term. The approach resembles that of sector models; however, we modify the actual portfolio weights in such a way that they can be viewed as the result of exposures to the risk factors related to specific strategies. The proposed model disentangles the contribution of each strategy in order to detect specific portfolio manager skills: (1) duration contribution, (2) curve contribution, (3) spread contribution, and (4) security selection. The proposed framework thus provides a clear interpretation of results of fixed-income portfolio managers.

As an empirical application of the model, we analyze the performance of a group of foreign exchange reserve managers that carry out the investment of the European Central Bank's (ECB) official reserves in US dollars, worth around USD43 billion,[2] using a new dataset that includes detailed portfolio holdings from 2006 to 2010.

We find that, first, the bond portfolio managers investing the ECB reserves in US dollars on aggregate outperform the active benchmark by around 10 basis points on a yearly basis net of transaction costs. This amounts to EUR39 million per year, which, based also on confidential data available to the authors, is well above management costs. It is worth mentioning that the governance structure of the ECB reserve management framework is based on a three-layer structure: a strategic benchmark, a tactical benchmark, and the actual portfolio managed by the national central banks (NCBs) involved in the active reserve management (see Sect. 3.3 for further details). Also, the tactical layer, implementing security selection strategies at each rebalancing date, allows for active management vis-à-vis the strategic benchmark, thus exploiting sources of excess returns and contributing to the overall alpha generation. If we measure the alpha of the aggregated portfolio vis-à-vis the strategic benchmark, it turns out to be positive and significant at the 1.6% significance level. On the other hand, if we measure the alpha of the aggregated portfolio vis-à-vis the tactical benchmark, it turns out to be positive, but is only significant at the 13% significance level. These two results, taken together, indicate that a component of security selection is absorbed by tactical choices.

Second, we attribute the extra performance to the ECB managers' specific strategies based on our performance attribution model, which employs portfolio holdings as well as the 'true' benchmark holdings. For this, we use weekly return data for the eight portfolios and the benchmark, plus the individual asset holdings. We have a specific interest in time periods shorter than one month, since the active benchmark is revised on a monthly basis. Under the hypothesis that portfolio managers have market-timing and selection skills, these should be revealed at very short time intervals. The analysis shows that, in the period under analysis, in the aggregate the main source of extra performance is related to security selection, followed by spread contribution. This approach also allows us to pinpoint the diversity of different investment styles across managers.

Overall our analysis shows that reserve managers adopt different investment styles and make a diversified use of the risk budget, which presumably results in a high number of independent bets on the aggregate portfolio. Our findings seem consistent with the 'law of active management' (Grinold 1989), according to which a high number of independent bets improves the information ratio of the aggregate portfolio. These results seem noteworthy, in consideration of the tightness of the portfolio contest.

Section 3.2 presents the methodology of the performance attribution model. Section 3.3 shows the main features of the ECB reserve management framework. Section 3.4 reports the empirical results. Section 3.5 concludes.

3.2 The Methodology

In this section, we present the methodological building blocks of the proposed performance attribution model. We develop an approach that tries to preserve the richness of performance attribution factor models without incurring the drawback of a large residual term. The approach resembles that of sector models; however, we modify the actual portfolio weights in such a way that they can be viewed as the result of exposures to the risk factors related to specific strategies. The proposed model disentangles the contribution of each strategy in order to detect specific portfolio manager exposure to (1) duration contribution, (2) curvature contribution, (3) spread contribution, and (4) security selection. The proposed framework thus provides a clear interpretation of results from a portfolio manager's perspective.

The total excess return is described by the following expression:

$$r^p = r_d^p + r_c^p + r_a^p + r_s^p$$

where, r^p is the total portfolio return in excess of the benchmark, r_d^p is the duration contribution, r_c^p is the curve contribution, r_a^p is the spread contribution, and r_s^p is the security selection contribution.

The duration contribution r_d^p captures the part of the excess return stemming from portfolio duration exposure different from that of the benchmark. The curve contribution r_c^p provides the result of the portfolio manager's choices in weighting the time buckets[3] differently from the benchmark without taking any duration exposure. The selection contribution r_a^p stems from strategies in weighting asset classes (indexed by *i*; e.g. Treasuries vs Agencies) within a specific time bucket *j* differently from the benchmark. The security selection contribution r_s^p is due to the activity of picking securities within a specific sector.

We start by building a sequence of virtual portfolios the weights of which represent the relevant strategies. As a first step, we build a virtual portfolio A, reflecting all the strategies implemented by the portfolio manager with the exception of security selection choices. By comparing the total return of the actual portfolio with that of portfolio A, we can isolate the security selection contribution r_s^p. Second, we build a virtual portfolio B the weights of which include only the portfolio manager's spread choices. By comparing the benchmark total return with that of the virtual portfolio B, we can thus disentangle the spread contribution r_a^p. Third, starting from the virtual portfolio B, we rearrange the weights in order to build a virtual portfolio C including also the curve exposure. By comparing the virtual portfolio B return with that of portfolio C, we obtain the curve contribution r_c^p. Finally, comparing the portfolio A with portfolio C, we obtain the duration contribution. By construction, this model presents no residual term.

We introduce the following definitions:

w_{ij}^{b} is the weight of sector *i* in time—bucket *j* of the benchmark;
R_{ij}^{b} is the return of sector *i* in time—bucket *j* of the benchmark;
MD_{ij}^{b} is the modified duration of sector *i* in time—bucket *j* in the benchmark;
pd_{ij}^{b} is the partial duration (or duration contribution) of sector *i* in time—bucket *j* in the benchmark; it is obtained as the product of benchmark weight w_{ij}^{b} times the modified duration of sector *i* in time—bucket *j*, MD_{ij}^{b};
w_{ij}^{p} is the weight of sector *i* in time—bucket *j* in the actual portfolio;
R_{ij}^{p} is the return of sector *i* in time—bucket *j* in the portfolio;
MD_{ij}^{p} is the modified duration of sector *i* in time—bucket *j* in the portfolio;
pd_{ij}^{p} is the partial duration of sector *i* in time—bucket *j* in the portfolio; it is obtained as the product between the actual portfolio weight w_{ij}^{p} and the modified duration of sector *i* in time—bucket *j*, MD_{ij}^{p}.

The total excess return of the portfolio is given by:

$$r^{p} = \sum_{i}\sum_{j} w_{ij}^{p} R_{ij}^{p} - \sum_{i}\sum_{j} w_{ij}^{b} R_{ij}^{b} \tag{3.1}$$

First, we build a virtual portfolio A which, by construction, has for each sector *i* in time—bucket *j* the same internal composition, modified duration, and return of the benchmark, while making sure that it has the same sector and time-bucket partial durations as the actual portfolio. This virtual portfolio includes all the choices of the reserve manager with the exception of the security selection component. Therefore, if we subtract the overall return of this portfolio from the overall return of the actual portfolio, we obtain the security selection contribution to the overall extra returns.

We compute the weights of the virtual portfolio as:

$$w_{ij}^{A} = \frac{pd_{ij}^{p}}{MD_{ij}^{b}}$$

Since the sum of the rearranged portfolio weights is not necessarily equal to 100%, we assume that we can use a cash account as an additional asset class in order to finance the position (if the sum of weights is larger than 100%) or to invest the cash (if the sum of weights is lower than 100%). We assume that the return on this cash account is equal to the overnight unsecured rate $r_{O/N}$. The weight of this cash account is equal to:

$$w_{\text{cash}}^{A} = 1 - \sum_{i}\sum_{j} w_{ij}^{A}$$

The overall extra returns can be split into two components.

$$r^{P} = \underbrace{\sum_{i}\sum_{j} w^{P}_{ij} R^{P}_{ij} - \left(\sum_{i}\sum_{j} w^{A}_{ij} R^{b}_{ij} + w_{cash}^{A} r_{O/N} \right)} + \underbrace{\sum_{i}\sum_{j} w^{A}_{ij} R^{b}_{ij} + w_{cash}^{A} r_{O/N} - \sum_{i}\sum_{j} w^{b}_{ij} R^{b}_{ij}}$$

This term represents the security selection component r_s^P

This term represents the sum of spread contribution, curve and duration contribution $r_d^P + r_c^P + r_a^P$

The asset class selection choices depend on the relative asset weighting (e.g. Treasury vs spread products) within each time bucket in terms of partial duration; the partial duration for each time bucket of the actual portfolio and the benchmark can be expressed by:

$$PD_j^p = \sum_{i=1} pd_{ij}^p \; (\text{portfolio})$$

$$PD_j^b = \sum_{i=1} pd_{ij}^b \; (\text{benchmark})$$

The relative asset class weight α_{ij}^p of the actual portfolio in terms of partial duration exposures for each asset class i and time bucket j is:

$$\alpha_{ij}^{p} = \frac{pd_{ij}^{p}}{PD_{j}^{p}}$$

Second, we build the weights of the virtual portfolio B, having the same time-bucket partial duration exposure as the benchmark, expressed by PD_j^b, but an exposure for each asset class i, in relative terms, equal to the one of the actual portfolio, as:

$$w_{ij}^B = \frac{PD_j^b \alpha_{ij}^p}{MD_{ij}^b}$$

Starting from Eq. 3.1, we add and subtract the overall return of the virtual portfolio B. As previously discussed with the virtual portfolio A, the sum of the rearranged portfolio weights is not necessarily equal to 100%; therefore, we introduce an additional cash account:

$$w_{\text{cash}}^B = 1 - \sum_i \sum_j w_{ij}^B$$

Again, we assume that the return of this cash account is equal to the overnight unsecured rate $r_{O/N}$. If we subtract the overall return of the benchmark from the virtual portfolio B return, we obtain the spread contribution to the overall extra returns. The difference between the return of portfolio A and the return of portfolio B represents the sum of the curvature and duration contribution.

$$\left(r_d^p + r_c^p + r_a^p\right) = \underbrace{\left(\sum_i \sum_j w^A{}_{ij} R^b{}_{ij} + w_{cash}{}^A r_{O/N}\right) - \left(\sum_i \sum_j w^B{}_{ij} R^b{}_{ij} + w_{cash}{}^B r_{O/N}\right)} + \underbrace{\left(\sum_i \sum_j w^B{}_{ij} R^b{}_{ij} + w_{cash}{}^B r_{O/N}\right) - \sum_i \sum_j w^b{}_{ij} R^b{}_{ij}}$$

This term represents the sum of curve and duration contribution to the overall extra–performance $r_d^p + r_c^p$	This term represents the spread contribution to the overall extra-performance r_a^p

Third, in order to disentangle the contribution stemming from exposure to curvature, we assume that the duration exposure is targeted through securities included in the time bucket with the highest duration exposure in the same direction (long or short) as the overall exposure. We note that the split among curve and duration is not unique; different assumptions may lead to different results. However, we believe that our choice is the most intuitive and suitable from a portfolio manager's perspective. The attribution of the overall duration exposure to the sector with the largest duration exposure is easier to understand compared to more sophisticated algorithms (for instance, based on principal component analysis), which might spread the duration exposure over different time buckets, sometimes also in a counter-intuitive manner. Therefore, we compute the differential time-bucket exposures (portfolio vs benchmark) in terms of partial duration; for illustrative purposes, assume that

- the portfolio exposure in terms of partial duration for the different time buckets is as given in Table 3.1;
- the benchmark exposure is as given in Table 3.2;
- then the differential exposure would be as given in Table 3.3.

Table 3.1 Portfolio

	1–3	*3–5*	*5–7*	*7+*	
Weights	19%	25%	31%	25%	100%
Modified duration	2	4	6	9	5.49
PD	0.38	1	1.86	2.25	5.49

Table 3.2 Benchmark

	1–3	*3–5*	*5–7*	*7+*	
Weights	25%	25%	25%	25%	100%
Modified duration	2	4	6	9	5.25
PD	0.5	1	1.5	2.25	5.25

Table 3.3 Differential exposure

	1–3	*3–5*	*5–7*	*7+*	
PD	−0.12	0	0.36	0	0.24

We identify the time bucket $\overline{j}$ with the largest exposure in the same direction as the overall exposure; in the example, the overall exposure is equal to 0.24 and the bucket with the largest exposure in the same direction as the overall exposure is the 5–7 time bucket.

Starting from the portfolio exposure, we assume that we sell or buy the overall exposure by means of the time bucket identified in the previous step in order to re-instate the benchmark overall exposure; we therefore compute

$$PD_j^{*p} = PD_j^p \forall j \neq \overline{j}$$

$$PD_{\overline{j}}^{*p} = PD_{\overline{j}}^{p} \pm \text{overall exposure}$$

and, with regard to the time bucket $\overline{j}$, we re-compute the asset class partial durations $pd_{ij}^{*} = \alpha_{i\overline{j}} PD_{\overline{j}}^{p} \pm \text{overall exposure}$ in such a way as to preserve the actual portfolio proportion to the overall time-bucket partial duration.

In the example, the partial duration of the 5–7 time bucket is adjusted accordingly (Table 3.4).

Notice that this portfolio has the same overall duration as the benchmark, but a different combination of partial duration exposure among different time buckets; therefore, it conveys only a curve exposure (Table 3.5).

We compute the weight of the virtual portfolio C including only curve and spread exposure in the usual way:

$$w_{ij}^{C} = \frac{pd_{ij}^{*}}{MD_{ij} b}$$

also including the cash account

$$w_{\text{cash}}^{C} = 1 - \sum_{i} \sum_{j} w_{ij}^{C}$$

In the example, considering only the total time-bucket weights and the cash account adjustment, the result is the following (Table 3.6):

Table 3.4 Portfolio adjusted—partial durations

	1–3	*3–5*	*5–7*	*7+*	
Modified duration	2	4	6	9	5.25
PD	0.38	1	1.62	2.25	5.25

Table 3.5 Differential exposure adjusted

	1–3	*3–5*	*5–7*	*7+*	
PD	−0.12	0	0.12	0	0

Table 3.6 Portfolio adjusted—weights

	0–1	*1–3*	*3–5*	*5–7*	*7+*	
Weights	4%	19%	25%	27%	25%	100%
Modified duration	0	2	4	6	9	5.25
PD	0	0.38	1	1.62	2.25	5.25

$$\left(r_d^p + r_c^p\right) = \underbrace{\left(\sum_i\sum_j w^A{}_{ij}R^b{}_{ij} + w_{cash}{}^A r_{O/N}\right) - \left(\sum_i\sum_j w^C{}_{ij}R^b{}_{ij} + w_{cash}{}^C r_{O/N}\right)}_{\text{This term represents the duration contribution component } r_d^p} + \underbrace{\left(\sum_i\sum_j w^C{}_{ij}R^b{}_{ij} + w_{cash}{}^C r_{O/N}\right) - \left(\sum_i\sum_j w^B{}_{ij}R^b{}_{ij} + w_{cash}{}^B r_{O/N}\right)}_{\text{This term can represents the curve contribution } r_c^p}$$

3.3 Main Features of the ECB Reserve Management Framework

Foreign exchange reserves worldwide are worth USD10.9 trillion[4] and are mainly invested in government bonds and other liquid instruments. For comparison, the global net assets of bond- and money-market funds is worth around USD14.5 trillion.[5] While the management and performance of private bond portfolio managers is the subject of a vast empirical literature, relatively little is known about the investment of foreign exchange reserves, owing mainly to confidentiality reasons.

The recent surveys on central bank reserve management mainly deal with strategy issues, such as the use of an ALM approach, and with governance issues (e.g. Borio et al. 2008a, b; Johnson-Calari et al. 2007; Nugée 2012). The composition of US dollar official holdings has been examined in some detail (McCauley and Rigaudy 2011). Not surprisingly, due to the prevalence of institutional reasons for the management of official reserves, their investment performance is rarely the subject of publicly available research (exceptions include Hu 2010; Vesilind and Kuus 2005).

The ECB reserve management framework is based on a three-layer structure: (1) a strategic level, which defines the strategic benchmark; (2) a tactical level, which sets up the tactical benchmark; and (3) the portfolio managers of NCBs involved in the active management of the reserves.

The strategic benchmark addresses the ECB's long-term risk-return preferences, the tactical benchmark seeks to exploit medium-term market movements, and portfolio managers attempt to outperform the tactical benchmark. It is important to highlight that the tactical level also seeks to generate portfolio outperformance by searching for strategies with positive alpha. At each rebalancing date, the tactical level defines a tactical benchmark composition with the goal of outperforming the strategic benchmark. In particular, the tactical layer tries to exploit market and security selection opportunities by deviating from the strategic benchmark within a defined risk budget by choosing a specific composition of eligible asset classes. In turn, portfolio managers try to outperform the tactical layer with active strategies that deviate from the tactical benchmark within specific limits. Consequently, a share of exploitable alpha is absorbed by the tactical level. The ECB sets a common tactical benchmark, thus generating competition among managers (Koivu et al. 2009; Manzanares and Schwartzlose 2009). Every month their individual performance is computed and made known by the ECB to all managers. An annual general report on the investment activities and risks is transmitted to the Governing Council of the ECB, including the individual performance figures and rankings of the NCBs. The assets under management reflect the share of each NCB in the ECB's capital.

The ECB reserves in US dollars must be invested in highly liquid fixed-income instruments. The eligible asset classes and the composition of the strategic benchmark, the tactical benchmark, and the actual portfolios managed by the NCBs reflect the objective of the ECB's foreign reserve portfolio to ensure that, whenever needed, the Eurosystem has a sufficient amount of liquid resources for its foreign exchange policy operations involving non-EU currencies. Indeed, for the ECB's foreign reserves, the portfolio management objective is to maximize returns through prudent portfolio management, subject to the stringent security and liquidity requirements that derive from the portfolio purpose. The eligible investment universe includes government bonds, agencies with government support, BIS instruments, bonds issued by supranational organizations, and deposits. No currency exposure and short selling of securities is allowed within this framework. The portfolio management framework reflects the idea that, within the tight constraints imposed by the framework, portfolio managers can add value to the portfolios over time.

Some factors make the investment contest of the ECB's reserve managers extremely challenging (Scalia and Sahel 2012). First, while private bond funds often lack formal benchmarks, in our case, the benchmark is tailor-made by the ECB to reflect its risk-return preferences and is actively managed, since the ECB may revise it based on the flow of new information on a monthly basis.[6] Second, the investment set is relatively small and risk limits are quite severe in comparison with the private sector. Third, reserve managers monitor each other's performance and ranking at monthly frequency. In practice, the ECB's reserve managers compete for a handful of basis points of performance in a tight competition. With reduced risk-taking opportunities, the market-timing ability of reserve managers plays a key role in securing extra returns.

In the sample period 2006–2010, the owner of the reserves delegated their investment to a group of managers located at eight NCBs of the Eurosystem, namely those of Belgium, France, Germany, Greece, Ireland, Italy, Luxembourg, and Spain.[7]

In the following section, we show the results of the application of the model of Sect. 3.2 to the aforementioned portfolio managers, treated anonymously and denoted by a random code ranging from M1 to M8.

3.4 Results

We apply the above model to a dataset of portfolio manager performance and positions related to the fixed-income portfolios of US dollar reserves managed by the NCBs.

The net asset value of the ECB US dollar tactical benchmark and aggregate portfolio during 2006–2010 is shown in Fig. 3.1. The return on the portfolio has exceeded the benchmark return in each year, and at the end of the period, the portfolio cumulative return was about 46 basis points above that of the benchmark.

The above figures are net of transaction costs, which are accounted for in the portfolio management system at each trade. The money equivalent

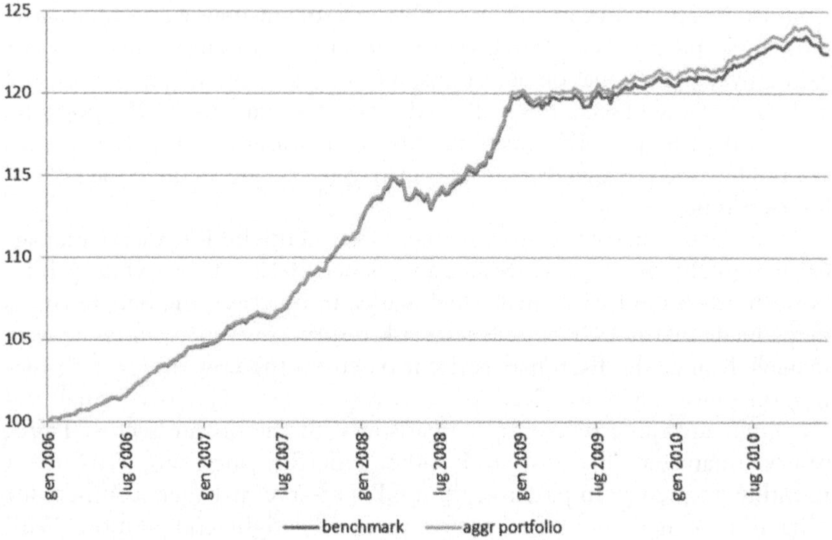

Fig. 3.1 Cumulative returns, ECB's US dollar reserves, 2006–2010: benchmark versus aggregated portfolio. On the y axis, cumulative returns are expressed as an index

of the yearly average extra performance is about EUR39 million. This figure is arguably well above the management costs (staff salaries, IT equipment, overhead) that are involved in the ECB reserve management framework, hence we have a case of positive net outperformance.

Owing to the weekly data frequency, security selection actually reflects not only the activity of 'pure' selection among different bonds, but it captures also the result of all the other positions (duration, curve, and spread) opened and closed in the same week, without altering the weights from one week to another. Furthermore, it includes the component of excess return that comes from the carry of deposits and repo market activity.[8]

We first examine the contribution to the excess return that accrues from duration management (Fig. 3.2).

It is interesting to notice that only one portfolio manager (M8) achieved a non-negligible positive result in duration management, while the other portfolio managers obtained negative results (M3, M4, and M7) or almost nil (M1, M2, M5, and M6).

Portfolio managers also show different styles in the use of risk budget, as can be argued by looking at the average and volatility of duration exposure for each portfolio manager (Fig. 3.3).

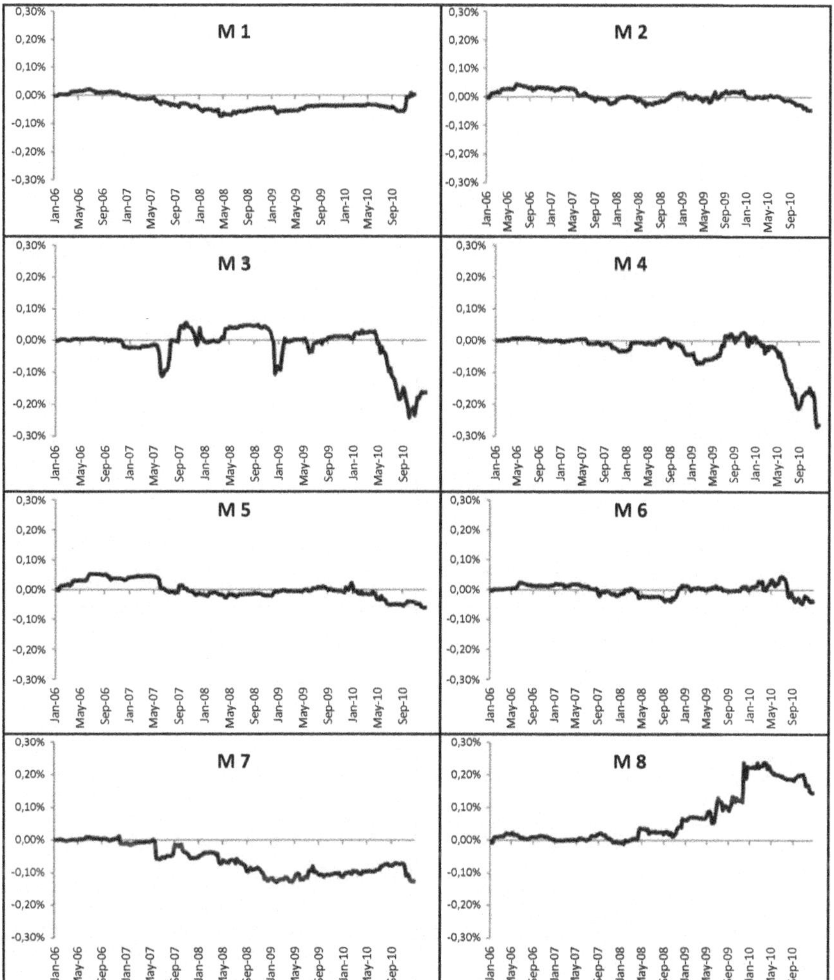

Fig. 3.2 Duration contribution to outperformance

We observe a relatively low exposure to duration bets, with the exception of a couple of portfolio managers (M3 and M4). However, we note that M4 shows a more active duration management only after 2008. The peaks of duration exposure of the other portfolio managers are of the order of 10 basis points only.

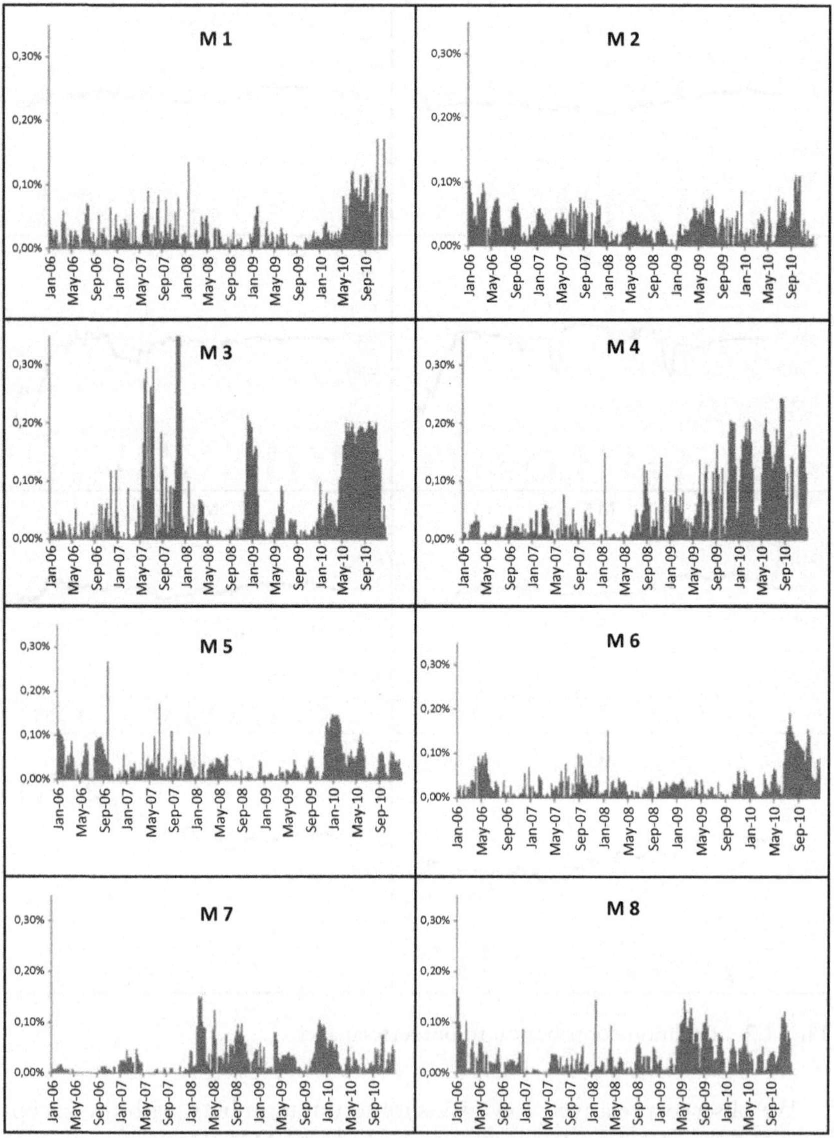

Fig. 3.3 Duration exposure

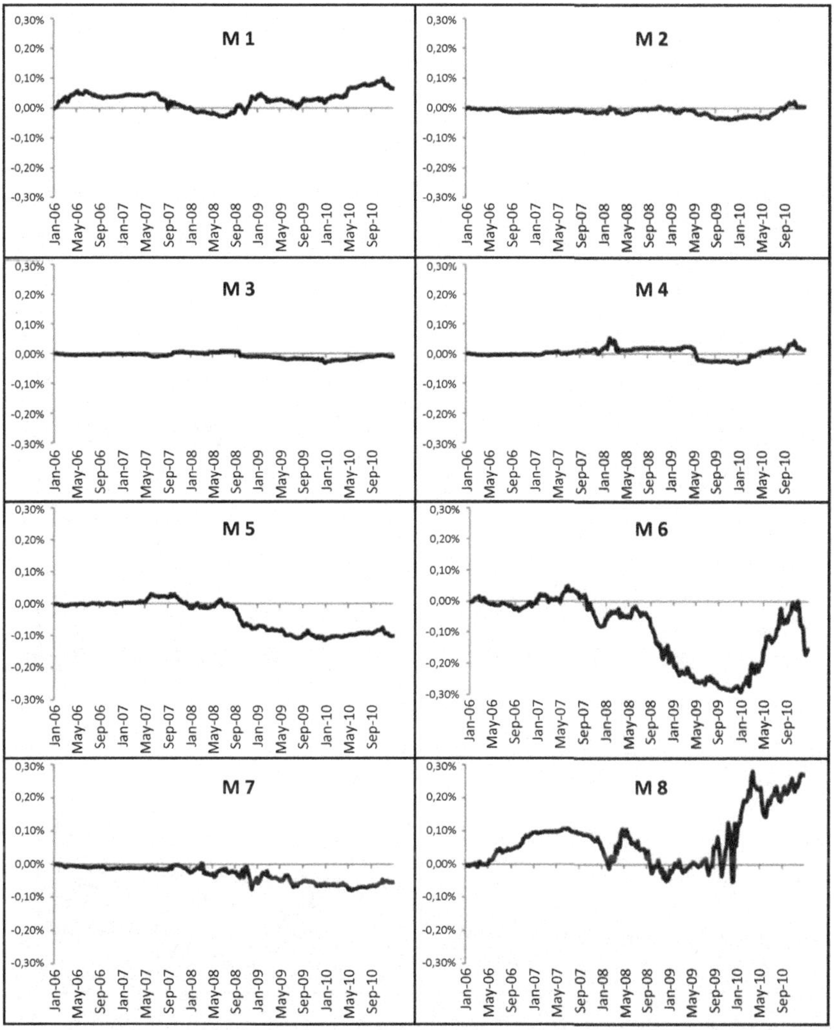

Fig. 3.4 Curvature contribution to outperformance

The curve contribution analysis shows a similar picture. Even in this case, only M8 achieved a sizeable excess return by loading on curvature (Fig. 3.4).

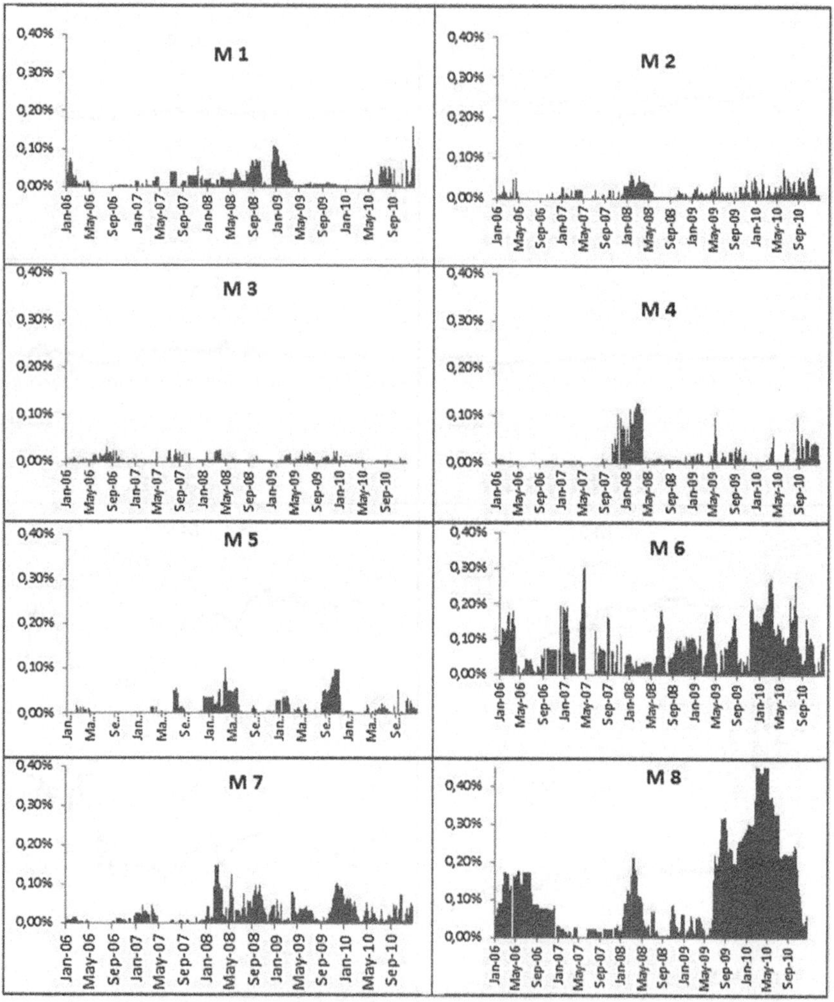

Fig. 3.5 Curvature exposure

M1 shows a slightly positive performance loading on curvature, with the other portfolio managers not taking appreciable curvature risk (M2, M3, and M4) or shorting curvature (M6, M5, and M7). Figure 3.5 illustrates a more diversified use of the risk budget in curve bets than in duration bets. In particular, some portfolio managers seem not to place curve bets (M2 and M3), and other managers take only moderate curve exposures (M1, M4, M5, and M7), while M8 (with exposure peaks at around 50 basis points) and M6 (with maximum exposure at around 30 basis points) show a very active curve management.

Spread exposure proved to be the most important active layer in terms of results and exposures along the sample period. Almost all portfolio managers achieved positive results, with the exception of M8, which was substantially aligned with the benchmark (Fig. 3.6).

In general, an important source of spread-related outperformance is related to the carry component. This component represents the yield pick-up earned by replacing government securities with spread products. The yield pick-up was very high during the financial crisis of 2007–2008, when swap spreads in the two-year tenor peaked at about 165 basis points. However, portfolio managers seem to have achieved these results not only by maintaining a long exposure to spread products, but also by actively trading spreads on both sides, long and short. The best performer in spread management are M1 and M6, which obtained an outperformance of around 40 basis points. M6 also showed an active style, by changing intensity in the usage of the risk budget (Fig. 3.7); M2, M4, M5, and M7 show a result of around 20 basis points, while the other managers obtained a slightly positive outperformance. Again, different styles can be traced: low active spread players (M2, M3, and M4), moderate active spread players (M5, M7), and strong spread players (M6 and M8) can be clearly identified (Fig. 3.7).

The most important source of outperformance proves to be security selection (Fig. 3.8).

The best performer is M6, which achieves an excess return of close to 60 basis points, followed by M7 (around 50 basis points) and M5 (40 basis points); M2 and M4 achieve around 20 basis points, while the results of M1 and M3 are close to zero. The only manager that reports a negative result is M8 (−20 basis points).

All the managers contribute to the outperformance while showing different skills or different ways to pursue returns in excess of the benchmark. Some portfolio managers prove to be more successful in duration bets, while others obtain better results in curve management, or loading on the spread component, or exploiting carry opportunities. Figures 3.3, 3.5, and 3.7 clearly show a different use of the risk budget among portfolio managers and a different attitude in changing it over time.

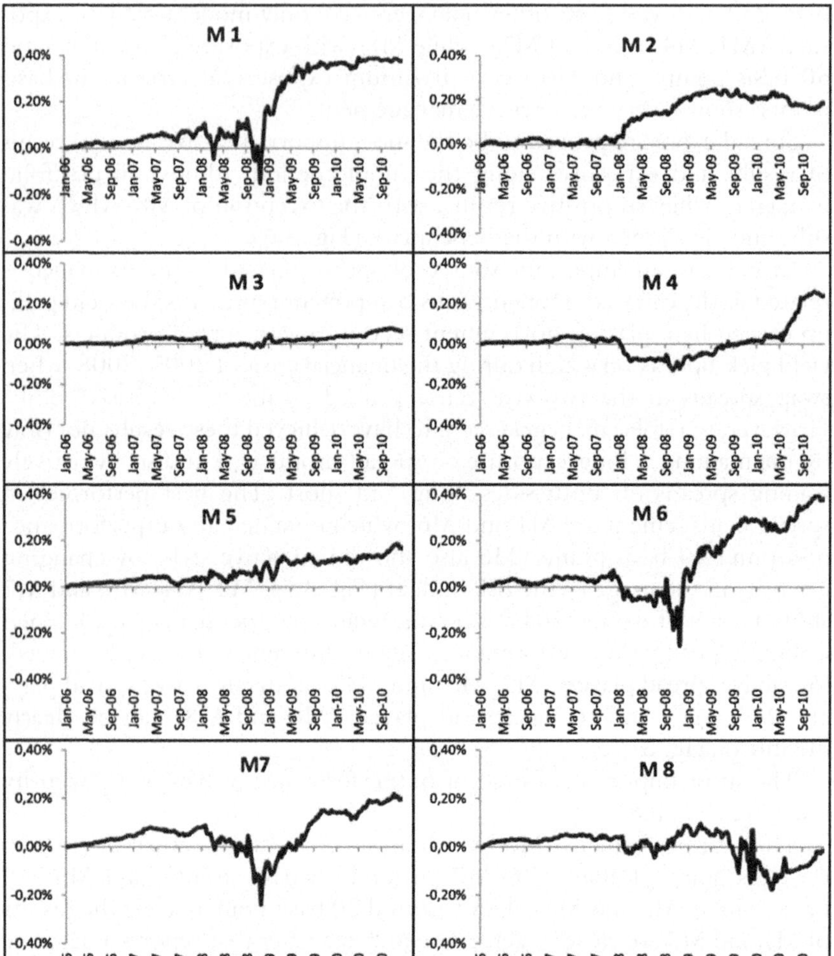

Fig. 3.6 Spread contribution to outperformance

Portfolio managers' also styles prove to be different in terms of some important indicators that may help to better qualify the attitude toward risk and the specific ability of portfolio managers to preserve capital. To illustrate this point, we selected a group of indicators: (1) the information ratio, measuring risk-adjusted performance; (2) the tracking error, giving

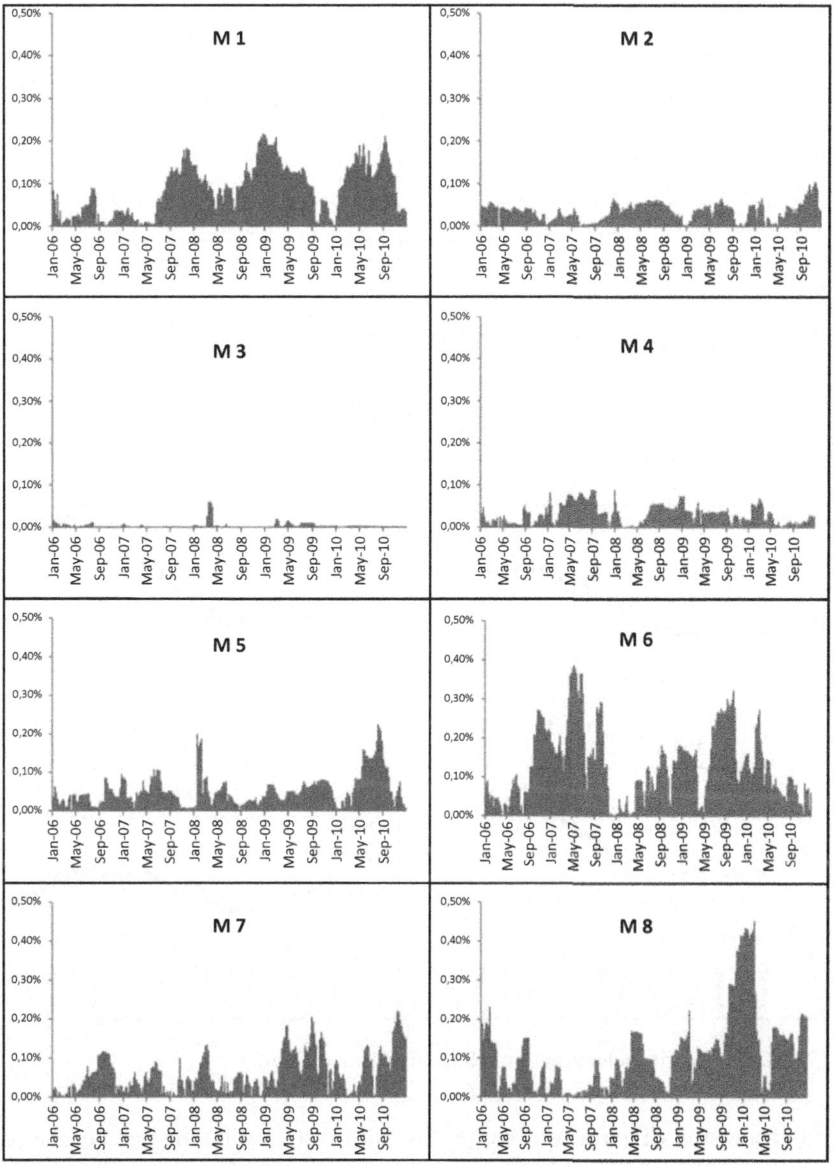

Fig. 3.7 Spread exposure

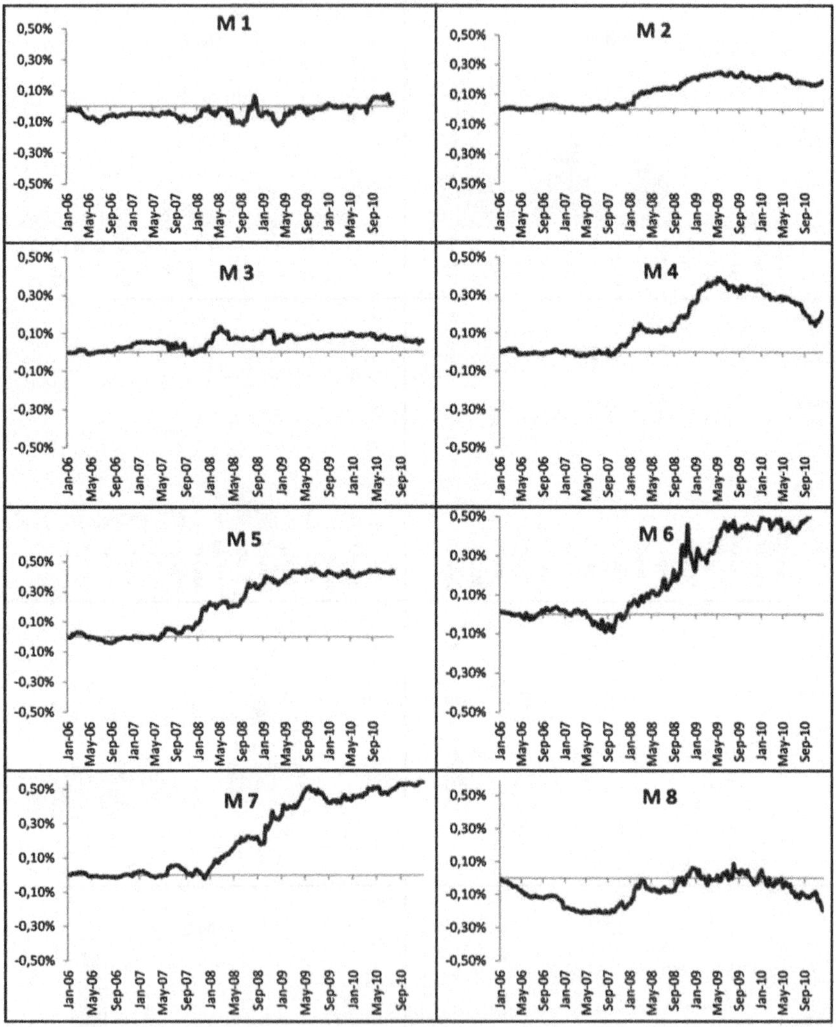

Fig. 3.8 Security selection contribution to outperformance

the dispersion of extra returns; (3) the hit ratio, that is, the percentage of winning bets over total bets; and (4) the max drawdown, measuring the largest cumulative loss from peak to trough over a period of time.

The ranking across these performance qualifiers sheds some light on the preferences of portfolio managers toward returns (high information ratio) or capital preservation (low drawdown risk). The hit ratio helps understand if the extra returns reflect a combination of a large number of winning bets (with low profits) and a small number of losing bets (with a higher loss) or a combination of a few winning bets (with high profits) with many losing bets (with low losses). The tracking error provides a useful indication about the confidence interval of returns around the mean, which may help distinguish whether the results depend on solid skills.

Tables 3.7 through 3.10 show a low degree of overlap among the ranking of portfolio managers across performance qualifiers and active layers,

Table 3.7 Duration exposure synthetic indicators

	M1	*M2*	*M3*	*M4*	*M5*	*M6*	*M7*	*M8*
Duration								
Information ratio (yearly basis)	0.02	−0.30	−0.35	−0.87	−0.36	−0.20	−0.56	0.40
Ranking	2	4	5	8	6	3	7	1
Tracking error (yearly basis)	0.03%	0.03%	0.10%	0.06%	0.03%	0.04%	0.05%	0.08%
Ranking	1	2	8	6	3	4	5	7
Hit ratio	45%	51%	49%	48%	47%	50%	56%	49%
Ranking	8	2	4	6	7	3	1	4
Max drawdown	−0.09%	−0.09%	−0.30%	−0.30%	−0.11%	−0.09%	−0.14%	−0.09%
Ranking	4	1	8	7	5	2	6	3

Table 3.8 Curve exposure synthetic indicators

	M1	*M2*	*M3*	*M4*	*M5*	*M6*	*M7*	*M8*
Curve								
Information ratio (yearly basis)	0.35	0.05	−0.18	0.09	−0.71	−0.33	−0.27	0.36
Ranking	2	4	5	3	8	7	6	1
Tracking error (yearly basis)	0.04%	0.02%	0.01%	0.03%	0.03%	0.10%	0.04%	0.15%
Ranking	5	2	1	4	3	7	6	8
Hit ratio	51%	53%	51%	50%	48%	49%	49%	54%
Ranking	3	2	3	5	8	7	6	1
Max drawdown	−0.09%	−0.04%	−0.04%	−0.09%	−0.14%	−0.34%	−0.08%	−0.18%
Ranking	5	2	1	4	6	8	3	7

thus supporting the idea of heterogeneous investment styles. The time horizon for active bets chosen by portfolio managers qualifies the investment style, discriminating between portfolio managers that prefer a low number of bets with a longer time horizon from those oriented toward a higher number of bets with a shorter time horizon.

Finally, Table 3.11 shows the average time horizon, in terms of weeks, for each single strategy across portfolio managers.[9] Portfolio managers are more resilient in changing positions of spread trades. This is in line with the idea that managers seek to fully exploit the carry component of spread

Table 3.9 Spread exposure synthetic indicators

	M1	*M2*	*M3*	*M4*	*M5*	*M6*	*M7*	*M8*
Spread								
Information ratio (yearly basis)	0.55	0.47	0.40	0.77	0.57	0.50	0.36	−0.01
Ranking	3	5	6	1	2	4	7	8
Tracking error (yearly basis)	0.14%	0.03%	0.03%	0.06%	0.06%	0.16%	0.12%	0.18%
Ranking	6	1	2	4	3	7	5	8
Hit ratio	57%	61%	57%	54%	55%	55%	61%	53%
Ranking	3	2	4	7	6	5	1	8
Max drawdown	−0.28%	−0.07%	−0.06%	−0.17%	−0.08%	−0.33%	−0.33%	−0.27%
Ranking	6	2	1	4	3	7	8	5

Table 3.10 Security selection indicators

	M1	*M2*	*M3*	*M4*	*M5*	*M6*	*M7*	*M8*
Security selection								
Information ratio (yearly basis)	0.04	0.77	0.18	0.68	1.13	0.76	1.21	−0.32
Ranking	7	3	6	5	2	4	1	8
Tracking error (yearly basis)	0.11%	0.05%	0.07%	0.07%	0.08%	0.16%	0.09%	0.13%
Ranking	6	1	2	3	4	8	5	7
Hit ratio	52%	55%	60%	51%	55%	55%	54%	44%
Ranking	6	2	1	7	2	2	5	8
Max drawdown	−0.19%	−0.09%	−0.09%	−0.25%	−0.07%	−0.23%	−0.09%	−0.28%
Ranking	5	3	2	7	1	6	4	8

Table 3.11 Active positions—average time horizon (weeks)

	M1	*M2*	*M3*	*M4*	*M5*	*M6*	*M7*	*M8*
Duration	4	10	5	5	6	6	6	6
Curve	11	6	4	6	7	10	7	9
Spread	24	13	2	15	24	22	13	18

products, which involves a preference for long spread positions and a bias toward a longer time horizon of spread strategies. The average holding period for curve strategies is shorter, and it ranges between four and eight weeks, showing mixed preferences in terms of holding period among portfolio managers. The time horizon for duration strategies is even shorter than that of curve strategies. The duration positions show a time horizon of slightly over one month, thus indicating that the monthly rebalancing represents a kind of 'catalyst' for duration bets.

These results confirm the idea that portfolio managers adopt different investment styles. The more diversified the investment styles of portfolio managers are, according to each active layer, the more likely it is that, in the aggregate portfolio, a higher number of independent bets are carried out. According to the 'law of active management' (Grinold 1989), other things being equal, the higher the number of independent bets, the higher the information ratio of the aggregated portfolio. In particular, the information ratio is defined as:

$$\mathrm{IR} = \mathrm{IC}^{*} \sqrt{BR}$$

where IC is the information coefficient, a measure of the level of skill, or the ability to forecast each asset residual return. It is defined as the correlation between the forecasts and the returns; *BR* represents breadth, or the number of independent bets in the managed portfolio. According to this formula, one way to improve the information ratio might be given by an increase in the number of independent bets, assuming a comparable level of skills. More independent positions among portfolio managers in terms of duration, curve, and timing may actually lead to a decrease in the absolute and relative risk of the aggregated portfolio, while the aggregate return can be expected to increase, hence improving the risk-return profile of the aggregate portfolio.

3.5 Conclusions

We develop a simple performance attribution model that has some advantages in comparison with existing factor models: it identifies the contribution of the key portfolio managers' strategies, it offers a clear interpretation of results from a portfolio manager's perspective, and it presents no residual term.

Applying our methodology to the managers of the ECB's foreign reserves, we find that among the active layers (duration, curve, and spread), the spread contribution seems the most relevant. Curve and duration bets, with some exceptions, have generally provided modest value addition. The analysis of the use of risk budget and the ranking across 'performance qualifiers' supports the view that portfolio managers adopt diversified investment styles. This may explain the non-negligible result of the aggregate reserve portfolio, averaging 10 basis points on an annual basis net of transaction costs. The more diversified the investment styles are, the more likely it is that portfolio managers place independent bets, which in turn may positively affect the risk-adjusted return of the aggregate portfolio.

Notes

1. Helpful comments by Christophe Beuve, Narayan Bulusu, Gioia Cellai, Francesco Daini, Maurizio Ghirga, Giuseppe Grande, Johannes Kramer, Philippe Muller, Franco Panfili, Tommaso Perez, Dario Ottaviani, Antonio Rossetti, Andrea Santorelli, Roberto Violi, and seminar participants at the Sixth BIS-World Bank-Bank of Canada Public Investors' Conference in Washington, ECB and Banca d'Italia are gratefully acknowledged.
2. At the end of 2010.
3. Bonds included in the benchmark can be grouped in pre-defined buckets, so called 'time buckets', according to their maturities (just for illustrative purposes, bonds with maturity ranging from zero to one year can be included in an hypothetical time bucket '0–1 year', and so on).
4. At first quarter 2017 (IMF COFER statistics: http://data.imf.org/?sk=E6A5F467-C14B-4AA8-9F6D-5A09EC4E62A4)
5. At first quarter 2017 (International Investment Funds Association: https://www.iifa.ca/files/1503579002_IIFA%20-%20Worldwide%20Open-End%20Fund%20Report%20-%20Q1%202017.pdf).
6. 'Virtual' trades for rebalancing the tactical benchmark are carried out at actual trading prices (including transaction costs).

7. The ECB's official reserves include also assets denominated in Japanese yen and gold. The other Euro-system NCBs were involved in the active management of the yen reserve portfolio. We refer to each central bank's desk involved in the management of the ECB reserves as a 'portfolio manager'. In practice, a small team usually works on the ECB reserves desk, comprising, for example, one manager and one or two dealers, in some cases devoting part of their work time to the ECB reserves and the remainder to the management of the foreign exchange portfolio owned by the NCB.
8. The extra return that comes from the carry of deposits is included in the security selection and not in the spread contribution, because deposit instruments are not classified as spread products.
9. The average time horizon is obtained by counting the number of inversions of sign of partial duration exposures related to each single strategy.

References

Blake, C. R., Elton, E. J., & Gruber, M. J. (1993). The performance of bond mutual funds. *Journal of Business, 66*(3), 371–403.

Boney, V., Comer, G., & Kelly, L. (2009). Timing the investment grade securities market: Evidence from high quality bond funds. *Journal of Empirical Finance, 16*(1), 55–69.

Borio, C., Ebbesen, J., Galati G., & Heath, A. (2008a). *FX reserve management: Elements of a framework*. BIS Papers, No. 38.

Borio, C., Galati, G., & Heath, A. (2008b). *FX reserve management: Trends and challenges*. BIS Papers, No. 40.

Brinson, G. P., Hood, L. R., & Beebower, G. L. (1986). Determinants of portfolio performance. *Financial Analysts Journal, 42*(4), 39–44.

Campisi, S. (2011). A sector based approach to fixed income performance attribution. *The Journal of Performance Measurement, 15*(3), 23–42.

Chen, Y., Ferson, W., & Peters, H. (2010). Measuring the timing ability and performance of bond mutual funds. *Journal of Financial Economics, 98*(1), 72–89.

Cici, G., & Gibson, S. (2012). The performance of corporate bond mutual funds: Evidence based on security-level holdings. *Journal of Financial and Quantitative Analysis, 47*(1), 159–178.

Elton, E. J., Gruber, M. J., & Blake, C. R. (1995). Fundamental economic variables, expected returns, and bond fund performance. *Journal of Finance, 50*(4), 1229–1256.

Ferson, W., Henry, T. R., & Kisgen, D. J. (2006). Evaluating government bond fund performance with stochastic discount factors. *Review of Financial Studies, 19*(2), 423–455.

Grinold, R. (1989). The fundamental law of active management. *The Journal of Portfolio Management, 15*(3), 30–37.

Hu, Y.-W. (2010). *Management of China's foreign exchange reserves: A case study on the state administration of foreign exchange (SAFE)*. European Commission Economic Papers, No. 421.

Huang, J.-Z., & Wang, Y. (2014). Timing ability of government bond fund managers: Evidence from portfolio holdings. *Management Science, 60*(8), 2091–2109.

Johnson-Calari, J., Grava, R., & Kobor, A. (2007). Trends in reserve management by central banks. In A. Bakker & I. van Herpt (Eds.), *Central bank reserve management*. Cheltenham: Edward Elgar.

Koivu, M., Monar, F., & Nyholm, K. (2009). Strategic asset allocation for fixed-income investors. In U. Bindseil, F. Gonzalez, & E. Tabakis (Eds.), *Risk management for central banks and other public investors*. New York: Cambridge University Press.

Lam, M. (1999). The performance of global bond mutual funds. *Journal of Banking and Finance, 23*(8), 1195–1217.

Manzanares, A., & Schwartzlose, H. (2009). Risk control, compliance monitoring and reporting. In U. Bindseil, F. Gonzalez, & E. Tabakis (Eds.), *Risk management for central banks and other public investors*. New York: Cambridge University Press.

McCauley, R., & Rigaudy, F. (2011). Managing foreign exchange reserves in the crisis and after. In *Portfolio and risk management for central banks and sovereign wealth funds. Proceedings of a joint conference organised by the BIS, the ECB and the World Bank in Basel*, 2–3 November 2010. BIS Papers, No 58.

Moneta, F. (2015). Measuring bond mutual fund performance with portfolio characteristics. *Journal of Empirical Finance, 33*, 223–242.

Nugée, J. (2012). *Foreign exchange reserves management*. CCBS Handbooks in Central Banking, No. 19.

Scalia, A., & Sahel, B. (2012). *Ranking, risk-taking and effort—An analysis of the ECB's foreign reserves management*. Bank of Italy Discussion Paper, No. 840.

Vesilind, A., & Kuus, K. (2005). *Application of investment models in foreign exchange reserve management in Eesti Pank*. Working Papers of Eesti Pank, No. 6.

CHAPTER 4

Sovereign Wealth Fund Investment Performance, Strategic Asset Allocation, and Funding Withdrawal Rules

Michael G. Papaioannou and Bayasgalan Rentsendorj

4.1 Introduction

In the past decade, we have observed shifts in the strategic asset allocations (SAAs) of many sovereign wealth funds (SWFs), manifested by a rather significant reduction in the share of public-market assets (publicly traded equity and fixed income) at the expense of an expansion of riskier private-market assets (alternatives, infrastructure, private equity, real estate, and so on). This trend has mainly been the result of SWFs' search for higher returns. The investment value chain has further evolved from the traditional asset owner and manager relationships to a business model of closer partnerships. This business model has gradually been adopted by traditional, mostly conservative SWFs, which have preferred a passive-benchmark

M. G. Papaioannou (✉)
International Monetary Fund (IMF), Washington, DC, USA
e-mail: mpapaioannou@imf.org

B. Rentsendorj
International Forum of Sovereign Wealth Funds (IFSWF), London, UK
e-mail: br@ifswf.org

N. Bulusu et al. (eds.), *Advances in the Practice of Public Investment Management*, https://doi.org/10.1007/978-3-319-90245-6_4

replication strategy over high-risk active asset management. In particular, newer SWFs' governance arrangements tend to be more receptive to higher risk and adopt in-house, active asset management approaches.

The change in many SWFs' risk appetite has primarily been triggered by a heightened observance of their fiduciary duty to build intergenerational equity—that is, a mandatory obligation to provide positive returns over a specified future period. Most SWF governance structures require careful consideration when adopting an enhanced role in the investment value chain in private markets by playing a more active general-partnership role rather than a limited-partnership role. Also, the search for higher returns leads to a more comprehensive governance map for SWFs, suggesting a more flexible operational framework than a traditional rule-based asset management framework. In turn, these developments imply that SWFs will likely become more active participants in the management of corporate businesses around the world by being directly involved rather than being silent or distant investors.

Although the number and size of established SWFs have increased dramatically over the past ten years, surpassing 90 in number at the end of 2015, with combined assets exceeding $7 trillion,[1] the adequacy of their operational independence is still in question. In particular, 14 SWFs have been set up in Africa, with a total of $114 billion in assets under management (ADB 2013); 11 in hydrocarbon (oil and gas)-exporting Arab countries; 12 in northern hemisphere countries, including Colombia and Panama; and 18 in Asian countries, including Thailand and Vietnam. This increase in the establishment of SWFs enhances the need for legitimacy (including the adoption of appropriate legal structures) and for assurances of sufficiently independent operational rules and relationships.

Our analysis suggests that many SWFs still lack coordinated, sustainable, and independent operational structures, as well as fiscal frameworks that support a comprehensive investment value chain that could enhance their return performance. Specifically, various perspectives have recently been offered for setting up "hybrid" SWFs, with multiple goals and a range of policy purposes, such as to attract strategic long-term investors for large-scale infrastructure or developmental projects, draw more foreign direct investment (FDI), enhance economic competitiveness, attain portfolio diversification, serve financial stability considerations, all while avoiding integrated budget implications. However, these designs often contradict some fundamental prerequisites and basic principles in establishing an SWF, including the establishment of clear objectives (such as stabilization, intergenerational savings, or explicit liability coverage (pensions) and/or development purposes, adoption of a well-defined governance structure, and implementation of transparent investment and risk management frameworks). These shortcomings in design do not only open the door to misappropriations of initial policy purposes and management ineffectiveness in the respective SWFs but also often complicate the execution of fiscal rules.

In general, our findings indicate that SWFs with a comprehensive governance structure that is in line with the SWF owner country's macrofiscal policy framework are better able to determine their dynamic asset allocations and experience investment performances closer to their strategic policy/benchmark target compositions. Suitable SWF funding and withdrawal rules are found to be critical components of an effective SWF governance structure. Also, a strong institutional development and risk management framework is typically required to ensure an appropriate timing and frequency of SAA changes, especially in periods of high or intensifying market volatility.

The chapter is organized as follows: Sect. 4.2 presents some stylized facts relating to changes in SWF SAAs over the period from 2008 to 2015, Sect. 4.3 outlines some determinants of SWF investment performance, Sect. 4.4 discusses some broad implications of the investment value change on SWFs' strategic asset allocation and investment performance, and Sect. 4.5 provides some concluding remarks on current challenges in SWF governance structures and their effects on investment performance.

4.2 Shifts in SWF Strategic Asset Allocations During 2010–15

As long-horizon investors, many SWFs are positioned to invest in ways that many short- and medium-horizon investors cannot. As such, certain investments and risk premia that are efficiently priced from the perspective of other long-term investors may also present value opportunities for SWFs. In principle, active ownership should not undermine the selection of the investment universe and, thus, the performance of the respective SWFs. However, SWFs should be resilient and able to overcome international and local business cycle challenges, including broad macroeconomic volatilities.

Figure 4.1 illustrates the percentage changes in allocation to asset classes for select SWFs between end-2015 (or latest available data) and end-2010 (or June 2011). Figures 4.2 and 4.3, respectively, contain the

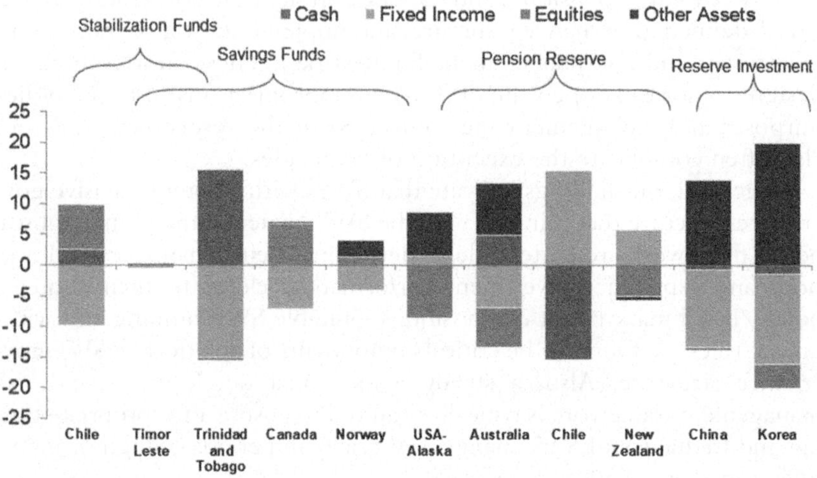

Fig. 4.1 Selected SWF SAA changes, 2015 versus 2010. The units of the Y-axis are %

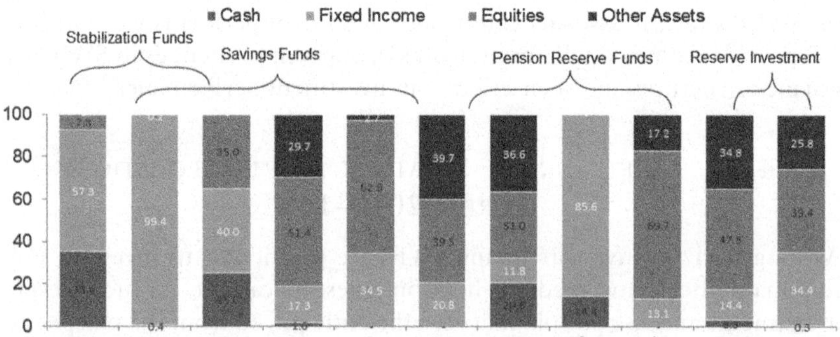

Fig. 4.2 Selected SWF SAAs, 2015. The units of the Y-axis are %

allocation by asset class at the end and beginning of the sample. Although the evidence is limited, the observed changes indicate, in general, that pension reserve and reserve investment funds have experienced more changes in their SAAs compared to stabilization funds.

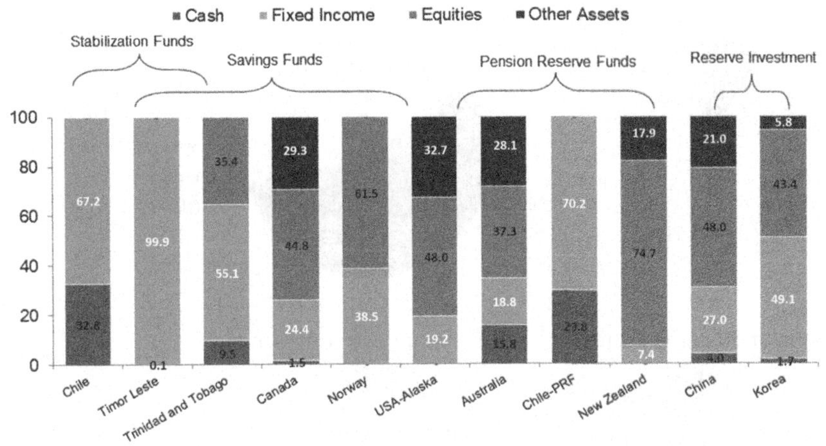

Fig. 4.3 Selected SWF SAAs, 2010. The units of the Y-axis are %

Although there is no uniform approach in selecting an SAA for an SWF, it is worth noting that multiple policy purposes or lack of clarity in objectives have been found to adversely affect the selection process of assets within the permissible investment universe. This usually leads to the choice of suboptimal and inconsistent instruments, which undermine investment performance. Also, the performance of SWFs tends to respond in accordance with the selection and implementation of SAAs (Hammer et al. 2008; Bodie and Briere 2013).

Further, an increasing number of newly established non-natural-resources-based strategic funds, mainly from indebted developing countries, now accounting for about half of all SWFs, are found to be vulnerable to respective country budget rules. This broad consideration of lack of independence or close macrofiscal integration should further be analyzed from the sovereign asset and liability management framework. Das et al. (2009) provide a comprehensive set of international good practices in setting up and managing SWFs, utilizing broad recommendations and guidelines outlined in the Santiago Principles.[2]

As indicated in Figs. 4.4 and 4.5, SWFs' asset allocations, and consequently their investment performance, depend mainly on their type. Also, their asset allocation trends indicate that they are largely leaning more toward private markets, which includes higher-yielding private equity and alternative investment vehicles, as part of their performance enhancement

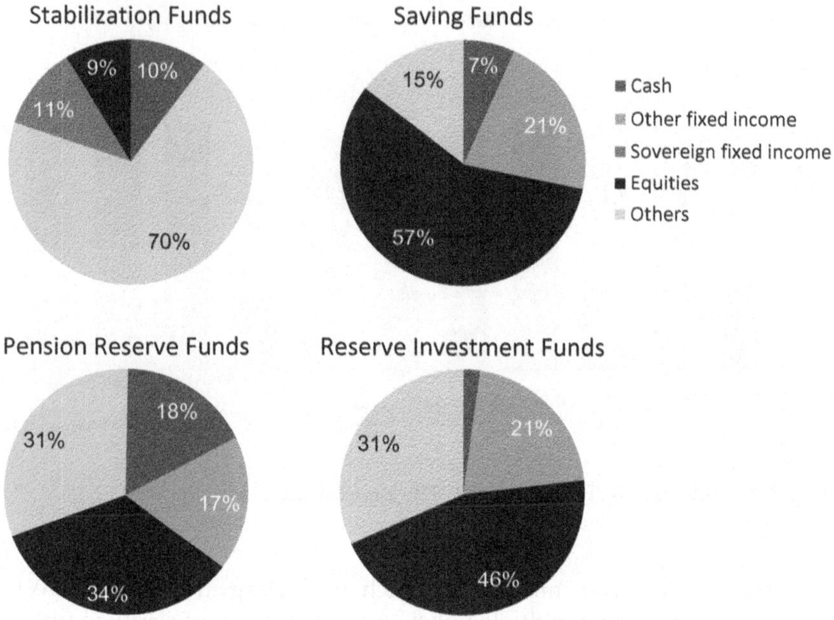

Fig. 4.4 SAAs by type of SWF, end-2015 (or latest available data)

strategies. However, a higher proportion invested in long-horizon assets entails bearing the risk of significant within-horizon drawdowns. It is thus critical for SWFs not only to measure and manage these risks, but also to communicate them clearly to stakeholders in advance. The increased need to better align with fellow institutional investors calls for closer partnerships in the changing investment-value-chain landscape.

Although SAAs depend on the SWF type, changes in SAAs have been observed across all types. SWFs, as long-horizon investors, have an advantage in that they require less liquidity than other investors. To the extent they invest in illiquid asset classes, SWFs should expect to earn a premium. Based on their unique liquidity profile, it is essential for SWFs to estimate the illiquidity premium they should demand to determine the appropriate exposure to illiquid investments. At any particular time, the risk premia of certain asset classes may represent better value opportunities than others for long-horizon investors.

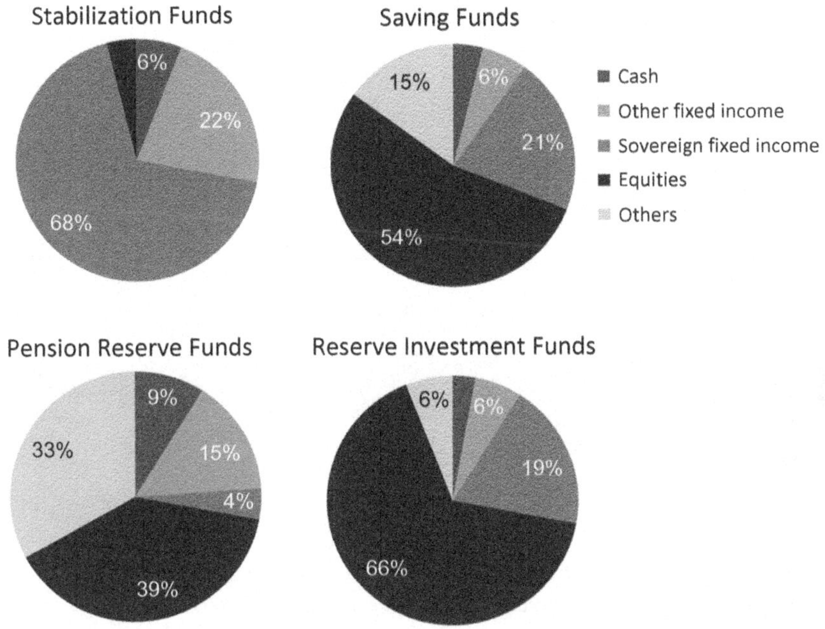

Fig. 4.5 SAAs by type of SWF, end-2010 (or June 2011)

4.3 SWF Investment Performance over the Last Decade

Arguably, the performance of an SWF should be compared against its objectives, often based on the persistent pursuit of its long-term investment beliefs. Although the overall trajectory is mostly determined by global financial market volatility, persistent long-term benchmarking along with an ability to operate independently of government fiscal fluctuations are also associated with high rates of investment returns. As indicated in Fig. 4.6 and Table 4.1, representative savings and pension reserve funds performed significantly better than other types of SWFs.

Well-defined SWF funding and withdrawal rules are critical for investment performance. In principle, these rules should depend on the individual SWF's objectives and the owner country's legal framework and general macroeconomic setting. While many established SWFs have fairly

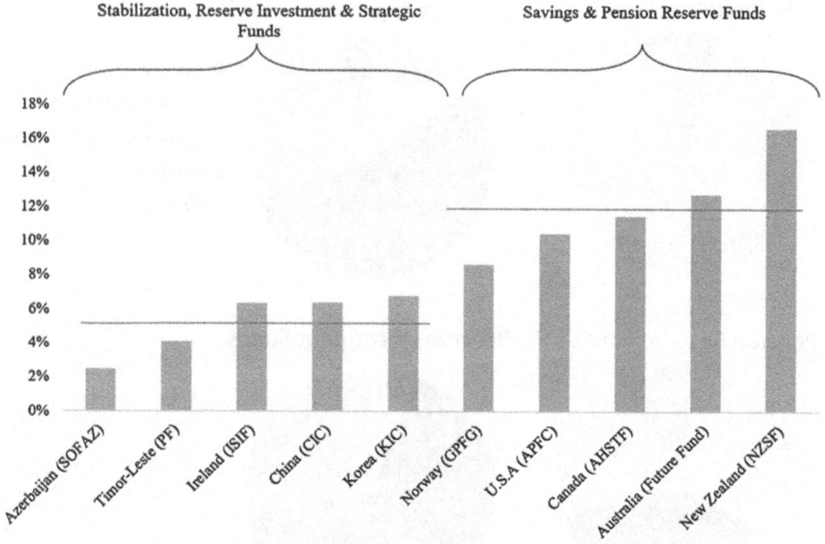

Fig. 4.6 Annualized (five-year) returns of selected SWF portfolios

transparent rules, our analysis shows that some newly-established SWFs need to strengthen their respective funding and withdrawal rules. Not implementing such rules may leave funds vulnerable to various macrofiscal shocks as well as common principal-agent problems between the government and the asset manager, where each would like to act in its own interests. Common examples include sudden fiscal shocks (i.e., to fulfill liquidity shortages), volatility in global commodity prices (i.e., sudden shortness in budget revenues—a gap-filler role), uneven financial market conditions (i.e., owing to government borrowing, cost increases, and/or currency short selling), and domestic macroeconomic pressures (i.e., exchange rate movements, Dutch-disease effects), which could adversely affect the realization of initial SWF objectives and policy mandates, as well as the intended accumulation of assets and investment performance) (Fig. 4.7).

Table 4.1 Historical returns of selected SWFs (percent)

Country (fund)	*2005*	*2006*	*2007*	*2008*	*2009*	*2010*	*2011*	*2012*	*2013*	*2014*	*2015*
Australia FF (Future Fund)		6.0	6.2	1.5	−4.2	10.6	12.8	2.1	15.4	14.3	8.4
Canada AHSTF (Alberta Heritage Savings Trust Fund)	15.2	12.4	−0.7	−18.1	17.8	10.4	10.4	8.2	16.0	12.5	4.7
Chile ESSF (Economic and Social Stabilization Fund)			8.9	7.6	2.3	1.8	3.5	1.0	−1.3	−1.7	−1.78
China CIC (China Investment Corporation)				−2.1	11.7	11.7	−4.3	10.6	9.3	5.5	−2.96
Ireland ISIF (Ireland Strategic Investment Fund)	19.6	12.4	3.3	−30.4	20.6	11.7	1.6	7.8	6.4	4.6	
Korea KIC (Korea Investment Corporation)			7.40	−17.5	17.6	8.2	−4.0	11.8	9.1	4.0	−3.0
Malaysia Khazannah				−35.7	43.9	33.4	−7.0	24.3	19.1	9.0	3.20
New Zealand SF (Superannuation Fund)	21.0	13.7	13.4	−12.9	−5.5	13.0	1.4	20.9	24.3	19.4	14.6
Norway GPFG (Government Pension Fund Global)	11.1	7.9	4.3	−23.3	25.6	9.6	−2.5	13.4	16.0	7.6	2.74
Singapore Temasek				7.0	−30.0	42.7	4.6	1.5	9.0	2.0	19
U.S.A. APFC (Alaska Permanent Fund Corporation)	10.16	10.82	17.06	−3.58	−18.0	11.8	20.6	0.02	10.9	15.5	4.91

Source: SWF annual reports, financial press information, and authors' calculations

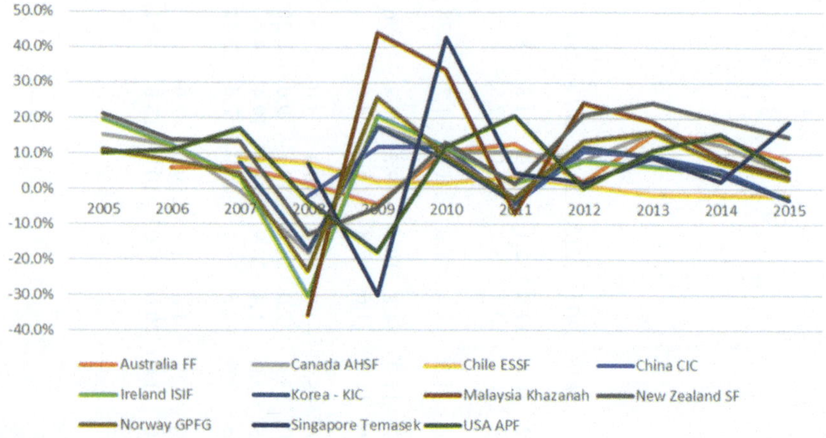

Fig. 4.7 Historical returns of selected SWFs

Especially for intergenerational savings SWFs, better prospects for investment performance can be established through well-defined governance, operational transparency, and independence in investment decisions. Our findings indicate that only a handful of sovereign funds have adopted comprehensive funding and withdrawal frameworks in line with their policy purposes, thus illustrating their high degree of vulnerability to potential government interference and consequent risks to their investment management sustainability (see Fig. 4.8).

An absence of these rules tends to hurt SWFs' long-term investment performance, which, along with maintaining their integrity and credibility within the country's fiscal regime, is typically their objective. Sustainable intergenerational wealth building requires primarily a commitment to a long-term investment horizon, which needs to take into consideration the country's macrofinancial conditions and the establishment of well-rounded funding and withdrawal frameworks that are well aligned with the country's fiscal management (Ang et al. 2009; Rozanov 2007).

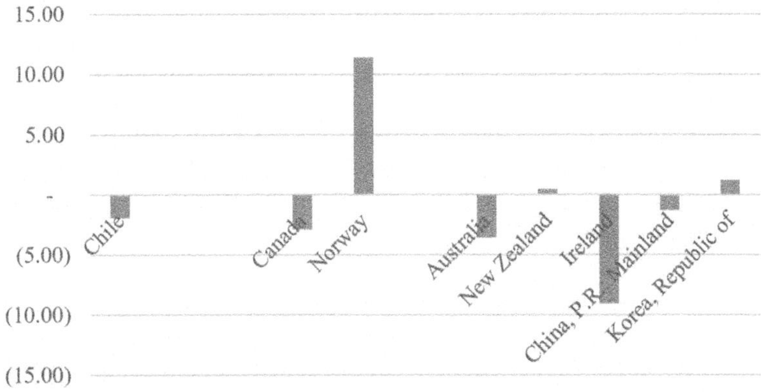

Fig. 4.8 Selected SWF owner countries' budget balances (annualized, five years)

4.4 SWF Investment Value Chain and Implications for SAAs and Investment Performance

4.4.1 Policy Objectives and Funding and Withdrawal Frameworks

The policy objectives of SWFs typically determine their funding and withdrawal frameworks and rules, which are often defined in their relevant legislations. Mixed policy objectives may undermine the clarity of incentives and, as a result, support inconsistent macroeconomic policies. In general, funding and withdrawal rules are connected to the main types of SWFs in the following ways:

- Stabilization funds usually have funding and withdrawal frameworks that are closely linked to the state of the fiscal policy through clearly predetermined rules.
- Reserve investment funds, often following the global diversification and high-return mandates of central bank reserves, have funding and withdrawal frameworks that are quite independent of the owner country's fiscal and/or other macroeconomic policies.
- Savings and pension funds have funding and withdrawal frameworks that reflect their respective objectives. In the case of pension funds with increasing uncertainty of future liabilities, the fund's manage-

ment becomes more complicated. In particular, a target obligation of higher returns in order to meet a predetermined pension fund value frequently leads to higher risk-taking than for stabilization funds.

- Development and strategic funds' funding and withdrawal frameworks tend to be simpler than those for other SWF types, as in many cases, they involve one-off state funding for specific strategic developmental purposes.

As can be seen in Table 4.2, hybrid-type funds have become increasingly popular. According to the IFSWF (2014), many SWFs have declared two or more mandates and policy purposes. Although this flexibility enhances the owner country's ability to maneuver in certain global and local economic conditions, it could also become a source of economic instability if funding and withdrawal rules are not strictly adhered to or are easily modified.

4.4.2 *Enhancing the Investment Value Chain Through Appropriate Funding and Withdrawal Rules*

A principal-agent problem may arise and the investment value chain may be undermined when SWFs do not have publicly disclosed mandates and operational independence of funding and withdrawal rules. Lack of well-defined and transparent rules could compromise SWFs' objectives by allowing governments' ad hoc policies to overrule SWFs' institutional mandate to act independently. Such institutional conflicts of interest may lead to moral-hazard issues. Sovereign funds may not act in the best interest of the country regarding value maximization of public assets, but may rather act in the service of other government aspirations, such as parking SWF assets for short periods of time and using them for the government's political and social agendas. To this end, the complexity of global financial markets and asymmetry of information may be used by different governments as excuses to make biased policy decisions on SWF SAAs so as to accommodate politically motivated SWF portfolio compositions. To avoid such challenges, governments need to institute operational independence of sovereign funds, with publicly disclosed fiscal, funding, and withdrawal rules. On this front, Chile (Fiscal Stability Law and Fiscal Rules) and Norway (Government Pension Fund Act) lead the way. Table 4.3 presents the fiscal rules of a selected group of countries with SWFs.

Table 4.2 Policy purpose and performance of SWFs

Sovereign wealth fund, inception year	*Stabilization*	*Reserve investment*	*Savings or pension*	*Development or strategic*	*Performance (average annual return since inception, percent)*
Angola FSDEA (Fondo Soberano de Angola), 2011		√		√	–
Australia FF (Future Fund), 2006			√		7.4
Azerbaijan SOFAZ (State Oil Fund of the Republic of Azerbaijan), 1999	√		√		2.42
Botswana PF (The Pula Fund), 1994		√			–
Canada AHSTF (Alberta Heritage Savings Trust Fund), 1976			√		7.0
Chile ESSF (Economic and Social Stabilization Fund), 2007	√				2.71
Chile PRF (Pension Reserve Fund), 2006			√		3.4
China CIC (China Investment Corporation), 2007		√			4.58
Iran NDFI (National Development Fund of Iran), 2001		√	√	√	–
Ireland ISIF (Ireland Strategic Investment Fund), 2014				√	10.8
Italy FSI (Fondo Strategico Italiano SpA), 2011				√	–
Kazakhstan S-K (Joint-Stock Company Samruk-Kazyna), 2008				√	–
Kazakhstan NIC (Joint-Stock Company National Investment Corporation of National Bank of Kazakhstan), 2012	√		√		–
Korea KIC (Korea Investment Corporation), 2005		√			3.23
Kuwait KIA (Kuwait Investment Authority), 1953		√			5
Libya LIA (Libyan Investment Authority), 2006		√			–
Malaysia Khazanah (Khazanah Nasional Berhad), 1993				√	14.1
Mexico FMPED (Fondo Mexicano del Petroleo para la Establizacion y el Desarrollo), 2008	√			√	–
Morocco FMDT (Fonds Marocain de Developpement Touristique), 2011				√	–

(continued)

Table 4.2 (continued)

Sovereign wealth fund, inception year	*Stabilization*	*Reserve investment*	*Savings or pension*	*Development or strategic*	*Performance (average annual return since inception, percent)*
New Zealand Superannuation Fund, 2001			√		10.1
Nigeria NSIA (Nigeria Sovereign Investment Authority), 2011		√		√	–
Norway GPFG (Government Pension Fund Global)[a], 1990			√		5.6
Oman SGRF (State General Reserve Fund), 1980		√			7.5
Palestine PIF (Palestine Investment Fund), 2003				√	–
Panama FAP (Fondo de Ahorro de Panama)[a], 2012	√		√		–
Qatar QIA (Qatar Investment Authority), 2005		√			–
Russia RDIF (Russian Direct Investment Fund), 2011				√	–
Rwanda AGACIRO (Agaciro Development Fund), 2012				√	–
Singapore GIC (Government of Singapore Investment Corporation Private Limited), 1981		√			4.9
Singapore Temasek (Temasek Holdings Private Limited)[a], 1974				√	–
Timor-Leste PF (Petroleum Fund), 2005	√	√			2.3
Trinidad and Tobago HSF (The Heritage and Stabilization Fund), 2007	√		√		1.7
UAE ADIA (Abu Dhabi Investment Authority), 1976			√		7.5
UAE Mubadala (Abu Dhabi Mubadala Development Company Private Joint-Stock Company)[a], 2002			√		–
USA APFC (Alaska Permanent Fund Corporation), 1976			√		10.6

Source: IFSWF, SWF Institute, and authors' calculations

Note: Policy purpose and performance is broadly referenced in the self-assessment of member SWFs of the IFSWF, Surveys of 2013 and 2015

[a]SWFs are not members of the IFSWF

Table 4.3 Fiscal rules in selected countries with SWFs

Country	*Expenditure rule*	*Revenue rule*	*Budget balance rule*	*Debt rule*	*Total rules in effect*
Australia	1	1	1	1	4
Botswana	1				1
Canada	1	–	1	1	3
Chile			1		1
Ireland	–	–	1	1	2
Italy	–	–	1	1	2
Mexico	1	–	1	–	2
Mongolia	1	–	1	–	2
New Zealand	–	–	1	1	2
Norway	–	–	1	–	1
Panama	–	–	1	1	2
Russia	1	–	–	–	1
Singapore	1	–	1	–	2

Source: Budina et al. (2012)

Lack of disciplined fiscal policy and budget management during natural resource booms often results in Dutch-disease effects due to the possible undertaking of procyclical and inefficient public investments, as such spending often distorts the economy by generating capital flow imbalances, exchange rate disparity, overheating of public investment, and consequent overcrowding of productive private sector. Although SWF funding and withdrawal rules vary across countries due to different macroeconomic objectives, fiscal systems, and legal frameworks, it is widely accepted that SWFs should embody the following macrofinancial characteristics:

- Avoidance of procyclical behavior and promotion of countercyclical policy actions through careful design and definition of the rules.[3]
- Consistency with the respective country's macroeconomic policy agenda through assessment of the long-term macroeconomic and stability implications of the funding and withdrawal rules (for instance, SWFs should not interfere with the country's macroeconomic policy agenda, including inflation targeting).
- Provisions for proper accounting of the budget surplus and sovereign fund transfers.
- Operation and implementation of these rules should be done within a well-established SWF framework, guarded by special laws and decrees to (1) ensure a clear definition of SWF objectives,

appropriate governance structure, prudent investment and risk management frameworks, and adequate reporting systems; (2) protect its operational independence (through an independent board and executive team); and (3) properly identify the implementation steps, including selection of investment managers, global financial markets, and asset classes that will be invested in.

For commodity-based SWFs, funding and withdrawal rules should be designed to fit the type and policy mandate of the specific SWF. Common types of arrangements typically include designs that allow predetermined transfers to budget from stabilization funds in the event of commodity declines and accumulation of assets for both stabilization and savings funds in case of commodity price increases. Table 4.4 provides an overview of the main types of funding and withdrawal arrangements for stabilization, savings, reserve investment, pension reserve, development, and strategic SWFs.

To establish long-term, sustainable macroeconomic growth and a budget framework that avoids principal-agent problems, countries need to ensure the development and institutionalization of strong budget governance and sound rules of intergenerational wealth creation—that is, by adopting proper SWF funding and withdrawal rules. In this context, it is critical that SWFs improve their investment value chain by adopting strong governance and an institutional framework that enhances the optimal strategy for natural resources, with the following general characteristics:

1. Set up a transparent, accountable budget governance (government) and institutional (SWFs) framework through the adoption of a specific budget law (fiscal responsibility law) or specific regulation (fiscal rules) to ensure open and fair funding and withdrawal relationships.
2. Publicly disclose government guidelines. The purpose and set priorities of SWFs can help to define a transparent investment strategy that meets explicit liabilities and other responsibilities as well as avoid procyclical bias in budget expenditures. Thus, they help better preserve natural resource revenue for future generations with the highest potential of return possible.
3. Adopt market-responsive, cyclically adjusted funding and withdrawal rules with adequate calculation formulas to optimize the stability and enhance the credibility of government fiscal policy.

Table 4.4 Types of funding and withdrawal rules

Type of SWF	*Common type of funding*	*Common type of withdrawal*	*Examples*
Stabilization Fund Countercyclical in construct, designed to offset macroeconomic volatility for both budget and overall economy Conservative investment behavior with short- to medium-term horizon	Depends on budget surplus/ deficit, in line with budget process and specific fiscal rule. Inflows come from: – Excess revenue Exceeding market price of an exported commodity from its reference price level	To finance budget deficit stemming from: – Shortfall of revenue – Special funding requirement Commodity price drop below "structured" price used to calculate budget expenditures	Chilean Fiscal Stability Fund
Savings Fund Intended to save proceeds for intergenerational purposes, addressing future explicit liabilities, market uncertainties and potential macrofinancial vulnerabilities	Mostly budget surplus (expected or unexpected) State enterprise revenue Current account surplus	Can be designed to allow the withdrawal of part or whole of the fund's returns, revenue or dividends to support the budget	• Australian Future Fund • Norwegian Government Pension Fund Global
Reserve Investment Funds Similar function to FX reserves Diversified portfolio, but preference for "safety, liquidity and return"; very limited use of derivatives or leverage may be allowed	Usually from excess official FX reserves Can be a special trust-account arrangement	During market turmoil or when official reserves deplete unexpectedly Can also be designed to withdraw the fund's returns, revenue or dividends	• Korea Investment Corporation
Pension Reserve Funds Seek to fulfill future explicit liabilities A long-term investment horizon while keeping a highly diversified portfolio	Mostly budget surplus When the market price of an exported commodity exceeds its structural price	To cover future pension obligations	• Chilean Pension Reserve Fund • New Zealand Superannuation Fund

(*continued*)

Table 4.4 (continued)

Type of SWF	*Common type of funding*	*Common type of withdrawal*	*Examples*
Development Funds Focus on financing local infrastructure investments; typically try to avoid Dutch disease, currency appreciation, and local asset boom	Budget or other forms of privatization proceeds Funding through, for example, co-investment, which is highly desirable	Within the government budget framework, consistent with local development priorities	• Fundo Soberano de Angola • Moroccan Tourism Development Fund • Nigeria Sovereign Investment Authority
Strategic Funds Specifically focused on strategic priority sectors and national interests Designed to leverage and to attract international investments, co-investments and similar partnership	Usually one-off type of government/public funding Continuous restructuring, as needed	Restricted withdrawal Potential benefits include the development of local strategic sectors, rather than future direct withdrawals from the SWF	• Fondo Strategico Italiano • Ireland Strategic Investment Fund • Russian Direct Investment Fund

Source: Authors

Although adopting hybrid policy objectives is common in some recently established SWFs, the following broader macroeconomic analytics should be taken into account for their optimum management, regardless of whether they concern stabilization, savings, development, or reserve investment funds:

- Macroeconomic uncertainties and stress test variations in response to market volatilities
- Different capital flows, FDI, exchange rate, and global interest rate variations
- Global commodity price trends and forecasts
- Countercyclical policy measures
- Developmental priorities and policy changes, such as expansionary fiscal or loose monetary policies
- Modifications in response to unforeseen economic events, seasonal adjustments, and/or changes in the owner country's medium-term budget projections and contingent liabilities

Our analysis of selected SWFs indicates that operational independence and adherence to Santiago Principles increase their accountability to both the owner country and external stakeholders. Also, institutional independence and efficient governance structures are found to determine to a large degree differences in SWF performance. This, in turn, depends on the clarity of the funding and withdrawal rules, as described in their legal frameworks ("organic" laws). Typically, SWFs are governed by their special legal frameworks, with different government bodies, such as the ministry of finance or a special board, exercising an ownership and/or supervisory role.

In line with their remarkable growth, SWFs' role in fiscal management has increased dramatically. Especially in economies dependent on natural resources, clear funding (asset accumulation) and withdrawal rules need to be developed in the early stages of SWF establishment as part of the owner countries' objectives for stable and countercyclical budget planning. In particular, SWF funding and withdrawal rules could be an integral part of well-defined fiscal rules that can positively affect sustainable budget planning and ensure sound macroeconomic policy. For example, in Kuwait, like in many other Arab countries with SWFs, a predetermined part of oil revenues is deposited in its SWF, the Kuwait Investment Authority. In Chile, funding accumulation (and withdrawal) in its SWFs, the Economic and Social Stabilization Fund and the Pension Reserve Fund, is based on a reference copper price determined annually by the authorities. Norway's SWF, Government Pension Fund Global, receives the net central government receipts from petroleum activities and transfers to the budget the amounts needed to finance the non-oil deficit. Thus, the net allocation to its SWF reflects predominantly the budget's overall balance.

Funding and withdrawal rules should also be consistent with the owner country's debt sustainability and be decided in a sovereign asset and liability management (SALM) framework (Das et al. 2012). Such a determination would evidently depend on the adopted type of SWF arrangement and its objectives.

Some common types of SWF funding sources and withdrawal rules, along with their relations to the budget, are outlined below (Fig. 4.9).

4.4.3 A Stylized Framework of Macrofiscal Linkages and Funding and Withdrawal Rules

The permanent income hypothesis (PIH) can be used to provide an analytical framework to identify the extent of the needed SWF accumulation and its performance to help maintain an overall sustainable budget. The PIH shows that while a non-resource primary balance can be in deficit

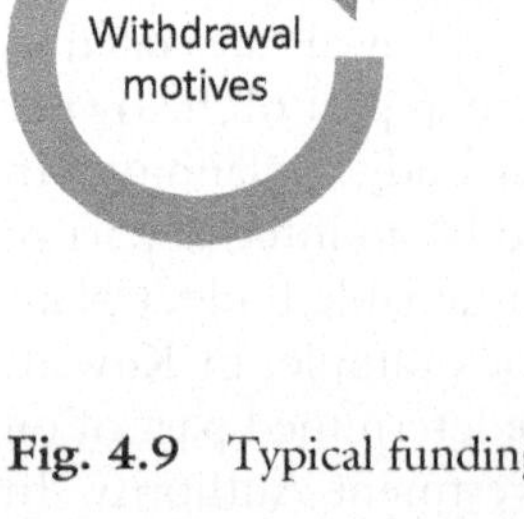

- *Royalty payments and mining related corporate tax and license fees*
- *Mining profit dividend and natural resource revenue transfer*
- *Difference between cyclically adjusted balance and actual government budget*
- *Excess tax revenue, after identifying temporary versus permanent revenue variables*
- *Excess international reserves, after determining international reserve adequacy for monetary/exchange rate policy purposes*

- *Intertemporal budget constraints*
- *Non-mining component of revenues falling short*
- *Various shocks to government budget*
- *Various effects from commodity price volatility*
- *Government liability increases above a sustainable level*
- *Meeting other liabilities, such as pension obligations*

Fig. 4.9 Typical funding sources and withdrawal motives

(which can incorporate an expenditure growth cap, restrictions on out-of-budget spending, and so on), the country can accumulate funds and maximize their returns for an overall fiscal balance (Baunsgaard et al. 2012):

$$\text{Fiscal balance} = R_{\text{resource}} + \left(R_{\text{non-resource}} - E\right) + \left(i^a A_{t-1} - i^d D_{t-1}\right)$$

Or, the fiscal balance is the sum of the resource revenue (R_{resource}), the non-resource primary balance ($R_{\text{non-resource}}$ − E), and the net interest earned on the country's sovereign portfolio ($i^a A_{t-1} - i^d D_{t-1}$). That is, the overall fiscal balance is expressed as the change in a country's net financial assets ($\Delta(A - D)$).[4]

Further, to satisfy intertemporal budget constraints, the sustainable long-term budget balance (in present value terms) should be higher or equal to the inflation-adjusted return on net wealth (the difference between the return on wealth and debt, or just debt in non-resource-abundant countries) (Montiel 2009).

To avoid overcrowding of the private sector and ignition of Dutch-disease effects (declines in non-resource output), as well as consequent inflationary pressures and exchange rate instability, resource-induced primary surpluses should preferably be kept in a separate external account (creation of an SWF). The respective funding (or saving) rules should take into account the country's specific development priorities (growth targets), related monetary policies (inflation targets), and sustainable budget frameworks. For example, Norway's non-oil central budget deficit cap is set at the long-term real rate of return of its SWF (4 percent). Other SWFs' funding and withdrawal frameworks can be found in Table 4.4.

As fiscal credibility and long-term budget sustainability require adoption of transparent SWF funding and withdrawal rules and robust policy frameworks, many resource-abundant countries have considered the PIH rule, within a comprehensive framework that limits current spending (expenditure rule) and determines proper accumulation for future generations (revenue rule) (Baunsgaard et al. 2012). Recent country experiences with SWFs offer some stylized facts on budget rules that are closely related to appropriate SWF funding or accumulation frameworks and ensure counter-cyclicality (see Table 4.5).

As countercyclical fiscal-policy tools, the fiscal rules mentioned above have proven to be effective, when enacted, in setting fiscal discipline and credibility. In particular, resource-abundant developing countries that

Table 4.5 Typical fiscal rules and SWF funding and withdrawal frameworks

Fiscal frameworks	*Policy*	*Implications*
Expenditure Rule	Sets benchmark limits for public expenditures in various forms	Necessary to prevent excessive withdrawals from SWFs
Revenue Rule	Sets limits for budget allocation and SWF accumulation for future generations	Regulates funding and procyclical accumulation of SWFs
Budget Balance Rule	Structurally regulates the general budget balance and sets a budget deficit limit, which is directly linked to the SWF accumulation framework and aims to avoid fiscal boom and bust cycles (and Dutch-disease effects)	Connected to both SWF funding and withdrawal frameworks
Debt Rule	Regulates public debt, with set limits based on budget or macrofinancial indicators	Sometimes associated with SWF withdrawal frameworks through budget regulation

Source: Baunsgaard et al. (2012)

tend to experience procyclical fiscal policy could benefit by adopting such rules for clear SWF funding and withdrawal. In this connection, the PIH, along with a comprehensive fiscal sustainability structure, could help ensure long-term fiscal solvency and provide a basic framework for sustainable SWF management.

4.5 Concluding Remarks

There are several challenges in carrying out SAA optimization to enhance performance, including the decisions about admissible asset classes, selection of benchmarks, determination of risk-tolerance levels for different asset classes, performance measurements, application of accounting standards, accepted rating(s) for investment instruments, and related market predictions. SWFs' mandates, given adopted fiscal rules, restrict the expansion of their investment value chain as well as the flexibility of shifts in their active asset management framework that could lead to ensuring higher returns over time. The adoption of a comprehensive framework for timely portfolio rebalancing is another challenge in managing a diversified global portfolio. A risk-return adjusted portfolio rebalancing would depend on the individual SWF's characteristics, including its asset size and risk-tolerance level (Papaioannou and Rentsendorj 2014, 2015).

Differences in SWF performance could illustrate the possibility of enhancing overall returns with a lower risk level, through (for example) a more comprehensive governance framework that is in line with the respective country's macrofiscal rules. Such independence and flexibility directly determine dynamic asset allocations that allow funds to perform in line with their strategic policy/benchmark target compositions. To ensure the appropriate timing and frequency of asset weight changes, especially in response to intense market volatility, a strong institutional development and risk management framework is required. For SWFs, which are long term in nature, changes in asset allocation that increase the equity composition over time are expected to pay off in the long term, by, for instance, harvesting illiquidity premia in the market that often yield higher returns.

Over time, we have observed shifts in strategic asset allocation trends within SWFs. Stabilization funds largely concentrate in fixed income, while reserve investment, pension, and future-generation savings funds actively explore new asset classes, particularly in alternative asset classes such as private equity, real estate, and infrastructure, after the current global macrofinancial developments.

As SWFs are a heterogeneous group, their funding and withdrawal rules reflect individual performance priorities that necessitate different SAAs. Intertemporal budget constraints and the PIH could be used to argue that a sustainable long-term budget balance should be equal to or higher than the inflation-adjusted return on net wealth. In this framework, the SWFs' performance should also be higher than the owner country's debt payments in order to satisfy the fiscal balance. In particular, it should be required that SWF funding and withdrawal rules be integrated within the respective country's fiscal frameworks with a clear mandate, but with less flexibility, and therefore adopting robust, preset rules to help sustain a long-term, high SWF performance.

With the accession of SWFs to a main institutional investor class in global financial markets, their role in the stability of both local and global markets has increased significantly. In this context, the development of proper SWF funding and withdrawal rules that ensure operations at an arm's length from the government is essential for their efficient build-up and is particularly important for the long-term stability of the fiscal and financial systems in which they function, as well as for global financial stability.

Our analysis shows that several savings and superannuation funds that adopt much stricter governance structures and stronger regulatory frameworks, as well as support the adoption of more diversified and expanded asset classes, perform generally better than stabilization, strategic, and other reserve investment funds. For example, the annualized returns of some SWFs, such as the New Zealand Superannuation Fund, the Australian Future Fund, and the Alaska Permanent Fund Corporation (which requires amendments to the Alaskan constitution, with substantial majority of house vote, to change existing funding and withdrawal frameworks) (APFC 2001) have generated returns well above 10 percent during the last five years.

Without publicly disclosed SWF funding and withdrawal rules, principal-agent problems and associated moral-hazard issues may arise that could undermine the integrity of the frameworks that they are part of. Inconsistent policy purposes, hybrid objectives, and a broad or flexible coverage in withdrawal and funding frameworks may undermine the SWFs' performance and operations. Specifically, natural-resource-based reserve investment and savings funds are far more at risk than the stabilization and pension reserve funds, with regard to certainty of funding and withdrawal rules that may affect the long-term efficiency (performance) of those respective types of funds. For example, the withdrawal mandates of the SWFs of Azerbaijan (SOFAZ) and Angola (FSDEA) are rather narrow and leave ultimate discretion to the president. This may adversely affect their long-term investment beliefs and increases the risk of an inappropriate SAA selection.

Furthermore, an increasing focus on enhancing the SWF owner country's strategic global positioning has been observed in recent years. For example, some pension reserve funds have started shifting their focus to supporting strategic investments. Notable examples include the Ireland National Pension Reserve Fund, which is changing its focus and is now reorganized as the Ireland Strategic Investment Fund. Italy's Cassa Depositi e Prestiti (CDP) decided to set up the Fondo Strategico Italiano to support Italy's private sector involvements globally. Such positioning enables strategic funds to focus on long-term strategic investments and ensures operational independence from the government that, from a theoretical SAA point of view, can assure a higher performance over longer periods (provided that private equities are a higher risk/return asset class than fixed-income or public equities). In this regard, operational independence of SWFs with transparent, publicly disclosed funding and withdrawal rules could help build long-term intergenerational equity, although it could undermine the ability of governments to access large pools of funds when they may be urgently needed.

Finally, our examination of different SWFs' funding and withdrawal rules indicates that there are inconsistencies and in some cases improper integrations with the owner countries' fiscal regimes. In particular, if the withdrawal rule is completely detached from the non-natural-resource fiscal deficit, the country could end up in a situation with a suboptimal management of the sovereign balance sheet. Some studies have shown that procyclical fiscal policy is quite common in natural-resource-exporting countries, including many oil-exporting countries during the 2008 oil-price boom (Villafuerte and Lopez-Murphy 2010). This budget procyclicality often relates to weak general and SWF institutional development, with short-sighted fiscal formulation and low integration of macroeconomic policies. In these cases, revamping the institutional structure of SWFs with well-integrated funding and withdrawal rules in the domestic macrofiscal policy setting and independent frameworks will help avoid domestic fiscal and financial fragilities and cope more effectively with international trade and financial market shocks.

Notes

1. Sources include the International Forum of Sovereign Wealth Funds (IFSWF) Secretariat and ESADEgeo SWF reports.
2. The Santiago Principles are a set of voluntary principles on the establishment and management of SWFs. These principles were prepared and adopted by member SWFs of the IFSWF in 2008, with the collaboration and coordination of the IMF.
3. For a documentation of pro-cyclical behavior of SWFs, as well as of other institutional investors, during the recent financial crisis, see Papaioannou and others, 2013.
4. For an exposition of the macro-financial linkages of the SAAs of commodity-based SWFs, see Brown and others, 2009.

References

African Development Bank Group (ADB). (2013, January 11). *The boom in African sovereign wealth funds*. Abidjan: ADB. Retrieved from http://www.afdb.org/en/blogs/afdb-championing-inclusive-growth-across-africa/post/the-boom-in-african-sovereign-wealth-funds-10198/.

Alaska Permanent Fund Corporation (APFC). (2001, February 16 and March 6). *Learn about the constitutional amendment to inflation-proof the fund*. Press release. Juneau, Alaska: APFC. Retrieved from http://www.apfc.org/home/

Content/pressroom/pressStory2009.cfm?story=10%20Q&As%20about%20the%20C-Ammendment&s=5&i=70.

Ang, A., Goetzmann, W. N., & Schaefer, S. M. (2009, December 14). Evaluation of active management of the Norwegian government pension fund–global. Retrieved from http://www.regjeringen.no.

Baunsgaard, T., Villafuerte, M., Poplawski-Ribeiro, M., & Richmond, C. (2012, May 16). *Fiscal frameworks for resource rich developing countries*. IMF Staff Discussion Note SDN/12/04, International Monetary Fund, Washington, DC.

Bodie, Z., & Briere, M. (2013). *Sovereign wealth and risk management: Optimal asset allocation for sovereign wealth funds*. Boston University School of Management Research Paper No. 2013–11. Retrieved from SSRN: https://ssrn.com/abstract=2344747.

Brown, A., Papaioannou, M., & Petrova, I. (2009). *Macrofinancial linkages of the strategic asset allocation of commodity-based Sovereign Wealth Funds*. IMF Working Paper WP/10/9, International Monetary Fund, Washington, DC.

Budina, N., Kinda, T., Schaechter, A, & Weber, A. (2012). *Fiscal rules at a glance: Country details from a new dataset*. IMF Working Paper WP/12/273, International Monetary Fund, Washington, DC.

Das, U. S., Lu, Y., Mulder, C., & Sy, A. (2009). *Setting up a Sovereign wealth fund: Some policy and operational considerations*. IMF Working Paper WP/09/179, International Monetary Fund, Washington, DC.

Das, U. S., Lu, Y., Papaioannou, M. G., & Petrova, I. (2012). *Sovereign risk and asset and liability management: Conceptual issues*. IMF Working Paper WP/12/241, International Monetary Fund, Washington, DC.

Hammer, C., Kunzel, P., & Petrova, I. (2008, September 15). *Sovereign wealth funds: A survey of current institutional and operational practices*. International working group for Sovereign Wealth Funds, Washington, DC. Retrieved from http://www.iwg-swf.org/pubs/eng/swfsurvey.pdf.

Montiel, P. (2009). *Macroeconomics in emerging markets*. Cambridge: Cambridge University Press.

International Forum of Sovereign Wealth Funds (IFSWF). (2014). *Santiago principles: 15 case studies—How IFSWF members implement the Santiago principles*. Published at the IFSWF's 6th Annual Meeting in Doha, November. Retrieved from http://www.ifswf.org/sites/default/files/Publications/SantiagoP15CaseStudies1.pdf.

Papaioannou, M., Park, J., Pihlman, J., & van der Hoorn, H. (2013). *Procyclical behavior of institutional investors during the recent financial crisis: Causes, impacts, and challenges*. IMF Working Paper WP/13/193, International Monetary Fund, Washington, DC.

Papaioannou, M., & Rentsendorj, B. (2014). *Sovereign wealth fund investment performance: Some stylized strategic asset allocation results*. BAFFI Center on International Markets, Money and Regulation, Sovereign Investment Lab, Annual Report 2013 (43–48).

Papaioannou, M., & Rentsendorj, B. (2015). Sovereign wealth fund asset allocations—Some stylized facts on the Norway pension fund global. *Procedia Economics and Finance, 29*, 195–199.

Rozanov, A. (2007). *Sovereign wealth funds: Defining liabilities.* Boston, MA: State Street Global Advisors.

Villafuerte, M., & Lopez-Murphy, P. (2010). *Fiscal policy in oil producing countries during the recent oil price cycle.* IMF Working Paper WP/10/28, International Monetary Fund, Washington, DC.

PART II

Asset Allocation and Interest Rate & Credit Risk Environment

CHAPTER 5

A Macro-Based Process for Actively Managing Sovereign Bond Exposures

Jacob Bjorheim, Joachim Coche, Alex Joia, and Vahe Sahakyan

5.1 Introduction

The success of any active management approach, that is, any approach that aims at generating outperformance relative to a benchmark, depends crucially on the quality of expectations about the excess returns (the return over and above the short rate) of the managed assets. Only if expected excess returns are fair estimates of subsequently realised excess returns, is added value from active management possible.

To derive expectations on the excess returns of sovereign bonds of different maturities, we propose a macro-based yield-curve model in which we assume that current bond yields are determined—amongst other factors—by expected macroeconomic developments and their future values can be estimated by projecting these macro expectations forward. The link

J. Bjorheim
Faculty of Business and Economics, University of Basel, Basel, Switzerland

J. Coche (✉) • A. Joia • V. Sahakyan
Bank for International Settlements (BIS), Basel, Switzerland
e-mail: Joachim.Coche@bis.org; Vahe.Sahakyan@bis.org

N. Bulusu et al. (eds.), *Advances in the Practice of Public Investment Management*, https://doi.org/10.1007/978-3-319-90245-6_5

between macroeconomic variables and bond yields is evident by decomposing the yield into two components:

- The short-rate expectations component. This part of the yield on a long-dated bond reflects the expected return from rolling investments in the short rate through to the maturity of the long bond. As argued below, this component is closely related to macroeconomic conditions; and
- The term premium component. This part is the remainder, or the actual yield on the long-dated bond less the short-rate expectations component. The term premium reflects the additional return that investors demand for investing in the long-dated bond over and above the expected return from rolling investments in the short rate.

The sovereign short rate is assumed to be the monetary policy rate of the central bank, which in turn is assumed to be set in reaction to prevailing and expected macroeconomic developments. The central bank sets its policy rate based on its policy objectives, for example, full employment and price stability for the US Fed. Policy makers would tend to reduce the rate if consumer price inflation or employment is expected to undershoot their targets and increase the rate if inflation or employment is expected to overshoot. The conduct of monetary policy therefore ensures a link between the yields of long-dated bonds (notably the short-rate expectations component) and macroeconomic developments. We model this link through a modified Taylor (1993) rule.

In the aftermath of the Great Financial Crisis, the so-called zero lower bound, which describes the situation in which the central bank is unwilling or unable to set a negative policy rate, resulted in the policy rate being maintained at a level above where it would ideally be based purely on the inflation and employment objectives of the central bank. This introduces an additional challenge in the modelling of the policy rate as the policy rate is insensitive to improvement/deterioration in macroeconomic variables in the short run. This challenge is addressed by the introduction of a shadow short rate that can be negative while the actual policy rate remains above or at zero. The shadow short remains responsive to changes in macroeconomic conditions, while the actual monetary policy rate remains at its lower bound. Eventually, after sufficient improvement in macroeconomic conditions, the shadow short rate will increase sufficiently to allow the actual policy rate to "lift-off" from its lower bound.

Over the past few years, a rich literature on zero-lower-bound modelling has emerged; see among others Bauer and Rudebusch (2016), Christensen and Rudebusch (2014), Feunou et al. (2015), Krippner (2013, 2014, 2015b), Wu and Xia (2016) for the US market, and Lemke and Vladu (2016) for the Euro area. Loosely speaking, this literature adopts the concept of a shadow short rate, in the spirit of Black (1995), as an unconstrained random variable that maps to the observed short rate via a static truncation function. These approaches are static with regard to the applied truncation function that does not depend on the state of the economy. This has often led empirical studies to uncover a somewhat counter-intuitive time-series trajectory for the shadow short rate process on US data (see, e.g. Krippner 2014, 2015a). For example, the estimated US shadow short rate path has been difficult to reconcile with survey- and market-based expectations of the policy rate path generally agreed among investment professionals, where the Fed eased or tightened policy stance through unconventional programmes (i.e. forward guidance and large-scale asset purchase programmes). These discrepancies motivated Krippner (2014) to advocate the use of two-factor models, instead of the more commonly applied three-factor models (Wu and Xia 2016).

We use a flexible three-factor model proposed by Coche et al. (2017b) that produces an economically intuitive shadow short rate path before, during, and after the zero-lower-bound period. This approach rests on a flexible truncation function, where the mapping from the unobserved shadow short rate to the observed short rate depends on the state of the economy, via the term structure of the yield curve.

The remainder of this chapter is organised as follows. Section 5.2 introduces the model set-up and Sect. 5.3 presents the data and discusses the estimation technique. A detailed assessment of the model's excess return predictability is presented in Sect. 5.4. Section 5.5 discusses the relevance of possible sources of excess return predictability and offers some thoughts on the application of the proposed model for real-world portfolio management. Section 5.6 concludes.

5.2 Model Set-Up

The macro-based yield-curve projections are based on a variation of the widely used dynamic Nelson-Siegel model proposed by Diebold and Li (2006), with three modifications. First, instead of the factor-loading structure of the original model of Nelson and Siegel (1987), we use a rotated version with the first factor being the short rate. Second, in order to better capture the dynamics of this factor near the effective lower bound, we use a shadow rate concept. Third, we model the dynamics of the shadow short rate factor using a modified version of the Taylor rule. These modifications are discussed below in detail.

Equation 5.1 shows the rotated loading structure for yield-curve factors $\boldsymbol{\beta}_t$ as proposed by Nyholm (2015). Consequently, the estimated factors proxy the short rate, slope, and curvature of a yield-curve structure $\boldsymbol{y}_t$ at a time t opposed to the long-term rate, slope, and curvature in the classical Nelson-Siegel loadings. We deviate from Nyholm (2015), in assuming the functional relationship between factors and yields in the shadow rate space rather than in the observed-rate space. Thus yields $\tilde{y}_t$ and factors $\tilde{\beta}_t$ represent shadow values. τ denotes maturity, and we set parameter λ to 0.71:

$$\tilde{y}_t(\tau) = \tilde{\beta}_{t,0} + \tilde{\beta}_{t,1}\left(1 - \frac{1 - e^{\lambda\tau}}{e^{\lambda\tau}}\right) + \tilde{\beta}_{t,2}\left(\frac{1 - e^{\lambda\tau}}{e^{\lambda\tau}} - e^{\lambda\tau}\right) \tag{5.1}$$

The link between the observed space and the shadow space is provided by the flexible truncation function in Eq. 5.2, with parameter A dependent on the curve's slope and curvature. Here $\bar{y}_t(\tau)$ denotes the estimated observed yields and y_L is the assumed effective lower bound.

$$\bar{y}_t(\tau) = y_L + \frac{\tilde{y}_t(\tau) - y_L}{1 - e^{-A(\tilde{\beta}_t)(\tilde{y}_t(\tau) - y_L)}} \tag{5.2}$$

We base our model choice of A on the premise that once the observed rate is close to the effective lower bound, the shadow rate goes deeper into negative territory with a flattening of the observed curve as longer-maturity yields get pushed down against the lower bound in the expectation that the short rate will remain at the zero bound for an extended period (factor $\beta_{t,1}$ decreasing) and lower observed curvature ($\beta_{t,2}$ decreases) and vice versa. This premise is reflected in Eq. 5.3 using the product of two hyperbolic tangent functions. Consequently, parameter A is allowed to fluctuate between K and $K + 4$ as a function of slope and curvature as illustrated in Fig. 5.1. The exact nature of the dependence is controlled in addition by parameters p_1, p_2, q_1, and q_2.

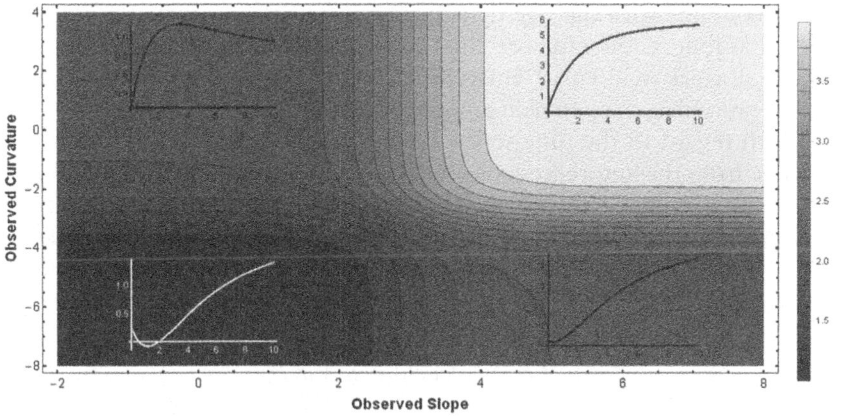

Fig. 5.1 Illustration of parameter A

Illustration of how parameter **A** *fluctuates as a function of observed slope and curvature given* $p_1 = 1$, $q_1 = 3$, $p_2 = 1$, *and* $q_2 = -3$. *The x-axis shows possible values of the observed slope in the range between −2 and 8, and the y-axis values for the observed curvature in the range between −8 and 4. Different pairs of slope and curvature values, in combination with the short rate being anchored to the effective lower bound, imply different yield-curve shapes, four of which are depicted in inset figures. In addition, the coloured areas indicate the values that parameter* **A** *takes as a function of slope and curvature. The corresponding numerical values can be read from the legend on the right*

$$A\left(\tilde{\beta}_t\right) = \frac{\tanh\left(p_1\left(\tilde{\beta}_{t,1} + \min\left(\tilde{\beta}_{t,0} - y_L, 0\right)\right) + q_1\right) + 3}{2} \times \frac{\tanh\left(p_2\tilde{\beta}_{t,2} + q_2\right) + 3}{2} + K \qquad (5.3)$$

In Eq. 5.3, the observed slope is proxied by the sum of the lower-bound constrained shadow short rate and the shadow slope ($\tilde{\beta}_{t,1} + \min\left(\tilde{\beta}_{t,0} - y_L, 0\right)$).

The set-up in Eqs. 5.1 to 5.3 follows closely the model proposed in Coche et al. (2017b), which provides the arbitrage-free version of the above specifications, and also shows that the implied shadow rate dynamics are broadly in line with the rate dynamics of the Krippner (2014) two-factor model as long as the rates are close to the effective lower bound but that under normal yield-curve environments, the three-factor Nelson-Siegel specification has a superior fit to observed yields.

With regard to the time-series dynamics of the shadow short rate, we deviate from the autoregressive specification in Diebold and Li (2006) by assuming a modified Taylor rule (Eq. 5.4 below) with a contemporaneous dependence of the short-rate factor on inflation expectations π_t^e relative to a target inflation π^* and output gap x_t as well as a policy inertia term ($d_0\,\tilde{\beta}_{t-1,0}$).

$$\tilde{\beta}_{t,0}^{US} = a_0 + b_0\left(\pi_t^e - \pi^*\right) + c_0\, x_t + d_0\, \tilde{\beta}_{t-1,0}^{US} + \epsilon_{t,0} \tag{5.4}$$

While Eq. 5.4 represents the choice of the short-rate dynamics for the US market (with a similar specification for Japan), the US shadow short rate is introduced as an additional explanatory variable in the short-rate dynamics of the German and UK markets.

$$\tilde{\beta}_{t,0} = a_0 + b_0\left(\pi_t^e - \pi^*\right) + c_0\, x_t + d_0\, \tilde{\beta}_{t-1,0} + e_0 \beta_{t,0}^{US} + \epsilon_{t,0} \tag{5.4a}$$

where superscripts UK and EA are omitted for simplicity.

For the slope factor, we assume an autoregressive model with exogenous variables (ARX) specification with the output gap x_t as an explanatory variable (Eq. 5.5), and for the curvature factor, we assume it follows a simple autoregressive process (Eq. 5.6).

$$\tilde{\beta}_{t,1} = a_1 + c_1\, x_t + d_1\, \tilde{\beta}_{t-1,1} + \epsilon_{t,1} \tag{5.5}$$

$$\tilde{\beta}_{t,2} = a_2 + d_2\, \tilde{\beta}_{t-1,2} + \epsilon_{t,2} \tag{5.6}$$

As there are contemporaneous relationships between the first two factors and the output gap and inflation, projections of these macro variables are required. Either judgement-based or model-based projections for these macro variables can be used. The model-based projection of inflation is based on an autoregressive process of order p on monthly inflation rates from which expectations on year-on-year inflation rates π_t^e are derived.

The model-based projection of the output gap $x_t = GDP_t / PGDP_t - 1$ assumes separate processes for the growth rates of GDP and potential GDP. That is, we assume that the GDP growth rate follows again an autoregressive process of order p. The growth rate of potential output $R_{t,PGDP}$ is modelled as an exponentially smoothed average of actual realised GDP growth rates $R_{t-1,GDP}$ and the previous period's output gap (Eq. 5.7).

$$R_{t,PGDP} = (1-w) R_{t-1,PGDP} + w\, R_{t-1,GDP} + v\, x_{t-1} \tag{5.7}$$

An illustration of this stepwise approach to the projection of yield-curve factors is provided in Fig. 5.2.

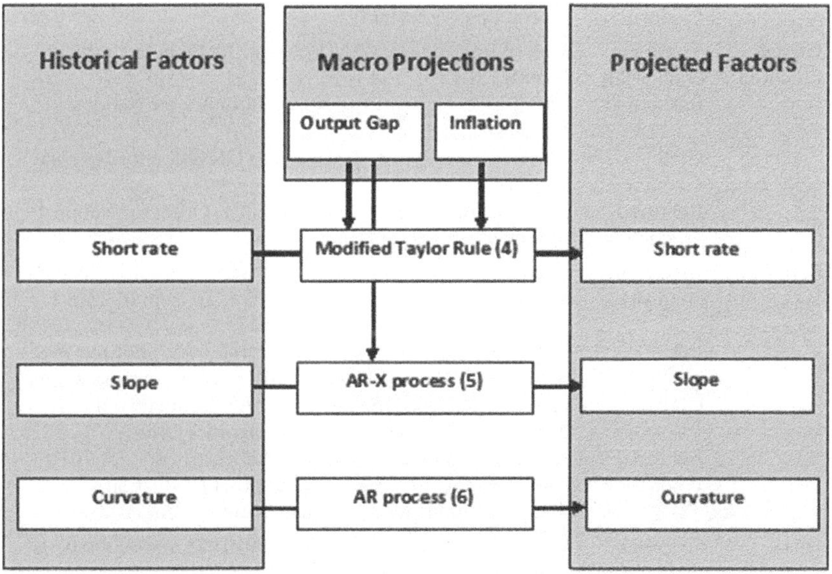

Fig. 5.2 Illustration of factor projection

5.3 Data and Estimation

Table 5.1 summarises the data sources for growth, inflation, and the yield curve used for the model estimation. In order to obtain long data histories, various sources are combined for some of the series. Combined series are in particular used for the euro area where German inflation and growth

Table 5.1 Data sources

Country	*Type*	*Source and start dates*
United States	Sovereign bond yields	US Federal Reserve Board (H.15) from 03/1953 and Bloomberg Curve I111 from 01/2000
	Inflation	US PCE Personal Consumption Expenditures Ex Food and Energy Deflator SA (US Bureau of Economic Analysis)
	GDP	Real Gross Domestic Product, Billions of Chained 2009 Dollars, Seasonally Adjusted Annual Rate (US Bureau of Economic Analysis)
	Industrial Production	Industrial Production Index (Board of Governors of the Federal Reserve System)
United Kingdom	Sovereign bond yields	Bank of England from 01/1970 and Bloomberg Curve I22 from 01/2012
	Inflation	UK CPI EU Harmonized NSA (UK Office for National Statistics)
	GDP	UK Real GDP Seasonally Adjusted (UK Office for National Statistics)
	Industrial Production	UK Industrial Production SA Real (UK Office for National Statistics)
Euro area	Sovereign bond yields	German government bond yields based on Bundesbank data from 08/1974 and Bloomberg Curve I16 from 01/2012 onwards
	Inflation	ECB Harmonised Consumer Price Index SA, prior to 1995 German CPI (ECB, Eurostat, BBK, German Statistics Office)
	GDP	Euro area Real GDP SA, prior to 1995 German GDP (Eurostat, Bundesbank), German Statistics Office)
	Industrial Production	Eurozone Industrial Production ex Construction SA 2010 Prices, prior to 1995 German Industrial Production (Eurostat, Bundesbank, German Statistics Office)
Japan	Sovereign bond yields	Ministry of Finance (Japan) from 09/1974 and Bloomberg Curve I18 from 01/2012
	Inflation	Japan CPI Nationwide General (Ministry of Internal Affairs and Communications)
	GDP	JP Real GDP Seasonally Adjusted (Economic and Social Research Institute Japan)
	Industrial Production	Japan Industrial Production SA Real (Ministry of Economy Trade and Industry Japan)

data are used as proxies prior to 1995. Furthermore, the German government yields are used as proxy for euro-area yields.

As the model is estimated on the basis of monthly data, frequency adjustment of quarterly GDP data is performed using industrial production as an instrument variable. As shown in Eq. 5.8, the proxied monthly GDP growth rates r_{GDP}^{M} correspond to the monthly growth rates of industrial production r_{IP}^{M} plus an adjustment term which ensures that the aggregated monthly GDP growth rate corresponds to the observed quarterly growth rate r_{GDP}^{Q}.

$$r_{GDP}^{M} = r_{IP}^{M} + \frac{r_{GDP}^{Q} - \sum r_{IP}^{M}}{3} \tag{5.8}$$

The shadow rate curves (Eqs. 5.1 to 5.3) are estimated statically—thus for each month individually—by minimising the sum of squared deviations of estimated yields $\overline{y}_t(\tau)$ from observed yields $y_t(\tau)$. For this, we assume a fixed set of parameters $p_1 = 1$, $q_1 = 3$, $p_2 = 1$, $q_2 = -3$ and $K = 0$. The effective lower bound y_L is set to the minimum observed short rate minus 0.25. The resulting estimates of shadow rate factors are shown in Fig. 5.3.

The model equations governing the time-series dynamics (Eqs. 5.4 to 5.6) are estimated individually using maximum likelihood estimation on the full data history. For the estimation of the modified Taylor rule (Eqs. 5.4 and 5.4a), we omit the explicit policy targets π^*, which thereby are assumed to be reflected in the estimated intercepts. Table 5.2 provides the estimated parameters.

5.4 Excess Return Predictability

In this section, we perform an assessment of the model's excess return predictability, which goes beyond the standard criteria typically used for the assessment of yield-curve models such as root-mean-squared errors and mean absolute deviations (e.g. Diebold and Li 2006; Johannsen and Mertens 2016). Notably, we first analyse predictability over time, that is, the extent to which a signal S_t derived from the model at time t predicts a bond's excess return realised over the subsequent 12 months. Second, we analyse the model's cross-sectional properties by constructing portfolios of US, German, UK, and Japanese bonds using bond rankings based on the model signals.

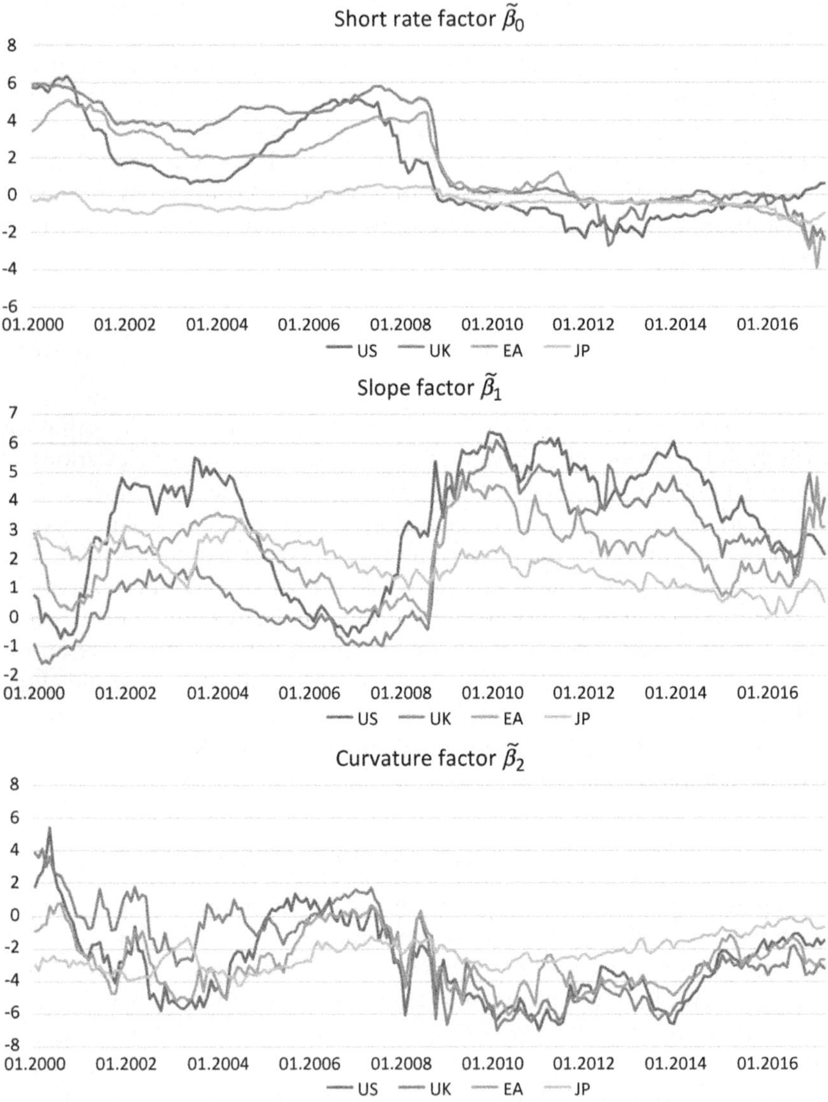

Fig. 5.3 Evolution of estimate shadow-curve factors. The units of the Y-axis are %

Table 5.2 Coefficient estimates governing the time-series dynamics (Eqs. 5.4 to 5.6)

	Intercept	π_t^e	x_t	$\tilde{\beta}_{t-1,0}^{x}$	$\tilde{\beta}_{t,0}^{US}$	R^2
US						
$\tilde{\beta}_{t,0}^{US}$	−0.019	0.048***	0.019***	0.969***		0.98
	(0.030)	(0.013)	(0.005)	(0.007)		
$\tilde{\beta}_{t,1}^{US}$	0.099***		−0.023***	0.948***		0.95
	(0.026)		(0.005)	(0.010)		
$\tilde{\beta}_{t,2}^{US}$	−0.020			0.903***		0.82
	(0.043)			(0.016)		
UK						
$\tilde{\beta}_{t,0}^{UK}$	0.100**	0.027***	0.031***	0.902***	0.091***	0.97
	(0.057)	(0.010)	(0.011)	(0.016)	(0.017)	
$\tilde{\beta}_{t,1}^{UK}$	0.075**		−0.039***	0.929***		0.91
	(0.038)		(0.011)	(0.015)		
$\tilde{\beta}_{t,2}^{UK}$	−0.338***			0.833***		0.70
	(0.094)			(0.023)		
Euro area						
$\tilde{\beta}_{t,0}^{EA}$	0.080**	0.053***	0.061***	0.899***	0.064***	0.98
	(0.041)	(0.020)	(0.012)	(0.014)	(0.009)	
$\tilde{\beta}_{t,1}^{EA}$	0.021		−0.032***	0.965***		0.95
	(0.029)		(0.011)	(0.010)		
$\beta_{t,2}^{EA}$	−0.311***			0.860***		0.74
	(0.074)			(0.022)		
Japan						
$\tilde{\beta}_{t,0}^{JP}$	0.066***	0.011	0.016***	0.953***		0.99
	(0.021)	(0.017)	(0.004)	(0.011)		
$\tilde{\beta}_{t,1}^{JP}$	0.140***		−0.008***	0.921***		0.94
	(0.028)		(0.003)	(0.015)		
$\tilde{\beta}_{t,2}^{JP}$	−0.346***			0.841***		0.71
	(0.072)			(0.024)		

***p<0.01, **p<0.05, *p<0.1

Two signals are extracted from the model. The first is the expected return for different (constant) maturity zero-coupon bonds calculated based on the projected evolution of the yield curve.[1] The second is the term premium estimated from the prevailing yield at a given maturity and the projected short rate over the maturity. We compare the predictive power of these signals to the carry signal, which has been shown to imply predictive power for a number of markets including government bonds (e.g. Koijen et al. 2016). Carry is calculated as the yield plus the return component from rolling down an unchanged yield curve.

The model performance is analysed under two macro assumptions: first, that inflation and GDP growth are mean reverting, and second, under the assumption of perfect foresight on these macro variables. For the mean-reverting macro assumption, inflation and GDP growth revert to equilibrium values in an autoregressive process. For the perfect foresight macro assumption, we use the subsequently realised 12-month-ahead inflation and GDP growth.

We backtest asset-return predictability both in sample and out of sample. For the in-sample backtest, we use a long data history going back to 1953 for the US and to 1970 for the German, UK, and Japanese markets. Subsequently, we assess the bias of the in-sample results by successively re-estimating model parameters in an out-of-sample setting starting in 1990.

5.4.1 *In-Sample Backtesting*

For the in-sample assessment of the model, we estimate the parameters making use of the full data history.

To analyse the model properties with regard to predicting the excess return over time, we present regression statistics in Table 5.3. For this, a regression of signal $S_{i,t}$ —either the term premium or expected excess return—for bond i is performed on the excess returns $R_{i,t\to t+k}$ earned by the bond over the subsequent $k = 12$ months.

$$R_{i,t\to t+k} = a + b \times S_{i,t} + \epsilon_{t\to t+k} \tag{5.9}$$

In the calculation of t-statistics, the Hansen and Hodrick (1980) correction is applied to account for overlapping data windows. In addition, accuracy and *F1* score measures are reported to assess the quality of the approach to correctly predict the sign of excess returns. Accuracy is defined as the ratio of correctly forecasted signs (i.e. forecasted and realised excess return either both positive or both negative) to total observations. The *F1* score (Rijsbergen 1979) considers both the forecast precision P (defined as true positives as a percentage of predicted positives) and recall R (defined as true positives as a percentage of actual positives). Based on this, the *F1* score is defined as $2PR/(P+R)$.[2]

Table 5.3 shows the regression statistics for both macro assumptions. Under the assumption of mean-reverting macro, the expected return signal

Table 5.3 In-sample backtest full period

Bond	*Mean-reverting macro assumption*					*Perfect foresight macro assumption*				
	b	*t(b)*	R^2	*Accuracy*	*F1 score*	*b*	*t(b)*	R^2	*Accuracy*	*F1 score*
					Expected return					
US 2Y	0.65	(2.14)**	0.10	0.64	0.27	0.98	(5.10)***	0.31	0.71	0.44
US 5Y	0.63	(1.82)*	0.08	0.60	0.40	1.26	(5.50)***	0.32	0.68	0.50
US 10Y	0.70	(1.91)*	0.09	0.58	0.49	1.36	(5.11)***	0.33	0.72	0.65
DE 2Y	0.43	(1.45)	0.05	0.53	0.31	0.93	(4.52)***	0.27	0.80	0.60
DE 5Y	0.42	(1.32)	0.04	0.61	0.23	1.13	(4.95)***	0.25	0.79	0.46
DE 10Y	0.47	(1.41)	0.04	0.61	0.33	1.03	(3.30)***	0.17	0.74	0.46
UK 2Y	0.51	(2.12)**	0.07	0.58	0.44	0.73	(4.26)***	0.20	0.66	0.52
UK 5Y	0.50	(2.20)**	0.06	0.59	0.36	1.22	(6.89)***	0.29	0.68	0.39
UK 10Y	0.46	(2.09)**	0.06	0.56	0.37	1.22	(6.55)***	0.25	0.67	0.41
JP 2Y	1.01	(3.26)***	0.21	0.72	–	1.49	(5.22)***	0.51	0.85	0.51
JP 5Y	0.74	(3.27)***	0.16	0.71	–	1.19	(5.13)***	0.39	0.78	0.27
JP 10Y	0.58	(3.57)***	0.14	0.66	0.26	0.89	(4.56)***	0.28	0.72	0.38
					Term premium					
US 2Y	1.11	(3.28)***	0.16	0.66	0.36	1.49	(6.15)***	0.30	0.71	0.45
US 5Y	1.14	(2.27)**	0.10	0.61	0.37	1.98	(5.61)***	0.32	0.66	0.45
US 10Y	1.33	(1.66)*	0.07	0.57	0.39	2.23	(4.38)***	0.25	0.67	0.52
DE 2Y	0.69	(1.84)*	0.06	0.59	0.35	1.26	(4.02)***	0.19	0.69	0.44
DE 5Y	0.73	(1.53)	0.05	0.57	0.27	1.78	(4.85)***	0.25	0.77	0.49
DE 10Y	0.73	(1.04)	0.03	0.59	0.34	1.66	(3.30)***	0.16	0.73	0.45
UK 2Y	1.42	(4.73)***	0.25	0.65	0.51	1.81	(6.88)***	0.44	0.70	0.57
UK 5Y	1.22	(3.18)***	0.12	0.61	0.38	2.05	(5.89)***	0.32	0.70	0.51
UK 10Y	0.79	(1.44)	0.03	0.57	0.37	1.47	(2.63)***	0.11	0.65	0.44
JP 2Y	1.74	(4.01)***	0.37	0.77	0.38	1.95	(4.62)***	0.53	0.79	0.45
JP 5Y	1.53	(3.94)***	0.23	0.71	–	2.10	(4.73)***	0.44	0.77	0.37
JP 10Y	1.25	(3.24)***	0.13	0.68	0.12	2.06	(4.68)***	0.29	0.76	0.34

***p<0.01, **p<0.05, *p<0.1

produces R^2s in the range between 4% and 21%. The weakest results are observed for the German curve and the strongest results for Japan. The regression coefficients are statistically significant for the UK and Japan curves, weakly significant for the US curve, and not significant for the German curve. Switching the signal to term premium implies generally higher R^2s and higher significance levels.

Under the assumption of perfect macro foresight, the model shows substantially increased explanatory power and statistical significance. The regression coefficients are significant at high confidence levels consistently across maturities and markets, and R^2s increase to between 11% and 53%. Also accuracy and F1 scores improve for all maturities. Under this assumption, the term premium and expected return signals show broadly comparable characteristics.

Table 5.4 offers a comparison of the model's properties to the carry signal. Over the full period and across all markets and maturities (left panel of Table 5.4; period consistent with the in-sample period used for Table 5.3), carry has a signal quality comparable with the model under the mean-reverting macro assumption. However, under the perfect macro foresight assumption, the model clearly shows superior properties in terms of significance levels and R^2s. Also the model shows generally better Accuracy and *F*1 scores (with the exception of Japan). It is noted here that the results for the model are subject to in-sample bias, while the model-free carry signal is not. To correct for this, we perform below (see Table 5.7) a proper out-of-sample analysis, to be compared with the right panel of Table 5.4.

To test the model's cross-sectional properties and the model's fitness to serve as a basis for portfolio construction, we assess the effectiveness of a number of duration-neutral strategies. To this end, the model is used to choose from 10 bonds, with maturities ranging from one to ten years for each of the four government bond markets, a universe of 40 bonds in total. In each month over the full sample, the 40 bonds are ranked using one of the term premium, the expected return, or the carry signal. On the basis of this ranking, five portfolios—representing distinct investment strategies—are constructed:

- Three quantile portfolios that comprise the lower third of the ranked bonds (Portfolio P1), the middle third (P2), and the upper third (P3).[3] The bonds within each quantile portfolio are equally weighted. As the bonds are duration adjusted, each quantile portfolio has duration equal to one.

Table 5.4 Carry

Bond	*Full period*					*1990–2016*				
	b	*t(b)*	R^2	*Accuracy*	*F1 score*	*b*	*t(b)*	R^2	*Accuracy*	*F1 score*
US 2Y	0.84	(2.27)**	0.06	0.65	0.19	0.25	(0.44)	0.01	0.74	0.09
US 5Y	1.35	(3.04)***	0.10	0.59	0.29	0.65	(1.13)	0.04	0.70	–
US 10Y	2.45	(3.70)***	0.14	0.58	0.34	1.54	(2.24)**	0.09	0.69	0.06
DE 2Y	0.48	(1.24)	0.05	0.69	0.33	0.47	(1.05)	0.05	0.71	0.23
DE 5Y	0.88	(1.67)*	0.08	0.71	0.28	0.82	(1.58)	0.08	0.73	0.05
DE 10Y	1.85	(2.32)**	0.14	0.67	0.25	1.76	(2.35)**	0.15	0.69	0.04
UK 2Y	0.27	(0.93)	0.02	0.60	0.46	0.24	(0.84)	0.02	0.59	0.32
UK 5Y	0.41	(1.03)	0.02	0.59	0.39	0.47	(1.25)	0.03	0.61	0.36
UK 10Y	1.01	(1.64)	0.04	0.61	0.42	0.96	(1.56)	0.06	0.62	0.40
JP 2Y	0.82	(1.49)	0.09	0.86	0.56	0.75	(0.74)	0.06	0.90	0.25
JP 5Y	1.15	(1.82)*	0.10	0.83	0.29	0.92	(1.16)	0.07	0.86	0.13
JP 10Y	2.00	(2.30)**	0.12	0.79	0.25	1.64	(1.59)	0.10	0.80	0.09

***p<0.01, **p<0.05, *p<0.1

- One long-short difference portfolio of the highest signal quantile portfolio (P3) minus the lowest signal quantile portfolio (P1). This long-short portfolio has zero duration.
- One long-short factor portfolio similar to Asness et al. (2013), where the weight $w_{i,t}$ of bond i is determined according to its signal rank. With this portfolio, the sum of the long positions is 1 and the sum of the short positions is −1 and the sum of all weights is zero. This long-short portfolio has zero duration.

$$w_{i,t} = \frac{rank(S_{i,t}) - \sum_i rank(S_{i,t}) / N}{\sum_i \left[\left| rank(S_{i,t}) - \sum_i rank(S_{i,t}) / N \right| \right] / 2} \tag{5.10}$$

Bonds in these portfolios are duration adjusted to have duration equal to one. For example, the duration-adjusted two-year bond has a 50% weight to the two-year bond and a 50% weight to cash, while the duration-adjusted five-year bond has 20% weight to the five-year bond and an 80% weight to cash. As a result, and noting that cash has zero excess return, the excess return on (say) the five-year duration-adjusted bond is 20% of the excess return on the five-year unadjusted bond.

Each portfolio is re-constructed on a monthly basis based on signals for the 40 bonds at the end of each month. Based on the re-constructed portfolios at the end of the month, the returns for the five portfolios/strategies is determined for the subsequent month.

The performance of the five portfolios/strategies is compared with an equally weighted benchmark of all 40 bonds. The benchmark is also used to estimate the portfolio's alphas and betas and to calculate tracking error and the information ratio. For the monthly rebalancing of the five portfolios as well as the benchmark, transaction costs of 2.5 basis points are assumed on each round trip (buy and sell).

Each portfolio is comprised of bonds denominated in different currencies. Assuming hedging costs reflect short-rate differentials, the excess return a bond earns over the short rate in its domestic currency is the excess return that a foreign exchanged (FX)-hedged investment in that bond will earn reflected in any base currency. The excess returns presented below reflect FX-hedged returns.

There is evidence of excess return predictability across all signals. Tables 5.5 and 5.6 show increasing excess return with signal strength, with the mean excess returns of P3 portfolios consistently higher than those of P2

Table 5.5 In-sample backtest expected return—part 1

	P1 (lowest signal)	*P2*	*P3 (highest signal)*	*P3 – P1*	*Factor*	*Benchmark*
Term premium (mean-reverting macro assumption)						
Mean (t-stat)	−0.031% (−0.29)	0.16% (1.60)	0.54% (3.81)***	0.57% (4.99)***	0.57% (5.06)***	0.28% (2.75)***
Standard deviation	0.83%	0.77%	1.11%	0.89%	0.88%	0.81%
Sharpe ratio	−0.04	0.21	0.49	0.64	0.65	0.35
Alpha (t-stat)	−0.29% (−5.35)***	−0.089% (−2.13)**	0.19% (3.02)***	0.48% (4.33)***	0.48% (4.40)***	
Beta (t-stat)	0.89 (46.96)***	0.87 (58.32)***	1.2 (54.27)***	0.34 (8.60)***	0.35 (8.99)***	
Tracking error	0.42%	0.34%	0.52%	1.00%		
Information ratio	−0.68	−0.26	0.37	0.48		
Expected return (mean-reverting macro assumption)						
Mean (t-stat)	0.043% (0.48)	0.28% (2.62)***	0.42% (3.05)***	0.38% (3.50)***	0.38% (3.64)***	0.28% (2.75)***
Standard deviation	0.71%	0.84%	1.07%	0.84%	0.82%	0.81%
Sharpe ratio	0.06	0.34	0.39	0.45	0.47	0.35
Alpha (t-stat)	−0.16% (−3.16)***	0.00072% (0.02)	0.065% (1.36)	0.23% (2.43)**	0.24% (2.59)***	
Beta (t-stat)	0.72 (39.32)***	1 (83.01)***	1.3 (72.73)***	0.53 (15.72)***	0.52 (15.83)***	
Tracking error	0.46%	0.26%	0.42%	0.82%		
Information ratio	−0.36	0.00	0.15	0.28		
Carry						
Mean (t-stat)	0.08% (0.71)	0.25% (2.39)**	0.39% (3.05)***	0.31% (2.73)***	0.3% (2.61)***	0.29% (2.84)***
Standard deviation	0.88%	0.82%	1.01%	0.90%	0.88%	0.80%
Sharpe ratio	0.09	0.31	0.39	0.35	0.33	0.36
Alpha (t-stat)	−0.19% (−3.11)***	−0.022% (−0.53)	0.07% (1.16)	0.26% (2.27)**	0.25% (2.19)**	
Beta (t-stat)	0.92 (42.43)***	0.94 (62.96)***	1.1 (51.46)***	0.19 (4.65)***	0.17 (4.22)***	
Tracking error	0.47%	0.33%	0.48%	1.10%		
Information ratio	−0.40	−0.07	0.15	0.24		

***p<0.01, **p<0.05, *p<0.1

Table 5.6 In-sample backtest expected return—part 2

	P1 (lowest signal)	*P2*	*P3 (highest signal)*	*P3 – P1*	*Factor*	*Benchmark*
Term premium (perfect foresight macro assumption)						
Mean (t-stat)	−0.091% (−0.82)	0.21% (1.95)*	0.62% (4.55)***	0.71% (5.93)***	0.73% (6.22)***	0.3% (2.87)***
Standard deviation	0.87%	0.84%	1.06%	0.93%	0.92%	0.80%
Sharpe ratio	−0.10	0.25	0.58	0.76	0.80	0.37
Alpha (t-stat)	−0.36% (−6.07)	−0.069% (−1.47)	0.28% (4.15)***	0.64% (5.43)***	0.66% (5.72)***	
Beta (t-stat)	0.91 (42.99)***	0.94 (56.28)***	1.2 (48.18)***	0.24 (5.64)***	0.23 (5.53)***	
Tracking error	0.47%	0.37%	0.53%	1.10%		
Information ratio	−0.77	−0.19	0.52	0.58		
Expected return (perfect foresight macro assumption)						
Mean (t-stat)	−0.027% (−0.30)	0.35% (2.95)***	0.49% (3.48)***	0.51% (4.75)***	0.48% (4.42)***	0.3% (2.87)***
Standard deviation	0.70%	0.92%	1.09%	0.84%	0.85%	0.80%
Sharpe ratio	−0.04	0.38	0.45	0.61	0.57	0.37
Alpha (t-stat)	−0.24% (−4.58)	0.041% (0.82)	0.12% (2.14)**	0.35% (3.80)***	0.32% (3.41)***	
Beta (t-stat)	0.71 (38.41)***	1 (57.53)***	1.3 (65.25)***	0.54 (16.32)***	0.55 (16.62)***	
Tracking error	0.46%	0.39%	0.46%	0.81%		
Information ratio	−0.51	0.10	0.25	0.44		

***p<0.01, **p<0.05, *p<0.1

portfolios that in turn are consistently higher than those of P1 portfolios. At the same time, the P3 portfolios appear to be riskier with higher volatilities, Sharpe ratios, and higher betas in regressions of excess returns on the benchmark. The quantile portfolios based on the expected return signal show the greatest spread in betas with 0.7 for the P1 and 1.3 for the P3 portfolio. The P3 portfolios based on the term premium signal (under both the mean reverting and perfect macro foresight scenarios) and expected return signal (under the perfect macro foresight scenario) show significant positive alphas.

Also the results for long-short portfolios, the difference portfolios (P3 – P1) and the factor portfolios, indicate excess return predictability, with statistically significant mean excess returns and significant, positive alphas. At the same time, despite these being zero-duration portfolios, all long-short portfolios show significant, positive betas. Compared with the carry signal, the term premium signal with mean-reverting macro variables implies higher levels of alphas and betas and higher significance levels.

Results under the perfect macro foresight assumption indicate the scope for further improvements in alpha and risk-adjusted returns based on accurate macroeconomic forecasts. The alphas of the difference portfolio are higher by 12 and 16 basis points, respectively, for the expected return and term premium signals. The information ratios increase from 0.28 to 0.44 and from 0.48 to 0.58 for the expected return and term premium signals, respectively.

Figure 5.4 shows the evolution of the cumulative excess return of the factor portfolio over time. This portfolio shows a meaningful increase in the cumulative excess return after 1970 (the point in time when data on all four markets is available; prior to this, only US data is available). In contrast, the cumulative return of the carry-based strategy shows a continuous increase only from the early 1980s onwards, possibly coinciding with start of the secular decline in interest rates (see Coche et al. 2017a).

5.4.2 *Out-of-Sample Backtesting*

To better assess the suitability of the model to support real-world decision-making, we repeat the analysis of time-series properties by successively re-estimating model parameters in an out-of-sample setting. That is, starting in January 1990, monthly re-estimations of the model parameters are performed, and expected returns and term premia are calculated on the

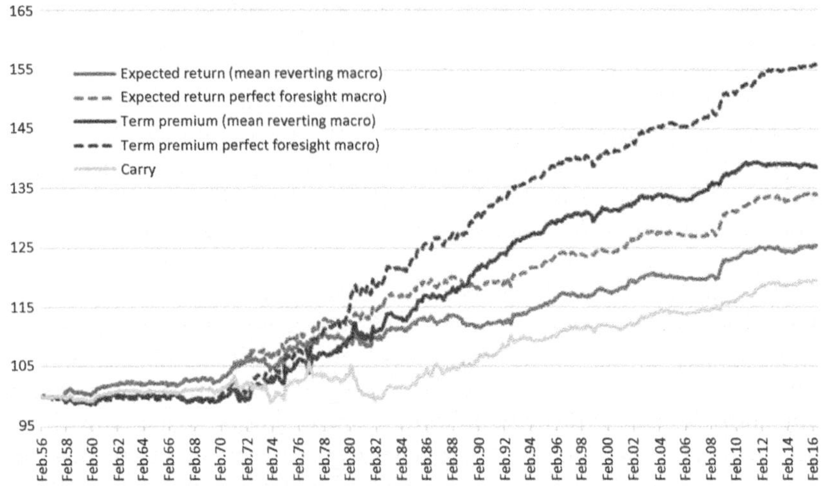

Fig. 5.4 Cumulative return of factor portfolios

basis of market information available at that point in time.[4] As before, the projection horizon to derive the return expectations is the subsequent 12 months. Results of this analysis are shown in Table 5.7.

The properties of the term premium signal in the out-of-sample setting are broadly in line with the in-sample forecasts over the same period. Comparing Tables 5.7 and 5.8 of the Annex with in-sample statistics starting in 1990, we find that the level and significance of coefficients in the regressions of the term premium on excess returns are of similar magnitude, both for mean reverting and perfect foresight macro. Further, R^2s, accuracy numbers and *F1* scores are comparable. However, the statistical significance and explanatory power of the expected return signal appears to be weaker in the out-of-sample setting.

Compared with the carry signal (right panel of Table 5.4), the expected return and the term premium signals both under the mean reverting and under the perfect foresight macro scenarios show higher significance levels and higher explanatory power.

Table 5.7 Out-of-sample backtest (1990 to 2016)

Instrument	*Mean-reverting macro assumption*					*Perfect foresight macro assumption*				
	b	*t(b)*	R^2	*Accuracy*	*F1 score*	*b*	*t(b)*	R^2	*Accuracy*	*F1 score*
					Expected return					
US 2Y	0.47	(0.99)	0.04	0.68	0.36	0.87	(2.11)**	0.16	0.76	0.41
US 5Y	0.71	(1.69)*	0.11	0.61	0.48	0.93	(2.43)**	0.22	0.73	0.50
US 10Y	0.65	(1.87)*	0.11	0.65	0.45	0.80	(2.43)**	0.20	0.71	0.44
DE 2Y	0.53	(1.80)*	0.07	0.36	0.39	1.06	(4.37)***	0.38	0.54	0.47
DE 5Y	0.62	(1.66)*	0.08	0.33	0.35	1.10	(4.27)***	0.32	0.39	0.37
DE 10Y	0.36	(1.17)	0.02	0.40	0.41	0.67	(2.98)***	0.12	0.47	0.44
UK 2Y	0.75	(3.59)***	0.33	0.62	0.47	0.86	(5.73)***	0.50	0.70	0.51
UK 5Y	0.60	(4.67)***	0.28	0.64	0.45	0.66	(6.82)***	0.38	0.69	0.45
UK 10Y	0.39	(3.74)***	0.16	0.61	0.44	0.44	(5.72)***	0.23	0.68	0.48
JP 2Y	0.73	(2.10)**	0.15	0.41	0.13	0.87	(3.69)***	0.34	0.60	0.17
JP 5Y	0.76	(2.74)***	0.27	0.30	0.19	0.74	(3.61)***	0.36	0.50	0.26
JP 10Y	0.46	(1.96)*	0.10	0.31	0.31	0.43	(2.18)**	0.12	0.46	0.31
					Term premium					
US 2Y	1.46	(1.71)*	0.10	0.70	0.31	2.16	(3.92)***	0.29	0.81	0.38
US 5Y	3.42	(3.35)***	0.22	0.73	0.51	3.76	(7.59)***	0.44	0.82	0.41
US 10Y	5.32	(4.13)***	0.25	0.65	0.48	4.66	(5.73)***	0.35	0.80	0.38
DE 2Y	0.78	(1.69)*	0.06	0.30	0.37	1.42	(3.18)***	0.36	0.54	0.48
DE 5Y	2.84	(3.09)***	0.22	0.26	0.35	1.76	(3.00)***	0.38	0.61	0.48
DE 10Y	4.57	(3.92)***	0.20	0.25	0.36	1.51	(2.33)**	0.17	0.69	0.55
UK 2Y	1.43	(3.83)***	0.35	0.58	0.49	1.53	(5.46)***	0.53	0.65	0.51
UK 5Y	2.34	(5.72)***	0.35	0.50	0.47	2.10	(5.98)***	0.45	0.70	0.54
UK 10Y	3.40	(6.28)***	0.26	0.45	0.48	2.18	(4.94)***	0.23	0.72	0.56
JP 2Y	1.47	(2.54)**	0.20	0.41	0.14	1.60	(4.21)***	0.40	0.59	0.18
JP 5Y	2.91	(4.83)***	0.43	0.43	0.19	1.94	(4.85)***	0.41	0.66	0.28
JP 10Y	4.24	(5.25)***	0.39	0.42	0.30	2.16	(3.96)***	0.28	0.68	0.34

***$p<0.01$, **$p<0.05$, *$p<0.1$

5.5 Discussion

Asset prices are driven by a wide range of factors. The role of the active portfolio manager is to develop a good understanding of these return drivers in order to understand and manage the risks embedded in the portfolio and to seek to add value (outperformance) relative to the benchmark.

Macroeconomic cycles—with fluctuations in inflation and the output gap—and future prospects for the economy have a fundamental influence on bond prices. Data relating bond prices to the macroeconomic state of the economy is available over many decades—and this relationship is captured by the model we have presented.

We have shown that with perfect foresight on macro developments, the model can generate statistically significant excess returns. Nevertheless, the model also generates significant excess returns with a naïve (AR1) projection of macro variables—this is less expected and while the backtested results of the model are very encouraging, we need to guard against being overconfident in the ability of generating excess returns solely on the basis of a model. We should recognise that financial markets in general—and G7 government bond markets in particular—are likely to be, to a high degree, informationally efficient, with a large number of sophisticated players seeking to maximise profit. Thus, there should be no easy opportunities to outperform. This leads us to question the excess return generated by the model in our out-of-sample backtesting. We contemplate three possible explanations:

(1) Data mining—that is, we have changed the model specification until we found one that “works”;
(2) The model has identified risk factors that can be exploited for generating higher return by earning the risk premiums associated with these factors; and
(3) The model has identified inefficiencies in the market that can be exploited for generating excess return without additional risk.

A model that only works because of data mining is a useless model as it will stop working going forward. The economic rationale underpinning the model specifications adopted in this chapter (e.g. a Taylor rule approach for the short rate) and the fact that the “no-model” carry signal also generates excess return provide considerable confidence that data mining is not the dominant source of excess return predictability.

It is healthy to be sceptical of the suggestions that we have found a formula to generate excess returns without assuming additional risk in the very efficient government bond markets we are analysing. We would therefore lean towards the suggestion that the model exploits one or multiple risk premiums in generating excess returns.

Risk premiums are time-varying and not perfectly correlated across different markets. A signal (such as carry or the model expected return) that picks up on the size of the risk premium can then be used to take on additional (duration) risk when such risk is most rewarded and shed risk when it is poorly rewarded. We note the counter-cyclical nature of this strategy as more exposure is taken at a time when other investors shy away from assuming such exposure.

The results of backtesting the model show that excess returns could have been generated if we had had perfect foresight on macroeconomic developments. This is reassuring as it confirms that macro fundamentals are one driver of bond prices. Unfortunately, real-world portfolio managers do not have perfect foresight, and accurately forecasting the future state of the economy may be as challenging as accurately forecasting future bond prices. While portfolio managers will have developed their own view on the evolution of the economy, the market will already have "priced-in" some form of consensus view of future macroeconomic development into current bond prices, making outperformance difficult even with a well-informed outlook on the macro economy.

In using the model, we also need to recognise that the relationship between the state of the economy and bond prices may have evolved over time. Over the past 30 years we have witnessed a dramatic fall in yield levels in developed markets, it is believed that the real neutral rate has also fallen over this period.[5] Furthermore, the recovery following the 2007–2008 financial crisis has been particularly shallow and government bond markets have been distorted by large-scale purchases of longer-maturity bonds, with the specific objective of reducing long-term financing costs (i.e. reducing long-term yields and compressing the term premium).

For the above reasons, the model will always remain only one input to our active investment decision-making process—with the final decision ultimately being a judgement call made by the portfolio manager.[6] While model signals are not automatically implemented, the model signal provides a valuable indicator of current over- or under-valuation of bonds in a historical context and serves as a cornerstone for the financial market discussion and the investment decision-making that follows.

Beyond forecasting the return on bonds of different maturity, the shadow short rate modelling framework can provide the portfolio manager with some insight into the normalisation or "lift-off" of the policy rate, as progress towards the central bank's macroeconomic policy objectives results in the shadow short rate approaching the lower bound (from below) and eventually in an increase in the actual policy rate.

In this chapter, we focused on the application of the macro-based yield-curve model to support active decision-making within and across government bond markets. For the cross-market positions, we assumed that currency hedging costs are closely matched by short-rate differentials. The model could be extended to account for deviations from the covered interest rate parity in which the currency hedging cost differs from short-rate differential. The model could also be extended to model currency movements—which are in part conditioned by the evolution of short-rate differentials that is already modelled.

5.6 Conclusions

Active portfolio management is a difficult task, in particular, if it aims at outperforming a benchmark of securities in deep, liquid, and well-researched fixed-income markets. While current bond prices are observable, their future values are not. Expectations about the horizon value of bonds are thus required. In this chapter, we propose a model that estimates these future values by connecting a modified Taylor rule with a rotated Nelson-Siegel yield-curve model. This set-up evaluates a central bank's interest rate target in response to economic and inflation developments. Furthermore, the chosen approach allows for modelling a negative "shadow short rate" even when the actual policy rate is restricted by the zero lower bound. From the estimates of the monetary policy rate, the yield-curve model dynamically constructs the level, slope, and curvature of future term structures. By comparing the current bond prices with the future projections of these prices, return and term premium estimates are developed.

We show that there is value to be had from using the model's expected return and term premium signals to guide portfolio construction even under the naïve mean-reverting macro data assumption. The value of using the model to guide portfolio construction increases significantly with perfect foresight on the evolution of macro data. This result supports the integration of macro forecasts into the investment decision-making process.

Annex

Table 5.8 In-sample backtest (1990 to 2016)

Instrument	*Mean-reverting macro*					*Perfect foresight macro*				
	b	*t(b)*	R^2	*Accuracy*	*F1 score*	*b*	*t(b)*	R^2	*Accuracy*	*F1 score*
				Expected return						
US 2Y	1.61	(3.16)***	0.19	0.78	–	1.82	(7.97)***	0.50	0.82	0.24
US 5Y	1.56	(3.42)***	0.18	0.75	0.31	1.98	(6.68)***	0.41	0.81	0.32
US 10Y	1.51	(3.76)***	0.20	0.66	0.45	1.73	(4.61)***	0.29	0.79	0.44
DE 2Y	0.77	(1.53)	0.08	0.47	0.38	1.17	(5.78)***	0.57	0.83	0.68
DE 5Y	0.98	(2.85)***	0.11	0.58	0.31	1.60	(7.09)***	0.51	0.83	0.56
DE 10Y	0.83	(2.39)**	0.10	0.61	0.44	1.33	(4.58)***	0.27	0.79	0.58
UK 2Y	1.23	(4.08)***	0.28	0.60	0.51	1.01	(3.71)***	0.40	0.68	0.50
UK 5Y	1.06	(3.73)***	0.22	0.66	0.53	1.15	(5.63)***	0.37	0.74	0.43
UK 10Y	0.90	(4.26)***	0.19	0.58	0.52	0.91	(6.12)***	0.20	0.75	0.55
JP 2Y	1.29	(4.85)***	0.51	0.75	–	1.41	(5.91)***	0.58	0.83	–
JP 5Y	1.04	(5.31)***	0.44	0.70	–	1.12	(6.30)***	0.49	0.79	0.09
JP 10Y	0.77	(5.17)***	0.32	0.63	0.31	0.80	(5.30)***	0.35	0.69	0.28
				Term premium						
US 2Y	1.36	(1.85)*	0.11	0.76	0.14	2.05	(3.83)***	0.27	0.81	0.23
US 5Y	2.31	(2.92)***	0.18	0.76	0.16	3.24	(7.62)***	0.42	0.79	0.20
US 10Y	2.84	(3.23)***	0.16	0.73	0.29	3.18	(3.90)***	0.28	0.78	0.30
DE 2Y	0.84	(1.22)	0.07	0.56	0.40	2.19	(6.58)***	0.40	0.69	0.50
DE 5Y	1.53	(2.77)***	0.12	0.52	0.35	2.79	(7.98)***	0.56	0.80	0.57
DE 10Y	1.46	(1.90)*	0.07	0.57	0.44	1.97	(4.25)***	0.25	0.75	0.52
UK 2Y	1.28	(4.16)***	0.33	0.66	0.43	1.50	(6.22)***	0.52	0.69	0.46
UK 5Y	1.66	(4.15)***	0.26	0.66	0.50	1.80	(6.14)***	0.40	0.75	0.54
UK 10Y	1.88	(3.45)***	0.16	0.61	0.53	1.56	(4.54)***	0.17	0.71	0.49
JP 2Y	2.15	(5.01)***	0.56	0.74	0.02	2.41	(5.98)***	0.66	0.75	–
JP 5Y	1.86	(5.50)***	0.47	0.70	–	2.09	(6.48)***	0.54	0.75	0.07
JP 10Y	1.71	(5.10)***	0.32	0.66	0.15	1.89	(5.12)***	0.35	0.75	0.24

***$p<0.01$, **$p<0.05$, *$p<0.1$

Notes

1. Determined by geometrically linking monthly returns of zero-coupon bonds of the target maturity (from one- to ten-year) at the start of the month.
2. The *F1 score* is applied to distinguish the assessed approaches from a simple strategy, which always assumes a positive excess return. The latter strategy would actually show good accuracy in an environment where negative excess returns are less frequent than positive excess returns, as this was the case for

the major bond markets since the early 1980s. However, the F1 score of such strategy would approach zero due to poor recall performance.

3. More precisely, P1 comprises bonds ranked 28 to 40 (13 bonds), P2 comprises rank 15 to 27 (13 bonds), and P3 comprises the first 14 ranked bonds.
4. The out-of-sample backtest is based on GDP data as available at the time. As GDP estimates are regularly revised and today's GDP estimates differ from estimates available at the time of decision-making, the out-of-sample backtest may be biased in this respect. However, the perfect foresight scenario is anyway seen as hypothetical ceiling analysis aimed at assessing improvements in the model's excess return predictability from having better macro forecasts.
5. In the practical application of the model presented in this chapter, we revise the estimated parameters of the modified Taylor rule to lower the implied real neutral rate of interest below historical values.
6. Having said this, we note that at some asset managers, investment decisions are almost entirely rule based, with, for example, the portfolio systematically tilted to higher carry instruments.

References

Asness, C. S., Moskowitz, T. J., & Pedersen, L. H. (2013). Value and momentum everywhere. *Journal of Finance, 68*(3), 929–985.

Bauer, M. D., & Rudebusch, G. D. (2016). Monetary policy expectations at the zero lower bound. *Journal of Money, Credit and Banking, 48*(7), 1439–1465.

Black, F. (1995). Interest rates as options. *Journal of Finance, 50*(5), 1371–1376.

Christensen, J. H. E., & Rudebusch, G. D. (2014). Estimating shadow-rate term structure models with near-zero yields. *Journal of Financial Econometrics, 13*(2), 226–259.

Coche, J., Knezevic, M., & Sahakyan, V. (2017a). *Carry on?* Working paper.

Coche, J., Nyholm, K., & Sahakyan, V. (2017b). *Forecasting the term structure of interest rates close to the effective lower bound.* Working paper.

Diebold, F. X., & Li, C. (2006). Forecasting the term structure of government bond yields. *Journal of Econometrics, 130*(1), 337–364.

Feunou, B., Fontaine, J.-S., Le, A., & Lundblad, C. (2015). *Tractable term-structure models and the zero lower bound.* Bank of Canada Staff Working Paper, No. 2015-46.

Hansen, L. P., & Hodrick, R. J. (1980). Forward exchange rates as optimal predictors of future spot rates: An econometric analysis. *Journal of Political Economy, 88*(5), 829–853.

Johannsen, B. K., & Mertens, E. (2016). *The expected real interest rate in the long run: Time series evidence with the effective lower bound.* FEDS notes. Washington: Board of Governors of the Federal Reserve System.

Krippner, L. (2013). *A tractable framework for zero lower bound Gaussian term structure models.* Reserve Bank of New Zealand Discussion Paper Series DP2013/02.

Krippner, L. (2014). *Measuring the stance of monetary policy in conventional and unconventional environments.* Centre for Applied Macroeconomic Analysis Working Papers 2014–06.

Krippner, L. (2015a). A *comment on Wu and Xia (2015), and the case for two-factor Shadow Short Rates.* Centre for Applied Macroeconomic Analysis Working Papers 2015–48.

Krippner, L. (2015b). *Zero lower bound term structure modelling: A practitioner's guide. Applied Quantitative Finance.* New York: Palgrave Macmillan.

Koijen, R. S. J., Moskowitz, T. J., Pedersen, L. H., & Vrugt, E. B. (2016). *Carry.* Fama-Miller Working Paper. Retrieved from SSRN: https://ssrn.com/abstract=2298565.

Lemke, W., & Vladu, A. L. (2016). *Below the zero lower bound: A shadow-rate term structure model for the euro area.* Bundesbank Discussion Paper No. 32/2016. Retrieved from SSRN: https://ssrn.com/abstract=2848045.

Nelson, C., & Siegel, A. F. (1987). Parsimonious modeling of yield curves. *The Journal of Business, 60*(4), 473–489.

Nyholm, K. (2015). *A rotated dynamic Nelson-Siegel model with macro-financial applications.* ECB Working Paper No 1851.

van Rijsbergen, C. J. (1979). *Information retrieval* (2nd ed.). London: Butterworth.

Taylor, J. (1993). Discretion vs policy rules in practice. *Carnegie-Rochester Conference Series on Public Policy, 39,* 195–214.

Wu, J. C., & Xia, F. D. (2016). Measuring the macroeconomic impact of monetary policy at the zero lower bound. *Journal of Money, Credit and Banking, 48*(2–3), 253–291.

CHAPTER 6

Carry On?

Joachim Coche, Mark Knezevic, and Vahe Sahakyan

6.1 Introduction

For institutional investors, factor-based investing has become a significant innovation in recent years. Factor-based investing aims at improving risk-adjusted returns, and it can be applied with a systematic approach at various levels in the investment decision-making process. For instance, a factor-based approach can be applied at the Strategic Asset Allocation (SAA) level and at the Tactical Asset Allocation (TAA) level. At the strategic level, a factor-based approach replaces, in the allocation decision, asset classes by risk factors. The value of this is that, as illustrated during the Great Financial Crisis in 2008–2009, asset class returns have been seen to be driven by common risk factors, so that portfolios traditionally considered to be diversified (based on an analysis at the asset class level) may not be as diversified as we might like to believe. Meanwhile, correlations across risk factors could be somewhat lower than across asset classes. Diversification derived at the risk factor level should therefore be more robust to market

J. Coche (✉) • V. Sahakyan
Bank for International Settlements (BIS), Basel, Switzerland
e-mail: Joachim.Coche@bis.org; Vahe.Sahakyan@bis.org

M. Knezevic
Bank for International Settlements (BIS), Hong Kong, China

N. Bulusu et al. (eds.), *Advances in the Practice of Public Investment Management*, https://doi.org/10.1007/978-3-319-90245-6_6

turbulence compared to diversification derived by looking at the asset class level only (Page and Taborsky 2011).

Ang et al. (2009), when reviewing the performance of the external active managers of the Norwegian Government Pension Fund (NGPF) with particular reference to the volatile period associated with the Great Financial Crisis, found that a significant part of the total NGPF returns represented by the external active managers is actually explained by a number of well-known risk factors. One consequence for the institutional investor is that rather than relying on external active managers to provide alpha, who in practice actually may just implement what amounts to something like factor-based investment strategies anyway (albeit for an active management fee), the institutional investor could more simply and transparently invest in (or, for the sufficiently sophisticated investor, construct for themselves) rules-based portfolios or index products with factor tilts.

At the tactical level, the factor-based approach implements rules that are used to build portfolios by choosing and/or sorting assets based on whether they exhibit particular characteristics. The idea of developing and implementing a rules-based approach that provides a premium to a classic passive weighting scheme—say market capitalization—by way of exposure to a particular factor, or suite of factors, clearly has some attraction for the tactical investment process; although to harvest the factor premiums, a long-term investment horizon may be needed (Blitz 2012). In any event, many studies, cited below, have shown that factor-based investing can produce excess risk-adjusted returns.

A key question then is whether there are factors that can provide an improvement to risk-adjusted returns and that can be applied on a systematic basis (whether at the strategic or tactical level). The question of whether such factors exist originally was of academic interest after researchers found factors that were anomalies in the framework of the classic asset pricing models (and so appeared to question the validity of such models). These factors—variables that had no special standing in classic asset pricing theory—appeared to be systematically and persistently associated with excess returns. Much work has gone into trying to explain their existence including the following: (1) that an asset pricing model is simply not capturing a component of systematic risk, (2) that they do in fact represent compensation for risk consistent with the Efficient Markets Hypothesis (EMH), or (3) they represent behavioural aspects of agents operating in markets (Moskowitz 1999).

As Koedijk et al. (2016) discuss, typical factors can be classified as economic (e.g. inflation, GDP growth), stylistic (e.g. value, growth momentum, term premium, volatility, and liquidity), or strategic (e.g. carry, trends, and calendar anomalies). A large body of research has been devoted to the topic over the last few decades. The above-mentioned factors, particularly value and momentum, seem to be mainstays in the literature, but the amount of research dedicated to uncovering new factors has expanded dramatically over the last decade, underlying its importance and interest from academics and practitioners alike. The meta-study by Harvey et al. (2016) catalogues 316 factors (in equity markets) and includes many "non-traditional" concepts, relying on novel proxy data, such as "company media coverage", "investor sentiment", and "fraud probability". Not surprisingly, the above study points out that the supposed significant results for such factors may be a spurious result of data mining.

At the tactical level, equity portfolios have received a lot of research focus, but the literature on bond markets still goes back some decades. It originated with tests of the Expectations Hypothesis (EH) of the term structure (Fama and Bliss 1987; Campbell and Shiller 1991). Evidence of return predictability, based on a factor, could be construed as violating theory (or require a reworking of the theory). By the late 1990s, the line of research seemed to suggest that there was widespread agreement that the EH model was deficient, implying risk premiums are time-varying. The focus shifted to determining what, and to what extent do, factors drive premia (Deaves 1997) and provide meaningful economic returns. To cite some recent research, several studies have looked at macroeconomic factors and the US Treasury market (Rezende 2015; Ludvigson and Ng 2009; Piazzesi and Swanson 2004; Ghysels et al. 2014). Other studies conduct analysis across markets looking at factors such as the ratio of past wealth to current wealth, a bond's relationship to the stock market, the term premium, the real bond yield (Ilmanen 1995; Silva et al. 2003), and value and momentum (Asness et al. 2013). Finally, many studies test a range of factors including forward spreads and macroeconomic variables (Gargano et al. 2014; Engsted et al. 2013). Lin et al. (2014) look at liquidity and credit spread factors, among others, in the US corporate bond market; Greenwood and Vayanos (2014) find that bond supply appears to predict long-term bond returns even after controlling for other factors.

6.1.1 *Carry*

In this study we aim to assess at a tactical level the quality of carry as a factor for bond market portfolios. The fundamental question is whether adopting carry investment strategies could improve portfolio performance in terms of both risk and returns. The attraction of carry—given its broad definition that it is the return on the forward if the spot price of the asset stays the same over the holding period—is that it has the benefit of being a model-free signal so there is no uncertainty on model parameters and no dependence on macroeconomic data, so that we may be more confident about back-testing a carry strategy rather than for more complex strategies and models. It also has a straightforward application to fixed income assets as detailed below. We acknowledge that the concept of carry as a factor is not particularly new, but would point at that its application has historically been limited largely to carry trades in foreign exchange markets.[1] Moreover, recently carry has received some renewed attention as evidence shows it can be a successful strategy for a number of asset classes, in addition to the currency carry trade.

One recent study is Koijen et al. (2018), in which carry is analysed across markets and asset classes (bonds, equities, currencies, commodities, credit, and equity index options). Ten sovereign bond markets are studied for the ten-year maturity. The authors find that carry strategies show evidence of excess returns and provide properties that are not explained by other factors (such as value and momentum). Furthermore, carry strategies (across all asset classes analysed) appear to coincide with deteriorating aggregate states of the global economy and periods of higher volatility, so that returns to carry strategies may be compensation for time-varying risk premia. The authors find that this appears to be a global phenomenon, so there may be a common risk faced by all carry strategies across all asset classes.

Ahmerkamp and Grant (2013a) examine carry and momentum across markets and asset classes. Both factors separately, and combined, show evidence of return predictability across asset markets. Their analysis for bonds looks at only five of the largest bond markets but for several maturities. The authors show that returns on carry strategies cannot be explained by other risk factors; momentum strategies are highly co-moving with carry strategies; and a combination of carry, momentum and long-only strategies appears to explain a significant proportion of variability in returns for a number of hedge fund index strategies.[2] In a follow-up paper by Ahmerkamp and Grant (2013b), the authors find that the segmented markets thesis[3] may explain the success of carry, where carry-strategy returns are related to hedge fund capital flows—and future expected returns tend to decrease as hedge funds' funds under management, assumed to be deployed for the purposes of the related strategy, increase.

Baz et al. (2015) show that carry is a meaningful signal for range of asset classes. This study uses interest rate swap markets, but examines ten developed markets and, interestingly, four emerging market economies (Hungary, Poland, South Africa, and the Philippines).

6.1.2 *Our Research*

We examine carry in sovereign bond markets of developed economies and attempt to add to recent studies for this particular asset class. The focus on a single asset class allows a deeper and more specialized investigation. We utilize a larger data set spanning a longer time period (for periods encompassing both increases and decreases in general interest rates) across a wide number of government bond markets. We also construct yield curves to be able to calculate carry signals for a larger number of maturity points for the markets in question. In addition, we take into account the effect of transaction costs, a variable which previous studies have generally not examined, but one that is obviously key when considering the economic effectiveness of an investment strategy.

The rest of this chapter is set out as follows. Sect. 6.2 summarizes the methodology and data applied. Sect. 6.3 provides the empirical findings and draws out some implications and interpretations of the results. Sect. 6.4 concludes this chapter.

6.2 Methodology and Data

To assess the carry strategy (taking into consideration concepts of continuousness, time-persistence, and pervasiveness[4]), we break down our analysis into three parts: cross-market, cross-curve, and cross-market and cross-curve. We first conduct a cross-market analysis for all markets (the USA, Germany, the UK, Japan, Canada, Switzerland, Australia, Sweden, Norway, and New Zealand) for two-year, five-year, and ten-year maturities. In this case, a portfolio is constructed based on the relative carry of markets, though the portfolio can only invest in one bond maturity in each market.[5] Second, for four major bond markets that have the longest time series data available (the USA, Germany, the UK, and Japan), we examine carry strategies across the curve (from the one-year to the ten-year maturity at yearly increments) within each market. This setting restricts a portfolio to a single market, but within each market the portfolio invests in bonds across the curve according to a bond's carry signal. Third, for the same four major bond markets, we conduct a cross-market and cross-curve analysis. In this most unconstrained setting, a portfolio is constructed on the basis of the relative carry of bonds across the curve and across markets.

6.2.1 Data

The data sources are shown in Table 6.1. The yield data, on a monthly basis, for the ten markets is obtained from central bank websites, where available, and Bloomberg Valuation Service (BVAL) where necessary. Four major markets have data availability going back several decades, with the US Treasury market having the longest history. Using the yield data we utilize the Nelson–Siegel approach to construct the full-term structures of Zero Coupon (ZC) yields for all markets in the analysis.[6] The studies that calculate carry for fixed income usually utilize bond futures data where available, or construct synthetic futures data using ZC curves for markets that do not have large or liquid bond markets. Our approach enables us to calculate carry for any maturity point in the term structure. The analysis in terms of maturity points in bond markets, then, is not limited by the limited maturity points for bond futures markets (where even for the largest bond markets, at most, liquid bond futures are available for two-year, five-year, and ten-year maturity points). Table 6.2 provides summary statistics including returns, volatility (standard deviation), probability of loss, and VaR returns at the 99% confidence interval for the ten-year maturity of the markets used in the analysis, with the sample period beginning in 1975 for the four markets with data going back this far, and for the respective starting dates for the other markets (e.g. 1982 for Canada). The sample period ends in May 2016.

Table 6.1 Data sources of sovereign bond yields

Country	*Starting date*	*Source*
United States	June 1953	US Federal Reserve Board (H.15)
United Kingdom	January 1970	Bank of England
Germany	August 1974	Bundesbank
Japan	September 1974	Ministry of Finance (Japan)
Canada	June 1982	Bank of Canada
New Zealand	March 1985	Reserve Bank of New Zealand
Norway	December 1994	Norges Bank
Sweden	December 1995	Bloomberg (BVAL)
Australia	December 1995	Bloomberg (BVAL)
Switzerland	January 1998	Swiss National Bank

Table 6.2 Summary statistics for ten-year zero coupon bonds (annual basis)

	Average return (%)	*Volatility (%)*
USA	6.5	11.7
Germany	8.9	9.2
UK	10.8	11.9
Japan	6.6	7.9
Canada	11.1	11.1
New Zealand	10.8	11.9
Norway	6.9	7.3
Sweden	5.9	7.4
Australia	6.6	8.6
Switzerland	4.6	5.7

Start date of samples for markets according to data availability shown in Table 6.1

6.2.2 *Calculating Carry*

Carry corresponds to the bond's income plus the capital gain that arises from the slope of the curve when a bond rolls down the curve through time. Yield curves historically slope upwards, although the steepness of the slope undergoes significant change through the business cycle. As shown below, all things equal, the steeper the yield curve, the greater the carry.

Carry can be calculated from current spot and futures prices as shown in Koijen et al. (2018). The total return on an asset over a particular time period is given by

$$r_{t+1}^{TR} = \frac{X_t\left(1+r_t^f\right)+F_{t+1,t+1}-F_{t,t+1}-X_t}{X_t} = \frac{F_{t+1,t+1}-F_{t,t+1}}{X_t}+r_t^f \qquad (6.1)$$

where r_{t+1}^{TR} is the total return from the current period, t, to the next period, $t + 1$, $F_{t,\,t+1}$ is the current (t) price of a futures contract that expires in the next period ($t + 1$), X_t is the amount of capital that finances the investment in each futures contract, and r_t^f is the current risk-free rate. $F_{t+1,\,t+1}$ is then the next-period price of the futures contract that expires next period (i.e. the price of the futures contract at its expiry). The excess return is thus the total return over the risk-free rate, that is, subtracting r_t^f from (6.1) gives

$$r_{t+1}^{ER} = \frac{F_{t+1,t+1}-F_{t,t+1}}{X_t} \qquad (6.2)$$

The broad definition of carry provides that spot prices remain constant over the investment holding period. This implies that

$$S_t = S_{t+1} = F_{t+1,t+1} \tag{6.3}$$

As a result, carry C_t is calculated[7] as

$$r_{t+1}^{ER}\left(S_t = S_{t+1}\right) = \frac{S_t - F_{t,t+1}}{X_t} \tag{6.4}$$

A fully collateralized position provides that $X_t = F_{t,t+1}$. We now apply this general formulation to bond markets. In our setting we examine monthly data so the holding period, t to $t + 1$, will be one month. The current price of a bond futures contract, expiring in one month, for a bond maturing in τ-years is given by

$$F_{t,t+1} = \frac{\left(1+r_t^f\right)^{\frac{1}{12}}}{\left(1+y_t^\tau\right)^\tau} \tag{6.5}$$

Substituting this into Eq. 6.4, where 1 m represents one month, we get

$$C_t = \frac{S_t - F_{t,t+1}}{F_{t,t+1}} = \frac{\dfrac{1}{\left(1+y_t^{\tau-1m}\right)^{\tau-1m}}}{\dfrac{\left(1+r_t^f\right)^{\frac{1}{12}}}{\left(1+y_t^\tau\right)^\tau}} - 1 \tag{6.6}$$

This approximates (through Taylor series expansion) to a more intuitive expression

$$C_t \approx \underbrace{\frac{1}{12}\left(y_t^\tau - r_f^t\right)}_{\text{slope}} \underbrace{-D^{\text{mod}}\left(y_t^{\tau-1m} - y_t^\tau\right)}_{\text{rolldown}} \tag{6.7}$$

Ultimately, as Eq. 6.7 shows, carry can be decomposed into the slope of the yield curve, the difference between the bond yield maturing in τ-years and the short-term risk-free rate, and, as mentioned above, the price change from the bond rolling down the yield curve. As Eq. 6.7 shows, carry will be bigger when the slope is steeper.

For cross-curve comparability, we adjust position sizing of investments in different maturities so that all bonds have similar risk profiles. This is done by adjusting for duration, dividing the carry return for each maturity bucket by each bucket's duration.

Table 6.3 shows summary statistics (mean and volatility) of the carry signals for each of the markets in the analysis for all maturity points at yearly increments. Generally speaking, the carry signal strength increases for longer maturities across all markets.

Table 6.3 Summary statistics of excess carry signals by country and maturity

	1Y	*2Y*	*3Y*	*4Y*	*5Y*	*6Y*	*7Y*	*8Y*	*9Y*	*10Y*
USA	0.52	0.98	1.22	1.35	1.42	1.46	1.48	1.49	1.49	1.49
	(0.62)	(0.93)	(1.16)	(1.36)	(1.49)	(1.58)	(1.63)	(1.66)	(1.67)	(1.68)
DE	0.09	0.61	1.08	1.41	1.62	1.75	1.82	1.86	1.89	1.90
	(0.81)	(1.22)	(1.48)	(1.67)	(1.80)	(1.88)	(1.92)	(1.95)	(1.96)	(1.97)
UK	−0.34	0.00	0.36	0.64	0.82	0.93	0.99	1.02	1.04	1.05
	(1.55)	(1.75)	(1.77)	(1.93)	(2.13)	(2.27)	(2.37)	(2.43)	(2.46)	(2.48)
JP	−0.31	−0.03	0.32	0.60	0.79	0.91	0.98	1.02	1.04	1.05
	(0.85)	(1.18)	(1.33)	(1.43)	(1.49)	(1.53)	(1.56)	(1.57)	(1.58)	(1.58)
CA		0.60			1.22					1.37
		(1.20)			(1.59)					(1.70)
CH		−0.18			0.55					0.80
		(1.43)			(1.74)					(1.80)
AU		0.03			0.48					0.62
		(1.45)			(1.58)					(1.58)
NO		0.12			0.72					0.90
		(1.06)			(1.45)					(1.55)
NZ		−0.38			−0.15					−0.08
		(1.67)			(2.15)					(2.24)
SE		0.74			1.53					1.73
		(0.78)			(0.91)					(0.96)

Start date of samples for markets according to data availability shown in Table 6.1
Full-sample mean and standard deviation (in brackets), percentages

6.2.3 Constructing Carry Strategy Portfolios

We back-test the performance of the carry strategy by constructing portfolios whose composition reflects the relative strength of the carry signal (in the three settings as outlined above). We follow the scheme set out in Asness et al. (2013). Securities are ranked according to the strength of the carry signal. In the case of cross-market analysis, this means ranking across markets only for each bond maturity; for the cross-curve analysis, ranking occurs for bonds across the curve only, within each market.

For the portfolios, we construct three long-only portfolios or quantiles: a "high" carry quantile portfolio (designated P3), a "middle" carry quantile portfolio (P2), and a "low" carry quantile portfolio (P1). Assets falling in the high quantile demonstrate greater carry than assets in the other two quantiles. However, once assigned to a particular quantile, the assets in each quantile are equally weighted. The cut-off points, based on the carry signal, for the quantiles are assigned so that there are the same number of assets in each quantile (i.e. a lower third, a middle third, and an upper third, so the lower third assets will exhibit the lowest carry signal, and the upper third assets exhibit the highest carry signal). If carry is meaningful, the high-carry quantile portfolios should outperform the others. The quantile portfolios are rebalanced monthly on the basis of the relative carry between assets.

In addition to these long-only carry quantile portfolios, we construct a carry "factor portfolio", which is a long/short neutral portfolio, effectively to encapsulate a portfolio strategy that funds investments in high-carry assets by shorting low-carry assets. The factor portfolio takes a position in all assets (from $i = 1, \ldots, N$) weighted (and invested in or shorted) according to each asset's carry ranking relative to the average carry signal rank; so long positions are taken in high-carry-ranked assets, and short positions are taken in low-carry-ranked assets, as given by Eq. 6.8

$$w_{it}^{C} = c_t \left(\text{rank}\left(C_{it}\right) - \sum_{i} \text{rank}\left(C_{it}\right)/N \right) \tag{6.8}$$

where i denotes the particular asset, at time t, for the signal C (carry). A scaling factor c_t is included to scale the portfolio to one dollar long and one dollar short. Summing across all the weights $\left(w_{it}^{C}\right)$ results in zero at each point in time (thus, long-short neutral). The return for the factor portfolio is then just the sum of the return of each security scaled by the weight provided by Eq. 6.8. The factor portfolio, being long-short neutral, should have no explicit directional exposure to the underlying asset but only exposure to the factor itself. Following the formula above, the cut-off point between high-carry assets and low-carry assets will effectively be the mid-point in the asset ranking, so the factor portfolio, for each analytical setting, will be long in half of the assets (with higher carry signals) and short the other half. It may therefore be considered more of a "pure play" exposure to the signal. In addition to this long-short factor portfolio, we also construct a differential portfolio, which is defined as the highest carry quantile portfolio minus the lowest carry quantile portfolio (i.e. P3 − P1). The differential portfolio should have results similar to the long-short factor portfolio. Again, the factor portfolios and the differential portfolio are rebalanced monthly.

If carry "works", high carry strategies and the carry factor portfolio should outperform low-carry portfolios and the benchmark. For the benchmark, we construct an equally weighted long-only portfolio—that is, all the assets are equally weighted regardless of carry signal. The benchmark is also used to estimate the carry portfolios' alphas and betas and to calculate tracking errors and information ratios. The benchmark calculation will differ for each analytical setting. That is, for example, for the cross-curve setting, the benchmark comprises only the assets, equally weighted, in that particular market (so ten instruments from the one-year to the ten-year maturity equally weighted), whereas the benchmark for the cross-curve cross-market will equally weight 40 instruments (across the four countries for the ten assets in each country).

6.2.4 *Transaction Costs*

The bond markets we examine are mostly large and relatively liquid, but the impact of transaction costs (arising from the requirement to rebalance portfolios each month as relative carry between assets changes) still needs to be considered to get a true sense of the economic extent of potential excess returns from a carry-based strategy. As such, we impose a round-trip (buy and sell) transaction cost of 2.5 basis points for the most liquid markets (the USA, Germany, Japan, and the UK) and 5 basis points for the other, less liquid, markets. The transaction costs are applied for the monthly rebalancing for all portfolios. Given the equal application of the round-trip cost for all portfolios, overall transaction costs for each portfolio will then depend on the turnover. For the carry portfolios, this would largely reflect the relative change in the carry signal between the securities in the analysis. For instance, the high-carry quantile portfolio in the cross-curve analysis would likely incur more trading activity (and therefore higher trading costs) than the equal-weighted benchmark.

6.3 Results

The results are provided below in the three sub-sections for the (1) cross-market, (2) cross-curve, and (3) cross-market and cross-curve analysis. For each analytical setting, we calculate cumulative returns over the sample period and regress the returns of the carry portfolios on the market benchmark to estimate the relationship of returns between the strategy and the market (beta), any excess returns (alpha), and compare measures of risk-weighted returns, the Sharpe ratio, and information ratio. As a cross-check to the factor portfolio results, we construct a long-short portfolio from the high- and low-carry quantiles, which invests in the high-carry quantile and shorts the low-carry quantile. We construct a cumulative return series of the factor portfolio net of modelled benchmark returns to visualize the extent of the impact of benchmark returns for the carry investment strategy. Finally, we examine fluctuations in the correlation of the returns of carry strategies with benchmark (or market) returns to provide some insight into what may be driving compensation for carry.

6.3.1 Cross-Market

Figure 6.1 shows the cumulative returns for cross-market investment strategies for two-year, five-year, and ten-year maturities. Table 6.4 provides the related statistics for the three quantile portfolios, the P3 – P1 portfolio, the factor portfolio, and the benchmark. We present the strategy statistics both for the full data available and for a subset of the data starting from 1983 in Table 6.5 to facilitate a comparison to the analysis by Koijen et al. (2018).

According to Fig. 6.1, the high-carry quantile portfolios, namely P3, consistently outperform the lower quantile portfolios and the benchmarks for all three maturities. However for the portfolios P1 and P2, the ordering of the performances is not completely continuous. That is, over the full sample P1 outperforms P2 for the five-year and ten-year maturities, but for the five-year maturity the mean return of the P1 portfolio exceeds that of the P2 portfolio. Table 6.4 shows for portfolio P3 positive and significant alphas for the two-year and five-year maturities, but alpha is insignificant for the ten-year maturity. Beta is close to one for the two-year

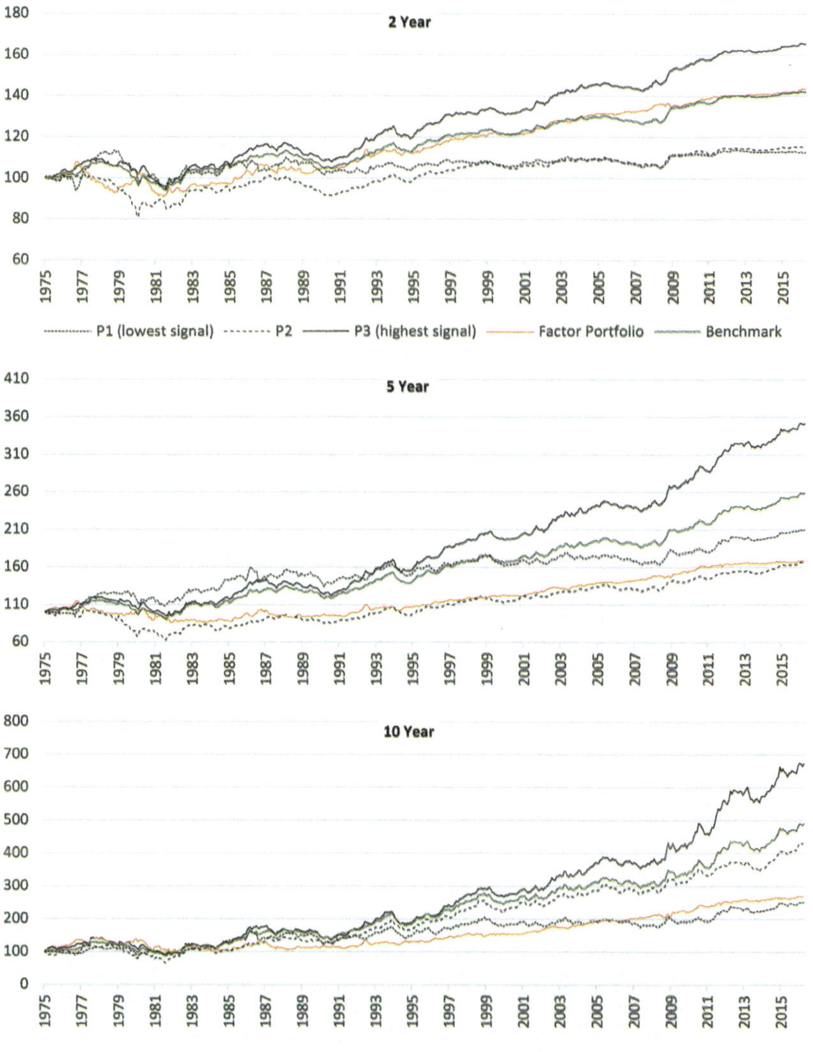

Fig. 6.1 Cross-market carry strategies: cumulative returns indices

Table 6.4 Cross-market carry strategies: full sample

	P1 (lowest signal)	*P2*	*P3 (highest signal)*	*P3 – P1*	*Factor*	*Benchmark*
			2 years			
Mean (t-stat)	0.33% (0.84)	0.36% (0.95)	1.2% (3.95)***	0.92% (2.35)**	0.92% (2.67)***	0.87% (3.23)***
Standard deviation	2.48%	2.43%	2.03%	2.52%	2.20%	1.72%
Sharpe ratio	0.13	0.15	0.61	0.37	0.42	0.50
Alpha (t-stat)	−0.52% (−1.80)*	−0.52% (−1.93)*	0.37% (2.27)**	0.89% (2.24)**	0.83% (2.41)**	
Beta (t-stat)	0.97 (20.35)***	1 (22.81)***	1 (37.27)***	0.041 (0.63)	0.096 (1.67)*	
Tracking error	1.83%	1.70%	1.04%	3.01%		
Information ratio	−0.28	−0.30	0.36	0.29		
			5 years			
Mean (t-stat)	1.9% (2.57)**	1.4% (1.59)	3.2% (4.71)***	1.3% (1.70)*	1.4% (2.15)**	2.4% (4.02)***
Standard deviation	4.82%	5.67%	4.36%	4.80%	4.19%	3.83%
Sharpe ratio	0.40	0.25	0.73	0.26	0.33	0.63
Alpha (t-stat)	−0.23% (−0.43)	−1.4% (−2.50)**	0.85% (2.41)**	1.1% (1.43)	1.4% (2.07)**	
Beta (t-stat)	0.9 (22.71)***	1.2 (28.25)***	0.98 (37.14)***	0.076 (1.36)	0.012 (0.24)	
Tracking error	3.40%	3.56%	2.24%	5.96%		
Information ratio	−0.07	−0.39	0.38	0.18		
			10 years			
Mean (t-stat)	2.6% (2.14)**	4.1% (2.68)***	5.1% (3.84)***	2.5% (1.93)*	2.7% (2.27)**	4.2% (3.83)***
Standard deviation	7.83%	9.80%	8.46%	8.17%	7.68%	6.99%
Sharpe ratio	0.33	0.42	0.60	0.30	0.35	0.60
Alpha (t-stat)	−0.78% (−0.92)	−0.43% (−0.44)	0.61% (0.97)	1.4% (1.10)	1.9% (1.61)	
Beta (t-stat)	0.81 (23.47)***	1.1 (27.17)***	1.1 (41.58)***	0.25 (4.96)***	0.19 (3.88)***	
Tracking error	5.54%	6.23%	4.02%	9.52%		
Information ratio	−0.14	−0.07	0.15	0.15		

*** Significantly different from zero at the 1% significance level
** Significantly different from zero at the 5% significance level
* Significantly different from zero at the 10% significance level

and five-year maturities and is slightly higher than one for the ten-year maturity. The alphas for P1 and P2 are negative across all maturities, but mostly insignificant. Beta is at least one or greater for P2, but consistently less than one across all maturities for P1. Sharpe ratios increase progressively from P1 to P3 for the ten-year maturity. The performance of the long-short portfolios is somewhat mixed across all maturities. The alphas are only significant for the two-year maturity for both, the alpha for the factor portfolio is statistically significant for the five-year maturity, and for the ten-year maturity, none of the alphas is significant.

The sub-sample results using data for 1983 and onwards, shown in Table 6.5, are more encouraging, and more in line with what is reported in the literature. Moving from P1 to P3 across the three maturities, the information ratios, Sharpe ratios, and alphas increase, generally moving from negative alpha for the low-carry portfolio P1 to positive (and more significant) alpha for the high-carry portfolio P3. Betas for all maturities are slightly higher for P3 (particularly for the two-year and ten-year maturities where beta is 1.1). The long-short portfolios also show improved statistics. Alpha is positive and significant for the P3 – P1 and the factor portfolios across all maturities, with the alpha estimates appearing to get larger as the maturity increases. Meanwhile, the beta estimates are not statistically significantly different from zero. The stronger results for this sub-sample appear to be more in line with the findings from Koijen et al. (2018) despite a few methodological differences, a data-set ending in September 2012, and no application of transaction costs in the Koijen study.

Figure 6.2 focuses on the performance of the factor portfolio versus the benchmark. The upper panel of Fig. 6.2 compares the monthly returns from the factor portfolio to the benchmark for the full data sample. There appear to be periods in which the returns tend to co-move—for instance, in the early 1980s—but then other periods when returns appear to be independent. In line with this observation, the middle panel shows fluctuations in the 36-month rolling correlation between returns from the factor portfolio and the benchmark (averaged over the three maturities). The correlation fluctuates alongside changes in the global carry signal, which is measured as the average carry across the three maturity points for all ten markets and using a 36-month rolling window. The relationship between the correlation of returns and the carry signal looks to be particularly strong up until the mid-1990s and again from the early 2000s. We observed similar phenomena for different time horizons.

Table 6.5 Cross-market carry strategies: 1983–2016

	P1 (lowest signal)	*P2*	*P3 (highest signal)*	*P3 – P1*	*Factor*	*Benchmark*
			2 years			
Mean (t-stat)	0.32% (1.05)	0.62% (2.37)**	1.4% (4.84)***	1.1% (3.26)***	1.2% (4.23)***	0.96% (4.10)***
Standard deviation	1.78%	1.51%	1.64%	1.87%	1.66%	1.36%
Sharpe ratio	0.18	0.41	0.84	0.56	0.73	0.71
Alpha (t-stat)	−0.59% (−2.74)***	−0.33% (−2.61)***	0.36% (2.54)**	0.96% (2.91)***	1.1% (3.89)***	
Beta (t-stat)	0.95 (21.10)***	0.98 (37.75)***	1.1 (35.01)***	0.099 (1.44)	0.079 (1.30)	
Tracking error	1.22%	0.71%	0.82%	2.23%		
Information ratio	−0.48	−0.46	0.45	0.43		
			5 years			
Mean (t-stat)	1.6% (2.25)**	2.2% (3.61)***	3.6% (5.34)***	2% (2.98)***	2% (3.44)***	2.7% (4.62)***
Standard deviation	4.18%	3.59%	3.88%	3.78%	3.37%	3.34%
Sharpe ratio	0.39	0.63	0.92	0.52	0.60	0.80
Alpha (t-stat)	−1.1% (−2.40)**	−0.31% (−1.08)	0.82% (2.62)***	1.9% (2.80)***	1.9% (3.25)***	
Beta (t-stat)	1 (27.11)***	0.96 (39.18)***	1 (39.13)***	0.026 (0.47)	0.022 (0.43)	
Tracking error	2.48%	1.64%	1.77%	4.99%		
Information ratio	−0.43	−0.19	0.47	0.38		
			10 years			
Mean (t-stat)	3% (2.30)**	4.6% (4.03)***	5.6% (4.40)***	2.5% (2.26)**	2.7% (2.65)***	4.6% (4.23)***
Standard deviation	7.64%	6.65%	7.34%	6.52%	5.90%	6.34%
Sharpe ratio	0.40	0.70	0.76	0.39	0.46	0.73
Alpha (t-stat)	−1.6% (−2.07)**	0.27% (0.52)	0.71% (1.31)	2.3% (1.98)**	2.4% (2.27)**	
Beta (t-stat)	1 (29.36)***	0.94 (40.44)***	1.1 (43.40)***	0.057 (1.10)	0.074 (1.60)	
Tracking error	4.30%	2.97%	3.09%	8.84%		
Information ratio	−0.37	0.09	0.23	0.26		

*** Significantly different from zero at the 1% significance level
** Significantly different from zero at the 5% significance level
* Significantly different from zero at the 10% significance level

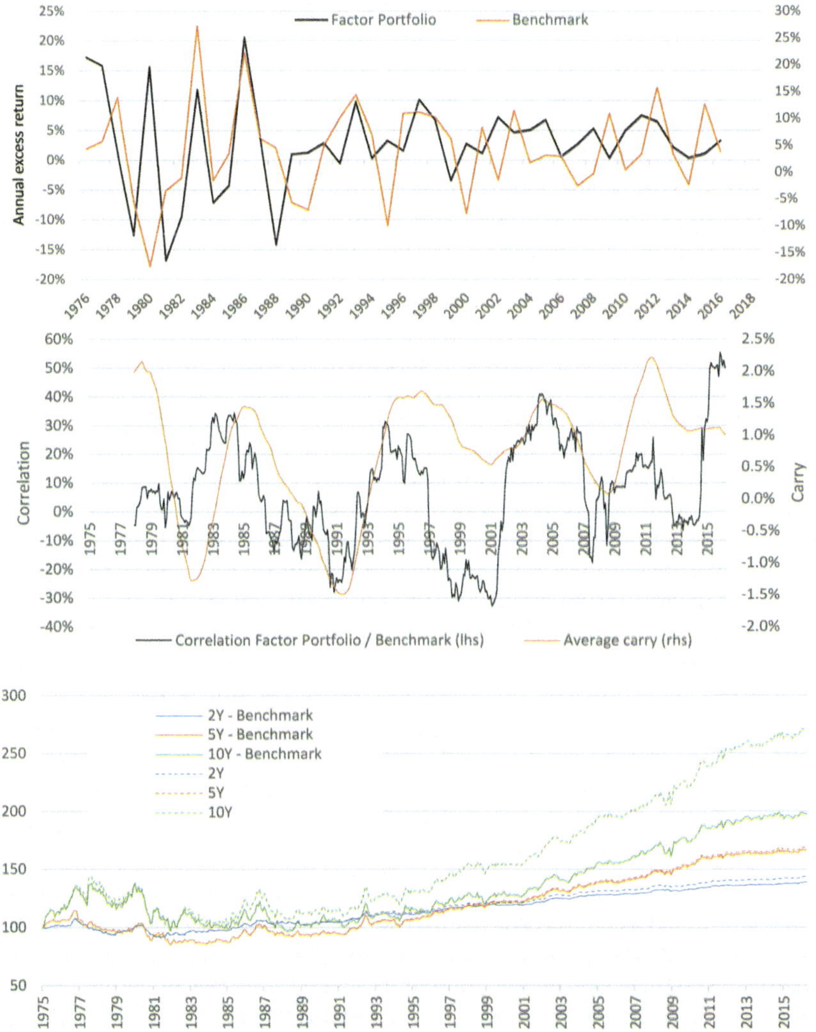

Fig. 6.2 Cross-market carry strategies: factor portfolio returns and correlations

The bottom panel of Fig. 6.2 compares the cumulative returns of the factor portfolios for the three maturities to the factor portfolios net of benchmark returns to assess the extent to which the return of the factor portfolio can be explained by benchmark returns. Essentially stripping out benchmark returns in this way, we find there is little impact on overall cumulative returns for the factor portfolios for two-year and five-year maturities. However, stripping out benchmark returns does have an impact on overall cumulative returns for the ten-year maturity. That is, for this maturity bucket, a significant portion of the factor portfolio's returns can be actually explained by the benchmark.

6.3.2 *Cross-Curve*

The top panel of Fig. 6.3 shows the cumulative returns of the factor portfolios for the cross-curve investment strategies for the USA, Germany, Japan, and the UK, starting from 1975. The UK factor portfolio shows the highest cumulative return of 15.4% over the period, but most of this return occurs in the first two years. For the USA and Germany, the strategy implies only modest total cumulative returns of 2.4% and 4.7%, respectively. Only for Japan does the strategy show significant and relatively steadily increasing cumulative returns for an overall return of 10.4%.

The statistics provided in Table 6.6 are consistent with this visual inspection. The alphas of the factor portfolios are only statistically significant for the UK and Japan. These markets also show significant betas (although negative in the case of Japan). For the USA and Germany, the alphas and betas of the factor portfolios are not statistically significantly different from zero and for the USA the low-carry P1 portfolio shows a higher mean return than P2.

The bottom panel of Fig. 6.3 shows, for each market, the 36-month correlation between returns from the factor portfolio and the related country benchmark, compared to the 36-month average carry across all maturities. Much like in the comparative results in the previous section, there is substantial variation in the correlation between benchmark and factor portfolio returns in the four markets over time, and, this coincides with the carry signal in each market (as shown in the lower four panels of Fig. 6.3). The relationship appears weaker in Japan (particularly from 1990 onwards) and there appears to be a structural break in Germany from around 2013 and onwards where the carry signal declined while correlation increased.

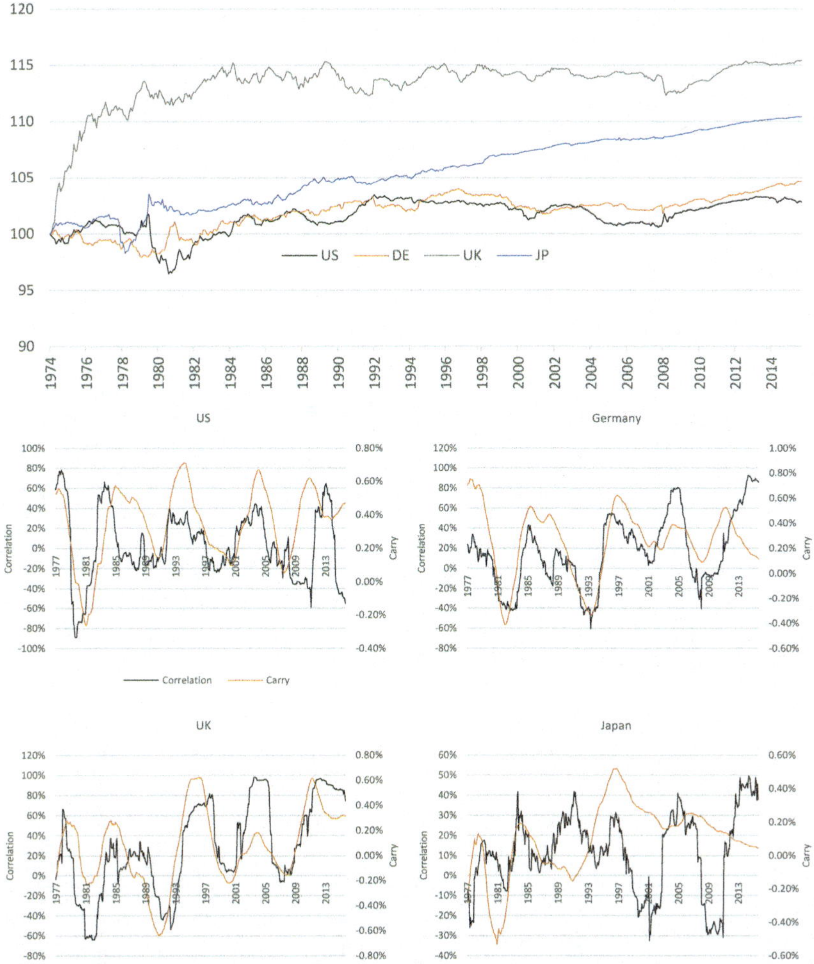

Fig. 6.3 Cross-curve carry strategies: cumulative returns and correlations

Table 6.6 Cross-curve carry strategies

	P1 (lowest signal)	*P2*	*P3 (highest signal)*	*P3 – P1*	*Factor*	*Benchmark*
			USA			
Mean (t-stat)	0.3% (1.99)**	0.25% (1.74)*	0.41% (2.76)***	0.11% (1.41)	0.11% (1.32)	0.36% (2.51)**
Standard deviation	1.18%	1.13%	1.18%	0.64%	0.65%	1.13%
Sharpe ratio	0.25	0.22	0.35	0.18	0.17	0.32
Alpha (t-stat)	−0.061% (−1.39)	−0.11% (−5.76)***	0.049% (1.27)	0.11% (1.35)	0.11% (1.29)	
Beta (t-stat)	1 (88.43)***	0.99 (208.98)***	1 (103.35)***	0.011 (0.55)	0.0071 (0.34)	
Tracking error	0.35%	0.15%	0.30%	1.29%		
Information ratio	−0.18	−0.73	0.16	0.09		
			DE			
Mean (t-stat)	0.41% (3.12)***	0.5% (3.96)***	0.55% (4.30)***	0.14% (1.71)*	0.11% (1.38)	0.53% (4.35)***
Standard deviation	0.85%	0.81%	0.83%	0.53%	0.53%	0.79%
Sharpe ratio	0.48	0.61	0.67	0.26	0.21	0.67
Alpha (t-stat)	−0.12% (−2.51)**	−0.039% (−1.59)	0.018% (0.46)	0.14% (1.66)*	0.11% (1.28)	
Beta (t-stat)	0.99 (57.10)***	1 (115.15)***	1 (72.89)***	0.0018 (0.06)	0.012 (0.40)	
Tracking error	0.31%	0.16%	0.24%	0.95%		
Information ratio	−0.40	−0.25	0.07	0.15		
			UK			
Mean (t-stat)	0.049% (0.25)	0.25% (1.29)	0.38% (1.79)*	0.33% (2.25)**	0.32% (2.22)**	0.3% (1.55)
Standard deviation	1.33%	1.35%	1.44%	1.00%	0.97%	1.30%
Sharpe ratio	0.04	0.19	0.26	0.33	0.33	0.23
Alpha (t-stat)	−0.22% (−2.53)**	−0.043% (−0.89)	0.065% (1.05)	0.29% (1.99)**	0.28% (1.98)**	
Beta (t-stat)	0.91 (47.01)***	1 (93.85)***	1.1 (76.61)***	0.15 (4.55)***	0.13 (4.15)***	
Tracking error	0.61%	0.33%	0.43%	1.48%		
Information ratio	−0.37	−0.13	0.15	0.19		

	JP					
Mean (t-stat)	0.11% (0.80)	0.26% (2.28)**	0.36% (3.03)***	0.25% (2.93)***	0.24% (2.71)***	0.3% (2.58)**
Standard deviation	0.86%	0.74%	0.76%	0.55%	0.57%	0.74%
Sharpe ratio	0.12	0.35	0.47	0.45	0.42	0.40
Alpha (t-stat)	−0.21% (−4.04)***	−0.025% (−0.88)	0.069% (1.84)*	0.28% (3.25)***	0.26% (2.93)***	
Beta (t-stat)	1.1 (53.15)***	0.97 (88.87)***	0.98 (67.36)***	−0.091 (−2.73)***	−0.067 (−1.95)*	
Tracking error	0.34%	0.18%	0.24%	0.98%		
Information ratio	−0.62	−0.14	0.29	0.28		

*** Significantly different from zero at the 1% significance level
** Significantly different from zero at the 5% significance level
* Significantly different from zero at the 10% significance level

6.3.3 *Cross-Market and Cross-Curve*

For the cross-curve, cross-market setting (again using the USA, Germany, Japan, and UK markets), portfolio P3 outperforms and the other portfolios, P1 and P2, underperform the benchmark as shown in the top panel of Fig. 6.4. From 1975 to the end of the sample period, P3 had a cumulative return of 31.4% compared to P1 and P2, which returned 5.9% and 18.1%, respectively. The factor portfolio returned 20.6%. Table 6.7 shows that moving from P1 to P2, mean returns, information ratios, and Sharpe ratios increase progressively. The betas for the three quantiles are positive and close to 1, with only the high quantile demonstrating positive alpha that is mildly statistically significant, with a beta of 1.1. The alphas also increase progressively, moving from negative to positive. The factor portfolio demonstrates a positive and highly significant alpha, high Sharpe ratio, and significant beta of 0.27. The bottom panel of Fig. 6.4 shows that after a sideways movement up to 1983, there is a fairly continuous increase in the cumulative returns of the factor portfolio. The cumulative returns of the total factor portfolio over the sample period are around 24% as compared to the returns of the factor portfolio net of benchmark returns, which are around 19%.

The second panel of Fig. 6.4 again shows significant fluctuation in the correlation between the factor portfolio and benchmark returns. For instance, the correlation touches cyclical lows in February 1980, July 1991, November 1998, and December 2007 and reaches cyclical peaks a few years after the lows in July 1984, December 1995, October 2004, and December 2011. Correlation has remained high in the years since 2011. The global carry signal touches cyclical lows in May 1982, October 1991, May 2001, and June 2008 and made cyclical peaks in January 1979, November 1985, December 1996, September 2004, and most recently in November 2011. While correlation has remained at an elevated level since 2011, the carry signal has declined somewhat, ranging around 0.24% since 2013.

6.3.4 *Time-Varying Fluctuations and the Carry Signal*

The fluctuation in rolling 36-month correlation between benchmark and factor portfolio returns was observed in each analytical setting. Mostly the fluctuations are large and coincide with changes in the carry signal (with the main exception of Japan in the cross-curve analysis).

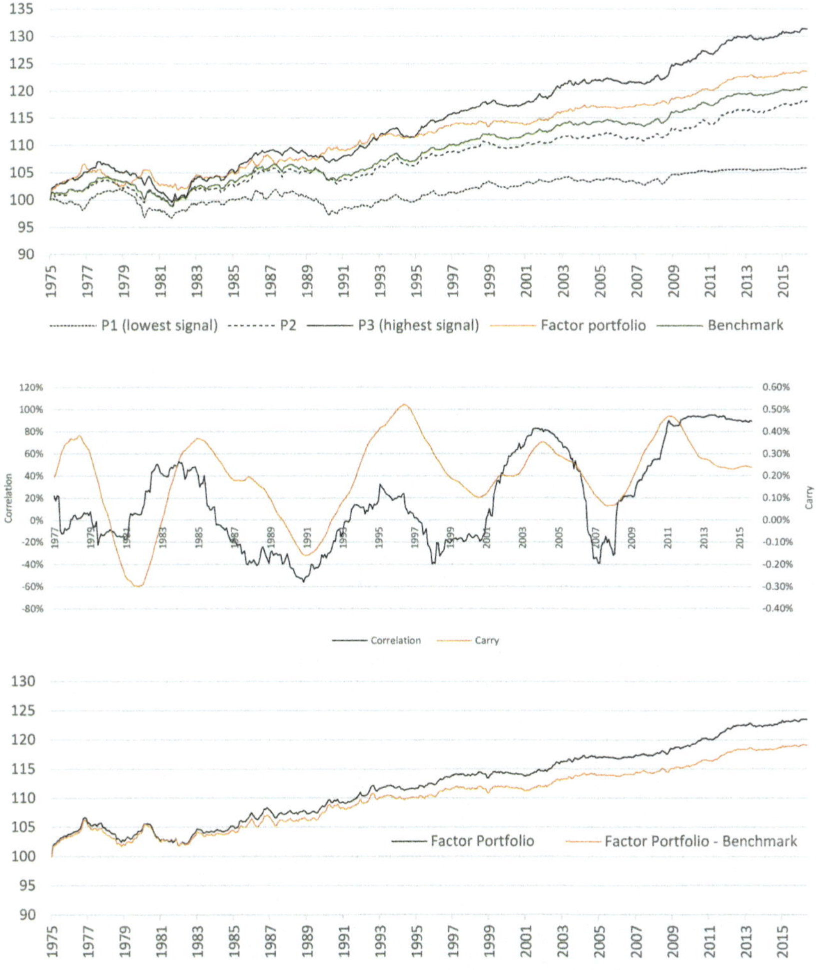

Fig. 6.4 Cross-curve and cross-market carry strategies: cumulative returns and correlations

Table 6.7 Cross-curve and cross-market carry strategies

	P1 (lowest signal)	*P2*	*P3 (highest signal)*	*P3 – P1*	*Factor*	*Benchmark*
			USA, DE, UK, JP			
Mean (t-stat)	0.031% (0.33)	0.19% (1.91)*	0.4% (3.36)***	0.36% (3.67)***	0.37% (3.74)***	0.25% (2.70)***
Standard deviation	0.76%	0.78%	0.93%	0.79%	0.79%	0.74%
Sharpe ratio	0.04	0.24	0.42	0.46	0.47	0.34
Alpha (t-stat)	−0.19% (−3.64)***	−0.057% (−1.48)	0.11% (2.11)**	0.3% (3.08)***	0.3% (3.15)***	
Beta (t-stat)	0.87 (43.39)***	0.97 (65.16)***	1.1 (56.23)***	0.26 (7.01)***	0.27 (7.08)***	
Tracking error	0.42%	0.30%	0.42%	0.94%		
Information ratio	−0.45	−0.19	0.26	0.32		

*** Significantly different from zero at the 1% significance level
** Significantly different from zero at the 5% significance level
* Significantly different from zero at the 10% significance level

We provide an interpretation of this as follows. The variations in monthly benchmark returns are mostly driven by changes in broad market yields. If this is the case, a reasonable assumption, positive correlation between the benchmark (as a proxy for broad market yields) and the factor portfolio implies that changes in yields of high-carry assets are larger than changes in yields of low-carry assets. So during the positive correlation phases, when benchmark yields are rising (and returns are negative), yields of high-carry assets will rise by more than yields of low-carry assets and the carry strategy would show weaker returns. Similarly, during periods when benchmark yields are falling (and returns are positive), yields of high-carry assets will fall by more than yields of low-carry assets and the carry strategy would show stronger returns. So, generally in times of positive correlation, the return of high-carry instruments tends to be more volatile than low-carry instruments. During times of negative correlation, the reverse would hold, and the return of high-carry instruments would tend to be less volatile than low-carry instruments.

We observed that the correlations between factor portfolio returns and benchmarks fluctuate through time. The observation that these fluctuations move alongside the strength of the carry signal may provide some insight into the sources of the strategies' excess returns. Correlations tend to be high when the carry signal is high (where high-carry assets appear to be more volatile) and correlations tend to be low (where high-carry assets appear to be less volatile) in times of low carry. We interpret this as indicating that the riskiness of carry strategies varies with its compensation—that is, as an indication of time-varying risk premium. That is, when the carry signal is high, it is high for a reason: to compensate for additional risk, for instance, the potentially greater losses accruing to a carry strategy, compared to the benchmark or low carry strategies, in the event that general market interest rates rise.

6.4 Conclusion

Our objective has been to analyse the properties of carry as a possible signal for a factor-based portfolio investment strategy. While carry has been analysed for a range of asset classes in several recent studies, in this chapter we have focused on carry strategies for sovereign bonds of developed economies. We split our analysis into three settings: (1) cross-market, (2) cross-curve, and (3) cross-curve and cross-market. For each setting, we used longer data histories than previously employed in the related literature and assessed the degree to which carry strategies result in performance that is continuous, time-persistent, and pervasive (across markets). We also took transaction costs into account.

In terms of the assessment of carry in relation to the criteria of continuity, persistency, and pervasiveness, to a large extent, though with some exceptions, we find continuity in all three settings where it is shown that risk/return attributes generally improve when progressively moving from the low-carry portfolios to the high-carry portfolios. The average return differences between low- and high-carry portfolios are mostly statistically significant. The evidence for the other two criteria, time-persistency and pervasiveness, is less supportive for carry. Extending the data history to the mid-1970s—thereby including a period of broadly increasing yields—we find sideways movements in cumulative excess returns. In particular, with the cross-market as well as the cross-curve and cross-market analysis, cumulative excess returns show steady increases only from the mid-1980s onwards, that is, during the period of a broad decline in interest rates. There are also marked differences for the cross-curve strategy for different markets with only modest, not statistically significant, performances for the USA and Germany.

Further, in contrast to Koijen et al. (2018) we report, for a number of strategies, significant betas for the factor portfolios. Again, this observation is made when the data history is extended to the mid-1970s. As a result, some of the reported performance of the factor portfolio might be a result of exposure to the market benchmark. The strategies also exhibit considerable fluctuations in the correlation between returns on the factor portfolio and the benchmark returns. These fluctuations co-move with the size of the global carry signal, so that correlations are high when the global carry signal is high and vice versa. Our analysis and conclusion here is based on the carry factor only with respect to the long-only passive benchmark and does not take into consideration a broader set of factors, as in other studies, such as for instance value and momentum. Our purpose for this study has been to focus on carry alone, but we would look to augment our analysis in future studies to look at the impact of other factors.

Overall, to the question "is carry on?" we answer a conditional "yes" in the sense that over long horizons and across markets there is some evidence of excess returns of carry strategies, and there is some indication of time-varying compensation for the related risks. But as highlighted above, there are important caveats to bear in mind. Our results, for instance, depend on the prevailing yield environment. During the period of rising interest rates in the late 1970s and early 1980s, carry strategies underwhelmed. In environments when the carry signal is high—likely when the yield curve is steep—some of the performance of carry strategies may be a result of exposure to the market risk factor. Overall, we might need to carry on with our research. It could be interesting to apply our methodology with a combination of factors with carry, such as momentum, value, the term premium, and other macroeconomic variables, as well as conduct further analysis into the underlying drivers of carry.

Notes

1. The carry trade in foreign exchange markets relates to borrowing a low-yielding currency and investing in a high-yielding currency. According to uncovered interest parity (UIP) gains from the interest rate differential (the carry) should be offset by a depreciation in the investment (high yielding) currency. However empirically, the reverse seems to hold true and the investment currency tends to appreciate a little (Brunnermeier et al. 2008).
2. This may be consistent with the broader analysis of factor-based investing relative to active investment management as provided by Ang et al. (2009).
3. The segmented markets thesis states that changing availability of capital that can be deployed for arbitrage trades (i.e. hedge fund capital) can impact the profitability of related trading strategies. This may arise, for instance, because investors are active in different markets and have limited risk bearing abilities (Shleifer and Vishny 1997).
4. Merton (2014) provides an overview of what constitutes a quality factor. A strategy is continuous if the relative strength of the strategy signal translates to the relative size of returns, so that, for instance, the more positive the signal, the more positive the return. The strategy is time-persistent if the strategy works through time, and thus in potentially different market conditions. The strategy is pervasive if the signal works in different markets, for instance, across geopolitical borders (or indeed across different asset classes). Consistency refers to whether and to what extent a strategy is supported by theory. If not underpinned by some rationale, the strategy could merely be a statistical artefact and more a result of data mining.
5. As the properties of the carry portfolios are assessed on the basis of their returns in excess of the respective short rates, the cross-market strategies imply the assumption that any exchange rate risk is fully hedged whereby the costs of the hedge correspond to the short-rate differentials between the markets (i.e. the covered interest rate parity holds).

6. The Nelson–Siegel formula is given by $y_t^{\tau} = \beta_t^1 + \beta_t^2 \cdot \left(\frac{1-e^{-\lambda\cdot\tau}}{\lambda\cdot\tau}\right) + \beta_t^3 \cdot \left(\frac{1-e^{-\lambda\cdot\tau}}{\lambda\cdot\tau} - e^{-\lambda\cdot\tau}\right)$ where the observed spot rate y for maturity τ years at t is explained by three parameters, the level (β_t^1), slope (β_t^2), and curvature (β_t^3) as well as λ. λ is fixed at 0.7173 calculated in terms of years (0.0609 calculated in months) across countries and across time following a standard estimation technique (Diebold and Li 2006). All quantitative work in this study, including calculation of zero coupon yields using the Nelson–Siegel approach and calculation of returns to carry-focused portfolios, is undertaken using the BIS Asset Management Asset Allocation Module (BAAM), a Matlab-based module developed jointly by the BIS Asset Management and Banco Central do Brasil.
7. Koijen et al. (2018) show how this equation is consistent even when calculating carry for assets denominated in different currencies, where the assumption, consistent with unchanging market conditions, is that the exchange rate stays the same from one period to the next.

References

Ahmerkamp, J., & Grant, J. (2013a). *The returns to carry and momentum strategies*. Imperial College London Working Paper.

Ahmerkamp, J., & Grant, J. (2013b). *Optimal carry and momentum returns in futures markets: A compensation for capital constrained hedge funds?*. Imperial College London Working Paper.

Ang, A., Goetzmann, W., & Schaefer, S. (2009). *Evaluation of active management of the norwegian government pension fund—Global*. Columbia Business School Working Paper.

Asness, C., Moskowitz, T., & Pedersen, L. (2013). Value and momentum everywhere. *Journal of Finance, 68*(3), 929–985.

Blitz, D. (2012). Strategic allocation to premiums in the equity market. *Journal of Index Investing, 2*(4), 42–49.

Brunnermeier, M. K., Nagel, S., & Pedersen, L. H. (2008). Carry trades and currency crashes. *NBER Macroeconomics Annual, 23*(1), 313–348.

Baz, J., Granger, N., Harvey, C., Le Roux, N., & Rattry, S. (2015). *Dissecting investment strategies in the cross section and time series*. SSRN Working Paper.

Campbell, J., & Shiller, R. (1991). Yield spreads and interest rate movements: A bird's eye view. *Review of Economic Studies, 58*(3), 495–514.

Deaves, R. (1997). Predictable excess fixed-income returns: The Canadian case. *Journal of Fixed Income, 7*(2), 61–66.

Diebold, F., & Li, C. (2006). Forecasting the term structure of government bond yields. *Journal of Econometrics, 130*(2), 337–364.

Engsted, T., Moller, S., & Sander, M. (2013). *Bond return predictability in expansions and recessions.* Aarhus University Center for Research in Econometric Analysis of Time Series, Research Paper, No. 2013–13.

Fama, E., & Bliss, R. (1987). The information in long-maturity forward rates. *American Economic Review, 77*(4), 680–692.

Gargano, A., Pettenuzzo, D., & Timmermann A. (2014). *Bond return predictability: Economic value and links to the macroeconomy.* Brandeis Working Paper Series No. 75.

Ghysels, E., Horan, C., & Moench, E. (2014). *Forecasting through the rear-view mirror: Data revisions and bond return predictability.* Federal Reserve Bank of New York Staff Reports, No. 581.

Greenwood, R., & Vayanos, D. (2014). Bond supply and excess bond returns. *Review of Financial Studies, 27*(3), 663–713.

Harvey, C., Liu, Y., & Zhu, H. (2016). … and the cross-section of expected returns. *Review of Financial Studies, 29*(1), 5–68.

Ilmanen, A. (1995). Time-varying expected returns in international bond markets. *Journal of Finance, 50*(2), 481–506.

Koedijk, K. G., Slager, A. M., & Stork, P. A. (2016). Investing in systematic factor premiums. *European Financial Management, 22*(2), 193–234.

Koijen, R., Moskowitz, T., Pedersen, L., & Vrugt, E. (2018). Carry. *Journal of Financial Economics, 127*(2), 197–225.

Lin, H., Wang, J., & Wu, C. (2014). Predictions of corporate bond excess returns. *Journal of Financial Markets, 21*, 123–152.

Ludvigson, S., & Ng, S. (2009). Macro factors in bond risk premia. *Review of Financial Studies, 22*(12), 5027–5067.

Merton, R. (2014). *Foundations of asset management goal-based investing: The next trend.* Presentation to the MIT Sloan Finance Forum.

Moskowitz, T. (1999). *An analysis of risk and pricing anomalies.* Center for Research in Security Prices Working Paper Series, No. 500, University of Chicago.

Page, S., & Taborsky, M. (2011). The myth of diversification: Risk factors versus asset classes. *Journal of Portfolio Management*, Invited Editorial Comment, *37*(4), 1–2.

Piazzesi, M., & Swanson, E. (2004). Futures prices as risk-adjusted forecasts of monetary policy. *Journal of Monetary Economics, 55*(4), 677–691.

Rezende, R. (2015). *Risks in macroeconomic fundamentals and excess bond returns predictability.* Sveriges Riksbank Working Paper Series, No. 295.

Shleifer, A., & Vishny, R. W. (1997). The limits of arbitrage. *Journal of Finance, 52*(1), 35–55.

Silva, F., Cortez, M., & Armada, M. (2003). *Bond return predictability: An investigation for the European market.* Universidade de Minho Working Paper.

CHAPTER 7

Short-Term Drivers of Sovereign CDS Spreads

Marcelo Yoshio Takami

7.1 Introduction

Given the size of the sovereign credit default swaps (CDS) market (currently at $1.6 trillion) and the valuable information it reveals about market expectations on the probability of default, there is great need for gaining understanding the determinants of CDS spreads (Alsakka and Gwilym 2010). CDS contracts are particularly useful for a wide range of investors, either for hedging existing exposures or for speculators who wish to take positions without the need to maintain the reference obligation on their

---

I am grateful to the Bank for International Settlement and, particularly, to Jacob Bjorheim and the Asset Management Unit of the Banking Department for their support. I thank for invaluable comments and suggestions received from Vahe Sahakyan, Narayan Bulusu, Joachim Coche, André Minella, Carlos Viana and Jacob Nelson. I thank Bilyana Bogdanova for her capable research assistance. All errors are my responsibility.

M. Y. Takami (✉)
Corporate Risk and Benchmarks Department,
Banco Central do, Brasília, Brazil
e-mail: marcelo.takami@bcb.gov.br

N. Bulusu et al. (eds.), *Advances in the Practice of Public Investment Management*, https://doi.org/10.1007/978-3-319-90245-6_7

books. This is one reason why the market of sovereign CDS is, in some cases, more liquid than the underlying sovereign bond market itself.[1] Moreover, CDS spreads may be monitored for gauging the market perception of the debt sustainability of specific governments, as they provide more timely and, arguably, within periods of crisis, more accurate, distress assessment than rating agencies, as conveyed by long-term ratings. Timely measures of credit risk are important, for example, to central banks concerned with the risk of their foreign reserves portfolios.

To account for model uncertainty, I fit all possible linear models using the chosen independent variables (which include both global and local factors), and choose the model specification with the best fit for 35 developed and emerging economies' sovereign CDS spreads (please see Table 7.1 for the full list). Identifying the best model separately for each country might prove useful for risk assessment and, eventually, for forecasting purposes. This procedure also allows us to gain insights about the relative importance of each of the factors considered. The most important result I find is that the S&P 500 index is contemporaneously negatively related to the CDS spreads for most of the countries. Further, the coefficients of the S&P 500 are higher for emerging markets than they are for advanced economies. I also conduct multiple robustness checks, all of which confirm the main result of this chapter.

It must be stressed that the proposed framework is not necessarily meant to either predict crises or enhance financial investment efficiency; however, it might prove useful for supporting short-term sovereign risk assessment. This chapter is closely related to Westerlund and Thuraisamy (2016) and Longstaff et al. (2011), but differs from these studies in the following aspects: (1) focus on the short-term relationship between spreads and drivers, and (2) comparing the drivers of CDS spreads in developed and emerging economies.

This chapter is organized as follows: Sect. 7.2 revises the related literature; Sect. 7.3 presents a short description of the CDS market; Sect. 7.4 describes the data; Sect. 7.5 provides the empirical strategy, the results, and the robustness assessment; and finally Sect. 7.6 concludes this chapter.

Table 7.1 Classification of sovereigns according to investment class

Investment class	*Countries*	*Rating*
SDR (Special Drawing Right) basket	Germany	Aaa
	France	Aa2
	Italy	Baa2
	Spain	Baa2
	Belgium	Aa3
	Netherlands	Aaa
	Austria	Aa1
	Portugal	Ba1
	Ireland	A3
	Finland	Aa1
	Japan	A1
Other G20 countries	Australia	Aaa
	China[2]	Aa3
	Korea	Aa2
	Turkey	Ba1
	Indonesia	Baa3
	Russia	Ba1
	South Africa	Baa2
	Brazil	Ba2
	Mexico	A3
Other highly rated countries	Denmark	Aaa
	Sweden	Aaa
	New Zealand	Aaa
	Hong Kong	Aa1
	Chile	Aa3
Other emerging markets	Israel	A1
	Poland	A2
	Czech Republic	A1
	Hungary	Ba1
	Peru	A3
	Slovakia	A2
	Philippines	Baa2
	Malaysia	A3
	Thailand	Baa1
	Colombia	Baa2

Source: Moody's, Sep/2016

7.2 Related Literature

In the spirit of Westerlund and Thuraisamy (2016), I test many models with different combinations of multiple drivers, instead of solely testing a specific model, for each sovereign. Applying a bootstrap-based panel predictability test, Westerlund and Thuraisamy (2016) find that the global drivers are the best predictors. In line with this analysis, I find that the S&P 500 is statistically significant across the board.

This chapter's results are also closely in line with Longstaff et al. (2011), who find that sovereign credit spreads are primarily driven by global macroeconomic forces and that the risk premium represents about a third of the credit spread.[3] Sixty-four per cent of the variations in sovereign credit spreads are accounted for by a single principal component which primarily loads on USA stock, high-yield markets and volatility risk premium (proxied by the VIX index). Instead of using principal components, this chapter tries to find the subsets of explanatory variables that can best explain short-term CDS spreads for each of the countries considered.

While this chapter focuses on the short-term determinants of sovereign risk, Remolona et al. (2008) are concerned with pricing mechanisms for sovereign risk and propose a framework for distinguishing market-assessed sovereign risk from its risk premia. They use a dynamic panel data model with a sample covering 16 emerging countries' sovereign CDS spreads. In contrast, I believe that this chapter provides a more comprehensive understanding of the determinants of credit risk, since this chapter's sample covers not only emerging countries but also advanced economies, summing up to 35 countries.

7.3 Description of the CDS Market

The sovereign CDS market grew from \$0.17 trillion (in terms of notional amounts outstanding) in December 2004 to almost \$2 trillion in December 2015.[4] During the same period, the credit derivatives market increased from \$6 trillion to \$15 trillion. Fig. 7.1 shows that positions in sovereign contracts have become an increasing part of the CDS market since December 2004, while total notional amount outstanding in the credit derivatives market as a whole has been declining markedly since 2007.[5]

CDS spreads indicate the cost of buying protection against the default of a reference entity. The protection buyer pays a premium or spread on a periodic basis and in exchange, upon the occurrence of a credit event (defined within the terms of a CDS contract), has the right to sell the

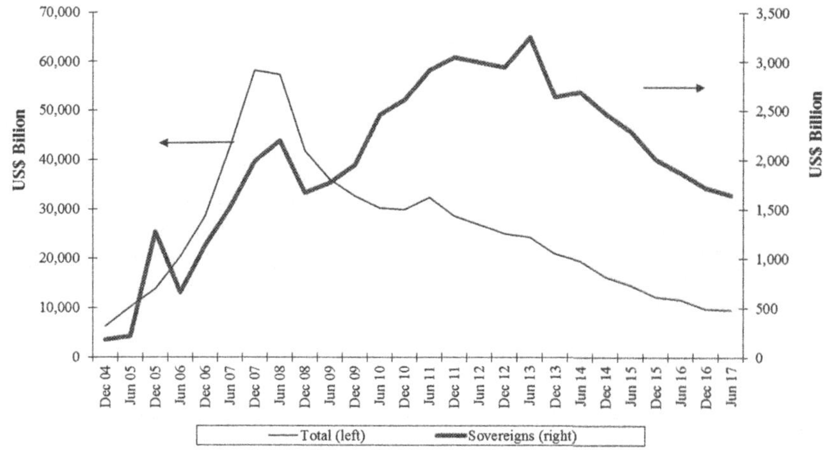

Fig. 7.1 Notional amount of CDS contracts outstanding: total versus sovereigns

bond to the protection seller at face value. CDS contracts are generally considered by market participants to be efficient and liquid instruments to mitigate credit risk. Further, they enable credit providers to diversify exposure and expand lending capacity. The protection seller, on the other hand, can take credit exposure over a customized term and earn the premium without having to fund the position. The spread is related to the expected loss of the bond: the higher the expected loss, the higher the spread. Since trades by market participants are more frequent than ratings (re)assessments by ratings agencies, CDS spreads are a more timely, though not necessarily a more accurate, way of gauging the market perception of credit conditions of specific entities.

Triggers for sovereign CDS contracts may be a failure-to-pay, a moratorium, or a restructuring. A failure-to-pay occurs when a government fails to pay part of its obligations in an amount at least as large as the payment requirement after any applicable grace period. A moratorium occurs when an authorized officer of the reference entity disclaims, repudiates, rejects, or challenges the validity of one or more obligations. A moratorium that lasts a pre-defined time period triggers a failure-to-pay event or a restructuring. Restructuring occurs when there is a reduction, postponement, or deferral of the obligation to pay the principal; when there is a change in priority ranking causing subordination to another obligation; or when there is a change in currency or composition of interest or principal payments to any currency which is not a permitted currency.

Upon default, there are two types of settlement: physical or cash. Both of them cause the termination of the contract. In the case of the physical settlement, the protection buyer delivers to the protection seller one of a list of bonds with equivalent seniority rights and the protection seller pays to the protection buyer the face value of the debt. In the case of cash settlement, the protection seller pays to the protection buyer the difference between the face value of the debt and its current market value.

7.4 Data

The dependent variable for each of the 35 investment-class markets listed in Table 7.1 is the change in its five-year CDS spreads, with the reference obligation being a deliverable senior dollar-denominated external debt of the sovereign. Table 7.2 shows descriptive statistics for the sovereign CDS spreads of the 35 selected countries.

I select the set of global and local explanatory variables that could potentially be used by investors and risk-managers who take short-term views on sovereign risk. The focus of this chapter is on establishing statistical relationships, and not on identifying the economic content of the variables considered. The slope, for example, not only provides an indirect indication of future tax revenues, as they are related to growth prospects through the business cycle, but also captures the risk premia embedded in long-term yields. Alternatively, it could convey information about the state of the economy with respect to growth prospects, risk aversion, banking system vulnerability, and business cycle. In this chapter, I do not take a stand on which of these interpretations matters more for the results.

In the following, I use *sp*500, *vix*, *Slope*, and *oil*, respectively, to refer to the S&P 500 index, VIX index, USA slope factor, and Brent oil price index. The local factors that I consider as presumably providing information on specific aspects related to debt sustainability or overall risk premium are the local stock index level ($stock_i$), exchange rate (xr_i), local two-year yield ($localTY_i$), local slope factor ($localSlope_i$), and the average of banks' CDS spreads (when available) of the banking system of the corresponding jurisdiction ($bank_i$). Given the reasonable assumption of persistence of CDS spreads, I include the lagged dependent variable in the regression. The description of the variables, the economic reasoning behind their inclusion, and data sources are described in detail in Table 7.3.

Table 7.2 Descriptive statistics for CDS spreads

	Mean	*Standard deviation*	*Minimum*	*Median*	*Maximum*	*# obs*
Germany	38.6	26.1	12.2	28.2	112.4	317
France	81.1	53.1	25.4	67.2	241.3	317
Finland	34.2	18.0	18.1	26.9	87.4	317
Netherlands	47.7	29.8	15.5	40.5	130.1	317
Austria	64.0	51.3	21.2	39.2	228.2	317
Belgium	107.0	83.0	31.8	62.2	381.6	317
Slovakia	100.0	70.2	38.2	81.3	315.0	317
Spain	222.0	136.0	58.6	217.7	613.1	317
Italy	222.1	126.9	85.3	173.1	566.6	317
Ireland	285.5	274.9	40.3	145.7	1207.3	317
Portugal	468.2	347.4	119.3	350.4	1615.0	317
Denmark	43.5	35.8	14.1	26.8	152.4	317
Sweden	27.4	16.4	13.1	20.6	80.8	317
Poland	116.2	61.1	53.7	87.6	318.8	317
Czech Rep.	74.0	33.2	38.5	59.7	189.8	317
Hungary	286.0	134.3	117.6	271.1	699.2	317
Turkey	204.3	49.5	112.9	200.6	327.7	317
Russia	227.5	94.8	120.3	198.8	615.5	317
Australia	48.7	15.4	28.2	45.0	103.5	317
New Zealand	52.5	20.1	27.7	45.6	117.8	317
Japan	67.7	26.9	32.5	63.4	152.0	317
Hong Kong	52.7	13.8	35.6	47.5	103.8	317
Korea	83.5	32.0	46.3	69.9	214.2	317
China	95.0	24.4	54.5	89.5	191.6	317
Philippines	121.4	30.5	79.9	113.5	255.1	317
Indonesia	174.8	37.5	121.6	165.0	296.9	317
Thailand	121.9	26.7	81.7	118.4	237.5	317
Malaysia	114.6	35.4	66.7	106.9	232.4	317
South Africa	190.8	55.1	109.6	180.6	376.3	317
Israel	115.9	39.3	64.7	114.7	209.0	317
Brazil	191.9	100.2	94.2	155.9	498.6	317
Mexico	120.2	30.3	66.1	114.8	221.1	317
Peru	131.5	30.1	77.6	129.6	221.6	317
Chile	90.7	21.1	57.5	84.9	156.8	317
Colombia	138.1	47.8	75.5	123.6	312.7	317

Source: Capital IQ

To avoid potential problems of non-stationarity of the variables in our study, I analyse the first differences of all the variables at the weekly frequency from July 2005 to July 2016. I perform the analysis at the weekly frequency to get a sufficient sample size. This, however, has the drawback of making it infeasible to use other macroeconomic sovereign credit-related

Table 7.3 Description of explanatory variables

Variable acronym	*Description and economic reasoning*	*Expected sign*	*Source*
$spread_i$	The CDS spread referencing country *i*'s debt stands as the last daily prices of a five-year senior dollar-denominated CDS contract. This is the dependent variable in the estimation; its lag is also included as an eligible explanatory variable in the estimation	Negative/positive	Capital IQ
*sp*500	The Standard & Poor's 500 Index is typically a gauge of the general state of the global economy	Negative	Bloomberg ticker: SPX
vix	VIX is a measure of market's expectation of stock market volatility. The positive variation of this index is associated with higher uncertainty and risk aversion among investors	Positive	Bloomberg ticker: VIX
Slope	The slope factor is set as the 10-Year USA Treasury Constant Maturity interest rates minus the three-month USA Treasury Constant Maturity interest rates. It presumably provides prospective information on the business cycle of the global economy. The slope factor is influenced positively by economic growth and by inflationary expectations; it is influenced negatively by risk aversion	Negative	Bloomberg tickers: H15T10Y and H15T3M
oil	The oil price is the last quoted price of the day of the London Brent Crude Oil Index. In general, increasing oil prices reflect both the surging of global economic activity or the impact of production shortfalls. As for the demand side, when the pace of economic expansion picks up, so is the global demand for energy expected to increase. Changes in oil prices might thus be deemed as a competing indicator of the state of the global economy as well as changes in S&P 500 or VIX indices	Negative	Bloomberg
$stock_i$	The local stock exchange index is expected to rise or remain stable when companies and the economy in general show positive prospects in terms of stability and growth. It is expected to decrease in periods of crisis. Then, it is an indicator generally used to gauge the overall economic health	Negative	Bloomberg

xr_i	The exchange rates are expressed in units of local currency per USA dollar. Arguably, currency devaluation might lead to additional charges for dollar-denominated indebted countries and for countries with negative balance of trade and highly dependent on import of manufactured products. On the other hand, as an indicator of relative international price competitiveness, currency devaluation might bring benefits derived from the international trade	Positive/ negative	Bloomberg
$localTY_i$	The two-year local government bond yield refers to the local currency denominated fixed rate government debt. All bond prices are mid-rates and are taken at the close of business in the local office for all markets. In general, high two-year yields are related to negative growth prospects in the near future. Moreover, high yields signal that the country might be struggling to attract investors to fund its expenses	Positive	Bloomberg
$localSlope_i$	The local slope factor is the difference between the interest rates on ten-year and two-year local government bonds. It is due to provide prospective information on the business cycle of the local economy. When the slope decreases or becomes negative, it indicates a slowdown in economic activity in the foreseeable future. On the other hand, higher slopes suggest expectations of increasing economic growth	Negative	Bloomberg
$bank_{i,t}$	Average of CDS spreads of banks comprising the banking system of a country *i*: the spreads stand as the last daily prices of a five-year senior CDS contract. The increasing deterioration of the banking system risk perception might be expected to spill over into the sovereign risk as long as its contingent liability becomes an ever growing part of the total government debt	Positive	Datastream

factors, such as deficit/GDP, debt/GDP ratios, or foreign reserves, as explanatory variables. These variables are available at best at a monthly frequency. I test as many as possible econometric models for a time period encompassing the period July 2005 to October 2012. The last 45 months (from November 2012 to July 2016) are set apart for calculating out-of-sample goodness-of-fit statistics.

7.5 Empirical Strategy and Results

First, in order to mitigate potential multicollinearity issues, I orthogonalized the variables most usually associated to the general economic conditions (*vix, oil*, and *stock*) to the S&P 500.

I begin the empirical analysis by attempting to narrow down the set of variables that could be included in the regressions, by means of the Granger-causality test (Granger 1969). This step is useful to reduce the computational time required for the analysis. I limit the set of eligible local explanatory variables to only endogenous and weakly exogenous ones, as given by the Granger-causality test. I narrow the set of variables because when estimating models with contemporaneous independent variables, a primary concern is the endogeneity of the regressors. For example, while weekly changes in the exchange rate may anticipate changes in CDS spreads, it could also be argued that currency changes might arise as a consequence of changes in CDS spreads. When associated with a negative outlook of government debt sustainability, increases in CDS spreads might lead currency depreciation as net capital outflows ensue. In order to mitigate such endogeneity issues, I run Generalized Method of Moments (GMM) estimations with instrumental variables for the endogenous variables. When the variable is set as exogenous *a priori* (this is the case for the global variables and the lagged dependent variable), I simply use it as instrument for itself; for the endogenous ones, I use their first lags as instruments. Non-exogenous and non-endogenous variables are not considered in the model specification. Therefore, by constraining the testable model specifications to a subset of only endogenous and exogenous variables, I can save computational cost. Parts A and B of Table 7.4 show chi-squared statistics for the Granger-causality test, respectively: (1) whether local variables anticipate changes in CDS spreads, and (2) whether the opposite holds true. A variable is deemed eligible when it is weakly exogenous or endogenous. Table 7.5 shows the subset of eligible variables for each country, that is, the weakly exogenous and endogenous variables

Table 7.4 Granger-causality test

	Part A					Part B				
	$stock_{i,t}$	$xr_{i,t}$	$localTY_{i,t}$	$localSlope_{i,t}$	$bank_{i,t}$	$stock_{i,t}$	$xr_{i,t}$	$localTY_{i,t}$	$localSlope_{i,t}$	$bank_{i,t}$
Germany	8.8	2.5	10.5*	11.5**	10.7*	6.5	12.7**	4.5	12.9**	4.4
France	5.1	2.6	7.9	11.9**	20.0***	9.5*	7.7	6.2	6.9	16.5***
Finland	5.0	5.7	4.5	7.2	8.9	7.2	19.4***	9.5*	3.5	28.9***
Netherlands	7.5	10.0*	9.6*	11.1**	5.6	9.9*	14.7**	14.1**	9.5*	6.1
Austria	8.5	3.8	10.5*	26.4***	13.2**	12.1**	8.8	11.9**	7.2	21.2***
Belgium	1.6	5.9	16.1***	30.3***	12.9**	5.7	11.9**	4.8	10.6*	11.9**
Slovakia	8.4	8.3	8.5	5.5		15.0**	5.6	8.8	28.4***	
Spain	4.5	6.3	7.7	17.5***	31.5***	1.8	4.6	9.8*	18.9***	29.5***
Italy	8.8	3.7	38.0***	29.1***	30.8***	10.0*	5.7	4.2	8.9	21.9***
Ireland	2.2	2.4	5.9	12.8**	7.8	7.8	10.4*	17.1***	24.5***	19.1***
Portugal	4.1	1.7	10.5*	19.9***	25.8***	12.8**	8.1	49.9***	50.7***	17.6***
Denmark	20.9***	4.8	17.3***	5.3	7.4	24.3***	13.8**	11.2**	1.6	8.3
Sweden	23.3***	18.5***	6.0	14.8**	11.6**	14.1**	19.9***	9.9*	0.8	25.7***
Poland	5.4	19.1***	13.7**	12.8**		9.4*	8.8	7.6	5.9	
Czech Rep.	5.7	33.4***	24.7***	1.6		44.6***	9.0	31.4***	4.9	
Hungary	6.9	20.5***	12.5**	10.0*		21.2***	25.5***	8.0	24.5***	
Turkey	11.8**	28.5***	16.7***	5.3	90.4***	12.6**	20.0***	8.9	12.4**	173.5***
Russia	36.1***	15.1**	10.5*	10.5*	52.8***	8.5	16.4***	4.2	4.3	85.8***
Australia	10.7*	4.5	18.4***	17.7***	38.8***	11.6**	15.3***	6.5	10.8*	12.9**
New Zealand	6.1	15.9***	2.4	6.1		7.3	7.1	0.6	6.4	
Japan	14.3**	3.7	4.1	1.9	7.9	6.3	2.3	3.0	6.1	15.8***
Hong Kong	22.2***	2.3	3.6	15.8***	27.9***	10.5*	6.5	6.8	21.4***	9.8*
Korea	39.5***	71.9***	5.2	11.0*	105.8***	11.5**	41.2***	19.8***	4.3	174.5***
China	12.6**	1.9	25.7***	7.0	17.4***	21.5***	9.8*	11.0*	5.0	64.8***
Philippines	33.5***	3.3	8.3	7.4		26.0***	15.5***	11.2**	14.1**	

(continued)

Table 7.4 (continued)

	Part A					*Part B*				
	$stock_{i,t}$	$xr_{i,t}$	$localTY_{i,t}$	$localSlope_{i,t}$	$bank_{i,t}$	$stock_{i,t}$	$xr_{i,t}$	$localTY_{i,t}$	$localSlope_{i,t}$	$bank_{i,t}$
Indonesia	42.5***	81.4***	117.7***	12.6**		42.8***	100.2***	62.0***	16.4***	
Thailand	27.4***	8.2	8.4	20.3***		43.8***	6.3	17.5***	2.0	
Malaysia	11.7**	18.4***	14.4**	14.1**	3.9	21.1***	6.9	4.2	7.8	38.3***
South Africa	15.3***	26.4***	11.7**	36.4***		14.8**	9.2	21.5***	0.9	
Israel	6.2	14.7**	6.3	5.3		13.6**	8.2	9.6*	2.5	
Brazil	13.9**	30.3***	5.3	1.9		10.2*	22.4***	7.5	9.4*	
Mexico	35.7***	34.6***	13.5**	3.9		13.1**	9.6*	4.7	2.5	
Peru	3.5	22.8***	16.0***	6.4		18.4***	7.8	10.7*	4.1	
Chile	23.5***	10.5*	14.8**	10.1*		7.9	8.8	14.2**	10.6*	
Colombia	11.2**	20.6***	17.5***	2.3		4.4	2.4	4.8	1.3	

Each column in Part A shows the chi-squared statistics with *n* degrees of freedom (χ_n^2) for the hypothesis test that the corresponding factor f_t does not "Granger cause" the first difference of CDS spreads of the country in the corresponding row. The Granger-causality test is a Wald test on the restrictions that the β_ls are jointly zero at the estimation of equation: $\Delta \mathbf{spread}_{i,t} = \alpha_0 + \sum_{k=1}^{5} \alpha_k \Delta \mathbf{spread}_{t-k} + \sum_{l=1}^{5} \beta_l \Delta f_{t-l} + \varepsilon_t$. Part B shows the chi-squared statistics for whether the opposite holds true, that is, for the hypothesis test that the first difference of CDS spreads of the country in the corresponding row does not "Granger cause" the corresponding factor f_t. The Granger-causality test is a Wald test on the restrictions that the δ_ls are jointly zero at the estimation of equation:

$$\Delta f_t = \gamma_0 + \sum_{k=1}^{5} \gamma_k \Delta f_{t-k} + \sum_{l=1}^{5} \delta_l \Delta \mathbf{spread}_{t-l} + \eta_t$$

Source: Capital IQ, Bloomberg, Datastream, and author's calculations

* Significant at the 10% level
** Significant at the 5% level
*** Significant at the 1% level

Table 7.5 Set of eligible explanatory variables

	Global variables				*Local variables*					
	$sp500_t$	vix_t	$Slope_t$	oil_t	$spread_{i,t-1}$	$stock_{i,t}$	$xr_{i,t}$	$localTY_{i,t}$	$localSlope_{i,t}$	$bank_{i,t}$
Germany	(*)	(*)	(*)	(*)	(*)			*	&	*
France	(*)	(*)	(*)	(*)	(*)				*	&
Finland	(*)	(*)	(*)	(*)	(*)					
Netherlands	(*)	(*)	(*)	(*)	(*)		&	&	&	
Austria	(*)	(*)	(*)	(*)	(*)			&	*	&
Belgium	(*)	(*)	(*)	(*)	(*)			*	&	&
Slovakia	(*)	(*)	(*)	(*)	(*)					
Spain	(*)	(*)	(*)	(*)	(*)				&	&
Italy	(*)	(*)	(*)	(*)	(*)			*	*	&
Ireland	(*)	(*)	(*)	(*)	(*)				&	
Portugal	(*)	(*)	(*)	(*)	(*)			&	&	&
Denmark	(*)	(*)	(*)	(*)	(*)	&		&		
Sweden	(*)	(*)	(*)	(*)	(*)	&	&		*	&
Poland	(*)	(*)	(*)	(*)	(*)		*	*	*	
Czech Rep.	(*)	(*)	(*)	(*)	(*)		*	&		
Hungary	(*)	(*)	(*)	(*)	(*)		&	*	&	
Turkey	(*)	(*)	(*)	(*)	(*)	&	&	*		&
Russia	(*)	(*)	(*)	(*)	(*)	*	&	*	*	&
Australia	(*)	(*)	(*)	(*)	(*)	&		*	&	&
New Zealand	(*)	(*)	(*)	(*)	(*)		*			
Japan	(*)	(*)	(*)	(*)	(*)	*				
Hong Kong	(*)	(*)	(*)	(*)	(*)	&			&	&
Korea	(*)	(*)	(*)	(*)	(*)	&	&		*	&
China	(*)	(*)	(*)	(*)	(*)	&		&		&
Philippines	(*)	(*)	(*)	(*)	(*)	&				
Indonesia	(*)	(*)	(*)	(*)	(*)	&	&	&	&	
Thailand	(*)	(*)	(*)	(*)	(*)	&			*	
Malaysia	(*)	(*)	(*)	(*)	(*)	&	*	*	*	
South Africa	(*)	(*)	(*)	(*)	(*)	&	*	&	*	
Israel	(*)	(*)	(*)	(*)	(*)		*			
Brazil	(*)	(*)	(*)	(*)	(*)	&	&			
Mexico	(*)	(*)	(*)	(*)	(*)	&	&	*		
Peru	(*)	(*)	(*)	(*)	(*)		*	&		
Chile	(*)	(*)	(*)	(*)	(*)	*	*	&	&	
Colombia	(*)	(*)	(*)	(*)	(*)	*	*	*		

(*) stands for exogeneity by assumption

* and & stand for weak exogeneity and non-weak exogeneity, as for the Granger-causality test, at 10% significance level, respectively

Blank accounts for non-significance at 10% significance level; in this case, the corresponding variable is not part of any estimation model for the corresponding country marked with the labels "*" and "&", respectively. Let's take the case of Italy. Their eligible variables are the global variables (*sp*500, *vix*, *Slope*, and *oil*) and the local variables $spread_i - 1$, $localTY_i$, $localSlope_i$, and $bank_i$. The first five variables are assumed to be exogenous *a priori*. Weak exogeneity is attributed to $localTY_i$ and $localSlope_i$, as their chi-squared statistics are significant at the 10% level in Part A (Table 7.4), while their Part B's (Table 7.4) chi-squared statistics are non-significant at the 10% level. $bank_i$ is set as endogenous, as their chi-squared statistics are significant at the 10% level in both Part A and Part B. When there is no label, the corresponding variable is not taken as eligible. Variables labelled as "(*)" in Table 7.5 are set as exogenous by assumption, that is, the global variables and the first lag of the dependent variable are not expected to be affected by the dependent variable in any sense.

I run the change in the weekly CDS spread over the four global factors (*sp*500, *vix*, *Slope*, and *oil*), the lagged first difference of the corresponding CDS spread, and the local factors chosen following Granger-causality test results. Second, I run the large-scale engine in Stata (Baum 2003) for choosing the best-fit model for each country *i*, testing as many econometric models as possible, according to Eq. (7.1):

$$\Delta\text{spread}_{i,t} = \alpha_i + \sum_{j=1}^{4} \beta_{i,j}.\Delta X_{j,t} + \lambda_i.\Delta\text{spread}_{i,t-1} + \sum_{k=1}^{5} \gamma_{i,k}.\Delta Z_{i,k,t} + \varepsilon_{i,t} \quad (7.1)$$

where α_i = constant term for country *i*, $X_{j,t}$ = set of global factors for week *t*: *sp*500, *vix*, *Slope*, or *oil*, $Z_{i,k,t}$ = set of local factors for country *i* and week *t*: $stock_i$, xr_i, $localTY_i$, $localSlope_i$, or $bank_i$, $\varepsilon_{i,t}$ = error term for country *i* and week *t*.

Variable transformations are such that "rate" variables are transformed first into absolute values, that is, CDS spreads, originally in basis points, are divided by 10,000; the other "rate" variables are divided by 100, when originally obtained in percentage format (*USA slope factor*, *Local Short-Term Yield*, and *Local slope* factor). "Price" variables are transformed into their logarithms: S&*P* 500 *index*, *VIX index*, *Oil price*, *Local Stock Index*, and *Exchange Rate*. I take the first differences of the resulting variables.

In the second step, I let the algorithm selects the model specification for each country constrained by the following pre-defined set of criteria.[6] First, I require that at least one variable with significance at the 10% level has the expected sign as in Table 7.3 is included in the model. Within the space of such models, I select the one with the highest Adjusted R^2 which is statistically superior to all possible nested models.[7] After testing 255 model specifications for Italy, for instance, the engine comes out with a model comprising *S&P500, Slope, spread* − 1, and *localTY* factors, as shown in Table 7.6. The Italy's S&P 500 estimator value of −0.025 means that a 1% weekly variation of the S&P500 index would be consistent, *ceteris paribus*, with a 2.5 basis points contemporaneous reduction in the Italy's CDS spreads. Blank cells in Table 7.6 mean that models including the corresponding factor are superseded by the prevailing model specification as presented in the table; or simply that this variable is not selected in the selection procedure. Finally, I assess the goodness-of-fit of the estimations and their forecast accuracy.

7.5.1 *Results*

The most striking result of Table 7.6 is that the *sp*500 estimator not only shows up as significant for most of the countries (22 out of 35), but one can also notice a remarkable difference in sensitivity magnitudes to this global factor between emerging markets and advanced economics. For countries where *sp*500 doesn't show up as statistically significant in the specification (Germany, the Netherlands, Austria, Portugal, Denmark, Poland, Turkey, Australia, Hong Kong, Korea, China, Mexico, and Chile), different combinations of global and local factors (*oil, spread* − 1, *xr, localTY*, and *bank*) are found by the algorithm to be their best-fit models. Quite noticeably, *vix, oil*, and *stock*, which are exactly the variables orthogonalized against *sp*500, barely show up as significant for any country's model specification.[8] In line with the usual finding that most emerging markets and advanced economies are typically well integrated into the global markets, no local variable shows up as a significant driver of sovereign CDS spreads for 16 out of the 35 countries.[9]

The pervasiveness of *sp*500 is consistent with the results reported by other authors (Longstaff et al. 2011; Pan and Singleton 2008). The results in Table 7.6 also confirm the intuition that CDS spreads of emerging market sovereigns are more sensitive to global factors than spreads of developed countries.

That the CDS spreads of Israel, Malaysia, South Africa, Mexico, Peru, Chile, and Colombia are significantly sensitive to the exchange rate is in line with the evidence (Broner et al. 2013; Broto et al. 2011; Calvo 2007) that emerging markets' debt riskiness is tightly linked to the dynamics of global capital flows or commodity prices.

Table 7.6 GMM results

	Const	Global variables				Local variables						Adj. R^2[c]	U_1[a,d]	U_2[a,d]	PHM[b,d]	#obs.[c]
		$sp500_t$	vix_t	$Slope_t$	oil_t	$spread_{i,t-1}$	$stock_{i,t}$	$xr_{i,t}$	$localTY_{i,t}$	$localSlope_{i,t}$	$bank_{i,t}$					
Germany	4.0E-06					0.26***						6%	0.749	0.777	42%	383
France	2.0E-05	−0.013***				0.09						19%	0.563	0.754	35%	374
Finland	9.0E-06	−0.007***	−0.0004									24%	0.608	0.792	44%	353
Netherlands	1.0E-05					0.18**						3%	0.818	0.787	53%	352
Austria	1.7E-05				−0.003*						0.28	39%	0.650	1.231	43%	241
Belgium	3.0E-05	−0.017***										13%	0.589	0.880	41%	383
Slovakia	4.0E-05	−0.022***										21%	0.618	0.987	42%	383
Spain	1.0E-04	−0.025***										10%	0.675	0.695	34%	313
Italy	6.9E-05	−0.025***		−0.16***		0.09			0.45***			44%	0.509	0.616	24%	383
Ireland	6.0E-05	−0.026***										3%	0.629	0.783	37%	353
Portugal	5.0E-05								0.84***	0.50		55%	0.305	0.469	25%	359
Denmark	1.0E-05					0.30***						8%	0.767	0.733	47%	352
Sweden	6.0E-06	−0.009***	−0.0008									17%	0.636	0.977	47%	353
Poland	3.0E-05								0.39***			10%	0.599	0.706	44%	378
Czech Rep.	3.0E-05	−0.022***										21%	0.622	0.872	34%	383
Hungary	1.0E-04	−0.040***				0.13			0.39***			51%	0.468	0.661	28%	295
Turkey	1.1E-04			−0.26					0.32***			36%	0.386	0.499	29%	333
Russia	4.0E-05	−0.033**		0.13			−0.014**	0.05	0.29**	0.17		99%	0.224	0.308	22%	96
Australia	8.0E-06	−0.008			−0.002*						0.38	39%	0.402	0.649	30%	252
New Zealand	2.0E-05	−0.012***										12%	0.541	0.705	36%	313
Japan	2.0E-05	−0.011***										19%	0.608	0.745	36%	383
Hong Kong	3.0E-06										0.28***	44%	0.643	0.726	42%	213
Korea	1.0E-05					−0.15					1.05***	87%	0.215	0.309	15%	252
China	2.0E-06					−0.31					1.03**	46%	0.315	0.481	19%	252
Philippines	−5.0E-05	−0.060***										32%	0.451	0.893	28%	383
Indonesia	2.0E-06	−0.092***	−0.0017									34%	0.461	0.764	32%	383

Thailand	3.0E-05	−0.036***							26%	0.454	0.646	31%	383
Malaysia	5.0E-05	−0.029***				0.04***			30%	0.405	0.597	24%	383
South Africa	−1.0E-05	−0.044***				0.04***		−0.12	59%	0.371	0.525	23%	206
Israel	4.0E-05	−0.018***	−0.0005	0.001		0.01*			25%	0.530	0.706	37%	383
Brazil	5.0E-06	−0.048***			−0.032				44%	0.471	0.563	28%	383
Mexico	−5.8E-05	−0.009				0.06**	−0.04		97%	0.352	0.502	26%	86
Peru	−6.0E-05	−0.042***				0.05**	−0.07		92%	0.415	0.633	30%	112
Chile	1.0E-05					0.05**		−0.29	43%	0.467	0.687	29%	84
Colombia	5.0E-06	−0.047***		−0.003	−0.006	0.02***	0.12***		49%	0.340	0.466	27%	372

This table reports, for each country, results of models: (1) with at least one 10%-significant coefficient with expected signs according to Table 7.3, (2) with the highest Adjusted R^2, and (3) statistically superior to all possible nested models. The dependent variable is the first difference of CDS spreads. Goodness-of-fit statistics are calculated for the estimation sample (July 2005 to October 2012) and out-of-sample (November 2012 to July 2016) periods. Only permutations of explanatory variables labelled with "(*)", "*", and "&" in Table 7.5 are taken as eligible estimation models. The explanatory variables were selected according to 10% significance level when applying the Granger-causality tests. The first lag of local variable is used as instrument for the corresponding local variable labelled with "&" in Table 7.5. As for variable transformation, I apply Δlog(.) to "price" variables (S&P 500 index, VIX index, Oil price, Local Stock Index, and Exchange Rate) and Δ(.) to "rate" variables (USA Slope, CDS spreads, Local Short-Term Yield and Local Slope). The variance-covariance matrices are estimated according to White (1980) robust estimation. *Vix* and *Local Slope* don't show up as significant for any country

Source: Capital IQ, Bloomberg, Datastream and author's calculations

* Significant at the 10% level

** Significant at the 5% level

*** Significant at the 1% level

[a]and [b] stand for Theil's U_i and percent hit misses, respectively

[b]and [d] stand for in-sample and out-of-sample calculations, respectively

Another interesting finding is that Portugal, Italy, Russia, Poland, Hungary, Turkey, and Colombia appear in Table 7.6 with local two-year yields being significant. While Portugal's and Italy's short-term debts might have been eventually under rollover risk between 2010 and 2012, as per the Eurozone debt crisis, the CDS spreads and yields co-movements of Russia, Poland, Hungary, Turkey, and Colombia are consistent with the usual view that a large part of their higher yields is presumably related to credit risk itself. In any case, these dynamics are arguably consistent with protection-sellers charging higher premiums on CDS contracts with those debts as reference obligations.

The fact that *bank* barely shows up as significant might be due to the general assessment that the transmission of distress from the banking sector to sovereign credit may occur more like a structural break than gradually over time.[10] It could perhaps have been expected that increases in *bank*, as a stress indicator of the banking sector, could have gradually spilled over into the risk perception of sovereign bonds. Thus, the apparent underpricing of the spillover effect from the financial stability stance to the sovereign debt risk during the period leading to the 2010–2012 European sovereign debt crisis can be tentatively explained by the expectation that governments would: (1) monetize their debts (perhaps more in the case of the USA than for Eurozone countries), (2) wipe out defaulted bank's shareholders and subordinated debtholders, or (3) be simply bailed out by economically stronger sovereigns. While not having been noticeably impacted by the global financial crisis, Hong Kong, Korea, and China are three jurisdictions where the banking sector remained relatively stable during the 2005–2012 period and where the governments are perceived to be very supportive of their domestic big banks. This may be the reason why, in these three cases, the sovereign and their banking system CDS spreads tend to co-move, that is, why their coefficients of the *bank* variable showed up as significant.

Next, I perform a goodness-of-fit analysis and compare the contemporaneous-variable model estimation outcomes with those of Autoregressive Moving Average (ARMA) structural models and lagged-explanatory variables specifications.

The goodness-of-fit of the GMM estimations is evaluated by means of Adjusted R^2, Theil's U_1, Theil's U_2, and percent hit misses (PHM) statistics. I calculate Adjusted R^2s for the in-sample period, whereas for calculating Theil's U_1, Theil's U_2, and PHM out-of-sample statistics, I use the first two-thirds of the data for estimation and perform out-of-sample tests on the remaining sample. Normalizing the root mean squared error by the dispersion of actual and forecasted series or calculating the root mean squared percentage errors relative to naive forecast (random walk), Theil's U_1 and Theil's U_2 stand, respectively, as intuitive assessments of forecast accuracy. PHM assesses whether the direction of the prediction is accurate or not, that is:

$$PHM = \#HitMisses / N$$

where *#HitMisses* = number of times the prediction does not have the same sign as the realized value and N = total number of observations.

It is well known that higher values of Adjusted R^2 imply better model fit; however, lower Theil's U_1, Theil's U_2, and PHM values indicate better forecasting ability.

The goodness-of-fit statistics of Table 7.6 suggest that emerging market economies' models presumably show more forecasting power than the developed countries'. Sorting into ascending (Adjusted R^2) or descending order (Theil's U_1, Theil's U_2, and PHM), these statistics confirm that countries at the bottom rows of the table, broadly composed of emerging market economies, are associated with better goodness-of-fit measures.

As a benchmark for this chapter's GMM estimations, ARMA model specifications are also estimated. The ARMA(p,q) process is estimated by full-information maximum likelihood estimation (FIMLE), following Box et al. (1994) and Enders (2004). I select the best model according to the following criteria: (1) the AR and MA terms are significant at the 10% level; (2) the residuals behave as a white-noise process (all autocorrelations of the residuals should be indistinguishable from zero), (3) the model has to have the lowest Bayesian Information Criteria (BIC) statistic, (4) it is non-degenerate, that is, there are no gaps within AR or MA terms, and (5) when (1) and (2) don't hold, then I only take criteria (3) and (4) into account. I use Ljung and Box (1978) Q-statistic in eq. (2) at 10% significance level for testing (2).

$$Q = T(T+2)\sum_{k=1}^{s} r_k^2 / (T-k) \tag{7.2}$$

If Q exceeds the critical value of χ^2 with $s - p - q$ degrees of freedom, then at least one value of r_k, which is the sample autocorrelation coefficient of order k, is statistically different from zero (*I* set s to 10).

Table 7.7 shows that the goodness-of-fit statistics (Adjusted R^2, Theil's U_1, Theil's, U_2 and PHM) of are noticeably worse than the respective contemporaneous model statistics (Table 7.6).

Table 7.7 ARMA results

	AR terms			*MA terms*					*Adj.* $R^{2[c]}$	$U_1^{a,d}$	$U_2^{a,d}$	$PHM^{b,d}$
	α_1	α_2	α_3	β_1	β_2	β_3	β_4	β_5				
Germany	0.3***								6%	**0.748**	**0.776**	**39%**
France				0.1					1%	0.862	0.778	35%
Finland				0.4***					10%	0.751	**0.748**	45%
Netherlands				0.2**					**3%**	**0.807**	**0.781**	**44%**
Austria				0.4***					11%	0.710	**0.780**	**38%**
Belgium				0.2*					3%	0.817	**0.755**	**40%**
Slovakia				0.3***					10%	0.767	**0.760**	51%
Spain				0.05					0%	0.948	0.744	39%
Italy	1.7***	−1.2***	0.2*	−1.7***	1.0***				8%	0.753	0.787	53%
Ireland				0.2***	−0.3				**10%**	0.733	0.798	50%
Portugal	1.0***			−0.8***	−0.4***	0.1	−0.1	0.2***	13%	0.691	0.929	39%
Denmark				0.3***					**9%**	**0.763**	0.738	**44%**
Sweden				0.3***	0.1	0.2			13%	0.765	**0.768**	**46%**
Poland				0.4***					**11%**	0.767	0.765	**42%**
Czech Rep.				0.4***					12%	0.804	**0.746**	56%
Hungary				0.3**	−0.1				11%	0.735	0.763	44%
Turkey				0.2	−0.3				8%	0.765	0.732	44%
Russia				0.2	−0.4	0.1	0.3**		22%	0.698	0.804	45%
Australia	0.3***								12%	0.732	0.788	42%
New Zealand	0.3***								9%	0.783	0.751	39%
Japan	0.1								0%	0.923	0.804	**34%**
Hong Kong				0.2*					4%	0.821	0.756	**39%**
Korea	−0.6***	−0.2		0.8***					11%	0.738	0.808	53%
China				0.3***	−0.3**				14%	0.724	0.822	49%
Philippines	−0.5***	−0.3		0.6***					11%	0.759	**0.807**	47%

Indonesia				0.3	−0.3*	16%	0.699	0.825	45%
Thailand	−0.6***	−0.2		0.8***		13%	0.741	0.838	48%
Malaysia	−0.6***	−0.3		0.7***		17%	0.711	0.812	45%
South Africa	0.2	−0.2	0.2*			11%	0.745	0.742	42%
Israel	−0.4**			0.7***		8%	0.756	0.776	42%
Brazil				0.2*	−0.2	9%	0.749	0.729	39%
Mexico	0.3*	−0.2				11%	0.741	0.737	47%
Peru	−1.1***	−0.7***		1.3***	0.8***	10%	0.737	0.745	43%
Chile	−0.7***			0.9***		6%	0.775	0.744	39%
Colombia	−1.1***	−0.7***		1.4***	0.8***	9%	0.728	0.746	42%

When the goodness-of-fit statistics are better than those of Table 7.6, they are highlighted in bold

This table reports, for each country, the ARMA coefficients α_i's and β_i's estimated from the FIMLE equation: $\Delta\text{spread}_{t,i} = \sum_{i=1}^{p} \alpha_i \Delta\text{spread}_{t-i} + \sum_{i=1}^{q} \beta_i \varepsilon_{t-i}$

Source: Capital IQ

***, **, and * stand for significance at the 1%, 5%, and 10% level, respectively

[a] and [b] stand for Theil's U_i and percent hit misses, respectively; [c] and [d] stand for in-sample and out-of-sample calculations, respectively

As for the lagged-factor specifications, Table 7.8 shows that they are noticeably less robust than those comprising contemporaneous factors. Except for a few occurrences (10 out of 124), the lagged-variable models' goodness-of-fit metrics are worse than those of contemporaneous-variable models (Table 7.6). Besides, the "best-fit" lagged-variable model specifications (which I am able to obtain for all but France, Italy, Spain, and Ireland) are even worse than those of ARMA models (Table 7.7).[11]

7.5.2 Robustness Check

This subsection shows that even altering the algorithm criteria significantly (changing the significance level of the Granger-causality test at which variables are included in the analysis, or substituting other goodness-of-fit statistics for the Adjusted R^2) or repeating the analysis across different sub-periods does not give rise to results substantially challenging this chapter's two main claims, that is, that the S&P 500 index is statistically significant and contemporaneously negatively related to the CDS spreads for most of the countries, and that emerging market's coefficients on the S&P 500 variable are higher in magnitude than those of advanced economies. To be sure, the S&P 500 coefficient's statistical significance and its magnitude do change when modifying the algorithm criteria or the sample period, leading to different country ranking orders. The coefficient on the S&P 500 for Russia (statistically significant and with the expected negative sign in Table 7.6), for instance, is not available in the July 2005–June 2010 and January 2008–December 2010 sub-periods' models, while ranging from −0.073 to −0.028 as for the other four sub-periods (Tables 7.15 and 7.16). Although the individual coefficient estimates somewhat vary between the different specifications, those of the S&P 500 remain higher (in absolute terms) for emerging markets.

Interestingly, eliminating the criterion (1) (choosing models with at least one coefficient significant at the 10% level with the expected sign) altogether from the algorithm, or modifying the restriction (2) (choosing models with the highest Adjusted R^2), the engine still generates models (see Tables 7.9, 7.10, 7.11, and 7.12) with statistically significant negative coefficients on the *sp*500 variable, higher in absolute terms for emerging market countries than for advanced economies. Table 7.9 shows that the characteristics of the sole 6 (out of 35 models; highlighted in bold) models which happen to be distinct from those of Table 7.6 don't lead to a different assessment regarding the coefficient of the *sp*500 variable. By the same token, no dramatic changes take place regarding the quantity and the magnitude of statistically significant *sp*500 coefficients. It continues to play a dominant role in explaining the CDS spreads in nearly all of our sample countries, and the higher sensitivity of emerging markets to this variable, when substituting other goodness-of-fit statistics for the Adjusted R^2 as a criterion for selecting the best-fit models (Tables 7.10, 7.11, and 7.12).

Aiming to evaluate, to a fairly large extent, whether changing the Granger-causality test significance level from 10% to 5% would lead to the rejection of this chapter's main claims, I ran the algorithm over the six sub-periods: (1) July 2005 to October 2012, (2) July 2005 to June 2010 (Before Jul 2010), (3) July 2010 to June 2014 (After Jul 2010), (4) July 2005 to June 2008 (Before Jul 2008), (5) January 2008 to December 2010 (Subprime Crisis), and (6) July 2010 to June 2013 (Euro Crisis). As it turns out, had I imposed a stricter cutoff (a 5% significance level, instead of 10%), it wouldn't materially have changed this chapter's main outcomes (Table 7.13).

Changing the significance level to 5% reduces the set of eligible variables either by excluding previously selected variables, or by switching previously endogenous variables to weakly exogenous ones. As expected, supressing previously elected variables from the set of eligible variables leads to the algorithm generating a different model. For instance, when excluding the *LocalTY* factor from the set of eligible variables, Portugal's alternative model (Table 7.14) ends up presenting a statistically significant S&P 500 estimator, when it was not the case previously (Table 7.6). Less obviously, when the changed cutoff of the level of significance switches a previously endogenous variable into a weakly exogenous one using the Granger-causality test, the algorithm may prefer a different model. The Netherlands' alternative model (Table 7.14), for example, shows a statistically significant coefficient on the S&P 500, when the previously endogenous variable *localSlope* (at the 10% significance level) turns into a weakly exogenous variable (at the 5% level) and further excluding *xr* and *localTY* from the set of eligible variables, even though none of these three variables were part of the originally selected model (see Table 7.6). As it turns out, this unintended consequence is due to the change in the instrumental variables setting: endogenous variables are transformed into lags when running the GMM regressions, while weakly exogenous ones are not.

Jointly, the results of Tables 7.15 and 7.16 show that the net effect of reducing the significance level from 10% to 5% in the Granger-causality test is almost neutral in terms of the quantity of statistically significant

Table 7.8 GMM results with lagged-explanatory variables

	const	*Global variables*				*Local variables*	
		sp500–1	*vix – 1*	*Slope – 1*	*oil – 1*	*spread – 1*	*stock – 1*
Germany	4.0E-06					0.26***	
Finland	5.0E-06					0.32***	
Netherlands	9.0E-06					0.18**	
Austria	1.0E-05					0.30***	
Belgium	2.0E-05		0.0001			0.17*	
Slovakia	2.0E-05					0.30***	
Portugal	1.0E-04			0.08		0.19*	
Denmark	1.0E-05					0.30***	
Sweden	3.0E-06					0.32**	
Poland	1.0E-05					0.29***	
Czech Rep.	1.0E-05					0.33***	
Hungary	1.0E-04						
Turkey	−1.0E-04	0.01	0.0007		−0.01*	0.50	0.024
Russia	5.0E-05					0.27*	
Australia	1.0E-05					0.35***	
New Zealand	1.0E-05					0.30***	
Japan	2.0E-05	−0.005***					
Hong Kong	1.0E-05	−0.01***					
Korea	1.0E-05	−0.02**	−0.002				
China	2.0E-05	−0.01**					
Philippines	−1.0E-04	−0.02*	−0.002				
Indonesia	−2.0E-05	−0.03*	−0.004			0.06	
Thailand	2.0E-05	−0.01*					
Malaysia	2.0E-05	−0.01*					
South Africa	1.0E-05						
Israel	4.0E-05	−0.01***					
Brazil	−1.0E-04	−0.01*	−0.001				
Mexico	−5.0E-05			−0.24*			
Peru	1.0E-06					0.14	
Chile	2.0E-05	−0.01***					
Colombia	−3.0E-05						

This table reports, for each country, the models' results with the same explanatory variables as in Table 7.6, but in lags. The dependent variable is the first difference of CDS spreads. Goodness-of-fit statistics are calculated for the estimation sample (July 2005 to October 2012) and the out-of-sample (November 2012 to July 2016) periods. The explanatory variable itself is used as instrument for the GMM estimation. As for variable transformation, I apply Δlog(.) to "price" variables (S&P 500 index, VIX index, Oil price, Local Stock Index, and Exchange Rate) and Δ(.) to "rate" variables (USA Slope, CDS spreads, Local Short-Term Yield, and Local Slope). The variance-covariance matrices are estimated according to White (1980) robust estimation. When the goodness-of-fit statistics are better than those of Table 7.6, they are highlighted in bold. The engine didn't generate any model specifications for France, Italy, Spain, and Ireland. ***Vix, stock, localSlope, and bank*** don't show up as significant for any country

Source: Capital IQ, Bloomberg, Datastream, and author's calculations

* Significant at the 10% level

** Significant at the 5% level

*** Significant at the 1% level

[a] and [b] stand for Theil's U_i and percent hit misses, respectively

[c] and [d] stand for in-sample and out-of-sample calculations, respectively

xr − 1	*localTY − 1*	*localSlope − 1*	*bank − 1*	*Adj.* $R^{2[c]}$	$U_1^{a,d}$	$U_2^{a,d}$	*PHM*[b,d]	*#obs.*[c]
				6%	0.749	0.777	42%	383
				10%	0.774	**0.746**	**44%**	352
				3%	0.818	0.787	53%	352
				9%	0.728	**0.783**	**37%**	383
				3%	0.826	**0.759**	43%	383
				9%	0.802	**0.751**	51%	383
				3%	0.801	0.825	42%	383
				8%	0.767	0.733	47%	352
				10%	0.775	**0.739**	50%	352
				8%	0.815	0.730	**42%**	383
				11%	0.834	**0.723**	53%	383
	0.20**			5%	0.803	0.767	46%	294
0.08			−0.8	31%	0.660	0.943	47%	240
	−0.24	−0.19		96%	0.799	0.699	56%	95
				12%	0.734	0.790	38%	312
				9%	0.785	0.753	39%	312
				3%	0.828	0.823	48%	383
				10%	0.740	0.768	46%	383
				4%	0.741	0.848	48%	383
				3%	0.826	0.754	49%	383
				2%	0.760	**0.804**	48%	383
				6%	0.776	0.816	48%	383
				2%	0.817	0.789	47%	383
				3%	0.824	0.775	49%	383
0.03***				10%	0.709	0.715	43%	383
				6%	0.731	0.791	49%	383
				3%	0.899	0.734	54%	383
	0.04			93%	0.820	0.750	53%	85
0.04*				5%	0.750	0.757	45%	383
				8%	0.775	0.763	46%	383
	0.10*			2%	0.781	0.666	46%	372

Table 7.9 GMM results without the criterion "with at least one 10%-significant coefficient with expected signs according to Table 7.3"

	const	*Global variables*				*Local variables*						*Adj.* $R^{2[c]}$	$U_1^{a,d}$	$U_2^{a,d}$	$PHM^{b,d}$	$\#obs.^{c}$
		$sp500_t$	vix_t	$Slope_t$	oil_t	$spread_{i,t-1}$	$stock_{i,t}$	$xr_{i,t}$	$localTY_{i,t}$	$localSlope_{i,t}$	$bank_{i,t}$					
Germany	4.0E-06					0.26***						6%	0.749	0.777	42%	383
France	**2.0E-05**	**−0.012**		**−0.07**						**0.03**	**0.09**	**37%**	**0.505**	**0.731**	**29%**	**252**
Finland	9.0E-06	−0.007***	−0.0004									24%	0.608	0.792	44%	353
Netherlands	1.0E-05					0.18**						3%	0.818	0.787	53%	352
Austria	**1.7E-05**	**−0.020*** **	**−0.002***									**24%**	**0.609**	**1.197**	**40%**	**383**
Belgium	3.0E-05	−0.017***										13%	0.589	0.880	41%	383
Slovakia	4.0E-05	−0.022***										21%	0.618	0.987	42%	383
Spain	1.0E-04	−0.025***										10%	0.675	0.695	34%	313
Italy	**6.0E-05**	**−0.026*** **		**−0.21*** **		**0.07**			**0.67*** **	**0.40*** *		**48%**	**0.420**	**0.536**	**21%**	**383**
Ireland	6.0E-05	−0.026***										3%	0.629	0.783	37%	353
Portugal	5.0E-05								0.84***	0.50		55%	0.305	0.469	25%	359
Denmark	1.0E-05	−0.010***	−0.001*									17%	0.648	0.979	47%	353
Sweden	6.0E-06	−0.009***	−0.0008									17%	0.636	0.977	47%	353
Poland	3.0E-05								0.39***			10%	0.599	0.706	44%	378
Czech Rep.	3.0E-05	−0.022***										21%	0.622	0.872	34%	383
Hungary	1.0E-04	−0.040***				0.13			0.39***			51%	0.468	0.661	28%	295
Turkey	1.1E-04			−0.26					0.32***			36%	0.386	0.499	29%	333
Russia	4.0E-05	−0.033**		0.13			−0.014**	0.05	0.29**	0.17		99%	0.224	0.308	22%	96
Australia	**5.0E-06**	**−0.008**									**0.37**	**38%**	**0.393**	**0.603**	**27%**	**252**
New Zealand	2.0E-05	−0.012***										12%	0.541	0.705	36%	313
Japan	2.0E-05	−0.011***										19%	0.608	0.745	36%	383
Hong Kong	3.0E-06										0.28***	44%	0.643	0.726	42%	213
Korea	1.0E-05					−0.15					1.05***	87%	0.215	0.309	15%	252
China	**2.0E-05**	**−0.023**		**−0.10**			**0.002**				**0.14**	**55%**	**0.450**	**0.586**	**26%**	**252**

Philippines	−5.0E-05	−0.060***								32%	0.451	0.893	28%	383
Indonesia	2.0E-06	−0.092***	−0.0017							34%	0.461	0.764	32%	383
Thailand	3.0E-05	−0.036***								26%	0.454	0.646	31%	383
Malaysia	5.0E-05	−0.029***					0.04***			30%	0.405	0.597	24%	383
South Africa	−1.0E-05	−0.044***					0.04***		−0.12	59%	0.371	0.525	23%	206
Israel	4.0E-05	−0.018***	−0.0005	0.001			0.01*			25%	0.530	0.706	37%	383
Brazil	1.0E-05	−0.048***				−0.032				44%	0.471	0.563	28%	383
Mexico	**−1.9E-05**	**−0.020**			**0.08**		**0.03**	**0.07**		**98%**	**0.346**	**0.463**	**27%**	**86**
Peru	−6.0E-05	−0.042***					0.05**	−0.07		92%	0.415	0.633	30%	112
Chile	1.0E-05						0.05**		−0.29	43%	0.467	0.687	29%	84
Colombia	5.0E-06	−0.047***		−0.003		−0.006	0.02***	0.12***		49%	0.340	0.466	27%	372

This table reports, for each country, results of models: (1) with the highest Adjusted R^2 and (2) statistically superior to all possible nested models. The dependent variable is the first difference of CDS spreads. Goodness-of-fit statistics are calculated for the estimation sample (July 2005 to October 2012) and out-of-sample (November 2012 to July 2016) periods. Only permutations of explanatory variables labelled with "(*)", "*", and "&" in Table 7.5 are taken as eligible estimation models. The explanatory variables were selected according to 10% significance level when applying the Granger-causality tests. The first lag of local variable is used as instrument for the corresponding local variable labelled with "&" in Table 7.5. As for variable transformation, I apply $\Delta\log(.)$ to "price" variables (S&P 500 index, VIX index, Oil price, Local Stock Index, and Exchange Rate) and $\Delta(.)$ to "rate" variables (USA Slope, CDS spreads, Local Short-Term Yield, and Local Slope). The variance-covariance matrices are estimated according to White (1980) robust estimation. When model specifications show up as different from Table 7.6, they are highlighted in bold. *Oil* doesn't show up as significant for any country. *Vix* and ***oil*** estimators aren't significant for any model

Source: Capital IQ, Bloomberg, Datastream, and author's calculations

* Significant at the 10% level

** Significant at the 5% level

*** Significant at the 1% level

[a] and [b] stand for Theil's U_i and percent hit misses, respectively

[c] and [d] stand for in-sample and out-of-sample calculations, respectively

Table 7.10 GMM results substituting Theil's U_1 for Adjusted R^2 in criteria (2) "with the highest Adjusted R^2"

	const	*Global variables*				*Local variables*						*Adj. $R^{2[c]}$*	*$U_1^{a,d}$*	*$U_2^{a,d}$*	*$PHM^{b,d}$*	*#obs.[c]*
		$sp500_t$	*vix_t*	*$Slope_t$*	*oil_t*	*$spread_{i,t-1}$*	*$stock_{i,t}$*	*$xr_{i,t}$*	*$localTY_{i,t}$*	*$localSlope_{i,t}$*	*$bank_{i,t}$*					
Germany	4.0E-06					0.26***						6%	0.749	0.777	42%	383
France	**−3.0E-05**		**−0.0006**		**−0.001**	**−0.07**				**0.10**	**0.85****	**18%**	**0.530**	**1.260**	**26%**	**252**
Finland	9.0E-06	−0.007***	−0.0004									24%	0.608	0.792	44%	353
Netherlands	**1.0E-05**	**−0.009*****	**−0.0003**									**17%**	**0.622**	**0.890**	**42%**	**353**
Austria	**7.0E-06**					**0.30*****						**9%**	**0.728**	**0.783**	**37%**	**383**
Belgium	**2.0E-05**	**−0.017*****				**0.16***						**15%**	**0.578**	**0.861**	**38%**	**383**
Slovakia	4.0E-05	−0.022***										21%	0.618	0.987	42%	383
Spain	1.0E-04	−0.025***										10%	0.675	0.695	34%	313
Italy	**6.5E-05**			**−0.20*****					**0.46*****			**33%**	**0.590**	**0.646**	**26%**	**383**
Ireland	6.0E-05	−0.026***										3%	0.629	0.783	37%	353
Portugal	5.0E-05								0.84***	0.50		55%	0.305	0.469	25%	359
Denmark	**1.0E-05**	**−0.010*****	**−0.0010**				**−0.001**					**17%**	**0.646**	**0.974**	**49%**	**353**
Sweden	6.0E-06	−0.009***	−0.0008									17%	0.636	0.977	47%	353
Poland	3.0E-05								0.39***			10%	0.599	0.706	44%	378
Czech Rep.	3.0E-05	−0.022***										21%	0.622	0.872	34%	383
Hungary	**1.4E-04**			**−0.26****					**0.56*****			**43%**	**0.528**	**0.692**	**36%**	**295**
Turkey	**−6.7E-05**					**−0.25**			**0.03**		**1.09*****	**49%**	**0.352**	**0.499**	**17%**	**241**
Russia	**−2.0E-05**	**−0.026***			**0.008**		**−0.016*****	**0.05**	**0.31****	**0.17**		**99%**	**0.222**	**0.308**	**24%**	**96**
Australia	8.0E-06	−0.008			−0.002*						0.38	39%	0.402	0.649	30%	252
New Zealand	2.0E-05	−0.012***										12%	0.541	0.705	36%	313
Japan	**2.0E-05**	**−0.011*****				**0.07**						**19%**	**0.596**	**0.731**	**34%**	**383**
Hong Kong	**3.0E-06**									**−0.05**	**0.29*****	**44%**	**0.639**	**0.729**	**40%**	**213**
Korea	1.0E-05					−0.15					1.05***	87%	0.215	0.309	15%	252
China	2.0E-06					−0.31					1.03**	46%	0.315	0.481	19%	252
Philippines	−5.0E-05	−0.060***										32%	0.451	0.893	28%	383
Indonesia	2.0E-06	−0.092***	−0.0017									34%	0.461	0.764	32%	383
Thailand	3.0E-05	−0.036***										26%	0.454	0.646	31%	383

Malaysia	5.0E-05	−0.029***				0.04***			30%	0.405	0.597	24%	383
South Africa	−1.0E-05	−0.044***				0.04***		−0.12	59%	0.371	0.525	23%	206
Israel	**4.0E-05**	**−0.018*****		**0.16**		**0.01***			**28%**	**0.510**	**0.719**	**34%**	**383**
Brazil	**−2.0E-05**	**−0.026**		**0.15***		**0.05**			**42%**	**0.397**	**0.499**	**24%**	**383**
Mexico	−5.8E-05	−0.009				0.06**	−0.04		97%	0.352	0.502	26%	86
Peru	**3.0E-05**	**−0.045*****				**0.06*****			**41%**	**0.384**	**0.574**	**25%**	**383**
Chile	**3.0E-05**	**−0.023*****			**−0.003**	**0.01****			**37%**	**0.401**	**0.510**	**27%**	**383**
Colombia	5.0E-06	−0.047***	−0.003		−0.006	0.02***	0.12***		49%	0.340	0.466	27%	372

This table reports, for each country, results of models: (1) with at least one 10%-significant with expected signs according to Table 7.3, (2) with the lowest Theil's U_1, and (3) statistically superior to all possible nested models. The dependent variable is the first difference of CDS spreads. Goodness-of-fit statistics are calculated for the estimation sample (July 2005 to October 2012) and out-of-sample (November 2012 to July 2016) periods. Only permutations of explanatory variables labelled with "(*)", "*", and "&" in Table 7.5 are taken as eligible estimation models. The explanatory variables were selected according to 10% significance level when applying the Granger-causality tests. The first lag of local variable is used as instrument for the corresponding local variable labelled with "&" in Table 7.5. As for variable transformation, I apply Δlog(.) to "price" variables (S&P 500 index, VIX index, Oil price, Local Stock Index, and Exchange Rate) and Δ(.) to "rate" variables (USA Slope, CDS spreads, Local Short-Term Yield, and Local Slope). The variance-covariance matrices are estimated according to White (1980) robust estimation. When model specifications show up as different from Table 7.6, they are highlighted in bold. *Vix* and *localSlope* estimators aren't significant for any model

Source: Capital IQ, Bloomberg, Datastream, and author's calculations

* Significant at the 10% level

** Significant at the 5% level

*** Significant at the 1% level

[a] and [b] stand for Theil's U_i and percent hit misses, respectively

[c] and [d] stand for in-sample and out-of-sample calculations, respectively

Table 7.11 GMM results substituting Theil's U_2 for Adjusted R^2 in criteria (2) "with the highest Adjusted R^2"

	const	*Global variables*				*Local variables*						Adj. $R^{2[c]}$	$U_1^{a,d}$	$U_2^{a,d}$	$PHM^{b,d}$	#obs.[c]
		$sp500_t$	vix_t	$Slope_t$	oil_t	$spread_{i,t-1}$	$stock_{i,t}$	$xr_{i,t}$	$localTY_{i,t}$	$localSlope_{i,t}$	$bank_{i,t}$					
Germany	4.0E-06					0.26***						6%	0.749	0.777	42%	383
France	2.0E-05	−0.013***				0.09						19%	0.563	0.754	35%	374
Finland	9.0E-06	−0.007***	−0.0004									24%	0.608	0.792	44%	353
Netherlands	**1.0E-05**	**−0.009*****	**−0.0003**									**17%**	**0.622**	**0.890**	**42%**	**353**
Austria	**7.0E-06**					**0.30*****						**9%**	**0.728**	**0.783**	**37%**	**383**
Belgium	**2.0E-05**			**−0.10*****								**2%**	**0.771**	**0.782**	**44%**	**383**
Slovakia	**2.0E-05**					**0.30*****						**9%**	**0.802**	**0.751**	**51%**	**383**
Spain	1.0E-04	−0.025***										10%	0.675	0.695	34%	313
Italy	6.9E-05	−0.025***		−0.16***		0.09			0.45***			44%	0.509	0.616	24%	383
Ireland	**5.0E-05**			**−0.21****	**0.002**	**0.15***						**2%**	**0.758**	**0.762**	**41%**	**352**
Portugal	**6.0E-05**			**−0.28*****					**0.82*****	**0.48**		**56%**	**0.298**	**0.459**	**19%**	**359**
Denmark	1.0E-05					0.30***						8%	0.767	0.733	47%	352
Sweden	6.0E-06	−0.009***	−0.0008									17%	0.636	0.977	47%	353
Poland	3.0E-05								0.39***			10%	0.599	0.706	44%	378
Czech Rep.	**3.0E-05**				**−0.004***							**1%**	**0.748**	**0.723**	**50%**	**383**
Hungary	**1.1E-04**	**−0.040*****							**0.42*****			**50%**	**0.471**	**0.667**	**31%**	**295**
Turkey	1.1E-04			−0.26					0.32***			36%	0.386	0.499	29%	333
Russia	4.0E-05	−0.033**		0.13			−0.014**	0.05	0.29**	0.17		99%	0.224	0.308	22%	96
Australia	8.0E-06	−0.008			−0.002*						0.38	39%	0.402	0.649	30%	252
New Zealand	**2.0E-05**	**−0.011*****	**−0.0006**									**12%**	**0.564**	**0.679**	**34%**	**313**
Japan	**2.0E-05**	**−0.011*****				**0.07**						**19%**	**0.596**	**0.731**	**34%**	**383**
Hong Kong	3.0E-06										0.28***	44%	0.643	0.726	42%	213
Korea	1.0E-05					−0.15					1.05***	87%	0.215	0.309	15%	252
China	2.0E-06					−0.31					1.03**	46%	0.315	0.481	19%	252

Philippines	−5.0E-05	−0.060***								32%	0.451	0.893	28%	383
Indonesia	2.0E-06	−0.092***	−0.0017							34%	0.461	0.764	32%	383
Thailand	3.0E-05	−0.036***								26%	0.454	0.646	31%	383
Malaysia	5.0E-05	−0.029***						0.04***		30%	0.405	0.597	24%	383
South Africa	**2.0E-05**	**−0.035*** **		**−0.04**				**0.03*** **		**48%**	**0.378**	**0.478**	**24%**	**383**
Israel										–	–	–	–	–
Brazil	**−2.0E-05**	**−0.026**				**0.15***		**0.05**		**42%**	**0.397**	**0.499**	**24%**	**383**
Mexico	**−6.0E-05**					**0.04**		**0.05*** **	**−0.04**	**97%**	**0.394**	**0.505**	**27%**	**86**
Peru	**3.0E-05**	**−0.045*** **						**0.06*** **		**41%**	**0.384**	**0.574**	**25%**	**383**
Chile	**3.0E-05**	**−0.023*** **					**−0.003**	**0.01** **		**37%**	**0.401**	**0.510**	**27%**	**383**
Colombia	5.0E-06	−0.047***			−0.003		−0.006	0.02***	0.12***	49%	0.340	0.466	27%	372

This table reports, for each country, results of models: (1) with at least one 10%-significant with expected signs according to Table 7.3, (2) with the lowest Theil's U_2, and (3) statistically superior to all possible nested models. The dependent variable is the first difference of CDS spreads. Goodness-of-fit statistics are calculated for the estimation sample (July 2005 to October 2012) and out-of-sample (November 2012 to July 2016) periods. Only permutations of explanatory variables labelled with "(*)", "*", and "&" in Table 7.5 are taken as eligible estimation models. The explanatory variables were selected according to 10% significance level when applying the Granger-causality tests. The first lag of local variable is used as instrument for the corresponding local variable labelled with "&" in Table 7.5. As for variable transformation, I apply Δlog(.) to "price" variables (S&P 500 index, VIX index, Oil price, Local Stock Index, and Exchange Rate) and Δ(.) to "rate" variables (USA Slope, CDS spreads, Local Short-Term Yield, and Local Slope). The variance-covariance matrices are estimated according to White (1980) robust estimation. When model specifications show up as different from Table 7.6, they are highlighted in bold. *Vix* and *localSlope* estimators aren't significant for any model

Source: Capital IQ, Bloomberg, Datastream, and author's calculations

* Significant at the 10% level

** Significant at the 5% level

*** Significant at the 1% level

[a] and [b] stand for Theil's U_i and percent hit misses, respectively

[c] and [d] stand for in-sample and out-of-sample calculations, respectively

Table 7.12 GMM results substituting percent hit misses (PHM) for Adjusted R^2 in criteria (2) "with the highest Adjusted R^2"

	const	*Global variables*				*Local variables*						*Adj. $R^{2[c]}$*	$U_1^{a,d}$	$U_2^{a,d}$	$PHM^{b,d}$	*#obs.*[c]
		$sp500_t$	vix_t	$Slope_t$	oil_t	$spread_{i,t-1}$	$stock_{i,t}$	$xr_{i,t}$	$localTY_{i,t}$	$localSlope_{i,t}$	$bank_{i,t}$					
Germany	4.0E-06					0.26***						6%	0.749	0.777	42%	383
France	**2.0E-05**			**−0.09*****		**0.12**				**0.07**		**5%**	**0.773**	**0.758**	**41%**	**374**
Finland	9.0E-06	−0.007***	−0.0004									24%	0.608	0.792	44%	353
Netherlands	**1.0E-05**	**−0.009*****	**−0.0003**									**17%**	**0.622**	**0.890**	**42%**	**353**
Austria	**7.0E-06**					**0.30*****						**9%**	**0.728**	**0.783**	**37%**	**383**
Belgium	3.0E-05	−0.017***										13%	0.589	0.880	41%	383
Slovakia	4.0E-05	−0.022***										21%	0.618	0.987	42%	383
Spain	1.0E-04	−0.025***										10%	0.675	0.695	34%	313
Italy	6.9E-05	−0.025***		−0.16***		0.09			0.45***			44%	0.509	0.616	24%	383
Ireland	6.0E-05	−0.026***										3%	0.629	0.783	37%	353
Portugal	**6.0E-05**			**−0.28*****					**0.82*****	**0.48**		**56%**	**0.298**	**0.459**	**19%**	**359**
Denmark	1.0E-05					0.30***						8%	0.767	0.733	47%	352
Sweden	6.0E-06	−0.009***	−0.0008									17%	0.636	0.977	47%	353
Poland	**4.0E-05**	**−0.034*****								**0.05**		**33%**	**0.554**	**0.894**	**33%**	**378**
Czech Rep.	3.0E-05	−0.022***										21%	0.622	0.872	34%	383
Hungary	**5.0E-05**	**−0.035*****				**0.21***			**0.74*****	**1.19**		**35%**	**0.513**	**1.091**	**24%**	**294**
Turkey	**−6.7E-05**					**−0.25**			**0.03**		**1.09*****	**49%**	**0.352**	**0.499**	**17%**	**241**
Russia	4.0E-05	−0.033**		0.13			−0.014**	0.05	0.29**	0.17		99%	0.224	0.308	22%	96
Australia	**1.5E-05**	**−0.013*****		**−0.05**						**0.17**		**26%**	**0.455**	**0.708**	**29%**	**313**
New Zealand	**2.0E-05**	**−0.011*****	**−0.0006**									**12%**	**0.564**	**0.679**	**34%**	**313**
Japan	**2.0E-05**	**−0.011*****				**0.07**						**19%**	**0.596**	**0.731**	**34%**	**383**
Hong Kong	**3.0E-06**									**−0.05**	**0.29*****	**44%**	**0.639**	**0.729**	**40%**	**213**
Korea	1.0E-05					−0.15					1.05***	87%	0.215	0.309	15%	252
China	2.0E-06					−0.31					1.03**	46%	0.315	0.481	19%	252
Philippines	−5.0E-05	−0.060***										32%	0.451	0.893	28%	383
Indonesia	2.0E-06	−0.092***	−0.0017									34%	0.461	0.764	32%	383

Thailand	3.0E-05	−0.036***							26%	0.454	0.646	31%	383
Malaysia	5.0E-05	−0.029***					0.04***		30%	0.405	0.597	24%	383
South Africa	**−3.0E-05**	**−0.039*****	**−0.0018**				**0.04****	**−0.03**	**56%**	**0.386**	**0.515**	**21%**	**240**
Israel	**3.0E-05**	**−0.020*****	**−0.0003**		**0.16**				**27%**	**0.524**	**0.719**	**32%**	**383**
Brazil	**−2.0E-05**	**−0.026**			**0.15***		**0.05**		**42%**	**0.397**	**0.499**	**24%**	**383**
Mexico	−5.8E-05	−0.009					0.06**	−0.04	97%	0.352	0.502	26%	86
Peru	**3.0E-05**	**−0.045*****					**0.06*****		**41%**	**0.384**	**0.574**	**25%**	**383**
Chile	**3.0E-05**	**−0.023*****				**−0.003**	**0.01****		**37%**	**0.401**	**0.510**	**27%**	**383**
Colombia	**3.0E-06**	**−0.047*****		**−0.002**		**−0.008****	**0.02*****		**48%**	**0.343**	**0.509**	**25%**	**383**

This table reports, for each country, results of models: (1) with at least one 10%-significant with expected signs according to Table 7.3, (2) with the lowest percent hit misses (PHM) and (3) statistically superior to all possible nested models. The dependent variable is the first difference of CDS spreads. Goodness-of-fit statistics are calculated for the estimation sample (July 2005 to October 2012) and out-of-sample (November 2012 to July 2016) periods. Only permutations of explanatory variables labelled with "(*)", "*", and "&" in Table 7.5 are taken as eligible estimation models. The explanatory variables were selected according to 10% significance level when applying the Granger-causality tests. The first lag of local variable is used as instrument for the corresponding local variable labelled with "&" in Table 7.5. As for variable transformation, I apply Δlog(.) to "price" variables (S&P 500 index, VIX index, Oil price, Local Stock Index, and Exchange Rate) and Δ(.) to "rate" variables (USA Slope, CDS spreads, Local Short-Term Yield, and Local Slope). The variance-covariance matrices are estimated according to White (1980) robust estimation. When model specifications show up as different from Table 7.6, they are highlighted in bold. *Vix, oil,* and *localSlope* estimators aren't significant for any model

Source: Capital IQ, Bloomberg, Datastream, and author's calculations

* Significant at the 10% level

** Significant at the 5% level

*** Significant at the 1% level

[a] and [b] stand for Theil's U_i and percent hit misses, respectively

[c] and [d] stand for in-sample and out-of-sample calculations, respectively

Table 7.13 5%-significant level Granger-causality test

	Global variables				*Local variables*					
	$sp500_t$	vix_t	$Slope_t$	oil_t	$spread_{i,t-1}$	$stock_{i,t}$	$xr_{i,t}$	$localTY_{i,t}$	$localSlope_{i,t}$	$bank_{i,t}$
Germany	(*)	(*)	(*)	(*)	(*)				&	
France	(*)	(*)	(*)	(*)	(*)				*	&
Finland	(*)	(*)	(*)	(*)	(*)					
Netherlands	(*)	(*)	(*)	(*)	(*)				*	
Austria	(*)	(*)	(*)	(*)	(*)				*	&
Belgium	(*)	(*)	(*)	(*)	(*)			*	*	&
Slovakia	(*)	(*)	(*)	(*)	(*)					
Spain	(*)	(*)	(*)	(*)	(*)				&	&
Italy	(*)	(*)	(*)	(*)	(*)			*	*	&
Ireland	(*)	(*)	(*)	(*)	(*)				&	
Portugal	(*)	(*)	(*)	(*)	(*)				&	&
Denmark	(*)	(*)	(*)	(*)	(*)	&		&		
Sweden	(*)	(*)	(*)	(*)	(*)	&	&		*	&
Poland	(*)	(*)	(*)	(*)	(*)		*	*	*	
Czech Rep.	(*)	(*)	(*)	(*)	(*)		*	&		
Hungary	(*)	(*)	(*)	(*)	(*)		&	*		
Turkey	(*)	(*)	(*)	(*)	(*)	&	&	*		&
Russia	(*)	(*)	(*)	(*)	(*)	*	&			&
Australia	(*)	(*)	(*)	(*)	(*)			*	*	&
New Zealand	(*)	(*)	(*)	(*)	(*)		*			
Japan	(*)	(*)	(*)	(*)	(*)	*				
Hong Kong	(*)	(*)	(*)	(*)	(*)	*			&	*
Korea	(*)	(*)	(*)	(*)	(*)	&	&			&
China	(*)	(*)	(*)	(*)	(*)	&		*		&
Philippines	(*)	(*)	(*)	(*)	(*)	&				
Indonesia	(*)	(*)	(*)	(*)	(*)	&	&	&	&	
Thailand	(*)	(*)	(*)	(*)	(*)	&			*	
Malaysia	(*)	(*)	(*)	(*)	(*)	&	*	*	*	
South Africa	(*)	(*)	(*)	(*)	(*)	&	*	&	*	
Israel	(*)	(*)	(*)	(*)	(*)		*			
Brazil	(*)	(*)	(*)	(*)	(*)	*	&			
Mexico	(*)	(*)	(*)	(*)	(*)	&	*	*		
Peru	(*)	(*)	(*)	(*)	(*)		*	*		
Chile	(*)	(*)	(*)	(*)	(*)	*		&		
Colombia	(*)	(*)	(*)	(*)	(*)	*	*	*		

Set of eligible explanatory variables

(*) stands for Exogeneity by Assumption. * and & stand for Weak Exogeneity and Non-Weak Exogeneity, as for the Granger-causality test, at 10% significance level, respectively. Blank accounts for non-significance at 10% significance level, in this case, the corresponding variable is not part of any estimation model for the corresponding country

Source: Capital IQ, Bloomberg, Datastream, and author's calculations

coefficients of the S&P 500 within each sub-period. What is more, the algorithm's outcomes still provide support to this chapter's two main findings. Tables 7.15 and 7.16 also show that the differences between the quantities of statistically significant S&P 500 estimators across the six sub-periods aren't large: 5, 1, 0, 0, 0, and 2 out of 35 countries, respectively, for the sub-periods July 2005–October 2012, Before July 2010, After July 2010, Before July 2008, Subprime Crisis, and Euro Crisis. Overall, whether or not the S&P 500 is selected by the algorithm does depend on the specific setting. Let's take the models for New Zealand and the Colombia models for the July 2005–June 2010 period ("Before Jul 2010" column in Table 7.16).[12] Supressing *localSlope* from the set of eligible variables for New Zealand gives rise to an alternative model where the previously non-significant coefficient of the S&P 500 (see the corresponding column in Table 7.15) now becomes statistically significant. In contrast, the S&P 500 is no longer selected by the algorithm for Colombia, when the Granger-causality test leads to the exclusion of the variable *stock* from the set of eligible variables. Quite conspicuously, apart from slight differences in other factor estimators for just three countries, the statistical significance of the coefficients of the S&P 500 is pretty much the same for the July 2005 to June 2008 ("Before Jul 2008" column in Tables 7.15 and 7.16).[13]

Ordering Adjusted R^2 statistics from low to high values and the other goodness-of-fit statistics (Theil's U_1, Theil's U_2, and PHM) the other way around (descending) according to the column "After Jul 2010", Tables 7.17, 7.18, 7.19, and 7.20 support the finding that emerging markets model specifications (mostly at the bottom rows of the tables) tend toshow better goodness-of-fit and forecast accuracy statistics as a group than advanced economies across all the different sub-periods.

Tables 7.21 and 7.22 show respectively that ARMA models' and lagged-variable models' goodness-of-fit statistics are mostly superseded by the contemporaneous models across the other five sub-periods as they are for the July 2005–October 2012 period.[14] However, comparing Table 7.21 values particularly with those of Tables 7.18 and 7.19, we find a couple of better ARMA Theil's U_1 values (highlighted in bold in Table 7.21, column "Before Jul 2008") and Theil's U_2 values (highlighted in bold in Table 7.21, columns "After Jul 2010" and "Euro Crisis"); yet this is the case for just less than half the number of countries. Showing mixed results in comparison to the corresponding ARMA-model statistics (Table 7.21)

Table 7.14 GMM results—5%-significant level Granger-causality-test set of eligible variables

	const	*Global variables*				*Local variables*						*Adj. $R^{2[c]}$*	$U_1^{a,d}$	$U_2^{a,d}$	$PHM^{b,d}$	*#obs.*[c]
		$sp500_t$	vix_t	$Slope_t$	oil_t	$spread_{i,t-1}$	$stock_{i,t}$	$xr_{i,t}$	$localTY_{i,t}$	$localSlope_{i,t}$	$bank_{i,t}$					
Germany	4.0E-06					0.26***						6%	0.749	0.777	42%	383
France	2.0E-05	−0.013***				0.09						19%	0.563	0.754	35%	374
Finland	9.0E-06	−0.007***	−0.0004									24%	0.608	0.792	44%	353
Netherlands	**1.0E-05**	**−0.009*** **	**−0.0003**									**17%**	**0.622**	**0.890**	**42%**	**353**
Austria	1.7E-05				−0.003*						0.28	39%	0.650	1.231	43%	241
Belgium	3.0E-05	−0.017***										13%	0.589	0.880	41%	383
Slovakia	4.0E-05	−0.022***										21%	0.618	0.987	42%	383
Spain	1.0E-04	−0.025***										10%	0.675	0.695	34%	313
Italy	6.9E-05	−0.025***		−0.16***		0.09			0.45***			44%	0.509	0.616	24%	383
Ireland	6.0E-05	−0.026***										3%	0.629	0.783	37%	353
Portugal	**1.0E-04**	**−0.029*** **	**0.0017**	**−0.25** **	**0.005**	**0.20***						**6%**	**0.671**	**0.773**	**28%**	**383**
Denmark	1.0E-05					0.30***						8%	0.767	0.733	47%	352
Sweden	6.0E-06	−0.009***	−0.0008									17%	0.636	0.977	47%	353
Poland	3.0E-05								0.39***			10%	0.599	0.706	44%	378
Czech Rep.	3.0E-05	−0.022***										21%	0.622	0.872	34%	383
Hungary	1.0E-04	−0.040***				0.13			0.39***			51%	0.468	0.661	28%	295
Turkey	1.1E-04			−0.26					0.32***			36%	0.386	0.499	29%	333
Russia	**3.0E-05**	**−0.073*** **	**−0.0022**			**0.12**		**0.06**				**25%**	**0.334**	**0.473**	**29%**	**383**
Australia	8.0E-06	−0.008			−0.002*						0.38	39%	0.402	0.649	30%	252
New Zealand	2.0E-05	−0.012***										12%	0.541	0.705	36%	313
Japan	2.0E-05	−0.011***										19%	0.608	0.745	36%	383
Hong Kong	**1.0E-05**						**−0.005*** **					**4%**	**0.799**	**0.771**	**49%**	**383**
Korea	1.0E-05					−0.15					1.05***	87%	0.215	0.309	15%	252
China	**2.0E-05**	**−0.026*** **										**34%**	**0.479**	**0.611**	**29%**	**383**
Philippines	−5.0E-05	−0.060***										32%	0.451	0.893	28%	383
Indonesia	2.0E-06	−0.092***	−0.0017									34%	0.461	0.764	32%	383

Thailand	3.0E-05	−0.036***							26%	0.454	0.646	31%	383
Malaysia	5.0E-05	−0.029***				0.04***			30%	0.405	0.597	24%	383
South Africa	−1.0E-05	−0.044***				0.04***		−0.12	59%	0.371	0.525	23%	206
Israel	4.0E-05	−0.018***	−0.0005	0.001		0.01*			25%	0.530	0.706	37%	383
Brazil	**−1.0E-05**	**−0.049*****			**−0.021*****				**46%**	**0.507**	**0.568**	**27%**	**383**
Mexico	**−1.5E-05**	**−0.022*****				**0.03*****	**0.08**		**98%**	**0.349**	**0.459**	**25%**	**86**
Peru	**−2.0E-05**	**−0.041*****				**0.05*****	**−0.03**		**92%**	**0.412**	**0.621**	**26%**	**119**
Chile	**3.0E-05**	**−0.026*****							**35%**	**0.451**	**0.566**	**28%**	**383**
Colombia	5.0E-06	−0.047***		−0.003	−0.006	0.02***	0.12***		49%	0.340	0.466	27%	372

This table reports, for each country, results of models: (1) at least one 10%-significant coefficient with expected signs according to Table 7.3, (2) with the highest Adjusted R^2, and (3) statistically superior to all possible nested models. The dependent variable is the first difference of CDS spreads. Goodness-of-fit statistics are calculated for the estimation sample (July 2005 to October 2012) and out-of-sample (November 2012 to July 2016) periods. Only permutations of explanatory variables labelled with "(*)", "*", and "&" in Table 7.13 are taken as eligible estimation models. Differently from the setting in Table 7.6, the explanatory variables were selected according to 5% significance level, instead of 10%, when applying the Granger-causality tests. Nine models (highlighted in bold) show up as different from those in Table 7.6. The first lag of local variable is used as instrument for the corresponding local variable labelled with "&" in Table 7.5. As for variable transformation, I apply Δlog(.) to "price" variables (S&P 500 index, VIX index, Oil price, Local Stock Index, and Exchange Rate) and Δ(.) to "rate" variables (USA Slope, CDS spreads, Local Short-Term Yield, and Local Slope). The variance-covariance matrices are estimated according to White (1980) robust estimation. *Vix* and *localSlope* don't show up as significant for any country

Source: Capital IQ, Bloomberg, Datastream, and author's calculations

* Significant at the 10% level

** Significant at the 5% level

*** Significant at the 1% level

[a] and [b] stand for Theil's U_i and percent hit misses, respectively

[c] and [d] stand for in-sample and out-of-sample calculations, respectively

Table 7.15 Coefficient estimators for $sp500_t$ across different sub-samples

	Jul 2005 to Oct 2012	*Before Jul 2010*	*After Jul 2010*	*Before Jul 2008*	*Subprime Crisis*	*Euro Crisis*
Australia	−0.008	−0.009***	−0.012***	−0.005	−0.008***	−0.006***
New Zealand	−0.012***		−0.013***			−0.018***
Ireland	−0.026***	−0.032***			−0.026***	
Sweden	−0.009***	−0.009***	−0.007***	−0.001*	−0.010***	
Germany		−0.003		−0.001***	−0.007***	
Finland	−0.007***	−0.004	−0.007***	−0.001***	−0.007***	
Denmark		−0.005*	−0.010***	−0.002*	−0.010***	
Netherlands		−0.008***	−0.002	−0.002***	−0.008***	−0.013***
Austria		−0.012	−0.012**	−0.002***	−0.013	−0.018*
France	−0.013***	−0.008***		−0.002***	−0.010***	
Belgium	−0.017***	−0.009***		−0.002***	−0.011***	
Hong Kong		−0.013***	−0.006***	−0.004**	−0.011**	−0.011***
Japan	−0.011***	−0.009***	−0.014***	−0.004**	−0.010***	−0.015***
Portugal		−0.017***	−0.046**	−0.004***		
Italy	−0.025***	−0.016***		−0.004***	−0.019***	
Slovakia	−0.022***	−0.017***	−0.023***	−0.005***	−0.018***	−0.033***
Spain	−0.025***	−0.017***	−0.028***	−0.005***	−0.018***	−0.057***
Czech Rep.	−0.022***	−0.020***		−0.006***	−0.017***	−0.020***
Israel	−0.018***	−0.013	−0.014***	−0.010***		−0.018***
Poland		−0.017***	−0.027***	−0.012***	−0.016***	
Chile		−0.025***	−0.022***	−0.012***	−0.030***	−0.022***
China			−0.022***	−0.014***		−0.023***
Korea			−0.025***	−0.017***		−0.031***
Malaysia	−0.029***	−0.031***	−0.023***	−0.019***	−0.042***	−0.016***
Thailand	−0.036***	−0.038***	−0.022***	−0.023***	−0.041***	−0.030***

Hungary	−0.040***	−0.026		−0.025***	−0.029	−0.061***
South Africa	−0.044***	−0.043***	−0.026***	−0.026***	−0.049**	−0.035***
Mexico	−0.009	−0.053***	−0.016*	−0.029***	−0.033***	−0.034***
Russia	−0.033**		−0.028	−0.029***		−0.030***
Turkey		−0.073***	−0.033***	−0.033***		−0.023***
Peru	−0.042***	−0.044***	−0.029***	−0.044***	−0.048***	−0.031***
Brazil	−0.048***	−0.053***		−0.052***	−0.053***	−0.033***
Philippines	−0.060***	−0.069***	−0.032***	−0.055***	−0.067***	−0.024***
Indonesia	−0.092***	−0.111***	−0.036***	−0.059***	−0.112***	−0.035***
Colombia	−0.047***	−0.053***	−0.028***	−0.062***	−0.051***	−0.032***

This table shows $sp500_t$ estimators ordered by the column "Before Jul 2008". Non-significant estimators are ranked as if they were not available. The columns show $sp500_t$ estimator values across six different periods: (1) July 2005 to October 2012, (2) July 2005 to June 2010 (Before Jul 2010), (3) July 2010 to June 2014 (After Jul 2010), (4) July 2005 to June 2008 (Before Jul 2008), (5) January 2008 to December 2010 (Subprime Crisis), and (6) July 2010 to June 2013 (Euro Crisis)

Source: Capital IQ, Bloomberg, Datastream, and author's calculations

***, **, and * stand for significance at the 1%, 5%, and 10% level, respectively

Table 7.16 Coefficient estimators for $sp500_t$ across different sub-samples 5%-significant level Granger-causality-test set of eligible variables

	Jul 2005 to Oct 2012	*Before Jul 2010*	*After Jul 2010*	*Before Jul 2008*	*Subprime Crisis*	*Euro Crisis*
Australia	−0.008	−0.009***	−0.006***	−0.005	**−0.009*****	**−0.017*****
New Zealand	−0.012***	**−0.010****	−0.016***			−0.018***
Ireland	−0.026***	**−0.025*****			−0.026***	
Sweden	−0.009***	−0.009***		−0.001*	−0.010***	
Germany		−0.003		−0.001***	−0.007***	
Finland	−0.007***	−0.004		−0.001***	**−0.005***	
Denmark		−0.005*		−0.002*	−0.010***	
Netherlands	**−0.009*****	−0.008***		−0.002***	**−0.009*****	**NA**
Austria		−0.012		−0.002***	−0.013	−0.018*
France	−0.013***	−0.008***		−0.002***	−0.010***	
Belgium	−0.017***	−0.009***		−0.002***	**−0.008*****	
Hong Kong		−0.013***	−0.011***	−0.004**	**−0.011*****	−0.011***
Japan	−0.011***	−0.009***		−0.004**	−0.010***	−0.015***
Portugal	**−0.029*****	−0.017***		−0.004***		
Italy	−0.025***	−0.016***		−0.004***	−0.019***	
Slovakia	−0.022***	−0.017***	−0.029***	−0.005***	−0.018***	−0.033***
Spain	−0.025***	−0.017***	−0.051***	−0.005***	−0.018***	**NA**
Czech Rep.	−0.022***	**−0.016*****	−0.019***	−0.006***	−0.017***	−0.020***
Israel	−0.018***	−0.013		−0.010***		−0.018***
Poland		−0.017***	−0.037***	−0.012***	−0.016***	
Chile	**−0.026*****	**−0.026*****	−0.022***	−0.012***	−0.030***	**−0.025*****
China	**−0.026*****		−0.023***	−0.014***		−0.023***
Korea			−0.029***	−0.017***		−0.031***
Malaysia	−0.029***	**−0.039*****	−0.029***	−0.019***	−0.042***	**−0.022*****
Thailand	−0.036***	−0.038***	−0.031***	−0.023***	−0.041***	−0.030***
Hungary	−0.040***	−0.026		−0.025***	−0.029	−0.061***

South Africa	−0.044***	**−0.044*****	−0.018***	−0.026***	−0.049**	**−0.044*****
Mexico	**−0.022*****	**−0.050*****	**−0.014*****	−0.029***	−0.033***	−0.034***
Russia	**−0.073*****		**−0.046*****	−0.029***		**−0.049*****
Turkey		**NA**	−0.013***	−0.033***		−0.023***
Peru	**−0.041*****	−0.044***	**−0.030*****	−0.044***	**−0.042*****	−0.031***
Brazil	**−0.049*****	**−0.055*****	−0.034***	−0.052***	−0.053***	−0.033***
Philippines	−0.060***	−0.069***	−0.035***	−0.055***	−0.067***	−0.024***
Indonesia	−0.092***	−0.111***	−0.036***	−0.059***	−0.112***	**−0.034*****
Colombia	−0.047***	**NA**	−0.032***	**−0.066*****	−0.051***	−0.032***

This table shows S&P500 estimators ordered by the column "Before Jul 2008". Non-significant estimators are ranked as if they were not available. In contrast to Table 7.15, in this case, the engine generated the models corresponding to the associated S&P500 estimators below from a set of variables elected by means of a 5%-significant level (instead of 10%, as for Table 7.15) Granger-causality test. The columns show S&P500 estimator values across six different periods: (1) July 2005 to October 2012, (2) July 2005 to June 2010 (Before Jul 2010), (3) July 2010 to June 2014 (After Jul 2010), (4) July 2005 to June 2008 (Before Jul 2008), (5) January 2008 to December 2010 (Subprime Crisis), and (6) July 2010 to June 2013 (Euro Crisis). When S&P500 estimators show up as different from Table 7.15, they are highlighted in bold

Source: Capital IQ, Bloomberg, Datastream, and author's calculations

***, **, and * stand for significance at the 1%, 5%, and 10% level, respectively. Blank cells and NA stand for "non-available"

Table 7.17 Adjusted R^2 across different periods

	Jul 2005 to Oct 2012	*Before Jul 2010*	*After Jul 2010*	*Before Jul 2008*	*Subprime Crisis*	*Euro Crisis*
Israel	25%	77%	3%	17%	7%	22%
Ireland	3%	73%	4%	89%	9%	3%
Denmark	8%	25%	4%	2%	16%	18%
Hungary	51%	41%	6%	24%	47%	22%
Netherlands	3%	17%	9%	8%	17%	20%
Sweden	17%	21%	9%	3%	22%	54%
Japan	19%	21%	10%	1%	24%	25%
Austria	39%	51%	11%	18%	51%	38%
Spain	10%	29%	13%	19%	40%	15%
Belgium	13%	24%	18%	20%	13%	35%
Czech Rep.	21%	34%	19%	20%	30%	21%
Portugal	55%	36%	21%	13%	14%	18%
Slovakia	21%	40%	22%	17%	42%	25%
Hong Kong	44%	39%	30%	14%	68%	32%
Germany	6%	5%	31%	9%	24%	2%
Poland	10%	45%	34%	24%	49%	4%
Italy	44%	26%	36%	25%	17%	35%
Thailand	26%	24%	37%	36%	26%	39%
Chile	43%	43%	39%	26%	38%	41%
Brazil	44%	47%	40%	35%	47%	47%
Korea	87%	88%	41%	31%	88%	44%
Philippines	32%	33%	42%	53%	31%	53%
New Zealand	12%	95%	43%	0%	96%	46%
Colombia	49%	50%	45%	49%	47%	49%
Indonesia	34%	38%	45%	45%	39%	52%
Finland	24%	32%	47%	5%	24%	48%
Malaysia	30%	28%	47%	33%	28%	73%
Peru	92%	93%	47%	27%	90%	80%
South Africa	59%	55%	49%	24%	66%	38%
China	46%	67%	51%	33%	65%	60%
Russia	99%	78%	54%	43%	78%	58%
France	19%	28%	62%	8%	30%	64%
Mexico	97%	45%	68%	52%	53%	60%
Australia	39%	31%	68%	30%	33%	71%
Turkey	36%	36%	76%	63%	44%	71%

This table shows the Adjusted R^2 statistics ordered (ascending) by the column "After Jul 2010". The columns show the Adjusted R^2 statistics across six different periods: (1) July 2005 to October 2012, (2) July 2005 to June 2010 (Before Jul 2010), (3) July 2010 to June 2014 (After Jul 2010), (4) July 2005 to June 2008 (Before Jul 2008), (5) January 2008 to December 2010 (Subprime Crisis), and (6) July 2010 to June 2013 (Euro Crisis). The explanatory variables for each period were selected according to 10% significance level when applying the Granger-causality tests. Countries at the bottom of the table, broadly composed of emerging market economies, are associated with better goodness-of-fit measures

Source: Capital IQ, Bloomberg, Datastream, and author's calculations

Table 7.18 Theil's U_1 across different periods

	Jul 2005 to Oct 2012	*Before Jul 2010*	*After Jul 2010*	*Before Jul 2008*	*Subprime Crisis*	*Euro Crisis*
Denmark	0.767	0.575	0.858	0.920	0.710	0.672
Israel	0.530	0.483	0.829	0.746	0.630	0.512
Sweden	0.636	0.474	0.805	0.838	0.467	0.568
Ireland	0.629	0.520	0.790	0.739	0.898	0.667
Belgium	0.589	0.765	0.784	0.678	0.827	0.535
Japan	0.608	0.676	0.692	0.732	0.673	0.477
Slovakia	0.618	0.629	0.650	0.664	0.593	0.650
Hong Kong	0.643	0.486	0.646	0.633	0.425	0.653
Czech Rep.	0.622	0.585	0.646	0.706	0.517	0.598
Italy	0.509	0.820	0.642	0.677	0.832	0.534
Hungary	0.468	0.351	0.641	0.739	0.331	0.520
Austria	0.650	0.498	0.619	0.841	0.477	0.620
Poland	0.599	0.436	0.584	0.649	0.413	0.746
Netherlands	0.818	0.721	0.583	0.872	0.689	0.645
Finland	0.608	0.553	0.571	0.705	0.633	0.602
Brazil	0.471	0.351	0.550	0.485	0.340	0.612
Spain	0.675	0.754	0.544	0.776	0.619	0.599
New Zealand	0.541	1.072	0.533	–	0.690	0.568
Germany	0.749	0.580	0.521	0.731	0.648	0.782
France	0.563	0.773	0.479	0.822	0.705	0.443
Colombia	0.340	0.359	0.470	0.447	0.340	0.576
Portugal	0.305	0.651	0.470	0.798	0.794	0.417
Malaysia	0.405	0.348	0.428	0.747	0.397	0.256
Chile	0.467	0.374	0.425	0.699	0.397	0.471
Thailand	0.454	0.438	0.396	0.707	0.442	0.529
Peru	0.415	0.439	0.386	0.477	0.396	0.620
South Africa	0.371	0.371	0.381	0.684	0.251	0.601
Korea	0.215	0.199	0.377	0.816	0.201	0.499
Mexico	0.352	0.382	0.348	0.575	0.331	0.449
Australia	0.402	0.347	0.347	0.553	0.265	0.445
Turkey	0.386	0.422	0.334	0.515	0.335	0.300
China	0.315	0.353	0.333	0.688	0.290	0.499
Philippines	0.451	0.438	0.318	0.553	0.424	0.361
Indonesia	0.461	0.500	0.310	0.629	0.488	0.374
Russia	0.224	0.237	0.305	0.838	0.225	0.286

This table shows the Theil's U_1 statistics ordered (descending) by the column "After Jul 2010". The columns show the U_1 statistics across the six out-of-sample periods: (1) November 2012 to July 2016, (2) July 2010 to December 2012, (3) July 2014 to July 2016, (4) July 2008 to November 2009, (5) January 2011 to June 2012, and (6) July 2013 to December 2014. These out-of-sample periods correspond, respectively, to the in-sample estimations over the periods: (1) July 2005 to October 2012, (2) July 2005 to June 2010 (Before Jul 2010), (3) July 2010 to June 2014 (After Jul 2010), (4) July 2005 to June 2008 (Before Jul 2008), (5) January 2008 to December 2010 (Subprime Crisis), and (6) July 2010 to June 2013 (Euro Crisis). The explanatory variables for each period were selected according to 10% significance level when applying the Granger-causality tests. Countries at the bottom of the table, broadly composed of emerging market economies, are associated with better goodness-of-fit measures

Source: Capital IQ, Bloomberg, Datastream, and author's calculations

Table 7.19 Theil's U_2 across different periods

	Jul 2005 to Oct 2012	*Before Jul 2010*	*After Jul 2010*	*Before Jul 2008*	*Subprime Crisis*	*Euro Crisis*
Slovakia	0.987	0.716	1.370	0.777	0.705	1.192
Austria	1.231	0.606	1.206	0.838	0.573	1.422
Czech Rep.	0.872	0.654	1.086	0.814	0.620	0.665
Poland	0.706	0.562	1.080	0.752	0.553	0.778
Germany	0.777	0.662	1.028	0.810	0.641	0.828
New Zealand	0.705	1.115	0.840	–	0.862	1.214
Finland	0.792	0.676	0.837	0.799	0.655	0.946
Spain	0.695	0.634	0.813	0.685	0.587	1.004
Japan	0.745	0.636	0.794	0.689	0.626	0.705
Hong Kong	0.726	0.598	0.792	0.686	0.550	0.834
France	0.754	0.668	0.788	0.836	0.623	0.815
Netherlands	0.787	0.660	0.782	0.804	0.629	1.215
Belgium	0.880	0.691	0.757	0.777	0.689	0.826
Sweden	0.977	0.656	0.748	0.811	0.646	0.740
Ireland	0.783	0.708	0.747	0.818	0.736	1.493
Israel	0.706	0.664	0.742	0.700	0.673	0.716
Hungary	0.661	0.512	0.733	0.740	0.483	0.758
Denmark	0.733	0.704	0.697	0.863	0.704	1.313
Italy	0.616	0.688	0.687	0.740	0.708	0.616
Korea	0.309	0.331	0.686	0.673	0.344	0.811
Portugal	0.469	0.650	0.664	0.705	0.712	0.601
Thailand	0.646	0.634	0.585	0.622	0.677	0.658
Malaysia	0.597	0.566	0.568	0.630	0.634	0.353
Australia	0.649	0.439	0.559	0.765	0.371	0.702
Brazil	0.563	0.577	0.558	0.589	0.575	0.599
Peru	0.633	0.619	0.517	0.572	0.560	0.661
Chile	0.687	0.552	0.514	0.663	0.635	0.564
Philippines	0.893	0.799	0.509	0.570	0.758	0.542
Indonesia	0.764	1.080	0.495	0.646	1.065	0.553
Colombia	0.466	0.623	0.490	0.568	0.583	0.616
China	0.481	0.579	0.460	0.666	0.499	0.629
South Africa	0.525	0.636	0.446	0.650	0.692	0.652
Mexico	0.502	0.618	0.437	0.653	0.590	0.576
Turkey	0.499	0.671	0.410	0.555	0.585	0.366
Russia	0.308	0.356	0.402	0.703	0.355	0.382

This table shows the Theil's U_2 statistics ordered (descending) by the column "After Jul 2010". The columns show the U_2 statistics across the six out-of-sample periods: (1) November 2012 to July 2016, (2) July 2010 to December 2012, (3) July 2014 to July 2016, (4) July 2008 to November 2009, (5) January 2011 to June 2012, and (6) July 2013 to December 2014. These out-of-sample periods correspond, respectively, to the in-sample estimations over the periods: (1) July 2005 to October 2012, (2) July 2005 to June 2010 (Before Jul 2010), (3) July 2010 to June 2014 (After Jul 2010), (4) July 2005 to June 2008 (Before Jul 2008), (5) January 2008 to December 2010 (Subprime Crisis), and (6) July 2010 to June 2013 (Euro Crisis). The explanatory variables for each period were selected according to 10% significance level when applying the Granger-causality tests. Countries at the bottom of the table, broadly composed of emerging market economies, are associated with better goodness-of-fit measures

Source: Capital IQ, Bloomberg, Datastream, and author's calculations

Table 7.20 PHM across different periods

	Jul 2005 to Oct 2012	*Before Jul 2010*	*After Jul 2010*	*Before Jul 2008*	*Subprime Crisis*	*Euro Crisis*
Belgium	41%	32%	53%	38%	38%	36%
Sweden	47%	31%	50%	33%	33%	48%
Israel	37%	27%	49%	32%	27%	34%
Denmark	47%	28%	46%	32%	38%	48%
Hungary	28%	15%	46%	34%	15%	42%
Ireland	37%	47%	45%	62%	42%	48%
Finland	44%	28%	44%	37%	40%	39%
Hong Kong	42%	32%	44%	25%	21%	43%
Germany	42%	26%	42%	38%	29%	34%
Slovakia	42%	31%	42%	27%	23%	42%
Austria	43%	25%	41%	32%	22%	39%
Japan	36%	37%	39%	34%	31%	32%
Spain	34%	28%	35%	32%	31%	40%
Czech Rep.	34%	25%	35%	34%	18%	29%
Netherlands	53%	36%	34%	38%	36%	43%
Italy	24%	28%	34%	30%	38%	23%
New Zealand	36%	29%	32%	0%	29%	38%
France	35%	33%	31%	34%	33%	29%
Portugal	25%	24%	31%	41%	23%	25%
Poland	44%	24%	30%	30%	21%	42%
Australia	30%	23%	29%	29%	17%	25%
Peru	30%	33%	28%	18%	30%	51%
Thailand	31%	29%	26%	29%	27%	40%
Russia	22%	22%	25%	25%	17%	26%
Philippines	28%	30%	24%	15%	28%	22%
Korea	15%	16%	23%	25%	14%	31%
Malaysia	24%	26%	22%	27%	27%	18%
Brazil	28%	25%	22%	18%	22%	38%
China	19%	22%	21%	29%	15%	27%
Indonesia	32%	32%	21%	25%	32%	29%
Colombia	27%	24%	20%	20%	23%	34%
South Africa	23%	20%	19%	25%	0%	36%
Mexico	26%	28%	19%	30%	21%	36%
Chile	29%	27%	17%	37%	27%	29%
Turkey	29%	32%	13%	9%	5%	10%

This table shows the percent hit misses (PHM) statistics ordered (descending) by the column "After Jul 2010". The columns show the PHM statistics across the six out-of-sample periods: (1) November 2012 to July 2016, (2) July 2010 to December 2012, (3) July 2014 to July 2016, (4) July 2008 to November 2009, (5) January 2011 to June 2012, and (6) July 2013 to December 2014. These out-of-sample periods correspond, respectively, to the in-sample estimations over the periods: (1) July 2005 to October 2012, (2) July 2005 to June 2010 (Before Jul 2010), (3) July 2010 to June 2014 (After Jul 2010), (4) July 2005 to June 2008 (Before Jul 2008), (5) January 2008 to December 2010 (Subprime Crisis), and (6) July 2010 to June 2013 (Euro Crisis). The explanatory variables for each period were selected according to 10% significance level when applying the Granger-causality tests. Countries at the bottom of the table, broadly composed of emerging market economies, are associated with better goodness-of-fit measures

Source: Capital IQ, Bloomberg, Datastream, and author's calculations

Table 7.21 ARMA models' goodness-of-fit statistics

	Before Jul 2010				*After Jul 2010*				*Before Jul 2008*				*Subprime Crisis*				*Euro Crisis*			
	Adj. R^2	U_1	U_2	*PHM*	*Adj. R^2*	U_1	U_2	*PHM*	*Adj. R^2*	U_1	U_2	*PHM*	*Adj. R^2*	U_1	U_2	*PHM*	*Adj. R^2*	U_1	U_2	*PHM*
Germany	**21%**	0.703	0.986	43%	2%	0.852	**0.739**	42%	5%	0.759	0.841	49%	16%	0.697	0.816	49%	2%	0.809	0.837	**32%**
France	14%	**0.735**	0.833	54%	0%	0.903	**0.728**	38%	−1%	0.942	0.887	41%	18%	0.750	0.822	47%	0%	0.882	0.842	30%
Finland	18%	0.669	0.819	38%	5%	0.838	**0.716**	**43%**	**19%**	**0.684**	0.972	51%	17%	0.679	0.798	**37%**	5%	0.783	**0.791**	43%
Netherlands	10%	0.751	0.771	40%	0%	0.932	**0.724**	48%	**13%**	0.899	0.881	54%	10%	0.752	0.767	40%	0%	0.923	**0.894**	**34%**
Austria	14%	0.689	0.794	41%	6%	0.784	**0.768**	41%	0%	0.891	0.864	42%	13%	0.694	0.777	45%	6%	0.758	**0.812**	**32%**
Belgium	12%	**0.719**	0.779	40%	2%	0.872	**0.709**	**43%**	**24%**	**0.627**	0.898	48%	**17%**	**0.717**	0.798	41%	1%	0.828	**0.819**	39%
Slovakia	16%	0.672	0.825	38%	7%	0.843	**0.696**	55%	14%	**0.641**	0.788	29%	15%	0.674	0.814	33%	7%	0.800	**0.748**	57%
Spain	18%	**0.644**	0.977	45%	−1%	0.964	**0.707**	42%	**33%**	**0.687**	1.086	49%	7%	0.741	0.711	40%	−1%	0.966	**0.835**	**36%**
Italy	9%	**0.742**	0.769	42%	1%	0.901	0.707	44%	**35%**	0.745	0.983	**53%**	9%	**0.743**	0.774	50%	0%	0.893	0.757	49%
Ireland	11%	0.694	0.792	**44%**	**14%**	**0.747**	0.935	51%	3%	0.842	0.845	51%	4%	**0.756**	**0.734**	42%	**14%**	0.690	**1.292**	60%
Portugal	19%	0.752	1.868	42%	5%	0.769	0.786	44%	**31%**	**0.711**	0.869	48%	12%	**0.709**	0.765	42%	4%	0.760	0.819	42%
Denmark	15%	0.698	0.805	36%	4%	0.861	**0.696**	47%	**46%**	**0.759**	1.091	48%	15%	**0.695**	0.788	**35%**	4%	0.808	**0.782**	**44%**
Sweden	10%	0.718	0.816	38%	9%	**0.796**	**0.739**	54%	**31%**	**0.701**	1.226	51%	10%	0.712	0.810	40%	10%	0.801	**0.733**	48%
Poland	14%	0.675	0.802	43%	5%	0.837	**0.714**	44%	6%	0.735	0.810	34%	13%	0.663	0.793	41%	**5%**	0.736	**0.766**	**39%**
Czech Rep.	18%	0.708	0.814	48%	7%	0.866	**0.645**	53%	**26%**	**0.658**	1.048	46%	17%	0.711	0.809	42%	1%	0.909	**0.653**	51%
Hungary	16%	0.704	0.860	38%	**6%**	0.815	**0.733**	49%	17%	**0.642**	0.748	39%	14%	0.716	0.848	37%	6%	0.773	0.772	42%
Turkey	9%	0.755	0.760	50%	0%	0.934	0.745	45%	3%	0.833	0.742	44%	11%	0.736	0.751	51%	0%	0.925	0.746	43%
Russia	24%	0.697	0.839	47%	2%	0.858	0.731	46%	4%	**0.827**	0.746	37%	23%	0.686	0.832	44%	1%	0.897	0.766	47%
Australia	15%	0.734	0.777	40%	2%	0.840	0.773	40%	**37%**	0.614	0.867	41%	15%	0.730	0.777	45%	2%	0.817	0.768	35%
New Zealand	10%	**0.756**	**0.768**	38%	2%	0.860	**0.729**	44%	**3%**	0.793	0.873	28%	10%	0.751	**0.770**	44%	2%	0.794	**0.817**	38%
Japan	0%	0.930	0.725	40%	−306%	0.807	2.348	56%	**10%**	**0.697**	1.160	56%	3%	0.844	0.725	42%	−306%	0.767	2.139	53%
Hong Kong	6%	0.793	0.745	49%	0%	0.925	**0.743**	44%	**23%**	0.647	1.037	43%	5%	0.803	0.747	53%	0%	0.927	**0.761**	44%
Korea	11%	0.720	0.797	48%	3%	0.828	0.737	46%	11%	**0.740**	0.733	32%	9%	0.725	0.800	49%	3%	0.806	**0.732**	51%

China	21%	0.670	0.851	45%	2%	0.863	0.732	42%	7%	0.774	0.760	39%	18%	0.664	0.828	46%	1%	0.854	0.759	48%
Philippines	11%	0.740	**0.772**	45%	4%	0.808	0.748	39%	2%	0.867	0.712	39%	12%	0.702	0.765	50%	3%	0.802	0.768	43%
Indonesia	17%	0.673	**0.794**	46%	5%	0.785	0.752	42%	3%	0.839	0.759	33%	18%	0.660	**0.789**	49%	6%	0.762	0.772	48%
Thailand	14%	0.721	0.807	48%	5%	0.781	0.779	40%	8%	0.801	0.734	42%	12%	0.675	0.779	50%	5%	0.773	0.770	43%
Malaysia	19%	0.699	0.825	44%	4%	0.793	0.760	40%	9%	0.754	0.709	35%	18%	0.704	0.834	46%	3%	0.812	0.749	42%
South Africa	12%	0.718	0.771	48%	0%	0.983	0.713	47%	13%	0.773	0.785	46%	11%	0.693	0.733	46%	−1%	0.984	0.752	52%
Israel	8%	0.742	0.758	45%	**4%**	**0.796**	**0.741**	52%	**23%**	**0.705**	0.972	49%	**8%**	0.738	0.773	45%	3%	0.782	0.816	35%
Brazil	11%	0.757	0.795	48%	1%	0.896	0.722	44%	4%	0.776	0.749	41%	16%	0.685	0.805	44%	1%	0.894	0.722	43%
Mexico	11%	0.735	0.781	49%	1%	0.902	0.714	48%	8%	0.737	0.772	34%	11%	0.727	0.776	46%	1%	0.892	0.723	49%
Peru	12%	0.725	0.805	47%	0%	0.913	0.737	43%	14%	0.825	0.806	49%	10%	0.746	0.770	50%	1%	0.904	**0.722**	49%
Chile	6%	0.756	0.812	54%	5%	0.810	0.733	42%	5%	0.798	0.754	41%	5%	0.762	0.831	49%	6%	0.817	0.741	43%
Colombia	11%	0.727	0.800	48%	1%	0.884	0.752	34%	2%	0.833	0.753	34%	−7%	0.751	1.680	58%	2%	0.894	0.744	47%

This table shows goodness-of-fit statistics for ARMA model specifications corresponding to five sub-periods: (1) July 2005 to June 2010 (Before Jul 2010), (2) July 2010 to June 2014 (After Jul 2010), (3) July 2005 to June 2008 (Before Jul 2008), (4) January 2008 to December 2010 (Subprime Crisis), and (5) July 2010 to June 2013 (Euro Crisis). The Adjusted R^2 is calculated over the in-sample period, whereas we adopted the two-part split of the data for calculating Theil's U_1, Theil's U_2, and percent hit misses (PHM) out-of-sample statistics: estimation (2/3 of data) and out-of-sample test (1/3 of data). Better statistics than the corresponding contemporaneous models are highlighted in bold

Source: Capital IQ

Table 7.22 Lagged-explanatory variable models' S&P500 estimators and goodness-of-fit statistics

	Before Jul 2010					*After Jul 2010*					*Before Jul 2008*
	$sp500_t$	*Adj.* R^2	U_1	U_2	*PHM*	$sp500_t$	*Adj.* R^2	U_1	U_2	*PHM*	$sp500_t$
Germany	−0.004***	**7%**	0.887	0.782	52%		3%	0.838	**0.741**	46%	
France	−0.004***	6%	0.937	0.746	52%	0.004	1%	0.675	0.813	37%	
Finland		14%	0.713	0.792	36%		5%	0.838	**0.717**	44%	−0.002***
Netherlands	−0.006***	9%	0.864	0.755	48%		2%	0.728	0.974	44%	
Austria		11%	0.730	0.789	42%		5%	0.775	**0.775**	42%	
Belgium	−0.006**	6%	0.935	0.770	51%	0.003	0%	0.693	0.811	47%	
Slovakia		11%	0.724	0.796	41%		7%	0.848	**0.699**	53%	
Spain		3%	0.846	0.725	46%	0.016	**2%**	0.743	**0.758**	**50%**	
Italy	−0.009***	5%	0.953	0.751	50%	0.040	−3%	0.758	0.787	44%	
Ireland		4%	0.815	0.753	**45%**		–	–	–	–	
Portugal		–	–	–	–		4%	0.810	0.793	44%	−0.003***
Denmark		12%	0.728	0.785	35%		4%	0.858	0.697	46%	
Sweden		10%	0.720	0.814	42%		9%	0.805	0.748	50%	
Poland		9%	0.764	0.792	45%		5%	0.857	**0.709**	51%	−0.007*
Czech Rep.		15%	0.736	0.777	48%		1%	0.791	**0.705**	47%	
Hungary	−0.032**	8%	0.796	0.836	46%		**6%**	0.807	0.734	50%	
Turkey		–	–	–	–		3%	0.809	0.750	46%	
Russia	−0.047*	8%	0.668	0.886	41%		20%	0.789	0.642	57%	−0.012***
Australia	−0.008***	7%	0.778	0.788	47%		1%	0.780	0.833	47%	
New Zealand	−0.004	94%	1.307	1.250	44%		3%	0.745	**0.744**	39%	
Japan	−0.005***	6%	0.856	0.729	48%		–	–	–	–	
Hong Kong	−0.009***	15%	0.731	0.778	47%		3%	0.858	**0.739**	50%	
Korea	−0.026**	5%	0.709	0.876	44%		3%	0.740	0.779	44%	−0.011***
China	−0.011**	5%	0.804	0.792	50%		1%	0.762	0.768	51%	−0.008***
Philippines	−0.022*	3%	0.738	0.832	48%		3%	0.842	0.748	44%	−0.017*
Indonesia	−0.052*	8%	0.686	**0.995**	48%		4%	0.818	0.752	41%	−0.018*
Thailand	−0.013*	3%	0.800	0.822	49%		4%	0.814	0.774	40%	
Malaysia	−0.015*	3%	0.763	0.819	50%		2%	0.765	0.775	50%	−0.011***
South Africa		29%	0.812	1.287	54%		3%	0.847	0.704	45%	
Israel		69%	0.716	0.819	48%		3%	0.829	0.742	49%	−0.008***
Brazil	−0.019**	4%	0.721	0.771	42%		2%	0.886	0.709	37%	
Mexico	−0.023**	7%	0.700	0.796	46%		15%	0.859	0.750	56%	
Peru		81%	0.652	0.677	33%		2%	0.829	0.744	47%	
Chile	−0.015***	15%	0.690	0.779	46%		5%	0.824	0.739	44%	−0.003*
Colombia	−0.019**	4%	0.721	0.778	45%		**45%**	0.821	0.680	59%	

This table shows S&P500 estimators and goodness-of-fit statistics for lagged-explanatory variable model specifications corresponding to five sub-periods: (1) July 2005 to June 2010 (Before Jul 2010), (2) July 2010 to June 2014 (After Jul 2010), (3) July 2005 to June 2008 (Before Jul 2008), (4) January 2008 to December 2010 (Subprime Crisis), and (5) July 2010 to June 2013 (Euro Crisis). The explanatory variables for each period were selected according to 10% significance level when applying the Granger-causality tests. The Adjusted R^2 is calculated over the in-sample period, whereas we adopted the two-part split of the data for calculating Theil's U_1, Theil's U_2, and percent hit misses (PHM) out-of-sample statistics: estimation (2/3 of data) and out-of-sample test (1/3 of data). Better statistics than the corresponding contemporaneous models are highlighted in bold

Source: Capital IQ, Bloomberg, Datastream, and author's calculations

***, **, and * stand for significance at the 1%, 5%, and 10% level, respectively

				Subprime Crisis					Euro Crisis				
Adj. R^2	U_1	U_2	*PHM*	$sp500_t$	*Adj. R^2*	U_1	U_2	*PHM*	$sp500_t$	*Adj. R^2*	U_1	U_2	*PHM*
4%	0.762	0.846	46%		13%	0.735	0.771	46%		2%	0.782	0.828	34%
–	–	–	–		7%	0.801	0.736	47%		1%	0.622	0.891	36%
8%	0.755	0.840	42%	−0.004***	8%	0.834	0.780	44%		5%	0.776	**0.792**	44%
–	–	–	–	−0.006***	8%	0.855	0.729	46%		2%	0.707	**0.940**	45%
–	–	–	–		10%	0.737	0.779	44%		1%	**0.576**	**0.804**	44%
10%	0.711	0.811	39%		9%	**0.776**	0.750	45%	0.004	0%	0.663	0.909	48%
10%	0.706	0.818	35%		10%	0.725	0.792	36%		7%	0.799	**0.748**	53%
13%	**0.744**	0.766	41%		3%	0.838	0.726	51%	0.019	2%	0.821	**0.934**	47%
11%	0.723	0.789	38%	−0.009***	4%	0.937	0.754	51%		2%	0.725	0.856	44%
88%	**0.696**	**0.575**	**49%**		3%	**0.837**	0.738	42%		–	–	–	–
8%	0.870	0.746	46%		–	–	–	–		4%	0.687	0.792	39%
–	–	–	–		12%	0.730	0.777	**36%**		1%	0.677	**1.051**	49%
–	–	–	–		10%	0.712	0.810	38%		10%	0.775	**0.729**	**44%**
5%	0.880	0.862	54%		8%	0.733	0.796	45%		4%	0.746	0.778	42%
4%	0.766	0.857	**32%**		13%	0.692	0.740	36%	0.001	1%	0.834	**0.634**	51%
6%	0.757	0.796	38%	−0.033**	7%	0.775	0.814	44%		–	–	–	–
3%	0.834	0.742	44%		–	–	–	–		–	–	–	–
7%	0.940	0.739	44%	−0.054**	8%	0.648	0.883	33%		3%	0.823	0.784	44%
29%	0.622	0.833	38%	−0.008***	7%	0.764	0.786	49%	0.004	3%	0.719	0.803	43%
–	–	–	–		94%	1.090	1.135	38%		3%	0.657	**0.873**	**36%**
–	–	–	–	−0.006***	8%	0.842	0.714	45%		–	–	–	–
8%	0.758	0.777	32%	−0.010***	16%	0.725	0.778	45%		1%	0.863	**0.798**	44%
11%	0.906	0.714	48%	−0.027**	5%	0.694	0.883	44%		3%	0.733	**0.720**	43%
10%	0.845	0.742	54%	−0.011**	6%	0.783	0.794	40%		1%	0.862	0.779	43%
3%	0.872	0.690	48%	−0.030*	3%	0.744	0.878	49%	0.008	2%	0.843	0.785	49%
3%	0.896	0.761	46%	−0.052*	7%	0.679	**0.985**	46%		5%	0.798	0.774	48%
9%	0.803	0.732	39%	−0.021*	4%	0.792	0.886	49%	0.007	4%	0.790	0.779	42%
11%	0.872	0.684	52%	−0.015*	3%	0.757	0.827	47%		3%	0.803	0.731	43%
11%	0.749	0.768	43%		22%	1.343	2.055	33%		–	–	–	–
10%	0.818	0.740	39%		6%	0.747	0.781	46%		2%	0.821	0.825	34%
4%	0.814	0.763	46%	−0.019*	5%	0.716	0.772	41%		4%	0.843	0.730	53%
8%	0.748	0.789	34%		13%	0.623	0.815	45%		13%	0.830	0.735	49%
6%	0.781	0.765	35%	0.019	33%	0.592	0.874	44%		74%	0.840	0.752	63%
99%	1.362	1.102	46%	−0.015***	9%	0.670	0.818	35%		6%	0.826	0.745	49%
2%	0.849	0.759	38%	−0.018*	4%	0.726	0.771	45%		–	–	–	–

for the periods "Before Jul 2010", "After Jul 2010", "Before Jul 2008", "Subprime Crisis", and "Euro Crisis", Table 7.22 indicates that the lagged-variable model statistics are worse than those of the ARMA models for the July 2005–October 2012 period and noticeably worse than the corresponding contemporaneous model statistics (Tables 7.17, 7.18, 7.19, and 7.20). In addition, one can also notice that no coefficient of the S&P 500 appears to be statistically significant for the two overlapping subperiods "After Jul 2010" and "Euro Crisis".

7.6 Conclusion

I find that the S&P 500 is significant in explaining CDS spreads across a range of countries, especially emerging markets. Moreover, the coefficients of *Exchange Rate* and *Local Two-Year Yield* variables have the expected sign, and are also significant for some important investable markets. On the other hand, variables such as *VIX, Oil, Local Stock index, Slope, Local Slope*, and *Banking System* are rarely found to be statistically significant in explaining sovereign CDS spreads. Strikingly, goodness-of-fit and forecast accuracy are much better for emerging markets than for developed countries. Models with contemporaneous variables provide better statistical fitness than lagged-variable models. As for ARMA models, except for a few occurrences, their goodness-of-fit and forecast accuracy statistics are worse than for contemporaneous fundamental models across the board. When generating fundamental models with lagged variables, however, the engine comes up with goodness-of-fit statistics even worse than those of pure time series-generated models (ARMA).

If the past is any guide (so far I still believe it is!) and risk assessments are to be made on a weekly basis, the proposed large-scale, econometric-based framework can be used as part of an early warning tool. While using this framework in practice, however, some caveats should be kept in mind. Models with contemporaneous variables need one-week-ahead predictions as inputs. Accordingly, the results point out that forecasting initiatives should be focused on global variables, particularly those conveying the overall risk aversion or the general state of the global economy, like the VIX or the S&P 500 factors. Not least, Longstaff et al.'s (2011) advice is worth considering: as the estimation period is "characterized by excess global liquidity, prevalence of carry trades and reaching for yield in thesovereign market", approaches like the one proposed in this chapter should be taken with a grain of salt when applied to periods not subject to those market forces. In addition, models based on historical information do not necessarily unveil the true relationship between variables under unusual circumstances, regardless of how sophisticated they are.

As for additional robustness assessments, I recommend applying randomization tests on a selected set of explanatory variables and compare the forecast accuracy ex-post. For example, if 60% of predictions of changes in S&P 500 had been correct, what would have been the value for PHM? Besides, while this chapter provides some evidence for the overall neutrality in terms of the quantity of statistically significant S&P 500 coefficients, there is an opportunity to more extensively check the robustness of the algorithm to potential unintended consequences when modifying the set of instrumental variables in the GMM estimation.

Finally, for future research, one could test other banking sector-related variables. While the well-functioning of the banking sector is key to fostering the economic development of any country, the opposite has proved so far to hold true: banking crisis can lead to economic recession. Not as a coincidence, the factor $bank_{i,\,t}$ strikes as indicating double causality between the sovereign and its corresponding banking system CDS spreads in almost all cases for which I could achieve data for banks' CDS spreads, as shown in Table 7.5.[15] As it turns out, distresses in the banking sector, when pervasive and impacting too-systemic-to-fail banks, as for the 2007–2009 crisis and the European debt crisis, might lead to negative views on the debt sustainability of the corresponding jurisdiction, which would presumably manifest themselves by increasing CDS spreads. Playing a pivotal role in paving the way for economic growth or where having a specific mandate for guaranteeing financial stability, central banks, as lenders of last resort, have an incentive to bailing the banking sector out. In this chapter, although using the average of banks' CDS spreads as a proxy for the distress in the banking sector, it didn't show up as significant in most of the cases.[16] I conjecture that movements in sovereign CDS spreads might not have fully captured the dynamics of the banking sector risk, as its transmission to sovereign credit deterioration may occur more like a structural break than continuously in time.

Notes

1. Arce et al. (2012) find that due to the higher liquidity of the sovereign CDS market, the sovereign bonds led the price discovery process during the recent global financial crisis.
2. The Chinese Renminbi was officially added to the SDR basket on October 2016, after the sample period chosen for this paper analysis.
3. Longstaff et al. (2011), "How Sovereign is Sovereign Credit Risk?"
4. Notional amounts outstanding are defined as the gross nominal or notional value of all deals concluded and not yet settled on the reporting date. These amounts provide a measure of market size and a reference from which contractual payments are determined in derivatives markets.
5. According to the BIS, these declines are largely due to terminations of existing contracts, by netting gross notional outstanding through portfolio compression and clearing.
6. The total number of models tested comprises all possible permutations of factors labelled as "(*)", "**", or "&" in Table 7.5. For example, in the case of Italy, I have a set of 8 eligible factors (Table 7.5):*sp500*,*vix*,*Slope*,*oil*, *spread* – 1, *xr*, *localTY*, *localSlope*, and *bank*. Then, the engine is due to test as many as $\begin{pmatrix}1\\8\end{pmatrix}+\begin{pmatrix}2\\8\end{pmatrix}+\begin{pmatrix}3\\8\end{pmatrix}+\begin{pmatrix}4\\8\end{pmatrix}+\begin{pmatrix}5\\8\end{pmatrix}+\begin{pmatrix}6\\8\end{pmatrix}+\begin{pmatrix}7\\8\end{pmatrix}+\begin{pmatrix}8\\8\end{pmatrix}=2^8-1=255$ models.
7. A model nests another one when the first contains the same terms as the second and at least one additional term. I use the F-test (see Greene 2007) for testing the null hypothesis that the more comprehensive model does not contribute with additional information. When I reject this hypothesis at 5% significance level, then the more comprehensive model is not rejected to be superior to the nested one.
8. The only exceptions are Austria (*oil*), Australia (*oil*), and Russia (*stock*).
9. France, Finland, Austria, Belgium, Slovakia, Spain, Ireland, Sweden, Czech Republic, Australia, New Zealand, Japan, Philippines, Indonesia, Thailand, and Brazil.
10. The only exceptions are Hong Kong, Korea, and China.
11. The ARMA-model statistics are better in comparison to the corresponding lagged model (Table 7.8) in 88 out of 124 goodness-of-fit statistic values.
12. The corresponding complete model specifications are not shown, but are available at request.
13. Even generating different models for Hungary, Israel, and Colombia, their S&P500 estimators differ by less than 5%.
14. The corresponding complete model specifications are not shown, but are available at request.

15. The exception is Germany, for which we cannot reject that the variable *bank* is weakly exogenous.
16. The exceptions are Hong Kong, Korea, and China.

References

Alsakka, R., & Gwilym, O. (2010). Leads and lags in sovereign credit ratings. *Journal of Banking and Finance, 34*(11), 2614–2626.

Arce, O., Mayordomo, S., & Peña, J.I. (2012). Credit-risk valuation in the sovereign CDS and bonds markets: Evidence from the Euro area crisis. Retrieved from SSRN: https://ssrn.com/abstract=1896297 or https://doi.org/10.2139/ssrn.1896297.

Baum, C. (2003). *An introduction to modern econometrics using Stata*. College Station: Stata Press.

Box, G., Jenkins, G., & Reinsel, G. (1994). *Time series analysis: Forecast and control*. Hoboken: John Wiley & Sons.

Broner, F., Didier, T., Erce, A., & Schmukler, S. (2013). Gross capital flows: Dynamics and crises. *Journal of Monetary Economics, 60*(1), 113–133.

Broto, C., Díaz-Cassou, J., & Erce, A. (2011). Measuring and explaining the volatility of capital flows toward emerging countries. *Journal of Banking and Finance, 35*(8), 1941–1953.

Calvo, G. (2007). *Crisis in emerging market economies: A global perspective*. NBER Working Paper No. 11305.

Enders, W. (2004). *Applied econometric time series*. Hoboken: John Wiley & Sons.

Granger, C. (1969). Investigating causal relations by econometric models and cross-spectral methods. *Econometrica, 37*(3), 424–438.

Greene, W. (2007). *Econometric analysis*. New York: Pearson.

Ljung, G., & Box, G. E. P. (1978). On a measure of a lack of fit in time series models. *Biometrika, 65*(2), 297–303.

Longstaff, F. A., Pan, J., Pedersen, L. H., & Singleton, K. (2011). How sovereign is sovereign credit risk? *American Economic Journal: Macroeconomics, 3*(2), 75–103.

Pan, J., & Singleton, K. (2008). Default and recovery implicit in the term structure of sovereign CDS spreads. *Journal of Finance, 63*(5), 2345–2384.

Remolona, E., Scatigna, M., & Wu, E. (2008). The dynamic pricing of sovereign risk in emerging markets: Fundamentals and risk aversion. *Journal of Fixed Income, 17*(4), 57–71.

Westerlund, J., & Thuraisamy, K. (2016). Panel multi-predictor test procedures with an application to emerging market sovereign risk. *Emerging Markets Review, 28*, 44–60.

White, H. (1980). A heteroskedasticity-consistent covariance matrix estimator and a direct test for heteroskedasticity. *Econometrica, 48*(4), 817–838.

CHAPTER 8

Long-Term Expected Credit Spreads and Excess Returns

Erik Hennink

8.1 Introduction

Expected credit spreads and excess returns of corporate bonds over government bonds could be used by investors to construct client portfolios. In this chapter, we estimate long-term expected credit spreads and excess returns for a variety of US corporate bond ratings and maturities. The long-term expected credit spreads and excess returns are estimated using an extension of the risk-neutral valuation model of Fons (1994). The model is calibrated on long historical data over the 1919–2014 period, a sample period that is much longer than used in most other papers analyzing credit spreads and excess returns.

The shape of the credit spread term structures (CSTS) has been shown to depend on the credit rating of the issuer. While the CSTS of high-quality corporate bonds could either be upward-sloping or hump-shaped, those for low credit quality corporate bonds are downward sloping; see

E. Hennink (✉)
Ortec Finance Research Center, Rotterdam, The Netherlands
e-mail: erik.hennink@ortec-finance.com

N. Bulusu et al. (eds.), *Advances in the Practice of Public Investment Management*, https://doi.org/10.1007/978-3-319-90245-6_8

Merton (1974) and Duffie and Singleton (1999). The shapes of the term structure of credit spreads have been confirmed by the empirical work of Sarig and Warga (1989), Fons (1994), and Bohn (1999).[1]

Investors in corporate bonds require a premium for default risk, referred to as the "default spread". It is well known that the default spread is only a small fraction of total spread (or the "corporate bond basis"); this is referred to as the "credit spread puzzle". Huang and Huang (2012) and De Jong and Driessen (2012) show that the corporate bond basis is related to liquidity effects, and Elton et al. (2001) show that a substantial part of the corporate bond basis can be explained by tax effects. Since long-term investors are expected to earn the corporate bond basis, we therefore include the basis in our estimation of the spread in our risk-neutral valuation model.

We find that investors require a higher default spread for investment grade (IG) corporate bonds than of high-yield (HY) corporate bonds for the same amount of default risk. This may be because investors appear to be more risk-averse when investing in IG corporate bond compared to HY bonds as investors: the risk-neutral default probabilities of IG- (HY-) rated bonds are 2.3 times (1.4 times) higher than their physical probabilities. These findings are similar to the existing literature; see, for example, Giesecke et al. (2011) and Driessen (2005).

We show that the shapes of the calibrated long-term (LT) expected CSTS are in line with the existing literature (Merton 1974; Duffie and Singleton 1999; Sarig and Warga 1989; Fons 1994). The shapes of the calibrated LT-expected CSTS are (1) upward-sloping for high credit ratings ranging from the AAA to BBB ratings, (2) humped-shaped for the BB and B middle-graded ratings, and (3) downward sloping for the CCC speculative rating. Furthermore, we find that the calibrated LT-expected CSTS are in line with the historical average CSTS over the 1988–2014 period and capture the positive skewness in the historical distribution of CSTS.

Table 8.1 presents the expected annualized buy-and-hold excess credit returns of ten-year corporate bonds in percentage and their corresponding par credit spreads, following the approach of De Jong and Driessen (2012) and Bongaerts et al. (2011). These estimates for the expected credit excess returns are in line with the findings of Hull et al. (2005) and Giesecke et al. (2011). Our expected excess returns for IG bonds are approximately 0.4% higher than historical average credit excess returns as documented by Ng and Phelps (2011) and Ilmanen (2011). The difference between the LT-expected buy-and-hold and historical average credit excess return for

IG bonds can largely be explained by the periodic rebalancing of constituents in the corporate bond benchmark as the result of rating upgrades and downgrades. Ng and Phelps (2011) show that relaxing the requirement of rebalancing gives 0.4% additional return for IG benchmark, which is approximately the documented difference between the LT-expected and historical average excess returns.

This chapter contributes to the existing literature in the following ways. First, the model is calibrated on much longer historical data sample. Second, we introduce a risk-neutral valuation model including the corporate bond basis, which captures the main stylized facts of CSTS and excess-return term structures and can straightforwardly be applied to determine expected credit spreads and excess returns for other regions than the US. Third, we extend the findings of the long-term expected credit spread and excess returns of Giesecke et al. (2011) by estimating the spreads and excess returns for multiple ratings and maturities. Fourth, our model can straightforwardly be applied to estimate the LT-expected credit spreads and excess returns for other regions than the US. These results have many uses for portfolio managers, for example, to construct efficient portfolios for long-term investors.

In the remainder of this chapter we provide more detail on these results. Section 8.2 introduces a risk-neutral model to calibrate long-term credit spreads and excess returns for multiple ratings and maturities. Section 8.3 outlines the data that is used to calibrate the risk-neutral model. Section 8.4 describes the calibration methods of the risk-neutral model. In Sect. 8.5, discusses the calibration results of the long-term expected credit spreads and excess returns for the US market. Finally, Sect. 8.6 concludes.

8.2 Risk-Neutral Valuation Model

8.2.1 *Defaultable Zero-Coupon Bond Excluding the Bond Basis*

The price of a default-free zero-coupon bond is equal to the discounted face value. Under the assumption of arbitrage-free and complete markets, the price of default-free zero-coupon bond with unit face value and maturity T at time t, $P(t,T)$, is given by

$$P(t,T) = \mathbb{E}_t^{\mathbb{Q}}\left[\frac{B(t)}{B(T)}\right] = B(t)\mathbb{E}_t^{\mathbb{Q}}\left[\exp\left(-\int_t^T r(s)\,\mathrm{d}s\right)\right],$$

where $\mathbb{Q}$ is the risk-neutral probability measure, $r(t)$ the instantaneous short-rate at time t, $B(t)$ is the money savings-account at time t. We define the initial money savings-account, $B(0)$, to be equal to 1.

The price of a defaultable zero-coupon bond is the sum of defaultable discounted face value plus the recovery value of the bond at an uncertain moment in time only when the issuer goes into default before the maturity of the bond. Under the assumption of fractional recovery of face value, Lando (1998) shows that the price of a defaultable zero-coupon bond with credit rating indexed by i, unit face value and maturity T at time t, $D_i(t, T)$, is given by

$$D_i(t,T) = \mathbb{E}_t^{\mathbb{Q}}\left[\frac{B(t)}{B(T)} 1_{(\tau>T)}\right] + \int_t^T \mathbb{E}_t^{\mathbb{Q}}\left[\frac{B(t)}{B(s)} R(s)\lambda_i^Q(s)\mathrm{d}s\right], \tag{8.1}$$

where τ is the time-of-default, $\lambda_i^Q(t)$ the instantaneous risk-neutral hazard rate of rating i at time t and $R(t)$ the recovery rate at time t.[2]

Next, we make the common assumptions as in O'Kane (2010) that the short rate process and hazard rate process are independent of each other and that the recovery rate is an exogenously given constant. Using these assumptions, we can write Eq. 8.1 as

$$D_i(t,T) = P(t,T)Q_i(t,T) + \bar{R}\int_t^T P(t,s)\lambda_i^Q(s)\mathrm{d}s, \tag{8.2}$$

where $\bar{R}$ is the expected recovery rate and $Q_i(t, T)$ the cumulative risk-neutral default probability of rating i up to time T. This expression assumes that investors are only compensated for interest rate and credit risk.

8.2.2 *Defaultable Zero-Coupon Bond Including the Bond Basis*

We include a maturity independent bond basis in our model by discounting corporate bond cash flows with an adjusted discount factor following Longstaff et al. (2005), which allows the model to capture any liquidity or other non-default-related components in corporate bond prices. We assume a maturity independent bond basis for simplicity and because there is at the moment no consensus in the literature whether liquidity premia are higher or lower for short-maturity compared to long-maturity corporate bonds.[3] We assume that the continuously compounded bond basis is an exogenously given constant depending on the rating *i*, defined as l_i^c. The expression of the defaultable bond price in Eq. 8.2 including the bond basis then becomes

$$D_i(t,T) = P(t,T)Q_i(t,T)Z_i(t,T) + \bar{R}\int_t^T P(t,s)Z_i(t,s)\lambda_i^Q(s)\mathrm{d}s,$$

with

$$Z_i(t,T) = \exp\left(-\int_t^T l_i^c \mathrm{d}s\right) = \exp\left[-l_i^c(T-t)\right],$$

where the continuously compounded bond basis l_i^c can be expressed in terms of *f*-frequency compounded bond basis l_i^f as follows:

$$l_i^c = f\log\left(1+\frac{l_i^f}{f}\right). \tag{8.3}$$

8.2.3 *Modeling Default Probabilities*

To model the physical and risk-neutral default probabilities of a reference entity, we use the first jump of a Poisson process with time-inhomogeneous intensities as in O'Kane (2010). The physical and risk-neutral probability that the reference entity with rating *i* survives up to time *T* at time *t*, $W_i(t, T)$, and $Q_i(t, T)$, respectively, are equal to

$$W_i(t,T) = \mathbb{E}_t^{\mathbb{P}}\left(1_{(\tau>T)}\right) = \exp\left(-\int_t^T \lambda_i^P(s)\mathrm{d}s\right),$$

$$Q_i(t,T) = \mathbb{E}_t^{\mathbb{Q}}\left(1_{(\tau>T)}\right) = \exp\left(-\int_t^T \lambda_i^Q(s)\mathrm{d}s\right),$$

where $\mathbb{P}$ is the physical probability measure and $\lambda_i^P(t)$ is the physical hazard rate of bond with rating *i* at time *t*.

The physical and risk-neutral default hazard rates are connected to each other through the Radon–Nikodym derivative, which allows us to change equivalent martingale measure $\mathbb{P}$ into $\mathbb{Q}$:

$$\Lambda_i^{\mathbb{P}\to\mathbb{Q}}(t) = \left.\frac{\mathrm{d}\mathbb{Q}}{\mathrm{d}\mathbb{P}}\right|_i = \exp\left[\int_0^t \left(\lambda_i^P(s) - \lambda_i^Q(s)\right)\mathrm{d}s\right].$$

For simplicity, we assume that the risk-neutral hazard rates are a constant multiple of the physical hazard rates, such that

$$\lambda_i^Q(t) = \theta_i \lambda_i^P(t),$$

where θ the price of risk parameter. With this assumption, the expression of the risk-neutral survival probability becomes,

$$Q_i(t,T) = \exp\left(-\theta_i \int_t^T \lambda_i^P(s)\,\mathrm{d}s\right) = W_i(t,T)^{\theta_i}. \tag{8.4}$$

8.2.4 *Defaultable Coupon-Paying Bond*

A defaultable coupon-paying bond can be decomposed as the sum of defaultable zero-coupon bonds. The price of a defaultable f-frequency coupon-paying bond with rating i, unit face value, annualized compounded coupon as percentage of the face value $c_i^f(T)$, and payment schedule[4] $T_1, \ldots, T_n$ at the time of the bond issuance $T_0 = t$, $V(t, T)$ is

$$\begin{aligned} V_i(t,T) = P(t,T)Q_i(t,T)Z_i(t,T) + c_i^f(T)\sum_{k=1} fP(t,T_k)Z_i \\ (t,T_k)Q_i(t,T_k) + \overline{R}\int_t^T P(t,s)Z_i(t,s)\lambda_i^Q(s)\,\mathrm{d}s, \end{aligned} \tag{8.5}$$

where $f = n/T$ is the accrual fraction equal to the coupon period of the bond such that $f = \frac{1}{2}$ denotes semi-annual coupons. Note that we assume that accrued coupons are not recovered. Substituting Eq. 8.4 in Eq. 8.5, we end up with the price of the defaultable coupon-paying bond

$$V_i(t,T) = P(t,T)W_i(t,T)^{\theta_i} Z_i(t,T) + c_i^f(T)\sum_{k=1}^{n} fP(t,T_k)Z(t,T_k)W_i(t,T_k)^{\theta_i} + \overline{R}\int_t^T P(t,s)Z_i(t,s)\theta_i\lambda_i^P(s)\mathrm{d}s. \tag{8.6}$$

The par coupon, $c_i^f(T)$, is defined as the coupon of a bond that equals the face value of the bond, that is, $V(t, T) \equiv 1$. We define the par coupon as the sum of the liquid default-free coupon, $r^f(T)$, and the par credit spread of the illiquid defaultable bond, $s_i^f(T)$. The par coupon is given by,

$$c_i^f(T) = r^f(T) + s_i^f(T) = r^f(T) + l_i^f + d_i^f(T), \tag{8.7}$$

where the par credit spread is decomposed into the bond basis l_i^f and par default spread $d_i^f(T)$.

8.3 Data

8.3.1 Raw Data

From exhibit 32 of Moody's default report (Ou 2015), we obtain historical global cumulative default probabilities for AAA, AA, A, BBB, BB, B, and CCC rated bonds for maturity from 1 to 20 years over the 1920–2014 period. Using exhibit 20 and 21 of the Moody's default report, we obtain annual average recovery rates of all bonds and senior unsecured bonds over the 1982–2014 period.

As a proxy for risk-free interest rates, we extract the monthly average of daily yields on US government bonds from the Federal Reserve Board's (FED) Selected Interest Rates H.15 statistical release for the three-month (3 M) and 6 M treasury bills and one-year (1Y), 2Y, 3Y, 5Y, 7Y, 10Y, 20Y, and 30Y constant maturities from April 1953 to December 2014. We extend the bond yields of all maturities except the 20Y and 30Y maturities further to April 1941 using GlobalFinancialData (GFD) and the 3 M and 10Y maturities further to January 1919.[5] We also obtain the monthly average yield on the composite of long-term government bonds with a maturity over ten years from the FED from January 1925 onward and from January 1919 to January 1925 from GFD. Using GFD, we follow Giesecke et al. (2011) and further extend the long-term composite government bond yield from March 1857 to December 1918 with yields on high-grade New England municipal bonds from March 1857 to December 1914 and the yield of high-grade Bond Buyer municipal bonds from January 1915 to December 1918. Finally, we extract the monthly weighted average life (WAL) maturity of the composite long-term government bond index from Bank of America Merrill Lynch (ML) from December 1988 to December 2014.[6]

The monthly average yields on Moody's US long-term corporate bond benchmarks of the four individual IG ratings are obtained from GFD over the period of January 1919 to December 2014. Using GFD, we follow Giesecke et al. (2011) and further extend the AAA corporate bond yield from March 1857 to December 1918 with the yield on long-term high-quality railroad bonds. From December 1988 to December 2014, we extract the monthly average yield and WAL maturity for the individual and composite US IG and HY ratings for multiple non-overlapping maturity bucket benchmarks (1–3Y, 3–5Y, 5–7Y, 7–10Y, 10–15Y, and 15Y+), the 10Y+ maturity bucket benchmark, and the combination of all-maturities bucket benchmarks from ML. From ML, we also obtain the option-adjusted credit spreads for the composite and individual IG and HY rating benchmarks and all the described maturity buckets from December 1996 to December 2014.

For historical measures of the bond basis of multiple ratings, we rely on the papers of Huang and Huang (2012), Chen et al. (2014), and De Jong and Driessen (2012) who quantify the bond basis. As an alternative measure for the bond basis, we calculate the average historical difference between the option-adjusted credit and credit default swap (CDS) spreads. As indicated by Ilmanen (2011), CDSs are more liquid and present a more generic view of a firm's default risk than corporate bonds. Therefore, we extract 5Y CDS spreads from Barclays Capital IG index and HY index that are available from March 2004 and September 2005 to December 2014, respectively.

8.3.2 *Smooth Marginal Default Probabilities*

The historical annual marginal default probabilities are not monotonous with term, in contrast to the popular assumption in the literature (see Duffie and Singleton 1999). For example, the marginal default probability of the AAA and AA ratings is higher in years 2–8 than for years 9–15. To prevent using data that do not conform to that commonly assumed in the theoretical literature we follow, we adjust the marginal default probabilities by fitting a smooth function through the raw data.

The estimation of smooth marginal default probabilities is set up as follows. A fully specified one-year Markov transition matrix is estimated by minimizing the weighted sum of the squared differences between the fitted and historical cumulative default probabilities. The weight assigned to each time period is the ratio of the largest cumulative default probability across all ratings and horizons divided by the cumulative default probability of a specific rating and horizon to ensure that each cumulative is relatively equally important in the minimization.[7]

$$
\begin{aligned}
\min_{\Gamma} \quad & \sum_{I=1}^{i-1}\sum_{j=1}^{H}\frac{d_{I-1,H}}{d_{i,j}}\left(\Gamma_{i,I}^{(j)}-d_{i,j}\right)^2 & & \\
\text{s.t.} \quad & 0 \le \Gamma_{k,l} \le 1, & & k,l = 1,\ldots,I \\
& \sum_{k=1}^{I}\Gamma_{i,k} = 1, & & k = 1,\ldots,I \\
& \Gamma_{I,k} = 0, & & k = 1,\ldots,I-1 \\
& \Gamma_{I,I} = 1, & &
\end{aligned}
\quad , \qquad (8.8)
$$

where $d_{i,j}$ is the historical j-year cumulative default probability of rating i, H the maximum horizon in years, I the number of ratings, and Γ the one-year Markov transition square $I \times I$-matrix. The rating letters correspond to rating numbers as follows: {AAA, AA, ..., CCC, D(efault)} = {1, 2, ..., 7, 8}. The last row of Γ is enforced to equal [0...0 1] which reflects the absorbing state of default.

The R^2 of the fitted marginal and cumulative default probabilities with respect to the original values per rating are reported in Table 8.2. The fitted cumulative default probabilities are close to the original ones as the R^2 is above 0.95 for each rating, indicating that our smoothed estimates do not greatly distort the overall pattern of default probabilities. The use of our smoothed estimates, however, has the advantage that it ensures that we obtain smooth CSTS.

8.3.3 Recovery Rates

There are only small differences between the average recovery rates of senior unsecured bonds and all bonds from 2000 onward. The average recovery rate of senior unsecured bonds across different ratings is around 38%, though it takes a few years to obtain the recovery. Including the delay in recovery, the discounted recovery rate is 35% for all senior unsecured ratings.

8.3.4 Government Bond Yields and Term Structure

We describe the risk-free yield term structure in a particular month using the Nelson–Siegel (NS) functional form:

$$y_t(T) = \beta_{1,t} + \beta_{2,t}\left(\frac{1-\exp^{-\lambda_t T}}{\lambda_t T}\right) + \beta_{3,t}\left(\frac{1-\exp^{-\lambda_t T}}{\lambda_t T} - \exp^{-\lambda_t T}\right), \tag{8.9}$$

where $y_t(T)$ the yield at time t for maturity T in years, $\beta_{i,t}$ latent dynamic factor i at time t and λ_t the exponential decay rate at time t. Following Diebold and Li (2006), we assume a fixed and exponential decay rate equal to $\lambda = 0.7308$. We estimate Eq. 8.9 in a particular month using all available constant maturities yields with ordinary least squares. The NS fitted yields are reported in Table 8.3. The fit of the NS term structures is generally high with an average (median) cross sectional R^2 of 0.92 (0.97) from 1941 onward.

8.3.5 Credit Spreads

8.3.5.1 Extended Sample of Option-Adjusted Credit Spreads

The most accurate measure of the credit spread is the option-adjusted spread (OAS) of ML as it is duration-matched and corrected for optionality. The ML OAS is available from December 1996 onward, and we extend the series up to December 1988 for all the available ML corporate bond maturity bucket benchmarks using the following estimation procedure inspired by Giesecke et al. (2011). In a particular month, we calculate the difference between the yield of the ML corporate bond maturity bucket benchmark and government bond yield that is estimated with Eq. 8.9 by using the WAL maturity of the corporate bond benchmark. For the 10Y+ and 15Y+ corporate bond maturity bucket benchmarks, we use the yield of the composite long-term government bond index as it better matches the duration of these maturity buckets than the government bond yield that corresponds to its WAL maturity. For the IG ratings, we obtain the longest available history of the OASs of the Moody's long-term corporate bond benchmarks by subtracting the LT composite government bond yields from the Moody's long-term corporate bond yields (as suggested by using Giesecke et al. 2011). Descriptive statistics of the constructed credit spread series are reported in Table 8.4, and Fig. 8.1 shows a graphical representation of the series.

Fig. 8.1 Graphical presentation of the credit spreads of the individual IG and HY rating for different sample periods

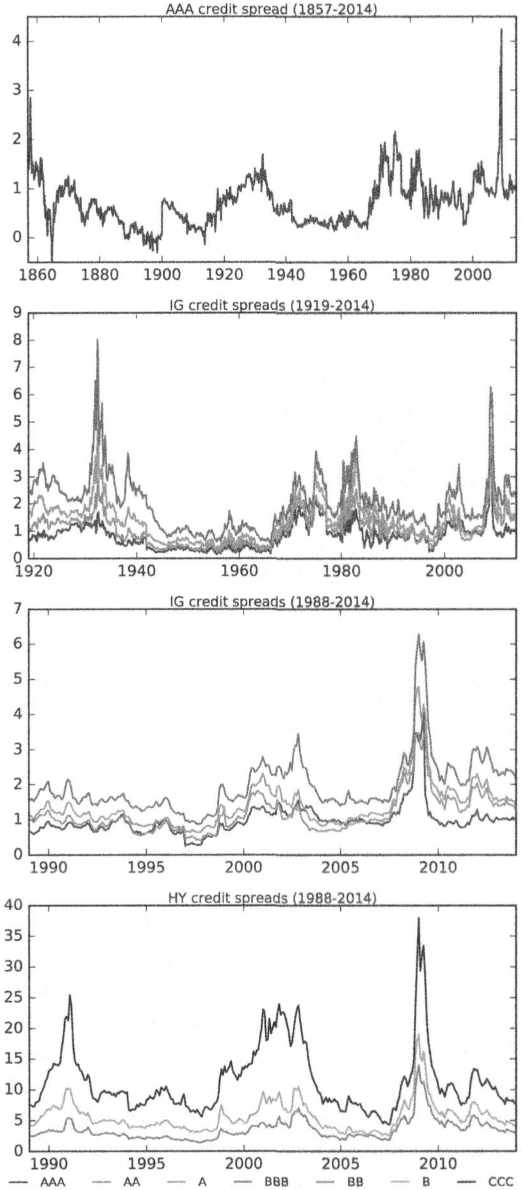

Credit spreads are positively skewed, such that average spreads are higher than median spreads. The average credit spreads of the A and BBB ratings are almost the same over the longest available sample compared to the 1988–2014 sample period, whereas the average credit spreads for the AAA and AA are lower for the 1998–2014 sample. The average of the average AAA and BBB credit spreads over 1919–2014 equals 144 bps, which is in line with Giesecke et al. (2011) who find an average credit spread of 153.3 bps over 1866–2008.

The average WAL maturities of the IG 10Y+ maturity bucket benchmarks are about 25 years over 1988–2014, whereas the WAL maturities of the HY all-maturity benchmarks range from 9 for BB to 7 for CCC. Although we do not have direct information of the WAL maturities regarding the corporate bond benchmarks before 1988, we examine the WAL maturity of the LT composite government bond index with maturities over ten years to get an indication for the WAL maturities of the IG corporate bond benchmarks before 1988. To get an indication of the WAL maturity of the LT composite government bond index before 1988, we compare the average yield of the LT government bond index with the average yield of the constant maturities indices using Table 8.3. Although the WAL maturity of the LT government bond index is above 20 years from 1988 onward, the average yield of the LT government bond index seems closer in line with the average yield of the 15-year constant maturity index for longer historical sample periods. Therefore, this might also suggest that the WAL maturities of the IG corporate bond benchmarks before 1988 are close to 15 years.

8.3.5.2 Credit Spread Term Structures

We construct NS CSTS for all individual corporate bond rating benchmarks from December 1988 to December 2014 in the same manner as for the government bonds in Eq. 8.9. For each rating, we take the credit spreads of all the available corporate bond non-overlapping maturity bucket benchmarks and their corresponding WAL maturities in a particular month and estimate the NS parameters using ordinary least squares. The cross-sectional explanatory power of the fitted CSTS is high with an average (median) R^2 of roughly more than 0.75 (0.80) for all individual ratings except for the AAA rating. The lower R^2 of the AAA rating might be caused by the fact that this rating contains the least number of issuers compared to all other individual ratings, especially for some particular maturity buckets. Although we do not use these constructed average

CSTS in the calibration of the pricing model of Sect. 8.2, we take them as reference to compare them with the LT-expected CSTS we construct in the remainder of this chapter.

8.3.6 *Bond Basis*

There are some papers that quantify the bond basis. Huang and Huang (2012) find that credit risk accounts only for about 20–30% of the observed credit spreads of IG bonds, whereas the fraction is higher for high yield spreads. Chen et al. (2014) document comparable results for the small fractions of pure default risk for IG bonds and higher fractions for HY bonds. De Jong and Driessen (2012) quantify that the liquidity risk premium of long-term IG and HY bonds is 60 bps and 150 bps, respectively. In Table 8.5, we summarize the main findings of Huang and Huang (2012), De Jong and Driessen (2012), and Chen et al. (2007) regarding the quantification of the bond basis. Based on the results of Huang and Huang (2012), De Jong and Driessen (2012), and Chen et al. (2007), the average bond basis is approximately 60, 66, 78, and 97 bps for the AAA, AA, A, and BBB ratings, respectively.

We compare these findings of the bond basis with an estimate for the bond basis that is calculated as the average difference between the 5Y spread of the credit default swap (CDS) index and 5Y credit spread of the corresponding composite corporate bond benchmark. We estimate an IG bond basis of 95 bps based on the average CDS-credit spread difference. As the composite IG benchmark is tilted to the A and BBB ratings, our estimate for the A and BBB bond basis of 78 and 97 bps, respectively, is in line with the alternative CDS-credit spread estimate of the IG bond basis.

8.4 Methodology

8.4.1 *Model Parameters*

Based on the historical data analysis, we assume some of the model parameters of the defaultable corporate coupon-paying bond in Eq. 8.6, namely:

1. We use the smoothed cumulative default probabilities estimated in Sect. 8.3.2 in place of the physical cumulative default probabilities $W_i(t, T)$.
2. The expected constant recovery rate $\bar{R}$ of 35% (see Sect. 8.3.3).

3. The par yields of 3 M, 10Y, and 20Y maturities of the risk-free interest rate term structure equal to 3.55%, 4.95%, and 5.95%, respectively. The risk-free par yield of 3 M and 10Y maturities is based on the historical average over the 1919–2014 period. The 20Y–10Y term spread is assumed to be 0.2%, which is in line with the longest available historical sample. With the assumptions of the three par yields, we solve the three NS β-parameters of Eq. 8.9 and determine the risk-free par yields $r^f(T)$ for all other maturities. The risk-free zero yields, required in $P(t, T)$, are obtained by bootstrapping the risk-free par yield term structure assuming annual coupons.
4. The par credit spreads $s_i^1(T)$ of 0.80%, 1.05%, 1.40%, and 2.05% of annual ($f = 1$) coupon-paying defaultable corporate bonds with AAA, AA, A, and BBB ratings, respectively, and a corresponding maturity of $T = 15$ years. The assumed par credit spreads of the individual IG ratings are based on the historical averages over the maximum overlapping sample from 1919 to 2014 and rounded to multiples of 0.05%. The assumption of the maturity of 15 years is based on paragraph 3.5.1.
5. The par credit spreads $s_i^1(T)$ of 3.50%, 5.55%, and 11.35% for annual coupon-paying defaultable corporate bonds with BB, B, and CCC ratings, respectively, and corresponding maturity of $T = 9$, 8, and 7 years, respectively. The assumed par credit spreads of the individual HY ratings are based on the historical averages over the maximum overlapping sample from 1988 to 2014 and again rounded to multiples of 0.05%. We assume that the individual HY average credit spreads over the 1988–2014 period would be approximately the same over the 1919–2014 period. This assumption is based on the observation that the average credit spreads of the A and BBB ratings are approximately the same measured over 1919–2014 and 1988–2014 sample periods. The assumptions of the WAL maturities are based on the historical average over the 1988–2014 period and rounded to whole years.
6. The par bond bases l_i^1 of 0.6%, 0.7%, 0.85%, 1.10%, 1.40%, 1.15%, and 1.00% for annual coupon-paying defaultable corporate bonds with AAA, AA, A, BBB, BB, B, and CCC ratings, respectively. These assumptions are based on the average bond basis of Huang and Huang (2012) and L. Chen et al. (2007) from Table 8.5 and rounded to 0.05%. We do not directly consider De Jong and Driessen (2012) as they do not report rating varying bond bases, although our assumptions for the bond basis of the aggregate IG

and HY benchmarks are in line with their results. With the assumed par bond bases l_i^f, we can calculate the continuously compounded bond basis l_i^c using Eq. 8.3 and $Z_i(t, T)$ discount factors.

Table 8.6 summarizes the model assumptions.

8.4.2 Calibration Credit Spread Term Structures

In order to calibrate the term structure of annual coupon-paying ($f = 1$) par credit spreads $s_i^1(T)$ per rating following Eq. 8.7, we only require information regarding the default spread $d_i^1(T)$ as we assume maturity independent bond bases per rating l_i^1 in Sect. 8.4.1. For every rating i, we assume a par credit spread $s_i^1(T)$ of the annual coupon-paying defaultable corporate bond for one particular maturity T. For the IG ratings, we made an assumption for the par credit spreads $s_i^1(T)$ for the $T = 15$-year maturity and we made par credit spreads assumptions for a maturity of $T = 9$, 8, and 7 year for the BB, B, and CCC ratings. Adding the par credit spread $s_i^1(T)$ to the assumption of the liquid default-free par coupon $r^1(T)$ gives to total par coupon $c^1(T)$ following Eq. 8.7. So, the total par coupon is assumed to be known for one particular maturity per rating and the other maturities have to be calibrated. In Sect. 8.4.1, we discussed assumptions regarding the prices of risk-free zero-coupon bonds $P(t, T)$, physical default probabilities $W_i(t, T)$, recovery rate $\bar{R}$, and additional discount factors $Z_i(t, T)$ so that we only need to calibrate the price of risk parameter θ_i before we can calibrate the full term structure of par default and credit spreads.

The price of risk parameter θ_i is calibrated as follows for a particular rating i. For every rating i, we assume the total par coupon $c^1(T)$ for one particular maturity T to be known. With this assumption and the other assumptions regarding $P(t, T)$, $Z_i(t, T)$, $W_i(t, T)$, and $\bar{R}$, only the price of risk parameter θ_i is the unknown parameter in the expression of the par bond price of the defaultable corporate bond of Eq. 8.6. We first discretize this expression of the par bond price of Eq. 8.6 with the trapezoidal rule as follows

$$
\begin{aligned}
V_i(t,T) &= P(t,T)W_i(t,T)^{\theta_i} Z_i(t,T) + c_i^1(T)\sum_{k=1}^{n} P(t,T_k)Z_i(t,T_k)W_i(t,T_k)^{\theta_i} \\
&\quad + \bar{R}\sum_{k=1}^{n}\frac{P(t,T_k)Z_i(t,T_k)+P(t,T_{k-1})Z_i(t,T_{k-1})}{2}\begin{bmatrix} W_i(t,T_{k-1})^{\theta_i} \\ -W_i(t,T_k)^{\theta_i}\end{bmatrix} \\
&= 1.
\end{aligned}
$$

We calibrate θ_i such that this expression equals 1.

With the calibrated θ_i, we calibrate the default spreads $d^1(T)$ for all other maturities using Eq. 8.7. The only unknown parameter for the corporate bond with particular maturity T is the par default spread $d_i^1(T)$. So, for every maturity T, we calibrate $d_i^1(T)$ such that the bond price equals 1. Adding the calibrated par default spread to the par bond basis gives the par credit spread.

8.4.3 Expected Credit Excess Returns

To estimate the expected excess returns of corporate bonds over government bonds, we follow the procedure of De Jong and Driessen (2012) and Bongaerts et al. (2011). The method works as follows. First, we approximate an annual coupon-paying defaultable bond with maturity T and rating i by a defaultable zero-coupon bond that has the same duration U as the coupon-paying defaultable bond. The price of the defaultable zero-coupon bond with maturity U equals

$$D_i(t,U) = P(t,U)Z_i(t,U)\left[Q_i(t,U) + \bar{R}\left(1 - Q_i(t,U)\right)\right] = \frac{1}{\left(1 + y_{iU}\right)^U},$$

where y_{iU} is the annual compounded yield of the defaultable bond with rating i and maturity U. This expression assumes that default losses are incurred at maturity. We express the price of the liquid default-free zero-coupon bond with maturity U as

$$P(t,U) = \frac{1}{\left(1 + y_{gU}\right)^U},$$

where y_{gU} is the annual compounded yield of the default-free government bond with maturity U. The expected real-world cumulative return of holding the defaultable zero-coupon bond at time t up to maturity U is

$$\left(1 + y_{iU}\right)^U \left[W_i(t,U) + \bar{R}\left(1 - W_i(t,U)\right)\right]. \tag{8.10}$$

Next, we annualize the expected cumulative return in Eq. 8.10 and subtract the annual expected return of the default-free zero-coupon government bond. This gives the annual expected real-world excess return of the defaultable zero-coupon bond with rating i and maturity U, $\mathbb{E}_t^{\mathbb{P}}\left(r_{iU}\right)$, as follows:

$$\mathbb{E}_t^{\mathbb{P}}\left(r_{iU}\right)=\left(1+y_{iU}\right)\left[W_i\left(t,U\right)+\bar{R}\left(1-W_i\left(t,U\right)\right)\right]^{1/U}-\left(1+y_{gU}\right). \quad (8.11)$$

Note that these are expected excess return for a buy-and-hold strategy of corporate bond investments. Portfolio rebalancing following upgrades and downgrades are not incorporated in these expected excess returns.

8.5 Results

8.5.1 Credit Spread Term Structures

The calibrated price of risk parameters θ_i per rating, reported in Table 8.7, is 4.44, 2.18, 2.36, 2.22, 1.54, 1.39, and 1.29 for the AAA, AA, A, BBB, BB, B, and CCC ratings, respectively.[8] Our calibrated price of risk parameters of the IG bonds is in line with the existing literature. Giesecke et al. (2011) find a price of risk parameter of 2.04 for the composite of IG bonds based over a 1866–2008 sample, and Driessen (2005) reports price of risk parameters of 1.83, 2.61, and 2.37 for AA, A, and BBB rated bonds, respectively, based on the 1991–2000 sample. The calibrated price of risk parameters indicates that investors in IG bonds are more risk-averse than for HY bonds.

Graphical presentations of the calibrated LT-expected par CSTS are shown in Fig. 8.2 and compared to the historical ones. The calibrated LT-expected par CSTS are (1) upward-sloping for high credit ratings ranging from AAA to BBB, (2) humped-shaped for the BB and B middle graded ratings, and (3) downward sloping for the CCC speculative rating. The shapes of these LT-expected par CSTS are consistent with the literature (Merton 1974; Duffie and Singleton 1999; Sarig and Warga 1989; Fons 1994). In addition, the historical CSTS have the same shape as the long-term expected CSTS for the IG and CCC ratings. On the other hand, the downward sloping shapes of the historical CSTS, containing both credit and basis components, of the BB and B ratings are

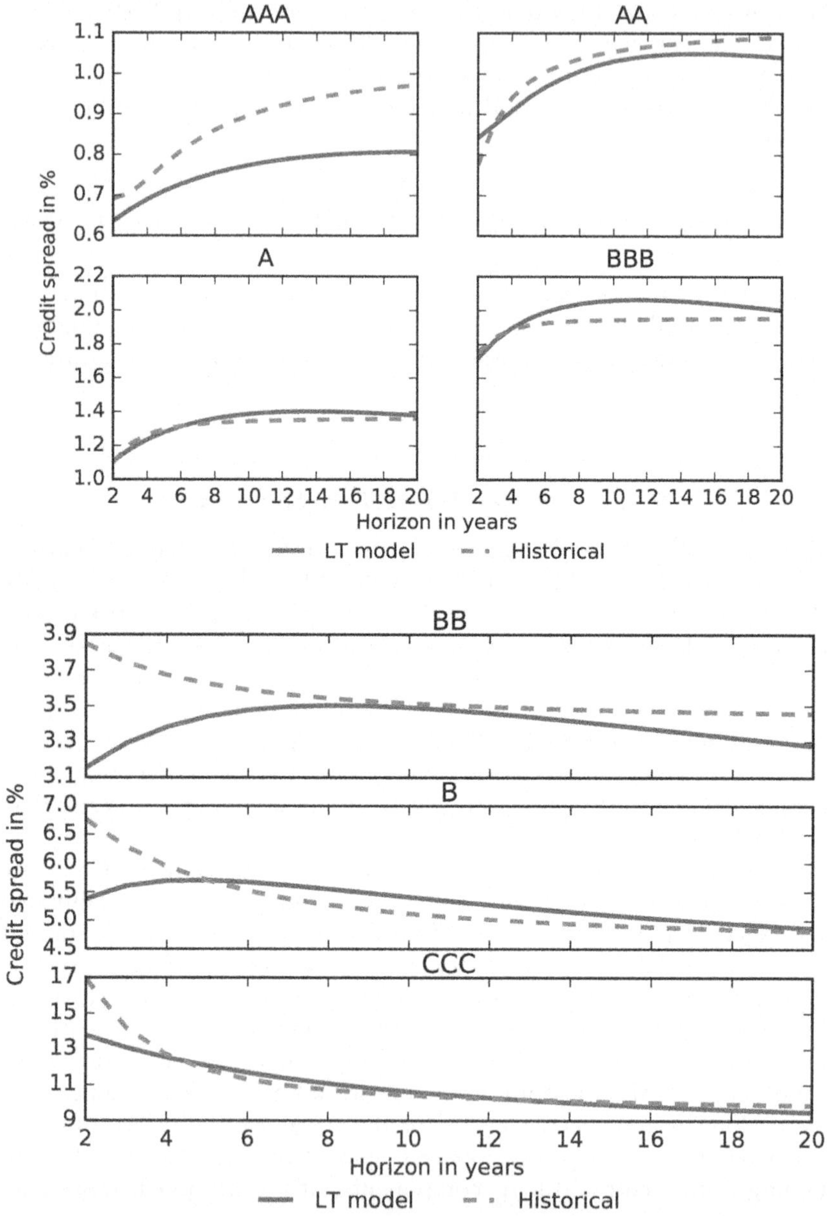

Fig. 8.2 A graphical presentation of the long-term (LT) model expected CSTS of the individual IG and HY ratings from Table 8.7

not in line with the theoretical hump-shape. This might be influenced by the liquidity of short-term BB and B bonds or the sample period that contain two crisis periods. Overall, we conclude that the shapes of the calibrated long-term expected par CSTS are in line with the literature and historical data.

In addition to the comparison with the literature, we also compare the shapes of the calibrated LT-expected par credit spread curves with the average historical CSTS of Sect. 8.3.5.2 in terms of correlation between the credit spreads for the 2–20-year maturities of both CSTS. We find high correlations above 0.95 for the individual IG ratings, which indicates that the shapes of the LT-expected and historical IG CSTS are strongly in line with each other. We observe lower correlations for the individual HY ratings, especially for the BB rating that shows a correlation of 0.40 between the LT-expected and historical average CSTS. On the other hand, the correlation between the LT-expected and historical average credit spreads for the CCC rating is high and equal to 0.93. The lower correlations for the BB and B ratings are mainly due to the differences between the shape of the short-end of the CSTS as seen earlier in this paragraph. Overall, we conclude that the calibrated LT-expected CSTS are in line with the estimated historical average CSTS.

Furthermore, we make a comparison between the LT-expected CSTS and the historical distribution of CSTS in Fig. 8.3. Although the figures show that the historical distribution of CSTS has a wide variation, the historical average CSTS are generally close to the 60%-percentile of the historical distribution which confirms that the historical distribution of CSTS has a positive skewness. The calibrated LT-expected CSTS are also generally close to the 60%-percentile of the historical distribution of CSTS, except for the AAA rating that is closer to the 40%-percentile of the historical distribution. This exception for the AAA rating is caused by the difference in sample means between 1988–2014 and 1919–2014 that we used for the calculation of the historical average CSTS and the calibrated one. Whereas the average historical BB and B CSTS is downward sloping, it is humped-shaped between the 40% and 60% percentiles of the historical distribution which is better in line with the theoretical and empirical literature. Overall, we conclude the calibrated LT-expected CSTS capture the positive skewness in the historical distribution of CSTS and are generally close to historical average CSTS.

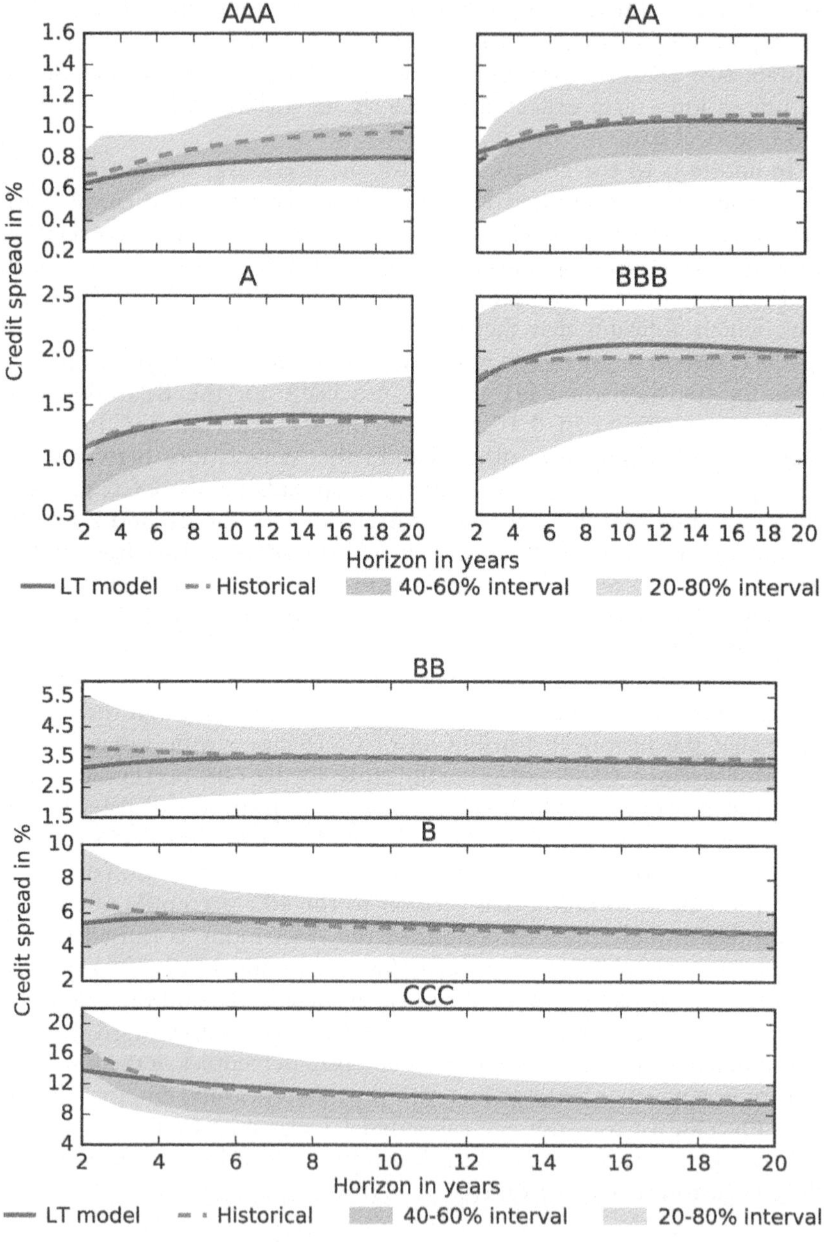

Fig. 8.3 A graphical presentation of the long-term (LT) model expected CSTS of the individual IG and HY ratings from Table 8.7, with confidence intervals

As a robustness check, we calibrated the LT-expected par CSTS over the same sample as the historical average CSTS in order to get a fairer comparison between both. Therefore, we calibrate the risk-neutral model on the 2000–2014 period by using different assumptions for the risk-free interest rates and credit par spreads. Based on unreported results (available upon request), we obtain almost the same historical average and LT-expected par CSTS if we calibrate the LT-expected par CSTS over the same sample that is used for the calculation of the historical average. This means that the LT-expected CSTS that we calibrate on the 1919–2014 sample is a good indication of the historical average CSTS over this period. So, our findings are robust to different model assumptions.

8.5.2 Credit Excess Returns

The calibrated LT-expected annualized buy-and-hold credit excess returns following the approach in Eq. 8.11 are reported in Table 8.8. We find that the LT-expected annual excess gross returns of ten-year coupon-paying corporate bonds of the AAA, AA, A, BBB, BB, B, and CCC ratings are 0.74%, 0.89%, 1.18%, 1.67%, 2.19%, 2.44%, and 3.23%, respectively. Our calibrated LT-expected excess returns are in line with the existing literature. For example, our findings generally only show differences with Hull et al. (2005) in the order of 0.05% for IG bonds and 0.2% for HY bonds.[9] Furthermore, Giesecke et al. (2011) find a long-term expected excess return of roughly 1% for IG bonds over the 1900–2008 period, which is close to the average of 1.1% of the calibrated LT-expected excess returns of the four individual IG ratings.[10]

In addition to the comparison with the literature, we compare the calibrated LT-expected excess returns with historical average excess returns. Ng and Phelps (2011) report historical arithmetic average excess net returns of about 0.7% (3%) for IG (HY) bonds over the 1990–2009 period and similar average returns are found by Ilmanen (2011) for longer historical periods. The historical average excess returns are about 0.4% lower (higher) than our calibrated LT-expected excess returns of IG (HY) bonds. Possible explanations for the difference in expected and historical average excess returns could be related to (a combination) of the following effects: more/less historical defaults than expected using our model; difference the actual and expected recovery rates; transaction costs that we do not incorporate in our model. The first two possible explanations for the difference between historical and expected defaults are probably more important for HY bonds than IG bonds as the default probability of HY bonds is higher than IG bonds. Our LT-expected credit excess return assumptions are derived for buy-and-hold investments, whereas typical corporate bond benchmarks are periodically rebalanced by removing constituents that no longer reflect the rating category of the benchmark as the result of rating upgrades and downgrades. Ng and Phelps (2011) show that relaxing the requirement of selling downgraded bonds for corporate bond benchmarks of IG ratings gives approximately 0.4% additional return compared to constrained indices. So, it seems that we can explain large part of the difference between the LT-expected and historical average excess returns of IG bonds to this rebalancing effect. Overall, we conclude that our calibrated LT-expected excess returns are generally in line with the historical average returns.

We observe a consistent increasing pattern in the expected credit excess return and the quality of the credit rating for every maturity. For every maturity, the AAA rated bond has the lowest expected credit excess return, followed by the AA rating, and so on. Within a rating category, we observe that the term structure of expected credit excess returns follows the shape as the term structure of par credit spreads. The expected credit excess returns of the individual IG ratings are within 1% of each other for all maturities which is approximately the same as the difference in expected par credit spreads. There are small differences of about 0.2% between the expected credit excess returns for the BB and B ratings. Depending on the maturity, the CCC rating has expected excess returns that are about 0.6–1.7% higher than that of the B rating. Overall, long-term investors could expect higher returns when investing in HY bonds compared to IG bonds though this coincides with higher risks.

8.6 Conclusion

In this chapter, we estimated LT-expected credit spreads and excess returns for multiple US corporate bond ratings and maturities using a risk-neutral model that is calibrated on historical data over the 1919–2014 period. The risk-neutral model incorporates the well-known credit spread puzzle by the addition of a maturity-independent constant that varies per rating.

We find that investors appear more risk-averse when investing in IG corporate bonds compared to HY bonds. In addition, we show that the shapes of the calibrated LT-expected CSTS are in line with the existing literature. The shapes of the calibrated LT-expected CSTS are (1) upward-sloping for high credit ratings ranging from the AAA to BBB ratings, (2) humped-shaped for the BB and B middle-graded ratings, and (3) downward sloping for the CCC speculative rating. Furthermore, we find that the calibrated LT-expected CSTS are in line with the historical average CSTS and capture the positive skewness in the historical distribution of CSTS.

We show that the expected annual excess gross corporate bond returns are in line with the empirical literature of expected credit excess returns of buy-and-hold investments. Our expected excess returns for IG (HY) bonds are approximately 0.4% higher (lower) than historical average credit excess returns. For HY, this difference could be due to a combination of effects. For IG, the difference could be related to benchmark construction. We obtain the returns of buy-and-hold benchmarks, whereas historical benchmarks are periodically rebalanced following rating upgrades and downgrades of constituents within a benchmark. Ng and Phelps (2011) show that relaxing the requirement of rebalancing gives 0.4% additional return for IG benchmark, which is approximately the documented difference between the LT-expected and historical average excess returns.

We extend the findings of Giesecke et al. (2011) for long historical average credit excess returns by determining the credit excess returns for ratings and maturities. Furthermore, we document two interesting patterns in the LT-expected credit excess returns. First, we find a consistent increasing pattern in the expected credit excess return and the quality of the credit rating for every maturity. So, long-term investors could expect higher returns when investing in HY bonds compared to IG bonds, though this coincides with higher risks. Second, we observe that within a rating category, the term structure of expected credit excess returns follows the same shape as the term structure of par credit spreads. Our findings are robust for different assumptions.

Acknowledgments I thank Alex Boer, Bert Kramer, and Martin van der Schans for very helpful comments and suggestions. Any remaining errors are my own.

Appendix

Table 8.1 The estimated long-term expected credit spreads and excess returns

Rating	*Credit spread*	*Excess return*
AAA	0.77	0.74
AA	1.03	0.89
A	1.39	1.18
BBB	2.06	1.67
BB	3.49	2.19
B	5.41	2.44
CCC	10.62	3.23

Source: Author calculations

Table 8.2 The R^2 of the marginal and cumulative default probabilities of the original Moody's data and the estimated model values from optimization of Eq. 8.8

Rating	*Marginal*	*Cumulative*
AAA	0.07	0.95
AA	0.63	1.00
A	0.89	1.00
BBB	0.87	1.00
BB	0.96	1.00
B	0.99	1.00
CCC	0.97	0.99

Source: Ou (2015) and author calculations

Table 8.3 The Nelson–Siegel fitted average of the US government bond yields of particular maturities for multiple samples

Sample	*3 M*	*1Y*	*5Y*	*10Y*	*15Y*	*20Y*	*30Y*	*LT (10Y+)*
1857–2014								4.70
1919–2014	3.55			4.96				5.03
1941–2014	4.00	4.32	5.13	5.41	5.51	5.56	5.61	5.48
1953–2014	4.60	4.97	5.81	6.07	6.17	6.22	6.26	6.08
1976–2014	4.95	5.32	6.38	6.79	6.93	7.01	7.08	6.93
1988–2014	3.29	3.51	4.63	5.18	5.40	5.50	5.61	5.7 (20.9)
2000–2014	1.90	1.96	3.16	3.89	4.18	4.32	4.47	4.36 (20.0)

In addition, we report the historical average yield of the long-term (LT) government bond index with a maturity over ten-years (10Y+). The weighted average life maturity of the LT government bond index is reported between parentheses

Source: GobalFinancialData, Federal Reserve Board and author calculations

Table 8.4 Descriptive statistics of the individual IG 10Y+ and HY all-maturity (all) rating benchmark for two sample periods

	AAA	*AA*	*A*	*BBB*	*BB*	*B*	*CCC*
Panel A: Descriptive statistics monthly credit spreads (1919–2014)							
Statistic	(10Y+)	(10Y+)	(10Y+)	(10Y+)	(All)	(All)	(All)
Mean	0.82	1.06	1.40	2.03			
Stdev	0.46	0.56	0.73	0.99			
Skew	1.43	0.78	1.09	1.40			
Kurt	8.83	3.85	5.10	7.14			
Min	0.14	0.23	0.32	0.51			
0.25	0.44	0.56	0.79	1.26			
0.50	0.82	1.03	1.33	1.93			
0.75	1.06	1.40	1.80	2.54			
Max	4.24	3.47	4.78	8.02			
Autocorr (1)	0.96	0.97	0.98	0.98			
Autocorr (12)	0.69	0.77	0.74	0.72			
Panel B: Descriptive statistics monthly credit spreads (1988–2014)							
Statistic	(10Y+)	(10Y+)	(10Y+)	(10Y+)	(All)	(All)	(All)
Mean	0.99	1.16	1.40	1.98	3.48	5.57	11.36
Stdev	0.46	0.54	0.64	0.81	1.74	2.45	5.40
Skew	3.54	1.80	2.46	2.51	2.57	2.14	1.74
Kurt	21.46	7.66	11.72	12.39	12.71	10.13	6.55
Min	0.25	0.39	0.63	0.86	1.41	2.54	4.37
0.25	0.78	0.80	1.01	1.52	2.44	3.92	7.71
0.50	0.93	1.01	1.22	1.70	3.03	4.93	9.60
0.75	1.07	1.40	1.60	2.35	4.09	6.60	13.25
Max	4.24	3.47	4.78	6.28	13.90	19.00	37.94
Autocorr (1)	0.96	0.97	0.98	0.98	0.96	0.96	0.96
Autocorr (12)	0.69	0.77	0.74	0.72	0.40	0.31	0.34
WAL maturity	25.2	24.2	23.9	23.5	9.2	7.5	6.8

The mean, standard deviation (stdev), skewness (skew), kurtosis (kurt), minimum (min), maximum (max), 25%, 50%, and 75% percentiles and monthly (1) and annual (12) autocorrelation (autocorr). In addition, we show the weighted average life (WAL) maturity for the 1988–2014 sample

Source: GobalFinancialData, Merrill Lynch and author calculations

Table 8.5 The findings of three papers that have quantified the liquidity premium in % of ten-year corporate bonds for different ratings

Number	*Paper*	*AAA*	*AA*	*A*	*BBB*	*BB*	*B*	*CCC*
1	Huang and Huang (2012)	0.53	0.77	1.00	1.38	1.28	0.82	
2	Chen et al. (2014)	0.63	0.63	0.76	0.93	1.22		
3	De Jong and Driessen (2012)	0.60	0.60	0.60	0.60	1.50	1.50	1.50
Mean	1 & 2	0.58	0.70	0.88	1.15	1.25		
Mean	1 & 3	0.57	0.68	0.80	0.99	1.39	1.16	
Mean	2 & 3	0.61	0.61	0.68	0.77	1.36		
Mean	1, 2 & 3	0.59	0.66	0.78	0.97	1.33		

The liquidity premium of Huang and Huang (2012) is taken from Table 8.2 of the paper by computing the difference between the ten-year maturity calculated credit spread and yield spreads. The liquidity premium of H. Chen et al. (2014) is taken from Table 8.5 of the paper by calculating the average difference between the credit spread and pure default spread of the bad (B) and good (G) state. Although De Jong and Driessen (2012) differentiate for the liquidity premium for different ratings, they do not report the actual numbers. Therefore, we decide to take the numbers they report

Source: Huang and Huang (2012), Chen et al. (2014), De Jong and Driessen (2012), and author calculations

Table 8.6 The assumptions for the par yield $c_i^f(T)$ of the defaultable corporate bond with annual, $f = 1$, coupon payments, rating i, and maturity T

i	T	$c_i^1(T)$	$r^1(T)$	$s_i^1(T)$	l_i^1	$d_i^1(T)$	$\frac{d_i^1(T)}{s_i^1(T)}$
AAA	15	5.88	5.08	0.80	0.60	0.20	25.0%
AA	15	6.13	5.08	1.05	0.70	0.35	33.3%
A	15	6.48	5.08	1.40	0.85	0.55	39.3%
BBB	15	7.13	5.08	2.05	1.10	0.95	46.3%
BB	9	8.41	4.91	3.50	1.40	2.10	60.0%
B	8	10.40	4.85	5.55	1.15	4.40	79.3%
CCC	7	16.14	4.79	11.35	1.00	10.35	91.2%

The par coupon is split into the risk-free par yield $r^f(T)$ and par credit spread $s_i^f(T)$. The par credit spread is decomposed into the bond basis l_i^f and default spread $d_i^f(T)$ assumptions of Eq. 8.7. In the last column, we report the par default spread as a percentage of the par credit spread

Source: Author calculations

Table 8.7 The long-term expected par credit spreads $s_i^1(T)$ of Eq. 8.7 for maturities T 1–10 years (panel A) and 11–20 years (panel B), and rating i

Panel A: $s_i^1(T)$ for maturities 1–10 years											
Rating i	θ_i	T=1	2	3	4	5	6	7	8	9	10
AAA	4.44	0.60	0.64	0.67	0.69	0.71	0.73	0.74	0.75	0.76	0.77
AA	2.18	0.80	0.84	0.87	0.91	0.94	0.97	0.99	1.01	1.02	1.03
A	2.36	1.01	1.11	1.18	1.23	1.28	1.31	1.34	1.36	1.37	1.39
BBB	2.22	1.57	1.72	1.82	1.90	1.95	1.99	2.02	2.04	2.05	2.06
BB	1.54	2.95	3.15	3.29	3.38	3.44	3.48	3.50	3.50	3.50	3.49
B	1.39	4.87	5.37	5.61	5.69	5.70	5.67	5.62	5.55	5.48	5.41
CCC	1.29	14.65	13.79	13.09	12.53	12.06	11.68	11.35	11.07	10.83	10.62
Panel B: $s_i^1(T)$ for maturities 11–20 years											
Rating i	ρ_i	11	12	13	14	15	16	17	18	19	20
AAA	0.99	0.78	0.79	0.79	0.80	0.80	0.80	0.80	0.81	0.81	0.81
AA	0.97	1.04	1.04	1.05	1.05	1.05	1.05	1.05	1.05	1.04	1.04
A	0.97	1.39	1.40	1.40	1.40	1.40	1.40	1.39	1.39	1.38	1.38
BBB	0.96	2.06	2.06	2.06	2.06	2.05	2.04	2.03	2.02	2.01	2.00
BB	0.40	3.48	3.46	3.44	3.42	3.40	3.37	3.35	3.32	3.30	3.28
B	0.66	5.34	5.28	5.21	5.15	5.10	5.04	4.99	4.95	4.90	4.86
CCC	0.93	10.44	10.27	10.13	10.01	9.89	9.79	9.70	9.62	9.55	9.48

In addition, we show the calibrated price of risk parameter θ_i of Eq. 8.4 per rating i in panel A. Finally, we calculate the correlation ρ_i between the 2–20 year maturities of the calibrated CSTS and the historical average CSTS over the 1988–2014 period from Sect. 8.3.5.2 for each rating i

Source: Author calculations

Table 8.8 The expected credit excess returns over government bonds based on Eq. 8.11 for maturities T 1–10 years (panel A) and 11–20 years (panel B)

Panel A: Expected credit excess returns for maturities 1–10 years										
Rating	1	2	3	4	5	6	7	8	9	10
AAA	0.60	0.63	0.65	0.67	0.69	0.70	0.71	0.72	0.73	0.74
AA	0.76	0.77	0.79	0.81	0.83	0.85	0.86	0.87	0.88	0.89
A	0.94	1.00	1.04	1.07	1.10	1.12	1.14	1.16	1.17	1.18
BBB	1.35	1.43	1.49	1.54	1.57	1.60	1.62	1.64	1.65	1.67
BB	1.93	2.00	2.05	2.09	2.12	2.14	2.16	2.17	2.18	2.19
B	2.15	2.29	2.36	2.40	2.42	2.43	2.44	2.44	2.44	2.44
CCC	3.85	3.71	3.60	3.51	3.45	3.39	3.34	3.30	3.26	3.23
Panel B: Expected credit excess returns for maturities 11–20 years										
Rating	11	12	13	14	15	16	17	18	19	20
AAA	0.75	0.76	0.76	0.77	0.77	0.78	0.78	0.79	0.79	0.79
AA	0.90	0.91	0.91	0.92	0.92	0.92	0.93	0.93	0.93	0.94
A	1.19	1.20	1.21	1.21	1.22	1.22	1.23	1.23	1.23	1.24
BBB	1.68	1.68	1.69	1.70	1.70	1.71	1.71	1.72	1.72	1.72
BB	2.20	2.20	2.21	2.21	2.21	2.22	2.22	2.22	2.22	2.22
B	2.43	2.43	2.42	2.42	2.41	2.41	2.41	2.40	2.40	2.40
CCC	3.21	3.18	3.16	3.15	3.13	3.12	3.11	3.10	3.09	3.08

Source: Author calculations

Notes

1. Helwege and Turner (1999) generated controversy with their findings of an upward-sloping credit spread term structure for low credit quality issuers. These findings have, however, been contradicted by Bohn (1999).
2. The assumption of fractional recovery of face value assumption is supported by empirical evidence; see Bakshi et al. (2001).
3. There exists considerable evidence of a short-term liquidity premium in the US sovereign debt market. See, for example, Nagel (2016) and the references therein.
4. Note that $T_n \equiv T$ with T equal to the bond maturity.
5. The historical interest rates obtained from GFD before April 1953 are based on Homer and Sylla (1996).
6. The yields of the composite of long-term government bonds index of Merrill Lynch are almost identical to the ones from the FED.
7. In our case, this is the 20-year cumulative default probability of the CCC rating.
8. Note that the price of risk parameter has no unit as it is a multiplication factor between the physical and risk-neutral hazard rates. For example, if the price of risk parameter is 4 then this means the risk-neutral investors perceive the risk-neutral default probabilities 4 times larger than the physical default probabilities.
9. Hull et al. (2005) find expected annualized excess returns of 0.81%, 0.86%, 1.12%, 1.58%, 2.03%, 1.36%, and 3.07% for the AAA, AA, A, BBB, BB, B, and CCC ratings, respectively. The authors define these excess returns over the swap rate.
10. Giesecke et al. (2011) report an expected annualized excess return of about 0.8%, which is based on a recovery assumption of 50%, an average credit spread of 1.53%, and average default loss rate of 1.5% measured over the period 1866–2008. However, the authors find that the annual default loss rate decreases by half to roughly 0.75% for the 1900–2008 period, which is a period that better corresponds to our 1919–2014 sample. Taking their finding of an average credit spread of 1.53% and default losses of 0.75% and our recovery assumption of 35% gives an expected excess return of 1.04%.

References

Bakshi, G., Madan, D. B., & Zhang, F. X. (2001). Understanding the role of recovery in default risk models: Empirical comparisons and implied recovery rates. *Finance and Economics Discussion Series, 2001–37,* Federal Reserve Board of Governors, Washington DC.

Bohn, J. (1999). Characterizing credit spreads. *Haas School of Business University of California Working Paper.*

Bongaerts, D., De Jong, F., & Driessen, J. (2011). Derivative pricing with liquidity risk: Theory and evidence from the credit default swap market. *Journal of Finance, 66*(1), 203–240.

Chen, L., Lesmond, D. A., & Wei, J. (2007). Corporate yield spreads and bond liquidity. *Journal of Finance, 62*(1), 119–149.

Chen, H., Sloan, I. T., Cui, N. R., & Milbrandt, N. K. (2014). Quantifying liquidity and default risks of corporate bonds over the business cycle. *National Bureau of Economic Research Working Paper No. 20638.*

De Jong, F., & Driessen, J. (2012). Liquidity risk premia in corporate bond markets. *Quarterly Journal of Finance, 2*(2), 1–34.

Diebold, F. X., & Li, C. (2006). Forecasting the term structure of government bond yields. *Journal of Econometrics, 130*(2), 337–364.

Driessen, J. (2005). Is default event risk priced in corporate bonds? *Review of Financial Studies, 18*(1), 165–195.

Duffie, D., & Singleton, K. J. (1999). Modeling term structures of defaultable bonds. *Review of Financial Studies, 12*(4), 687–720.

Elton, E. J., Gruber, M. J., Agrawal, D., & Mann, C. (2001). Explaining the rate spread on corporate bonds. *Journal of Finance, 56*(1), 247–277.

Fons, J. S. (1994). Using default rates to model the term structure of credit risk. *Financial Analysts Journal, 50*(5), 25–33.

Giesecke, K., Longstaff, F. A., Schaefer, S., & Strebulaev, I. (2011). Corporate bond default risk: A 150-year perspective. *Journal of Financial Economics, 102*(2), 233–250.

Helwege, J., & Turner, C. (1999). The slope of the credit yield curve for speculative grade issuers. *Journal of Finance, 54*(5), 1869–1884.

Homer, S., & Sylla, R. E. (1996). *A history of interest rates.* New Brunswick, NJ: Rutgers University Press.

Huang, J., & Huang, M. (2012). How much of the corporate-treasury yield spread is due to credit risk? *Review of Asset Pricing Studies, 2*(2), 153–202.

Hull, J. C., Predescu, M., & White, A. (2005). Bond prices, default probabilities and risk premiums. *Journal of Credit Risk, 1*(2), 53–60.

Ilmanen, A. (2011). *Expected returns: An investor's guide to harvesting market rewards.* Hoboken, NJ: John Wiley & Sons.

Lando, D. (1998). On Cox processes and credit risky securities. *Review of Derivatives Research, 2*(2–3), 99–120.

Longstaff, F. A., Mithal, S., & Neis, E. (2005). Corporate yield spreads: Default risk or liquidity? New evidence from the credit default swap market. *Journal of Finance, 60*(5), 2213–2253.

Merton, R. (1974). On the pricing of corporate debt: The risk structure of interest rates. *Journal of Finance, 29*(2), 449–470.

Nagel, S. (2016). The liquidity premium of near-money assets. *Quarterly Journal of Economics, 131*(4), 1927–1971.

Ng, K.-Y., & Phelps, B. D. (2011). Capturing credit spread premium. *Financial Analysts Journal, 67*(3), 63–75.
O'Kane, D. (2010). *Modelling single-name and multi-name credit derivatives.* John Wiley & Sons.
Ou, S. (2015). Annual Default Study: Corporate default and recovery rates 1920–2014. *Moody's Investor Services.*
Sarig, O., & Warga, A. (1989). Some empirical estimates of the risk structure of interest rates. *Journal of Finance, 44*(5), 1351–1360.

PART III

Portfolio Construction

CHAPTER 9

Regime Identification for Sovereign Bond Portfolio Construction

Santiago Alberico, Joachim Coche, Vahe Sahakyan, and Omar Zulaica

9.1 Introduction

Financial markets are closely linked to the business and credit cycles. They experience periods of persistent high or low volatility and go through risk-on and risk-off episodes. Certainly, return distributions vary with the state of the economy. As a consequence, the behaviour of portfolio returns can vary significantly over shifting economic and financial conditions—in other words, it can substantially change over each *regime*.

This chapter is based on a joint work by staff members from the Bank for International Settlements and Banco de México.

S. Alberico
Bank of France, Paris, France
e-mail: Santiago.ALBERICOLEZAMA.external@banque-france.fr

J. Coche • V. Sahakyan • O. Zulaica (✉)
Bank for International Settlements (BIS), Basel, Switzerland
e-mail: Joachim.Coche@bis.org; Vahe.Sahakyan@bis.org; Omar.Zulaica@bis.org

N. Bulusu et al. (eds.), *Advances in the Practice of Public Investment Management*, https://doi.org/10.1007/978-3-319-90245-6_9

Traditional asset allocation algorithms do not typically incorporate regime-specific information to construct optimal portfolios. In this chapter, we introduce a state-dependent investment strategy based on a set of indicators that we believe are useful in identifying economic and financial regimes. Importantly, it should be noted that the objective of this chapter is not normative. We are not proposing an alternative asset allocation approach; rather, our intention is to better compare the properties of portfolios which are, and are not, optimised taking state-conditional information into account.

To this end, we apply in this chapter a multi-step approach to portfolio construction. First, the state space is characterised by separating "regular" from "distressed" market environments, using a selected regime indicator. We then obtain distributions of asset class returns conditional on the regime indicator. Finally, we execute a dynamic asset allocation algorithm on the mean-variance space, optimising a portfolio over expected conditional return distributions.

While the existing literature on regime identification has focused, in particular, on equity markets, we illustrate this approach for an investment universe consisting of four of the most important and liquid developed government bond markets: the United States, the United Kingdom, Germany, and Japan. Furthermore, we analyse the properties of the portfolio construction method for different assumptions on currency numeraires (specifically, those often used by sovereign investors), different utility concepts and different levels of risk tolerance. Then, we compare these results with traditional asset allocation methodologies, such as simple mean-variance and Bayesian optimisation.

We show that the portfolios optimised across regimes have properties markedly different from those optimised using conventional asset allocation approaches. They imply diversified bond weightings with a lower inclination to corner solutions, and display higher mean returns at broadly comparable volatilities. Accordingly, the Sharpe ratios of the regime-optimised allocations indicate better risk-adjusted returns. Yet, as we show, they imply fatter-tailed return distributions. These findings may indicate that the regime-optimised allocations are exposed to an additional risk factor that, when priced, could give rise to an expected excess return over standard portfolios. From a theoretical perspective, this makes sense: if the optimised portfolios are adequately diversified within each financial or economic regime, resulting risk exposure must be mostly of systematic nature and thereby should carry a premium.

The rest of this chapter is organised as follows: Sect. 9.2 provides a brief literature review documenting the notion of economic regimes and the issues that arise when applying the concept to the analysis of financial markets. In Sect. 9.3 we propose three indicators for identifying regimes. Section 9.4 first demonstrates that these three measures are useful in characterising the future return distributions of our universe of developed market sovereign bonds, and then describes and applies our regime-optimal asset allocation framework. Section 9.5 concludes.

9.2 Regime Identification

The term *regime* has been used extensively in various fields: in finance, in economics, and even in politics.[1] The concept of multiple regimes received early formal treatment by Nicholas Georgescu-Roegen (1951) in a study of linear economic models. The author discussed the idea that different phases of the business cycle could be represented in a multiple regime model.

Later on, regime identification was addressed by Goldfield and Quandt (1973). They were among the first to incorporate the concept of regime switching into an econometric model. This approach was later popularised by Hamilton (1989), who explicitly modelled two states representing the aggregate business cycles: expansion and recession.

On an ex-post basis, for example, information published by the National Bureau of Economic Research (NBER)—responsible for determining official recessionary periods in the United States—could be used to identify regimes.[2] Based on this classification, return distributions of financial assets could be estimated separately for periods when the US economy is expanding or when it is contracting (Fig. 9.1). Though simple-sounding, several issues arise when applying such an approach to investment decision making. First, the expansion regime takes up most of history (e.g., about 80% of the past 26 years). Clearly, not all expansions since 1990 have been characterised by the same asset class behaviour. Second, asset classes can sometimes behave as if there is a looming recession, though macroeconomic data may not reflect so. To illustrate this point, we fit the NBER recession probability using two different probit models: one purely based on macro data and another using market indicators (Fig. 9.2). In both cases, the empirical probability of facing an economic downturn presents a spike when the NBER says the US economy is contracting.

However, the market-based model presents additional spikes in the last couple of years; the period going from October 2015 to February 2016 stands out the most. During this time, oil prices experienced one of the sharpest falls in history, sparking deflationary pressures. At the same time, investors were worried that China's economy may face a hard landing.

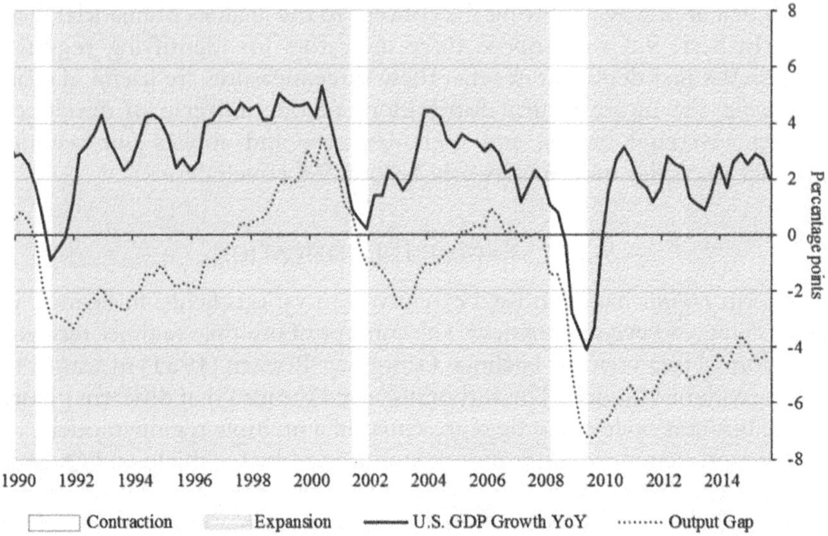

Fig. 9.1 US real GDP quarterly annualised GDP growth and output gap

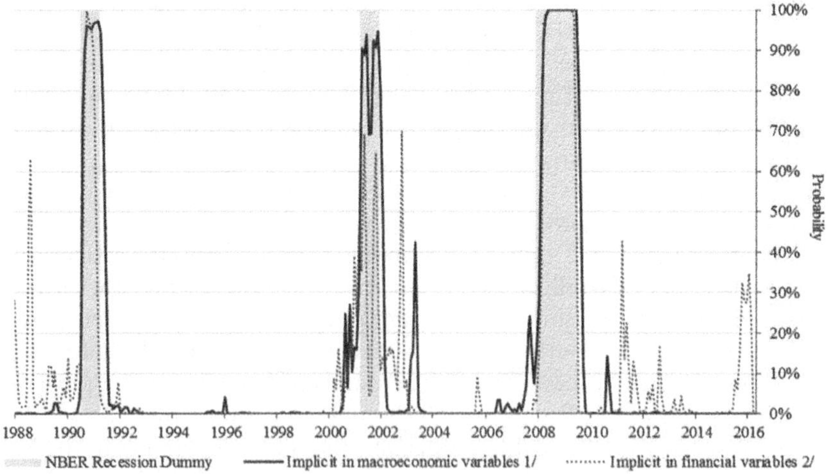

Fig. 9.2 US probability of recession implicit in selected variables

Though these worries later dissipated, market-based measures appeared to be pricing it in. Yet, the US recession probability based in macroeconomic data remained close to zero as economic fundamentals in the United States were not deteriorating. In conclusion, using the NBER classification as a regime indicator to model financial markets' behaviour, our forecasts would miss the changes in the conditional distribution of asset reeturns observed in the data.

Third, because the NBER classifies a period as either expansion or recession after it already happened (often, quite late), its data is actually of little use for real-life asset allocation purposes. A similar case can be made for most *ex-post* and macro-based dummy variables (i.e., financial crises, stages of the interest rate, or business cycles). This was pointed out by Blitz and van Vliet (2011), who propose a timelier leading indicator of the US business cycle that allows to split the state space into finer scenarios. However, we believe their approach still does not control for other important issues, such as country-risk concentration, which we discuss later on.

A fourth important point is that the frequency of the data can affect estimation results. Sometimes, in asset allocation, the periodicity of a sample is chosen in order to reflect the length of the investment horizon. To capture the phases of the business cycle, it would make sense to use a quarterly or annual frequency. However, this can introduce a small-sample bias to our estimations. By using a quarterly sample (e.g., when basing our estimations on GDP data), very few observations become available, making it harder to make adequate and trustworthy statistical inference. From the point of view of regime identification, this means that we receive the *regime signals* less frequently—an unattractive feature. The appropriate data frequency thus involves a trade-off between sample size and investment horizon.

Finally, the choice of the appropriate regime indicator is complicated by the fact that the regimes of different asset classes may not be perfectly synchronised. Even if assuming that one state variable is sufficient to summarise the regime in a particular country, relying on only one economy's data (in this case, the United States), may not be appropriate for portfolios with assets from multiple geographies. Including multiple state variables, one for each of the different regimes governing the assets in a global portfolio is difficult due to multiple reasons. Not least of which is the difficulty in estimating the joint probability distribution of the multiple state variables.

9.3 Alternative Regime Indicators

For market participants, it can be a daunting task to characterise the financial and economic environment given the wealth of data that is published every day. Not accounting for outliers in the data can easily lead to misspecification of conditional asset return distributions. For example, practitioners may be faced with investor preferences to use a well-known market indicator such as the VIX index or a corporate credit spread to define the states of the world; however, these indices are restrictive in nature as they only consider asset- and country-specific behaviour. For a multi-asset, multi-country investor, objective measures to define states of the world are much harder to find.

To achieve a regime identification process that is *rule-based, systematic, transparent,* and *less subjective*, we introduce in this section mathematical models that capture the underlying data structure. With the objectives of summarising a broad group of signals, achieving a fine enough partition of the state space and avoiding ambiguity in its interpretation, we propose the following three measures.

(a) Macro Fragility Index

The Macro Fragility Index (MFI) is defined as the variance explained by the principal components of a chosen set of macroeconomic indicators.[3] The time series plots the MFI obtained using monthly industrial production and consumer price indices for a set of developed countries (the United States, Canada, the United Kingdom, Germany, and France), beginning 1975 (Fig. 9.3). A 36-month rolling window is applied to estimate a time series of the measure.

If the total variation in this group of economic variables can be explained to a large degree by a few factors, then this is an indication of higher macro risk concentration. Additionally, this measure offers a way to summarise the economic cycle of multiple economies simultaneously.

(b) Financial Turbulence Index

The Financial Turbulence Index (FTI) is the time series of the Mahalanobis distance (i.e., the square root of the multivariate Z-score) of the return matrix of several asset classes.[4] The FTI is estimated from monthly returns of global bonds, equities, and commodities starting in 1977 (Fig. 9.4).[5] The

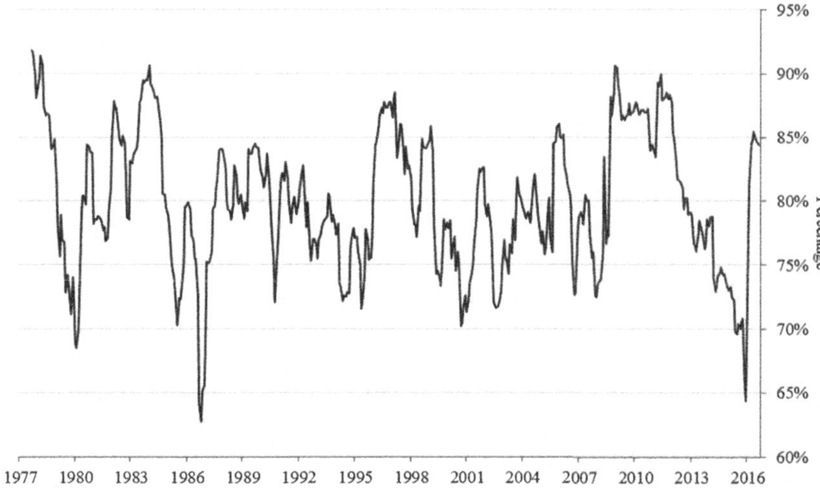

Fig. 9.3 Macroeconomic fragility index

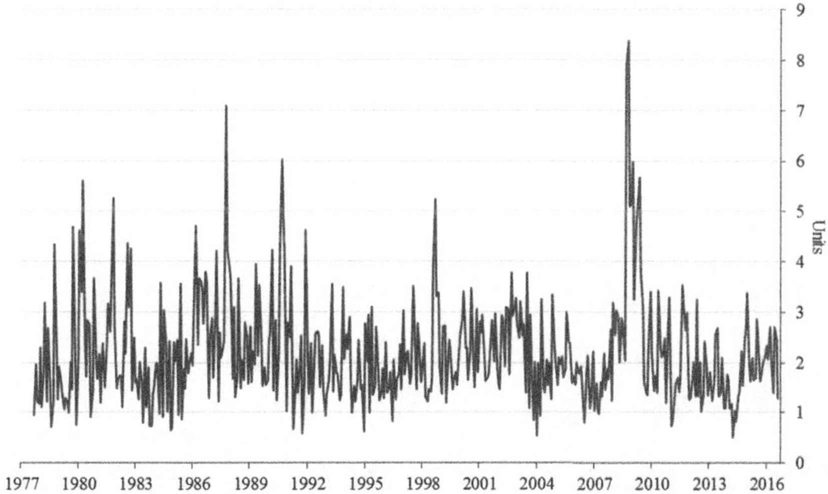

Fig. 9.4 Financial turbulence index

higher the FTI is, the more it signals an extraordinary realisation of joint returns away from the average. In this sense, the measure can prove helpful in defining regimes under which the market is more ***turbulent***.

(c) Systemic Risk Index

In a similar fashion to the MFI, the Systemic Risk Index (SRI) is defined as the variance explained by the first factor of a principal component analysis over the return matrix of a selected set of asset classes (Fig. 9.5). High values of this index indicate periods in which the returns are well explained by only one factor. This means that the multi-country, multi-asset class volatility is concentrated which may indicate systemic risk. As in the case of the MFI, a three-year rolling window is used for the estimation. Opposed to the FTI it does not measure ***concentration***, but the ***level*** of risk in the financial system.

As noted, these measures are estimated at a monthly frequency. Note, however, that these measures could be constructed at a weekly, and even daily, frequency, depending on the availability of underlying data. Higher frequency indicators may have some applications such as for early-warning indicators. However, higher frequency indicators must be used with caution, because daily data may contain greater noise.

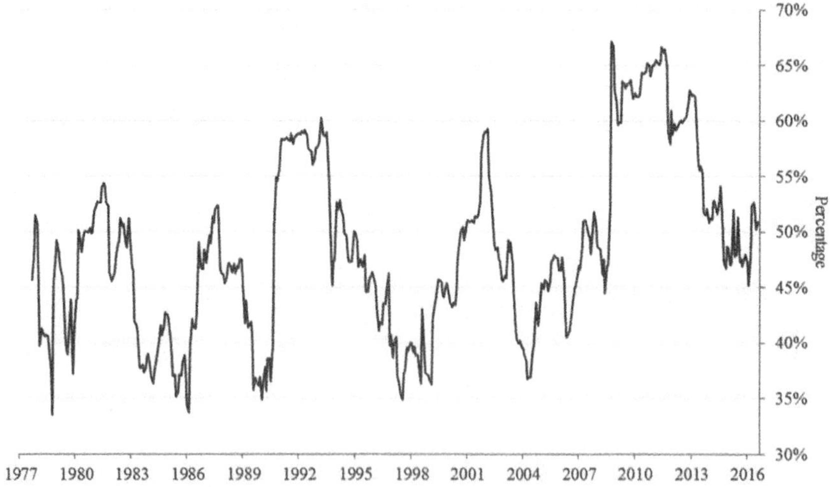

Fig. 9.5 Systemic risk index

9.4 Empirical Analysis

In this section, we assess the fitness of the proposed regime indicators for predicting future bond return distributions over several investment horizons. Subsequently, we attempt to construct regime optimised portfolios using an out-of-sample approach.

9.4.1 *Predictive Power of the Regime Indicators*

Now that systematic indicators have been defined—and before constructing an *ex-ante* investment strategy—the properties of these measures to characterise future returns are assessed. This analysis is performed for an investment universe comprising government bonds from four markets: the United States, the United Kingdom, Germany, and Japan, with constant durations ranging from one to ten years in one-year steps.

Using the full available data history from January 1975 to August 2016, the following predictive regression for the monthly local currency returns is performed:

$$r_t^i = \alpha + \beta I_{t-k} + \varepsilon_t.$$

Here, r_t^i is the month over month total return of the i-year government bond $i \in \{1,2,3,\ldots,10\}$ and I_{t-k} is the k-th lag of regime indicator $\in \{MFI, SRI, FTI\}$, $k \in \{1,3,6,9,12\}$. That is, the regime indicators' predictive power is tested for 1, 3, 6, 9, and 12 month-ahead returns. ε_t is the regression error.

SRI and FTI show some predictive power (Table 9.1).[6] Concretely, the SRI seems to do a decent job in explaining short-end bond returns across all economies and several months ahead. Additionally, the relationship between this indicator and total returns seems to be inverse and decreasing along term. However, the FTI can explain some returns in both Germany and the United Kingdom, especially in the medium term, and the relationship between them and financial turbulence appears positive. In contrast, the MFI does not perform well-explaining future returns for any investment horizon.

As a mean-variance algorithm will be used to construct portfolios, it is also important to explore if the MFI, SRI, and FTI can predict future volatility. To this end, predictive regressions of the following form are performed:

Table 9.1 T-statistics of β coefficient in the predictive regression using monthly local currency returns

		MFI				*SRI*				*FTI*			
	k=	1	3	6	12	1	3	6	12	1	3	6	12
US	1 year	0.04	0.20	0.78	0.44	−2.94***	−3.55***	−4.00***	−3.80***	1.26	−0.09	0.10	−0.68
	2 years	−0.25	−0.11	0.93	0.37	−1.57	−2.26**	−2.74***	−2.34**	1.49	−0.06	0.32	−0.68
	3 years	−0.43	−0.31	1.00	0.38	−0.75	−1.41	−1.89*	−1.45	1.53	−0.12	0.32	−0.61
	4 years	−0.52	−0.41	1.01	0.41	−0.28	−0.91	−1.36	−0.89	1.52	−0.22	0.21	−0.57
	5 years	−0.56	−0.46	0.99	0.43	−0.04	−0.63	−1.06	−0.53	1.49	−0.32	0.05	−0.55
	6 years	−0.58	−0.48	0.96	0.44	0.09	−0.47	−0.88	−0.28	1.47	−0.40	−0.12	−0.53
	7 years	−0.59	−0.48	0.93	0.44	0.15	−0.39	−0.78	−0.11	1.44	−0.48	−0.28	−0.52
	8 years	−0.59	−0.47	0.89	0.44	0.18	−0.35	−0.71	0.01	1.42	−0.53	−0.44	−0.51
	9 years	−0.59	−0.46	0.86	0.43	0.20	−0.32	−0.67	0.10	1.40	−0.58	−0.57	−0.50
	10 years	−0.58	−0.45	0.83	0.42	0.20	−0.31	−0.64	0.17	1.38	−0.61	−0.69	−0.49
Germany	1 years	0.82	0.46	0.51	0.68	−4.59***	−4.47***	−4.71***	−4.72***	0.64	0.30	−0.24	−0.54
	2 years	0.96	0.27	0.26	0.70	−3.32***	−3.35***	−3.42***	−3.37***	1.61	0.40	−0.68	−0.97
	3 years	1.02	0.13	0.07	0.76	−2.25**	−2.30**	−2.36**	−2.27**	1.69*	0.16	−1.03	−1.05
	4 years	1.10	0.06	−0.01	0.86	−1.57	−1.56	−1.68*	−1.54	1.57	−0.17	−1.31	−1.01
	5 years	1.19	0.03	−0.02	0.99	−1.14	−1.06	−1.27	−1.07	1.41	−0.48	−1.54	−0.97
	6 years	1.28	0.03	0.01	1.10	−0.85	−0.73	−1.01	−0.75	1.25	−0.74	−1.74*	−0.92
	7 years	1.36	0.03	0.07	1.19	−0.64	−0.50	−0.84	−0.52	1.09	−0.93	−1.89*	−0.89
	8 years	1.42	0.05	0.14	1.26	−0.49	−0.33	−0.71	−0.36	0.94	−1.08	−2.00**	−0.85
	9 years	1.47	0.06	0.20	1.31	−0.37	−0.20	−0.62	−0.23	0.79	−1.18	−2.08**	−0.82
	10 years	1.50	0.08	0.26	1.34	−0.27	−0.10	−0.55	−0.13	0.66	−1.26	−2.13**	−0.79
UK	1 year	0.54	0.52	−0.04	−0.40	−2.47**	−3.29***	−3.65***	−4.01***	1.45	0.16	0.04	−0.53
	2 years	0.75	0.46	−0.88	−0.61	−1.16	−1.64	−2.38**	−2.30**	1.27	0.48	0.41	−0.94
	3 years	0.87	0.41	−1.40	−0.46	−0.40	−0.49	−1.55	−1.30	0.81	0.51	0.31	−0.99
	4 years	0.94	0.39	−1.45	−0.24	0.02	0.14	−1.06	−0.80	0.45	0.42	0.01	−0.90
	5 years	0.99	0.38	−1.21	−0.02	0.23	0.44	−0.78	−0.53	0.17	0.28	−0.37	−0.76

	6 years	1.03	0.37	−0.89	0.17	0.34	0.57	−0.62	−0.39	−0.06	0.15	−0.79	−0.61
	7 years	1.07	0.37	−0.59	0.33	0.39	0.61	−0.53	−0.31	−0.25	0.03	−1.19	−0.46
	8 years	1.09	0.37	−0.35	0.47	0.42	0.62	−0.47	−0.27	−0.40	−0.07	−1.55	−0.33
	9 years	1.10	0.38	−0.15	0.57	0.43	0.62	−0.44	−0.24	−0.53	−0.15	−1.87*	−0.21
	10 years	1.12	0.38	0.00	0.66	0.44	0.61	−0.41	−0.22	−0.63	−0.21	−2.13**	−0.12
Japan	1 year	0.85	0.60	0.42	0.18	−3.48***	−3.60***	−3.70***	−4.57***	0.81	0.22	0.48	0.09
	2 years	0.96	0.51	0.47	−0.20	−2.33**	−2.39**	−2.56**	−3.84***	1.19	0.45	0.16	0.23
	3 years	0.88	0.34	0.50	−0.44	−1.71*	−1.75*	−1.89*	−3.36***	1.33	0.41	−0.24	0.24
	4 years	0.75	0.16	0.48	−0.54	−1.37	−1.37	−1.48	−3.00***	1.40	0.26	−0.42	0.16
	5 years	0.60	−0.02	0.42	−0.54	−1.17	−1.12	−1.20	−2.72***	1.46	0.05	−0.39	0.04
	6 years	0.45	−0.19	0.33	−0.50	−1.05	−0.94	−0.99	−2.47**	1.52	−0.16	−0.27	−0.10
	7 years	0.31	−0.34	0.23	−0.43	−0.96	−0.80	−0.81	−2.25**	1.58	−0.35	−0.15	−0.24
	8 years	0.19	−0.48	0.12	−0.35	−0.89	−0.69	−0.67	−2.06**	1.63	−0.51	−0.03	−0.37
	9 years	0.07	−0.59	0.02	−0.28	−0.84	−0.60	−0.55	−1.89*	1.66*	−0.65	0.06	−0.48
	10 years	−0.03	−0.70	−0.08	−0.22	−0.81	−0.53	−0.44	−1.73*	1.69*	−0.76	0.14	−0.57

Source: Authors' calculations using return data from Bloomberg and Bank of America/Merrill Lynch

***$p < 0.01$, **$p < 0.05$, *$p < 0.1$

$$\sigma_t^i = \alpha + \beta I_{t-k} + \varepsilon_t.$$

Here, σ_t^i is the 12-month rolling volatility of local currency returns for the *i*-year government bond $i \in \{1,2,3,\ldots,10\}$. The corresponding *t*-statistics, adjusted for overlapping sample issues using Hansen & Hodrick (1980) procedure (Table 9.2).

In line with previous results, MFI does not show predictive power for the future return, except in some Japanese Government Bond cases (results available on request). However, SRI and FTI show significant statistical power. Specifically, the SRI has a positive relationship with the volatility of some short- and medium-term maturities across all countries. The FTI performs well in a greater part of the term structures and across most investment horizons. The relationship between this indicator and future bond return volatility is positive and increasing with duration.

9.4.2 *Portfolio Construction*

Given some evidence of predictive power of the previously introduced regime indicators, we now proceed to establish an investment strategy that is *regime-optimal*. We define a regime-optimal portfolio as the *best* asset allocation to hold during the predicted state of the regime space.

Past examples of applications of a state-space-based approaches for constructing portfolios can be found in the literature. Clarke and de Silva (1998) suggest a method to expand the optimal frontier when considering multiple regimes. We apply the approach of Ang and Bekaert (2004), who take into consideration the effect of high volatility environments on the equity market. Blitz and van Vliet (2011) use a modified version of the NBER economic cycle indicator described above to capture the time-variation of risk and return properties in US markets. More recently, and from a sovereign investor's perspective, Cruz-Lopez and Rivadeneyra (2014) set up an approach to maximise the expected value of international reserves in the states of the world where they are most likely to be liquidated. They choose foreign exchange rates as state variables to differentiate between different regimes.

Our approach offers a more general setting: by recognising that asset portfolio investors may have different objectives, goals, and reaction functions, we define our state space by using a set of indicators that encompass a broader amount of information.

Table 9.2 T-statistics of β coefficient in the predictive regression of 12-month rolling volatility using monthly local currency returns

		MFI				*SRI*				*FTI*			
	k=	1	3	6	12	1	3	6	12	1	3	6	12
US	1 year	0.31	−0.09	−0.43	−0.81	−1.12	−1.25	−1.33	−1.49	2.23**	1.90*	1.47	0.16
	2 years	0.22	−0.14	−0.47	−0.88	−1.71*	−1.87*	−1.87*	−1.72*	2.22**	1.93*	1.46	0.14
	3 years	0.20	−0.14	−0.45	−0.91	−1.85*	−2.02**	−2.00**	−1.75*	2.38**	2.15**	1.65*	0.22
	4 years	0.24	−0.09	−0.40	−0.93	−1.75*	−1.92*	−1.93*	−1.66*	2.67***	2.56**	2.02**	0.40
	5 years	0.31	−0.01	−0.31	−0.92	−1.48	−1.63	−1.71*	−1.51	3.09***	3.12***	2.56**	0.64
	6 years	0.39	0.09	−0.20	−0.91	−1.11	−1.25	−1.39	−1.31	3.53***	3.73***	3.18***	0.92
	7 years	0.46	0.20	−0.07	−0.87	−0.73	−0.84	−1.04	−1.07	3.83***	4.16***	3.70***	1.19
	8 years	0.52	0.29	0.06	−0.82	−0.39	−0.49	−0.70	−0.82	3.89***	4.25***	3.93***	1.39
	9 years	0.57	0.37	0.19	−0.76	−0.13	−0.20	−0.41	−0.58	3.75***	4.10***	3.90***	1.52
	10 years	0.60	0.44	0.30	−0.70	0.08	0.03	−0.17	−0.35	3.53***	3.87***	3.73***	1.59
Germany	1 year	1.61	1.46	1.35	0.62	−0.88	−0.86	−0.94	−1.10	2.95***	2.53**	1.59	0.76
	2 years	0.92	0.53	0.28	−0.42	−0.54	−0.56	−0.64	−0.73	3.15***	3.06***	2.09**	0.47
	3 years	0.83	0.40	0.13	−0.57	−0.40	−0.42	−0.56	−0.54	3.22***	3.20***	1.86*	0.24
	4 years	0.70	0.28	0.05	−0.66	0.08	−0.03	−0.32	−0.36	3.55***	3.61***	1.95*	0.29
	5 years	0.45	0.05	−0.12	−0.78	0.88	0.61	0.06	−0.18	3.98***	4.18***	2.31**	0.54
	6 years	0.29	−0.06	−0.16	−0.82	1.58	1.12	0.36	−0.07	4.15***	4.52***	2.74***	0.87
	7 years	0.33	0.04	0.01	−0.72	1.92*	1.33	0.46	−0.05	3.96***	4.55***	3.10***	1.17
	8 years	0.52	0.30	0.30	−0.53	1.95*	1.34	0.44	−0.06	3.60***	4.40***	3.36***	1.40
	9 years	0.75	0.58	0.61	−0.32	1.84*	1.26	0.39	−0.08	3.25***	4.20***	3.50***	1.56
	10 years	0.96	0.83	0.86	−0.13	1.69*	1.16	0.33	−0.10	2.97***	4.01***	3.56***	1.67*
UK	1 year	0.76	0.69	0.61	0.12	−1.49	−1.48	−1.53	−1.91*	1.43	1.99**	1.70*	0.97
	2 years	0.35	0.29	0.24	0.20	−1.76*	−1.82*	−1.95*	−2.09**	2.10**	2.59***	1.86*	0.66

(*continued*)

Table 9.2 (continued)

		MFI				*SRI*				*FTI*			
	k=	1	3	6	12	1	3	6	12	1	3	6	12
	3 years	0.09	0.05	0.04	0.14	−1.76*	−1.87*	−2.08**	−2.12**	2.08**	2.54**	1.81*	0.57
	4 years	−0.01	−0.03	−0.02	0.14	−1.67*	−1.80*	−2.05**	−2.05**	1.87*	2.41**	1.79*	0.61
	5 years	0.03	0.02	0.05	0.20	−1.50	−1.63	−1.90*	−1.92*	1.63	2.31**	1.83*	0.75
	6 years	0.16	0.16	0.21	0.30	−1.23	−1.35	−1.64	−1.73*	1.41	2.24**	1.94*	0.99
	7 years	0.33	0.34	0.42	0.41	−0.94	−1.02	−1.33	−1.53	1.23	2.18**	2.06**	1.27
	8 years	0.48	0.51	0.62	0.51	−0.66	−0.71	−1.02	−1.33	1.07	2.10**	2.14**	1.55
	9 years	0.62	0.66	0.80	0.60	−0.44	−0.45	−0.75	−1.16	0.95	2.01**	2.19**	1.78*
	10 years	0.73	0.78	0.94	0.67	−0.27	−0.25	−0.53	−1.02	0.86	1.93*	2.20**	1.97**
Japan	1 year	−0.37	−0.06	0.28	0.30	−1.63	−1.84*	−2.16**	−2.78***	0.73	0.88	0.89	−0.29
	2 years	−0.27	−0.19	−0.04	−0.34	−1.65*	−2.02**	−2.68***	−3.24***	1.13	1.28	1.22	0.12
	3 years	−0.21	−0.33	−0.43	−1.05	−1.76*	−2.17**	−2.94***	−3.42***	1.34	1.47	1.36	0.41
	4 years	−0.25	−0.45	−0.66	−1.42	−1.96*	−2.35**	−3.13***	−3.62***	1.45	1.59	1.47	0.58
	5 years	−0.34	−0.59	−0.82	−1.63	−2.14**	−2.52**	−3.27***	−3.80***	1.58	1.72*	1.57	0.71
	6 years	−0.47	−0.73	−0.97	−1.77*	−2.25**	−2.62***	−3.31***	−3.87***	1.71*	1.83*	1.66*	0.82
	7 years	−0.59	−0.84	−1.07	−1.82*	−2.31**	−2.67***	−3.28***	−3.87***	1.83*	1.91*	1.72*	0.91
	8 years	−0.69	−0.93	−1.13	−1.81*	−2.33**	−2.69***	−3.23***	−3.82***	1.91*	1.95*	1.75*	0.97
	9 years	−0.77	−0.99	−1.16	−1.75*	−2.34**	−2.69***	−3.18***	−3.75***	1.96*	1.97**	1.77*	1.01
	10 years	−0.82	−1.02	−1.16	−1.69*	−2.34**	−2.68***	−3.13***	−3.67***	2.00**	1.97**	1.76*	1.03

Source: Authors' calculations using return data from Bloomberg and Bank of America/Merrill Lynch

Note: All t-statistics are Hansen-Hodrick adjusted

***$p < 0.01$, **$p < 0.05$, *$p < 0.1$

Naturally, the definition of *best* can vary depending on the investor's preferences and constraints. For example, take an investor with mean-variance preferences and a one-month regime-predicting horizon looking to maximise risk-adjusted returns. If the regime split has two states of nature $\{s_1, s_2\}$ and he foresees that the second state will prevail during the following month, the best portfolio to hold over the next 30 days could be the one which delivers the highest Sharpe ratio during said regime. The investor can subsequently re-adapt the portfolio if he foresees another regime switch. Alternatively, the investor could determine the probability of observing each of the two states during the following month and weight two state-optimal portfolios accordingly.

This definition highlights the importance of the regime identification process, which is of dynamic nature: the distribution of future bond returns is conditional on the state of the world. Naturally, a succinct definition of the state space and a methodology for forecasting such regimes are required, and are detailed as part of our investment set-up. It is also important to note at this point that, the methodology under which a portfolio is optimised is assumed to work, in principle. We take as given the portfolio optimisation process, and instead focus on pinpointing the value added to sovereign bond portfolios through regime identification.

9.4.2.1 Methodology

Regime-optimal portfolios are constructed by performing standard mean-variance (SMV) optimisation separately on risk and return estimates obtained conditionally. That is, based on each regime indicator, the historical returns of every bond prior to January 2000 are classified into two states: a high (H) and low regime (L), using the indicator's medians—a rather simple two-state split. Subsequently, for each set of returns from the high (s_H) and low (s_L) states, separate mean-variance optimisations are performed.

As a robustness check, these optimisations are executed for different currency numeraires and apply different rules by which a portfolio is selected from the efficient frontier. Next, the weights of the low and high regime portfolios are averaged either statically or dynamically. In the static approach, a constant weight of 50% is assigned to the weights of the low and high regime portfolios, respectively; in the dynamic approach, the weight is based on the expected value of the regime indicator (Table 9.3) at a given point in time; means and covariances are estimated in the sample from January 1985 to January 2000.

Table 9.3 Alternative assumptions used for portfolio construction

Portfolio selection criterions	• Minimum volatility • Maximum return/volatility ratio • Maximum Sharpe ratio • Target durations of 2, 4 and 6 years • Target volatilities of 2%, 4% and 6% • Maximum annualised loss probability of 2%, 5% and 10%
Currency numeraire assumptions	USD, EUR, GBP, JPY, and SDR

In detail, this portfolio construction process consists of the following steps:

1. Classifying the historical asset returns into low (s_L) and high (s_H) regime observations for each of the three regime indicators: MFI, SRI, and FTI. Any historical return observation is considered a high regime observation if the respective regime indicator exceeds its median during that period, and vice versa. This is the definition of our state space $\{s_L, s_H\}$.
2. Calculating low and high regime conditional means ($\mu| s_i$) and covariances ($\Sigma| s_i$) for each indicator and currency numeraire (thus in total 2 (#of regimes) × 3 (# of indicators) × 5 (# of numeraires) = 30 sets of means and covariances).
3. Calculating mean-variance efficient frontiers for each set of means and covariances: a low regime efficient frontier and a high regime efficient frontier.
4. Selecting one portfolio from the set of mean-variance efficient portfolios. We show the alternative selection criteria (Table 9.3).
5. For each regime indicator, the weights to place on the low $\left(w_L^*\right)$ and high $\left(w_H^*\right)$ regime optimal portfolios $\left\{w_L^*, w_H^*\right\}$ are determined using either a static and dynamic approach. Under the static weighting scheme, the low and high regime portfolios are weighted by w_i^* = 50% each. With the dynamic weighting, the low and high regime portfolios are weighted based on the expected value of the corresponding regime indicator. The expected value is obtained from an autoregressive process of order 1 with a projection horizon of 12 months, and represents our regime forecasting algorithm.[7]
6. Finally, as an aggregation method for both the dynamic and static approach, "combined" regime optimised portfolios are calculated as weighted averages across the regime identification criteria.

The combined regime-optimal portfolios are compared to standard mean-variance (SMV) optimal portfolios and a Bayesian approach (BAY) where the first moment of the prior distribution of expected returns is obtained by scaling expected return with the corresponding volatility. To be comparable to the regime-optimal portfolios, these portfolios are determined using in-sample data up to January 2000.

9.4.2.2 Results

The regime-optimised portfolios show a degree of diversification in-between that observed for the SMV and BAY portfolios. We calculate the portfolio weights resulting from the alternative portfolio construction techniques for the selection criterion of a target duration of four years separately for the alternative numeraire assumptions (Fig. 9.6). Clearly, the SMV portfolios on the left show higher bond concentration with corner solutions: the allocation to a single yield curve node can go as high as 50% of the portfolio. Under the Bayesian approach, the portfolios appear to be well diversified with few asset classes at zero weight and maximum asset weights not much higher than 10%. The regime-optimised portfolios appear to be more diversified than the SMV but less than the BAY portfolios. Furthermore, the results hold for the average portfolio composition across *all* selection criteria. Again, the SMV approach also shows more concentration in comparison to the Bayesian optimisation and the regime-optimised allocation.

With regard to the portfolios' risk and return profile, we present the mean returns and conditional returns-at-risk at a 95% confidence level over the out-of-sample period (Fig. 9.7). The dots represent either the SMV optimal portfolios or the Bayesian portfolios and the static or dynamic regime-optimal portfolios. The individual dots for each optimisation approach refer to the combination of different numeraires (5) with different selection criterions (12)—thus 60 dots for each approach. The regime-optimal portfolios show different features than SMV and BAY portfolios.

Compared to the SMV optimisation allocations, the regime-optimal portfolios appear to show mostly superior risk-return combinations for both the dynamic and static approaches. This is evidenced by their corresponding dots, which are mostly northeast of those produced from the SMV approach (two upper panels of Fig. 9.7). However, compared to the Bayesian approach, the regime-optimised portfolios do not show superior risk-return properties. The static approach appears to show less favourable risk-return combinations than the Bayesian approach for some of the currency numeraires.

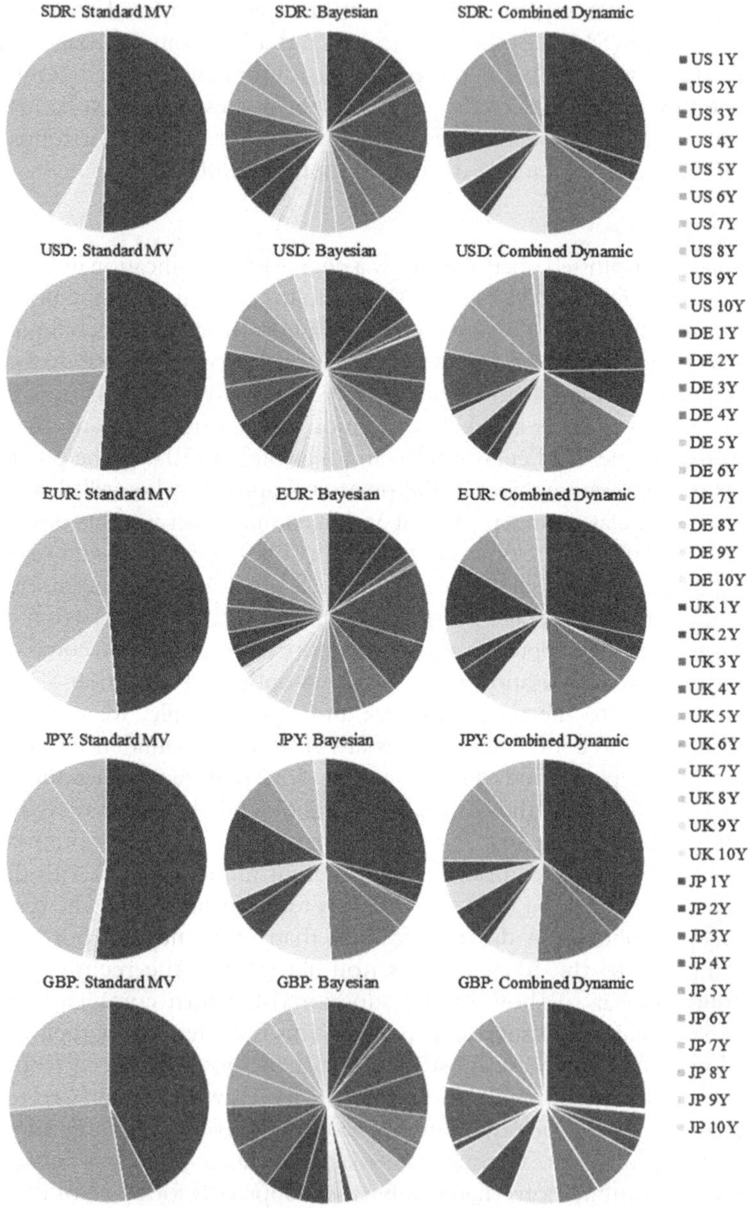

Fig. 9.6 Composition of optimised portfolios for a target duration of four years

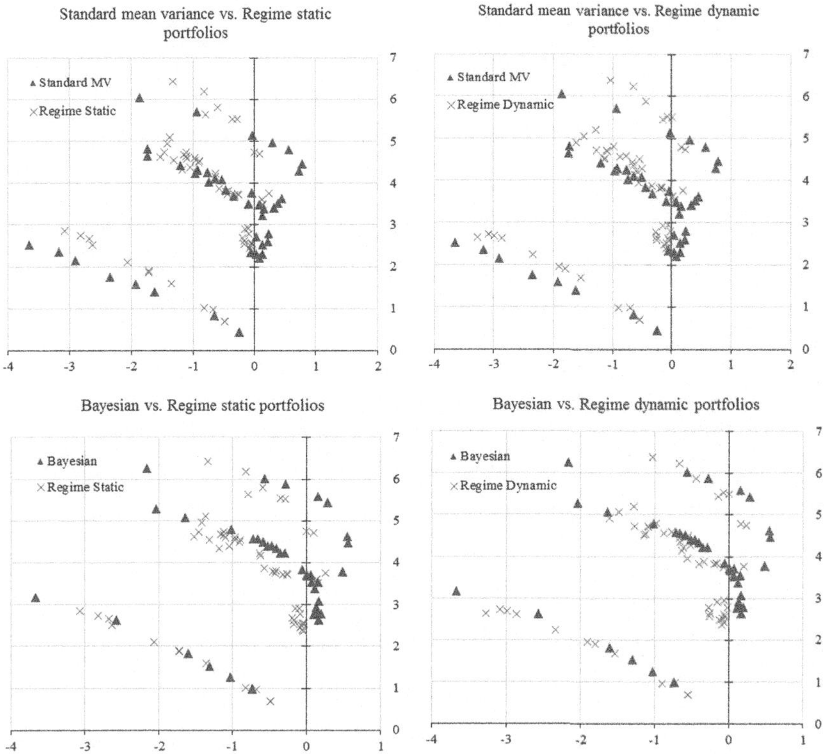

Fig. 9.7 Risk-return plots of regime portfolios versus standard mean-variance and Bayesian portfolios

Across the five numeraires, the combined regime portfolios (both static and dynamic) result in consistently higher mean returns than the full sample SMV and BAY optimisations (Table 9.4). At the same time, return volatilities of the combined static regime portfolios are broadly comparable to the SMV and BAY portfolios (slightly higher for the EUR and JPY numeraire and slightly lower for the GBP) while the combined dynamic portfolios tend to have, on average, slightly higher volatility. Also, average duration tends to be slightly higher for the combined regime portfolios—evidence of further risk taking.

Table 9.4 Absolute risk-return properties of standard, Bayesian, and regime portfolios

			MFI		*SRI*		*FTI*		*Combined*	
Numeraire/statistics	Standard MV	Bayesian	Static	Dynamic	Static	Dynamic	Static	Dynamic	Static	Dynamic
SDR										
Mean return	3.3%	3.6%	4.1%	4.0%	3.6%	3.5%	3.9%	4.3%	3.7%	4.0%
Volatility	2.1%	2.1%	2.4%	2.3%	2.0%	2.0%	2.3%	2.6%	2.1%	2.3%
Sharpe ratio	0.72	0.86	0.94	0.94	0.88	0.86	0.91	0.95	0.89	0.94
Return-at-risk	0.2%	0.3%	−0.1%	0.4%	0.2%	0.1%	−0.2%	−0.5%	−0.2%	0.0%
Cond. return-at-risk	−0.1%	0.0%	−0.5%	−0.1%	−0.4%	−0.4%	−0.6%	−1.1%	−0.5%	−0.5%
Loss prob.	3.2%	2.1%	5.8%	3.2%	4.7%	4.2%	5.3%	6.8%	5.3%	5.8%
Modified duration	4.0	4.1	4.9	5.2	3.8	3.9	4.5	5.2	4.2	4.5
USD										
Mean return	3.4%	3.7%	4.1%	4.1%	3.7%	3.6%	4.0%	4.4%	3.8%	4.0%
Volatility	2.2%	2.2%	2.3%	2.3%	2.1%	2.1%	2.4%	2.7%	2.2%	2.3%
Sharpe ratio	0.70	0.86	0.96	0.97	0.88	0.85	0.90	0.95	0.88	0.95
Return-at-risk	0.1%	0.1%	−0.1%	0.4%	0.0%	0.1%	−0.4%	−0.7%	−0.3%	−0.2%
Cond. return-at-risk	−0.3%	−0.2%	−0.5%	−0.1%	−0.4%	−0.4%	−0.8%	−1.3%	−0.6%	−0.6%
Loss prob.	4.7%	3.2%	5.3%	2.6%	5.3%	4.7%	5.8%	6.8%	5.8%	5.8%
Modified duration	4.2	4.4	4.9	5.1	4.0	4.0	4.7	5.5	4.3	4.5
EUR										
Mean return	3.4%	3.7%	4.1%	4.0%	3.6%	3.6%	3.9%	4.3%	3.8%	4.0%
Volatility	2.2%	2.3%	2.6%	2.5%	2.2%	2.2%	2.4%	2.7%	2.4%	2.5%
Sharpe ratio	0.68	0.75	0.84	0.82	0.76	0.74	0.80	0.86	0.78	0.82
Return-at-risk	0.3%	0.2%	0.0%	0.2%	−0.1%	−0.1%	−0.2%	−0.3%	−0.2%	−0.1%
Cond. return-at-risk	0.0%	−0.1%	−0.5%	−0.1%	−0.5%	−0.5%	−0.6%	−1.1%	−0.5%	−0.5%
Loss prob.	2.6%	2.1%	4.7%	2.1%	5.3%	6.3%	5.3%	6.8%	5.3%	5.3%
Modified duration	3.8	3.9	4.6	4.9	3.6	3.7	4.2	4.8	3.9	4.2

JPY										
Mean return	1.4%	1.7%	2.3%	2.3%	1.7%	1.6%	2.1%	2.5%	1.9%	2.1%
Volatility	1.3%	1.5%	2.1%	2.0%	1.5%	1.4%	1.9%	2.5%	1.7%	1.9%
Sharpe ratio	0.93	1.03	0.99	1.02	0.99	1.01	0.98	0.93	0.99	1.00
Return-at-risk	−1.0%	−0.7%	−1.0%	−1.0%	−0.8%	−0.7%	−1.1%	−1.7%	−0.9%	−1.2%
Cond. return-at-risk	−1.6%	−1.4%	−1.9%	−1.8%	−1.2%	−1.2%	−1.8%	−2.1%	−1.6%	−1.7%
Loss prob.	13.7%	12.6%	16.8%	13.7%	16.8%	16.8%	19.5%	19.5%	18.9%	16.8%
Modified duration	3.5	3.7	4.7	4.9	3.3	3.2	4.3	5.0	3.9	4.1
GBP										
Mean return	4.4%	4.9%	5.1%	5.0%	4.9%	4.8%	5.1%	5.5%	4.9%	5.1%
Volatility	2.5%	2.6%	2.7%	2.6%	2.5%	2.5%	2.7%	3.0%	2.5%	2.7%
Sharpe ratio	0.60	0.76	0.82	0.81	0.80	0.75	0.81	0.86	0.78	0.83
Return-at-risk	0.9%	0.9%	0.6%	1.1%	0.5%	0.5%	0.5%	0.1%	0.4%	0.5%
Cond. return-at-risk	0.4%	0.2%	−0.2%	0.4%	−0.2%	−0.2%	−0.4%	−0.9%	−0.3%	−0.2%
Loss prob.	0.0%	1.6%	2.6%	0.5%	2.6%	3.7%	4.2%	4.7%	4.2%	2.6%
Modified duration	4.6	5.0	5.1	5.2	4.4	4.5	5.1	5.7	4.7	4.9

Source: Authors' calculations using return data from Bloomberg and Bank of America/Merrill Lynch

Notes: Summary statistics for the absolute return distribution of portfolios averaged over the individual selection criterions for the respective optimisation approaches. The figures are annualised and the return-at-risk and conditional return-at-risk are calculated for a confidence level of 95%

Indeed, tail risks appear to be markedly higher for the combined regime portfolios. That is, the combined regime portfolios show almost consistently lower returns-at-risk and higher loss probabilities. However, these differences are larger than what can be attributed to observed differences in volatilities and durations. Risk-adjusted returns—measured on the basis of the Sharpe ratio—of the combined regime portfolios are consistently higher compared to the SMV portfolios and mostly higher compared to the BAY portfolios, with exception of the JPY numeraire.

Next, we turn to an excess return perspective to analyse how regime portfolios perform relative to their corresponding SMV counterparts. We also show the evolution of the cumulative excess returns of the regime portfolios—averaged for the individual regime indicators separately—over the in-sample and out-of-sample period (Fig. 9.8). While we observe a fairly continuous increase in the cumulative return of the combined regime portfolio, the allocations based on the individual regime indicators perform quite differently over time. Both the Macro Fragility and Financial

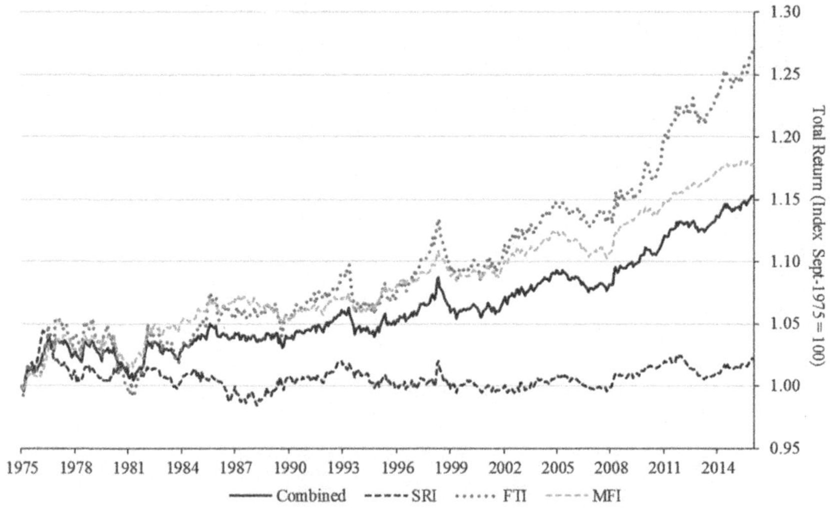

Fig. 9.8 Evolution of cumulative excess returns of regime portfolios over standard mean-variance portfolios

Turbulence-based portfolios show continuously increasing cumulative excess returns while the Systemic Risk-based portfolio implies essentially a sideways evolution of the cumulative excess return.

While taking a closer look to the summary statistics for the excess returns of the regime optimal and Bayesian optimal portfolios over SMV ones, we find that the combined regime portfolios consistently show positive excess returns for all numeraires with significance levels between 90% and 95%, and the excess returns of those dynamically rebalanced are slightly higher (Table 9.5). Nonetheless, the BAY portfolios show a consistent excess returns relative to the SMV portfolios. While the level of the excess returns is lower, they have higher statistical significance.

9.4.2.3 Stylised Facts

Regime-optimal portfolios demonstrate markedly different properties than portfolios based on SMV optimisation in an out-of-sample backtest. They imply more diversified holdings and show a lower inclination to corner solutions. In addition, the regime portfolios show higher mean returns at broadly comparable volatilities. Accordingly, their Sharpe ratios indicate better risk-adjusted returns. The excess returns of the combined regime portfolios compared are statistically significant and gradually increasing over time. At the same time, the tails of the regime portfolios are markedly fatter while return-at-risks are lower and loss probabilities are higher.

This combination of statistically significant excess returns, comparable return volatilities and fatter tail distributions may indicate that the regime portfolios constitute a factor. Arguably, positive factor returns could arise from a combination of two sources:

(a) SMV portfolios may turn out to be insufficiently diversified and risk-return inefficient in the out-of-sample period. The fact that the Bayesian portfolios show excess returns over them—at comparable volatilities and tail properties—may support this notion.
(b) Secondly, regime-optimised portfolios could be riskier than SMV portfolios, as indicated by fatter tails at comparable volatilities. The regime portfolios may therefore be compensated for the risk of regime switches in the asset return distributions. That is, the regime-based portfolios are a combination of allocations that are optimised for conditional asset return distributions in low and high fragility, turbulence,

Table 9.5 Excess returns relative to the standard mean-variance portfolio over the out-of-sample period

		MFI		*SRI*		*FTI*		*Combined*	
	Bayesian	Static	Dynamic	Static	Dynamic	Static	Dynamic	Static	Dynamic
SDR									
Mean	0.30%	0.77%	0.71%	0.32%	0.26%	0.58%	1.02%	0.44%	0.66%
T-statistic	(2.66)***	(2.70)***	(2.82)***	(1.51)	(1.37)	(2.37)**	(2.40)**	(2.01)**	(2.44)**
Standard deviation	0.46%	1.17%	1.04%	0.88%	0.78%	1.00%	1.74%	0.89%	1.11%
USD									
Mean	0.32%	0.70%	0.67%	0.31%	0.23%	0.59%	1.05%	0.39%	0.65%
T-statistic	(2.59)**	(2.47)**	(2.59)**	(1.52)	(1.29)	(2.34)**	(2.40)**	(1.85)*	(2.39)**
Standard deviation	0.50%	1.16%	1.05%	0.85%	0.74%	1.03%	1.80%	0.87%	1.12%
EUR									
Mean	0.22%	0.65%	0.54%	0.23%	0.17%	0.47%	0.88%	0.36%	0.53%
T-statistic	(2.73)***	(2.73)***	(2.64)***	(1.26)	(1.05)	(2.25)**	(2.33)**	(1.95)*	(2.32)**
Standard deviation	0.33%	0.97%	0.84%	0.73%	0.67%	0.85%	1.55%	0.76%	0.94%
JPY									
Mean	0.35%	0.87%	0.85%	0.29%	0.26%	0.75%	1.16%	0.54%	0.76%
T-statistic	(2.62)***	(3.00)***	(3.17)***	(1.42)	(1.40)	(2.45)**	(2.41)**	(2.28)**	(2.58)**
Standard deviation	0.55%	1.18%	1.10%	0.83%	0.75%	1.26%	1.97%	0.97%	1.20%
GBP									
Mean	0.41%	0.63%	0.57%	0.49%	0.39%	0.64%	1.07%	0.46%	0.67%
T-statistic	(2.69)***	(2.23)**	(2.31)**	(1.56)	(1.42)	(2.15)**	(2.17)**	(1.73)*	(2.09)**
Standard deviation	0.62%	1.17%	1.01%	1.29%	1.12%	1.22%	2.01%	1.08%	1.32%

Source: Authors' calculations using return data from Bloomberg and Bank of America/Merrill Lynch

***$p < 0.01$, **$p < 0.05$, *$p < 0.1$

and systemic risk regimes, respectively. However, the information on asset return distributions cross regimes, that is, unconditional volatilities and unconditional correlations, do not enter the portfolio construction.

In summary, the return distributions of regime-optimised portfolios differ significantly from those derived on the basis of standard techniques. The regime-optimised portfolios show superior Sharpe ratios—but contrary to our prior—they also imply fatter-tailed return distributions. With these results, regime-optimal portfolios appear to be a less obvious choice as a technique for robust optimisation. However, they may constitute an independent risk factor which could give rise to an expected excess return over standard portfolios.

9.5 Concluding Remarks

Regime identification algorithms can prove useful in many situations: for historical analysis, to better understand how financial markets have behaved under different scenarios; for forward-looking tests, because having the ability to foretell regimes could inform us about investor behaviour going forward; and, as shown in this chapter, for portfolio construction. By studying the properties and implications of regimes and regime changes, we can set up a state-dependent investment strategy.

A regime-based approach to portfolio construction has the flexibility to adapt to changing economic conditions. To perform it, indicators are required that allow to adjust in a timely fashion to changing states of the world. In this chapter, we propose three measures: the MFI, the FTI, and the SRI—all of which allow us to partition the state space into "low" and "high" risk states.

Furthermore, we show that the proposed regime indicators are useful in predicting future developed market government bond return distributions for several investment horizons. And, given some evidence of predictive power from the regime identification measures, we establish a multi-step algorithm to perform dynamic asset allocation.

This method seems to perform well when compared to SMV algorithms but faces challenges vis-à-vis a Bayesian approach. Though regime-optimal portfolios display higher Sharpe ratios, they represent higher tail-risk strategies, therefore being a less preferable choice when the investor's target is minimising the probability of loss. This is usually the case for more conservative sovereign investors. However, the higher excess returns delivered by regime-optimal portfolios appear to provide some evidence that they are a result of greater exposure to risk premia.

This approach can be used to support strategic or tactical asset allocation decisions; however, it should be adjusted for some practical issues. First, the usefulness of these (or other regime indicators) could be explored in a broader asset class universe; for example, one comprising equity, credit and even commodities markets, such as gold. Second, the dynamic optimisation methodology can be extended to allow for automatic updating of the optimal "high" and "low" regime return distributions, thereby permitting the conditional efficient frontiers to be refreshed as often as the portfolio is rebalanced. Third, a finer partition of the state space could be defined. Fourth, one could also try to calibrate the optimal rebalancing horizon—this could help minimise transaction costs and find statistical evidence of excess returns for medium and long-term investors. Finally, while our use of regime identification aimed to construct a dynamic portfolio *along* regimes—perhaps, one can try and construct a portfolio that is robust *across* different states of the world.

Notes

1. See Brida, Anyul & Punzo 2006. "A review on the notion of economic regime" for a review of the basic notions and definitions of economic regime and regime switching.
2. Refer to the website http://www.nber.org/cycles.html for the US Business Cycle Expansions and Contractions dates and durations.
3. Previous applications of principle component analysis for regime identification include Billio et al. 2010. "Measuring systemic risk in the finance and insurance sectors"; Pukthuanthong and Roll 2009. "Global market integration: An alternative measure and its application"; and Kritzman et al. 2011. "Principal components as a measure of systemic risk".
4. Mahalanobis 1927. "Analysis of race-mixture in Bengal", used several characteristics of the human skull to analyse dissimilarities between various castes and tribes in India. He later proposed a more generalised statistical measure, the Mahalanobis distance, which takes into account both the standard deviations of individual dimensions and the correlations between

dimensions (see Mahalanobis 1936. "On the generalised distance in statistics"). For applications of the measure in finance see Chow et al. 1999. "Optimal portfolios in good times and bad"; Kritzman and Li 2010. "Skulls, financial turbulence, and risk management" and references therein.

5. Specifically, we use the total return indices of U.S. Treasuries, investment grade global corporate bonds, the MSCI World U.S. and Non-U.S. equity indices and the GSCI Commodity Index.
6. For simplicity, only *t*-statistics and significance level for typical intervals are shown. The intercept and slope values are available upon request.
7. The expected value is normalised based on data from the in-sample period. The weight of the low-regime optimal portfolio corresponds to the normalised value of the expected regime indicator (x) and the weight of the high-regime portfolio corresponds to 1 minus the normalised value ($1 - x$). The dynamic regime optimal portfolio then is: $w^*_{\text{dynamic}} = x \cdot w^*_L + (1-x) \cdot w^*_H$.

References

Ang, A., & Bekaert, G. (2004). How regimes affect asset allocation. *Financial Analysts Journal, 60*(2), 86–99.

Billio, M., Getmansky, M., Lo, A., & Pelizzon, L. (2010). Measuring systemic risk in the finance and insurance sectors. *MIT Sloan Research Paper No. 4774–10.*

Blitz, D., & van Vliet, P. (2011). Dynamic strategic asset allocation: Risk and return across economic regimes, *Journal of Asset Management, 12*(5), 360–375.

Brida, J. G., Punzo, L. F. & Puchet Anyul, M. (2006). A review on the notion of economic regime, *International Journal of Economic Research, 5*(1), 55–76.

Chow, G., Jacquier, E., Lowrey, K., & Kritzman, M. (1999). Optimal portfolios in good times and bad. *Financial Analysts Journal, 55*(3), 65–73.

Clarke, R. G., & de Silva, H. (1998). State-dependent asset allocation, *Journal of Portfolio Management, 24*(2), 57–64.

Cruz-Lopez, J., & Rivadeneyra, F. (2014). *Foreign reserves and tail risks.* Mimeo: Bank of Canada.

Georgescu-Roegen, N. (1951). Relaxation phenomena in linear dynamic models. In T. C. Koopmans (Ed.), *Activity analysis of production and allocation.* New York: John Wiley & Sons.

Goldfeld, S. M., & Quandt, R. E. (1973). A Markov model for switching regressions. *Journal of Econometrics, 1*(1), 3–16.

Hamilton, J. D. (1989). A new approach to the economic analysis of nonstationary time series and the business cycle. *Econometrica, 57*(2), 357–384.

Hansen, L. P., & Hodrick, R. J. (1980). Forward exchange rates as optimal predictors of future spot rates: An econometric analysis. *Journal of Political Economy, 88*(5), 829–853.

Kritzman, M., & Li, Y. (2010). Skulls, financial turbulence, and risk management. *Financial Analysts Journal, 66*(5), 30–41.
Kritzman, M., Li, Y., Page S., & Rigson R. (2011). Principal components as a measure of systemic risk, *Journal of Portfolio Management, 37*(4), 112–126.
Mahalanobis, P. C. (1927). Analysis of race-mixture in Bengal. *Journal of the Asiatic Society of Bengal, 23*, 301–333.
Mahalanobis, P. C. (1936). On the generalised distance in statistics. *Proceedings of the National Institute of Sciences of India, 2*(1), 49–55.
Pukthuanthong, K., & Roll, R. (2009). Global market integration: An alternative measure and its application. *Journal of Financial Economics, 94*(2), 214–232.

CHAPTER 10

Benchmark-Relative and Absolute-Return Are the Same Thing: Conditions Apply

Robert Scott

10.1 Portfolio Objectives

Although they are both trying to maximise return for a given level of risk, benchmark-relative and absolute-return managers adopt different means for getting there. The benchmark-relative manager is maximising alpha, or return relative to the benchmark, subject to a tracking error limit, while the absolute-return manager is maximising total return subject to some risk limit such as a probability of loss or absolute volatility and so on. It might seem that the benchmark-plus-alpha that a benchmark-relative manager generates should be similar in magnitude to that which an absolute-return manager might deliver (at least during an up market); however, it turns out that this is not necessarily the case.

Our investigation is simulation-based, examining market views and optimal portfolios to test the impact of different investment objectives. The details of the simulation procedure can be found in the appendix and the specific objective functions and constraints for each strategy can be found in Table 10.1. Suffice it to say here that we have assumed that the

R. Scott (✉)
Official Institutions, Schroder Investment Management, London, UK
e-mail: robert.scott@schroders.com

N. Bulusu et al. (eds.), *Advances in the Practice of Public Investment Management*, https://doi.org/10.1007/978-3-319-90245-6_10

Table 10.1 Formal optimisation problems for absolute-return and benchmark-relative

Strategy	*Optimisation problem*
Absolute-return	Maximise $R_p = \beta_p F$ Subject to: $\sigma_{p,i} \leq$ Target max risk $i = 1 \ldots n$ where R_p is the return on the portfolio, β_p is the set of factor sensitivities in the portfolio, and F is the set of factor returns
Benchmark-relative	Maximise $\alpha_p = (\beta_p - \beta_{BM})F$ Subject to: $TE_p \leq$ Target max TE where α_p is the excess return of the portfolio over the benchmark and β_p and β_{BM} are the factor sensitivities in the portfolio and benchmark
Benchmark-relative, beta constrained	Maximise $\alpha_p = (\beta_p - \beta_{BM})F$ Subject to: $TE_p \leq$ Target max TE $\text{beta}_p = 1$ where beta_p is the overall beta of the portfolio relative to the benchmark (covariance divided by benchmark variance)
Benchmark-relative, risk capped	Maximise $\alpha_p = (\beta_p - \beta_{BM})F$ Subject to: $TE_p \leq$ Target max TE $\sigma_p \leq \sigma_{BM}$ where σ_p and σ_{BM} are the volatilities of the portfolio and benchmark

job of the benchmark-relative manager is to maximise their information ratio, and to apply this process to a multitude of similar portfolios, all with differing benchmarks and risk limits. For any one portfolio, the alpha is maximised subject to a tracking error (or other) limit. The alpha can be generated in the purest form by either market timing the beta (or betas) in the portfolio or through security selection.

In principle, the mandate can have a very low or a very high tracking error—there is nothing intrinsic to benchmark-relative investing that requires low tracking error. Absolute-return seeks to generate the highest return in the portfolio subject to a given risk limit, often captured as a measure of the probability of loss, or the likely frequency of losses over a particular horizon. By definition, for absolute-return investing, there is either no benchmark, or a margin over cash (or zero) is considered to be the benchmark. There is no requirement for return to be generated from either a single or multiple asset classes. We could therefore categorise absolute-return mandates into both single asset class (constrained) and multiple asset classes (unconstrained).

While maximising the Sharpe ratio or the information ratio might sound like very similar things, in fact, the process of maximising the information ratio does not deliver the highest possible Sharpe ratio for the end investor (see Roll 1992). For this reason, the opportunity set of possible returns for active investors are better under an absolute-return mandate than for a typical benchmark-relative strategy. This is true, so long as the benchmark is not mean-variance efficient: in other words, if the benchmark is not constructed by maximising returns as a function of risk. There is theoretical and empirical evidence in support of capitalisation-weighted benchmarks being inefficient (see Haugen and Baker 1991, 2010). The process of achieving the highest information ratio incentivises the portfolio manager to create portfolios that effectively "leverage" the beta in the benchmark to some degree as we show later. The end result is a higher information ratio, but a sub-optimal Sharpe ratio. Figure 10.1 shows the possible portfolios available to the investor for a given set of expected returns and risk tolerances: either total risk for absolute-return or tracking error for benchmark-relative. These possible portfolios are based on hypothetical risky assets with characteristics described in greater detail in the appendix. The portfolios constructed are based on maximising the expected return for absolute-return and expected alpha for benchmark-relative for the same set of expected asset returns. The only constraints for these initial portfolios are the risk limits (either total volatility or tracking error). If the benchmark-relative investor maximises alpha for a given level of tracking error, their resulting portfolio lies below an absolute-return portfolio with similar risks. Put another way, the Sharpe ratio is lower. Table 10.2 details some of the characteristics of the portfolios used to create the previous charts. In column one, we show that the benchmark is designed to have factor sensitivities, perhaps beta and duration derived from stocks and bonds. The next column makes clear that the absolute-return portfolio with similar risk levels to the benchmark has a higher expected return, this because it is constructed so as to be mean-variance efficient. The following two columns show some sample benchmark-return portfolios with different levels of tracking error. They are constructed to maximise the expected alpha subject only to the tracking error limit. Note the betas are fairly high, and the correlation between alpha and beta is also quite high. The information ratios, however, are the highest of all sample portfolios whereas the Sharpe ratios are among the lowest.

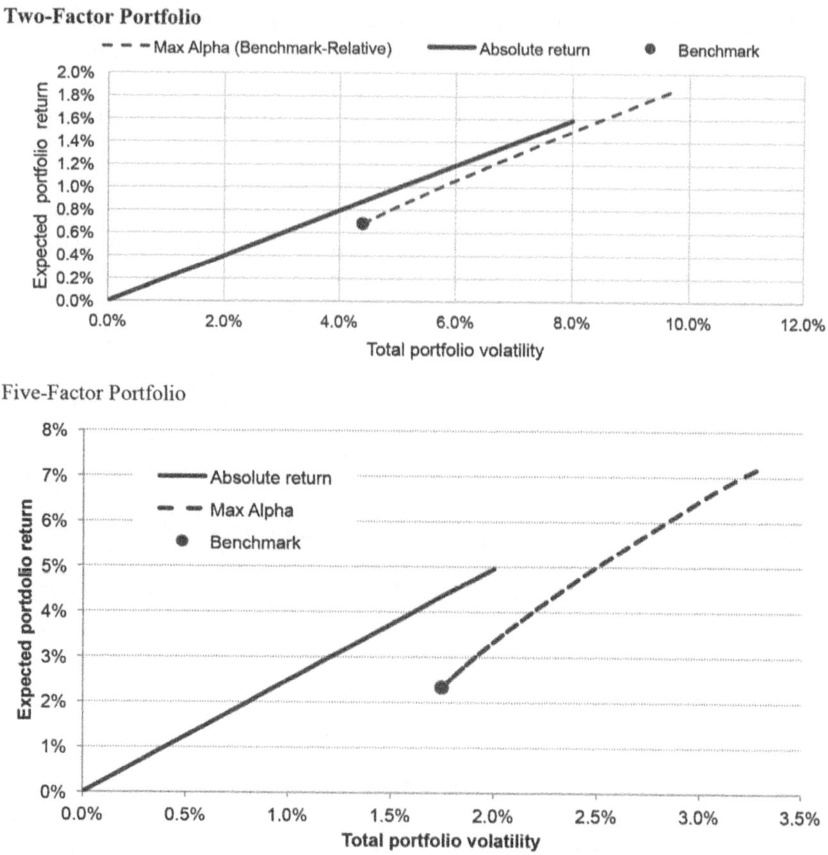

Fig. 10.1 Traditional benchmark-relative approaches lag absolute-returns for two- and five-factor portfolios. Two-Factor Portfolio

To improve the Sharpe ratio, an additional incentive is needed to induce the benchmark-relative active manager to improve the end investor's overall return for a given level of overall risk. One very effective method, we will argue, is for the investor to actually increase the constraints in the mandate.

Table 10.2 Sample portfolios under various constraints—two-factor model

	Benchmark	*AR risk = 4.4%*	*Max alpha TE = 90 bps*	*Max alpha TE = 3%*	*Beta = 1 TE = 90 bps*	*Beta = 1 TE = 3%*	*Risk < BM TE = 90 bps*	*Risk < BM TE = 3%*
Equity β	0.6	0.2	0.6	0.7	0.5	0.3	0.5	0.2
Bond β	2.0	4.6	2.9	5.1	3.0	5.3	2.9	4.6
α β correl		−33%	78%	78%	0%	0%	−10%	−33%
Beta	1	0.78	1.16	1.53	1.00	1.00	0.98	0.78
Total risk	4.4%	4.4%	5.1%	7.0%	4.5%	5.3%	4.4%	4.4%
Exp. ret.	0.68%	0.87%	0.86%	1.28%	0.80%	1.06%	0.78%	0.88%
Sharpe ratio	0.54	0.69	0.58	0.63	0.61	0.69	0.61	0.69
Alpha		0.19%	0.18%	0.60%	0.11%	0.37%	0.10%	0.19%
Tracking error		2.91%	0.90%	3.00%	0.90%	3.00%	0.90%	2.92%
Info. ratio		0.23	0.69	0.69	0.43	0.43	0.37	0.23

Source: Author's calculations. Note: All data are annualised and based on hypothetical returns and risks. See appendix for details of the simulation

10.2 Adding Constraints to Improve Performance

Conventional investment doctrine suggests that relaxing constraints is a way to improve performance. To test that dictum, we introduced two possible constraints (which we discuss below) on the benchmark-relative portfolio construction. Predictably, they reduced the amount of expected alpha for a given amount of tracking error, as shown in Fig. 10.2. Here we

Panel A: Two-Factor Portfolio

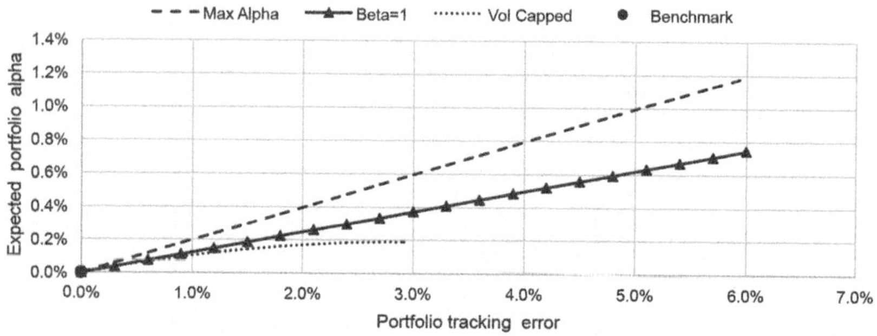

Panel B: Five-Factor Portfolio

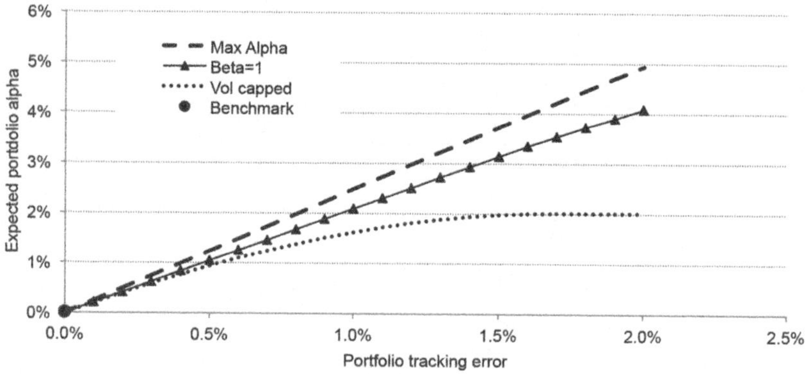

Fig. 10.2 Constraints tend to undermine information ratios—alpha and TEV for two- and five-factor portfolios

plot the unconstrained benchmark-relative optimal frontier from Fig. 10.1 in the space of tracking error vs. expected portfolio alpha, along with the frontiers for the two constrained portfolios, which we have called beta = 1 and vol-capped.

The first constraint we looked at, beta = 1, was originally proposed by Roll (1992) and can be formally defined in Eqs. 10.1 and 10.2 as:

$$\beta = \frac{\sigma_P \sigma_{BM} \rho}{\sigma_{BM}^2} \tag{10.1}$$

where $\sigma_P \sigma_{BM} \rho$ is the covariance of the portfolio with the benchmark and $\sigma^2{}_{BM}$ is the variance of the benchmark. In matrix terms using portfolio sensitivities, this is measured as:

$$\beta = F_P \Sigma F'_{BM} \big/ \sigma_{BM}^2 \tag{10.2}$$

where F_P is the set of portfolio factor sensitivities or betas and Σ is the covariance matrix of factor variances.

This forces the beta of the portfolio and that of the benchmark to be the same, which makes intuitive sense on many levels. Most importantly, it forestalls any attempt to substitute beta returns for alpha by making the portfolio a leveraged version of the benchmark. Any alpha will therefore be the result of genuine skill in stock selection or market timing and will be uncorrelated with beta. In fact, many active managers proclaim their objective to provide "uncorrelated alpha" so the constraint is within the spirit of active management.

The resulting portfolios at different levels of tracking error deliver lower alpha (and hence lower information ratios), as shown by the line in Fig. 10.2, but the overall Sharpe ratio of the portfolio is improved, and the set of possible portfolios is more efficient in terms of risk and return, as shown in Fig. 10.3. The reason for the improvement is that the Sharpe ratio combines three elements: the Sharpe ratio of the benchmark, the information ratio of the portfolio, and an element that equates to the correlation between the two, beta and alpha. If this correlation falls, as it is forced to in the beta = 1 portfolio, then the risk also falls and the total risk-adjusted return (Sharpe ratio) goes up.

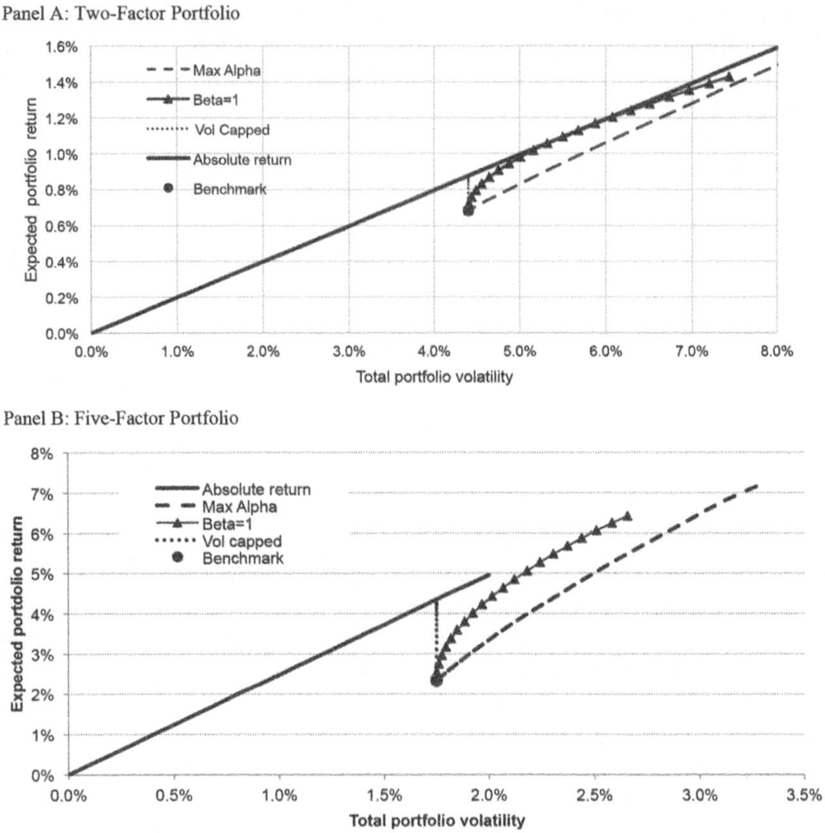

Fig. 10.3 Risk and return for two- and five-factor portfolios

Our second constraint is to restrict the total portfolio risk to a level no higher than that of the benchmark as originally proposed in Jorion (2003). We define the portfolio risk, benchmark risk, and the constraint as follows:

$$\sigma_p = \sqrt{F_P \Sigma F'_P} \tag{10.3}$$

$$\sigma_{BM} = \sqrt{F_{BM} \Sigma F'_{BM}} \tag{10.4}$$

$$F_P \Sigma F'_P - F_{BM} \Sigma F'_{BM} \leq 0 \tag{10.5}$$

This is also intuitive since it allows active positions, so long as the overall portfolio risk is not increased. Alpha-beta correlation under this scenario is typically zero or negative, which is also an attractive quality. As in the previous case, the total alpha delivered is lower for the same amount of tracking error as compared to an unconstrained portfolio, that is, the information ratio falls. But, again, the overall risk-return characteristics are improved and the set of possible portfolios is more efficient than the unconstrained approach, that is, their Sharpe ratio goes up.

To summarise, the unconstrained approach delivers the highest alpha, but at the expense of overall portfolio efficiency, while the two constrained approaches deliver less alpha, but also much less risk, so that the overall risk-return profile is better. For a given amount of total risk for the end investor, the constrained and absolute-return approaches all deliver higher returns. It is also noteworthy that at a certain level of tracking error, the constrained portfolios are as efficient as the set of possible absolute-return portfolios. We will discuss this in more detail in the next section.

10.3 Convergence of Benchmark-Relative and Absolute-Return Portfolios

We have shown that an investor is better served in the mean-variance framework by introducing a constraint into their mandate, either requiring that beta be equal to one or alternatively that total portfolio risk is never more than benchmark risk. In this section we will show some examples of what representative examples of these portfolios might look like under varying tracking error assumptions. One point to note, however, is that all these hypothetical portfolios assume the investor will receive positive returns from their constituent risk factors. We will deal with bear-market scenarios in the next section.

Revisiting Table 10.2, it is useful to compare the previously described basic portfolios with the constrained benchmark-relative ones. The beta = 1 portfolios (columns 5 and 6) have lower information ratios, but higher Sharpe ratios, and—as discussed earlier—the alpha-beta correlation is zero.

The last two columns display two sample portfolios where the overall risk is limited to the benchmark level (σ) or below: one for a tracking error (TE) of 1% and a second for a tracking error of 3.0%. Like the beta = 1 portfolios, these have higher Sharpe ratios and lower information ratios. The portfolio sensitivities for the TE = 3.0% portfolio are highly significant: *they are identical to the sensitivities of the absolute-return portfolio.* Put another way, a benchmark-return manager, operating within a tracking error and total risk constraint, while maximising alpha, has created an identical portfolio to that of an absolute-return manager (the two shaded columns). One final note. It is possible to show the same convergence for a beta = 1 portfolio, although at a much higher level of tracking error.

Thus far, we have demonstrated that it is possible to constrain a benchmark-relative manager in such a way that it induces them to improve the overall Sharpe ratio of their portfolio. In doing so, the portfolio ends up with identical characteristics to that of an absolute-return manager. However, there is one important proviso: returns for the risk factors must be expected to be positive. In an upcoming section, we will look at how a bear-market scenario affects these conclusions. Before turning to this point, however, the question arises as to how an investor can identify the amount of tracking error necessary to allow the portfolio exposure to be the same as the absolute-return portfolio. We will address this in the next section.

10.4 Identifying Optimal Tracking Error Levels

Figure 10.3 and Table 10.2 show that at some level of tracking error a constrained-alpha maximisation strategy will produce portfolios identical to absolute-return portfolios. The question arises as to what is the determinant of the required level of tracking error. We can borrow from Scott (2011) for the answer for this. Using the simulations from Fig. 10.3, the benchmark-relative portfolios that have identical characteristics to the absolute-return portfolios satisfy the criteria derived in Scott (2011), namely:

$$\lambda * = \frac{IR - \rho SR}{SR - \rho IR} \tag{10.6}$$

where $\lambda *$ is the optimal risk budget, determined as a function of the information ratio (IR), the Sharpe ratio (SR), and the correlation between alpha and beta. The risk budget is the ratio of the tracking error to the benchmark risk. A tracking error of 2% and 4% benchmark volatility would have a risk budget of 2%/4% or 0.5. Unfortunately, it is not possible to derive in advance what the impact of the constraint will be on the information ratio of the portfolio manager. This means that it is not likely practical to compute the optimal risk budget. Nevertheless, it is perhaps useful to indicate the general magnitude of tracking error necessary to produce the most efficient benchmark-relative portfolios. As we shall see in the next section, perhaps the more important decision on tracking error is driven by the desire to protect in a bear-market environment. We will turn to address this important issue in the next section.

10.5 How to Avoid Tracking Bears

As mentioned at the outset, one of the primary motivations for switching to an absolute-return strategy is to benefit from downside protection during a bear market. In principle, benchmark-constrained investments should be dragged into negative territory when the market falls. Even if the active manager has added alpha, (s)he may still have made losses in absolute terms. By contrast, an absolute-return manager with market-timing skill aims to anticipate bear markets and shift the portfolio into cash to avoid negative returns. The question then arises, what would a benchmark-relative manager do if they had the same skill and anticipated the same bear market? Depending on the tracking error, the optimal portfolio construction would be one as close to cash as the tracking error would allow. How do our constrained portfolios measure up to this ideal? To find out, we re-examined the outcomes in Fig. 10.3 under a bear-market scenario.

In all cases, we assumed that the absolute-return and the benchmark-relative managers had both correctly anticipated a bear market and had shifted to a portfolio structure consistent with their investment objectives. The former, since they are focused on capital preservation, would shift the portfolio into cash in an extreme case. Without the same room for manoeuvre, the latter would have to do different things, depending on the constraints they were working under.

In the simple case, where the (unconstrained) benchmark-relative manager is maximising alpha subject to a limit on tracking error, they would shift as close to cash as the tracking error would allow. This would be

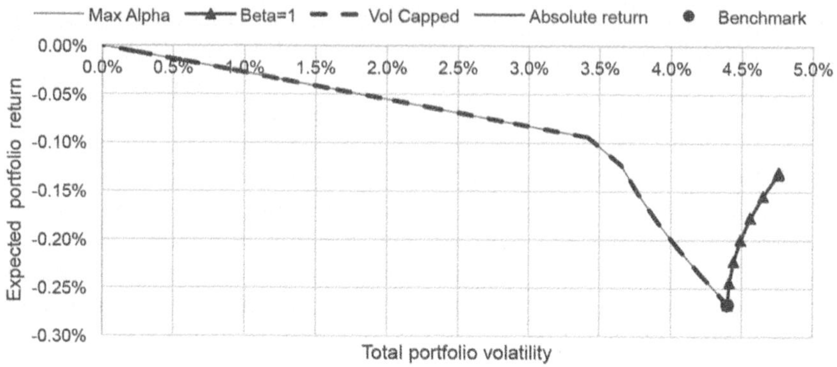

Fig. 10.4 The bear-market test

represented by the solid line in Fig. 10.4. The greater the tracking error, the further back up the solid line they would go and the lower the losses they would suffer. The constrained portfolio, where volatility must be no more than the benchmark volatility, would deliver the same portfolio as the unconstrained benchmark-relative strategy. Again, a higher tracking error would allow them greater leeway to move into cash. The reason they are identical is that both portfolios would be aimed at reducing risk in a bear market. However, the manager who has to hold the beta equal to one is labouring under an obvious disadvantage. Their performance must, perforce, be in line with the benchmark and therefore likely to be negative, depending of course on how much alpha they can derive from their asset mix and their security selection. The absolute-return portfolio is not visible on the graph, since, barring the ability to go short, the manager would be sitting completely in cash assuming all markets are producing negative returns.

The addition of one of the two constraints in a bull market environment clearly improves the efficiency and end-investor risk-adjusted return over an unconstrained benchmark-relative approach. In a bear market, however, the beta = 1 constraint is at a clear disadvantage to the total risk constraint. The total tracking error required to allow for an all cash position, however, is equal to the volatility of the benchmark, something that is higher than the conventional mandates might allow.

10.6 Implications for Investors and Conclusions

Investors who are interested in pursuing an absolute-return strategy either to improve portfolio efficiency or to avoid losses in bear markets are well served by making the switch, so long as the manager has the necessary market-timing skills. For those who would like the same benefits, but might wish—or be forced—to remain in a benchmark-relative framework, there are other options. This might be the case where the institution performs a strategic asset allocation and has budgeted risk and return to different investment teams for benchmark risks/returns and excess active risks/returns. The simplest prescription is to consider increasing tracking error of the mandate, allowing more defensive positions in a bear market. They could even consider non-traditional approaches like having asymmetric tracking error limits where the limit is large so long as the portfolio beta or total risk is being decreased. If the single most important element of absolute-return is loss-avoidance, then allowing enough tracking error to position in or close to a 100% cash holding would accomplish this.

Alternatively, the investor could add one of the restrictions mentioned in this chapter, while also allowing for enough tracking error to permit the benchmark-relative portfolio manager to move to the highest Sharpe ratio portfolio. The second constraint of limiting the total portfolio risk to no more than the benchmark risk has the added benefit of allowing the manager to move closer to cash ahead of an anticipated bear market.

Options for converting benchmark-relative mandates into absolute-return-like mandates:

1. Constrain total portfolio risk to being less than or equal to benchmark risk. Allow tracking error to be as large as the benchmark volatility. The large tracking error could result in aggressive positions, but only in the direction of defending the portfolio against losses. The downside is that the risk constraint tends to force a negative correlation between alpha and beta.
2. Constrain beta to be equal or less than one. Allow for a large tracking error. Constraining beta to one is fine in a bull market, but we saw that this was detrimental in a bear market. Changing the restriction to an inequality allows the manager to decrease overall risk in anticipation of a bear market.
3. Increase tracking error. In the absence of other constraints, the single easiest method for protecting downside in a bear market is to

allow the manager enough latitude to position the portfolio in cash without hitting any guideline constraints. Following this route alone does allow for the possibility of more severe losses in a bear market if the manger fails to correctly anticipate the decline.

None of these restrictions is commonplace. And they are likely to be met with resistance by some portfolio managers since they will force them to deliver a lower information ratio and perhaps lower alpha, which is often the basis for fees. Nevertheless, at a minimum, these arguments open a crack in the hitherto solid consensus that a benchmark-relative manager who maximises alpha is perfectly aligned with the interests of the end investor. There is perhaps room for improvement. One final note: This analysis is based on the assumption that there is market-timing skill. The decision to move from benchmark-relative to absolute-return will not in itself protect from losses. This is entirely dependent on a skilled portfolio manager correctly anticipating a bear market. These structures discussed above simply provide a framework to allow the skilled decisions to best be reflected in the construction of the portfolio.

Appendix: Simulation Details

Imagine a simple 60/40 stocks bonds portfolio where the stock component of the benchmark has a beta of one, meaning the benchmark has a beta of 0.6 (60% × 1) and the bond component is a simple 0–10-year universe of government bonds with a duration of 5, giving a benchmark duration of 2.0 (5.0 × 40%). We could simply describe this as a two-factor portfolio, and the decision for the portfolio manager is what the appropriate beta and duration are for the investment. There is a risk for each asset class (assumed to be 21% for the equity component and 3% for the bond component), and an expected return component. For equities, we have assumed an expected excess return over the risk-free rate of 7% and for bonds, 3%. Furthermore, we assume a correlation of 25% between stock and bond returns. It is important to note that the comparative results of this simulation are not sensitive to the actual expected returns, risks, or correlations (so long as they are not extremes, such as perfect positive or negative correlation, etc.). In an active process, the expected returns would change as the portfolio manager's views change, as well as possibly the expected correlation and volatilities. This information represents the minimum necessary to construct the best possible portfolio given a set of market views.

Under the absolute-return scenario, the possible portfolios are created using the highest expected return subject to a target or maximum portfolio volatility. The frontier of available portfolios then is the set of best possible portfolios assuming different levels of target risk. The simple benchmark-relative positions are the sensitivities that give the highest possible expected excess return over the benchmark (alpha), subject to a tracking error limit. It is important to point out here that these portfolios are based on the same market views. It is not feasible to have equities deliver 7% over cash for an absolute-return manager, and some other amount for a benchmark-relative manager. The market only has one outcome, although it can be measured against differing reference points. The constrained benchmark-relative simulations are based on the same framework and set of views as the unconstrained simulation but with the addition of beta = 1 in the first case and portfolio volatility ≤ benchmark volatility in the second case.

The simulation was repeated for five risk factors to ensure that the results were not unique to a two-asset portfolio, which produced similar results and identical conclusions.

References

Haugen, R. A., & Baker, N. L. (1991). The efficient market inefficiency of capitalization-weighted stock portfolios. *Journal of Portfolio Management, 17*(3), 35–40.

Haugen, R. A., & Baker, N. L. (2010). Case closed (Chapter 23). In J. Guerard Jr (Ed.), *The handbook of portfolio construction: Contemporary applications of Markowitz techniques* (pp. 601–619). New York: Springer.

Jorion, P. (2003). Portfolio optimisation with tracking-error constraints. *Financial Analysts Journal, 59*(5), 70–82.

Roll, R. (1992). A mean/variance analysis of tracking error. *Journal of Portfolio Management, 18*(4), 13–22.

Scott, R. (2011). Simple and optimal alpha strategy selection and risk budgeting. *Journal of Asset Management, 12*(3), 214–223.

CHAPTER 11

Factors and Sectors in Asset Allocation: Stronger Together?

Marie Brière and Ariane Szafarz

11.1 Introduction

Factor investing has recently become a huge success in asset allocation (Ang 2014). But its supposed superiority over other portfolio management techniques has yet to be proven. To fill that gap, we lay down a challenge to factor investing by organizing a contest pitting it against a well-established competitor, the classical industry-based approach to asset allocation (Sharpe 1992; Heston and Rouwenhorst 1994).[1] We compare the performance of factor-based and industry-based asset allocation strategies in the investment universe composed of US equities. We contrast the mean-variance performance of diversified portfolios made up of US industry sectors with diversified component portfolios of the five factors developed by Fama

M. Brière (✉)
Amundi, Paris, France

Paris Dauphine University, Paris, France
e-mail: marie.briere@amundi.com

A. Szafarz
Université Libre de Bruxelles (ULB), SBS-EM, Centre Emile Bernheim, Brussels, Belgium
e-mail: aszafarz@ulb.ac.be

N. Bulusu et al. (eds.), *Advances in the Practice of Public Investment Management*, https://doi.org/10.1007/978-3-319-90245-6_11

and French (2015). We duplicate all the trials for long-only portfolios (no short sales) and long-short ones (unlimited short sales accepted).[2] This duplication is a key aspect since factor-based asset management relies on short-selling and systematic portfolio rebalancing.

Our contest reveals no overall winner. In fact, we find superiority for each style depends on the specific time periods and investor restrictions. The alphas of factors with respect to the market inflate expected returns, while sectors reduce risks through high diversification potential. Factor investing tends to dominate when short sales are permitted. By contrast, when short-selling is excluded, industry-based allocation is preferable, especially for highly risk-averse investors. These results lead us to conjecture that factors and sectors could be complementary investing styles, and that combining them should help enhance financial performance, at least under some configurations of short-selling ability and/or risk preferences. Our empirical investigation suggests that composite portfolios made up of sectors and factors are particularly attractive under two types of circumstances. First, for long-only portfolios during non-crisis periods, a mixture of sectors and factors largely dominates both factor-only and industry-only investment styles. Second, unconstrained investors will find it best to combine sector and factor investments, especially during crisis periods. This chapter draws on the result that industry returns are difficult to explain using existing factors (Lewellen et al. 2010). It also confirms that industry portfolios can be used by investors facing portfolio restrictions (Bae et al. 2016). Further research is needed to investigate the optimal way to combine the different investing styles.

11.2 Data and Methods

Our investment universe is made up of US stocks listed on the NYSE, Amex, and Nasdaq, with a Centre for Research in Security Prices (CRSP) share code and positive book equity data over the period July 1963–December 2016. We use the risk factors proposed by Fama and French (1992, 2015) and Carhart (1997). All our data are retrieved from Kenneth French's website.[3] They include (1) the size factor, Small Minus Big (SMB), which is the return on a portfolio of small stocks (bottom 30% in terms of market capitalization) minus that of a portfolio of big stocks (top 30% capitalization); (2) the value factor, High Minus Low (HML), equivalent to the return of a portfolio made of "value" stocks, that is, those with a high (top 30%) book-to-market ratio (book value of common equity divided by the market equity) minus that of a portfolio of "growth" stocks (bottom 30% book-to-market ratio); (3) the momentum factor, Winners Minus Losers (WML), which is the return of a portfolio of best-performing stocks (top 30%) minus that of a portfolio of worst-performing stocks (bottom 30%) over the previous year; (4) the profitability factor, Robust Minus Weak (RMW), the difference between the returns on diversified portfolios of stocks with robust and weak operating profitability (the ratio obtained from dividing annual revenues minus cost of goods sold and expenses by book equity); and (5) the investment factor, Conservative Minus Aggressive (CMA), the difference between the returns on diversified portfolios of low- and high-investment stocks. For each of these five long-short factors, we extract the long-leg and short-leg components. For example, from the SMB factor, we make two factor components: the first is made up of small stocks only, while the second is restricted to large stocks. Splitting similarly the five factors of Fama and French leaves us with ten factor components, which are (1) small, (2) big, (3) value, (4) growth, (5) robust profitability, (6) weak profitability, (7) conservative investment, (8) aggressive investment, (9) high momentum, and (10) low momentum. These components are considered as the elementary assets in optimal factor-based allocation.

As for sector investing, the dataset includes ten industry-based indices made up of U.S. stocks listed on the NYSE, Amex, and Nasdaq. Our sector-based portfolios are constructed from ten sectors: (1) non-durable consumer goods, (2) durable consumer goods, (3) manufacturing, (4) energy, (5) high tech, (6) telecom, (7) shops, (8) health, (9) utilities, and (10) others (mines, construction, building materials, transportation, hotels, entertainment, finance, etc.). Finally, we recorded the market index returns (value-weighted returns of all NYSE, Amex, or Nasdaq-listed US firms) and risk-free interest rates (one-month Treasury bill rate from Ibbotson Associates). To scrutinize the sensitivity of our results to market conditions, we used three different sample periods: (1) the full sample period; (2) the crisis period, which combines the recessions dated by the National Bureau of Economic Research with the bear-market periods identified by *Forbes* magazine; and (3) the non-crisis period.[4] They include the oil-shock-driven financial crises in the 1970s, the 1987 stock market crash, the 1998 Asian crisis, the 2000 e-crash, and the recent subprime crisis (see Table 11.1). We are dealing with discontinuous crisis and non-crisis sample periods, this has become standard practice in the empirical literature on financial crises (Goetzman et al. 2005).

Table 11.1 Crisis periods

Start date	*End date*	*Crisis type*
Feb-66	Oct-66	Bear market
Nov-68	Nov-70	Bear market and recession
Jan-73	Mar-75	Bear market and recession
Jan-77	Feb-78	Bear market
Jan-80	Jul-80	Recession
Dec-80	Nov-82	Bear market and recession
Jul-83	Jul-84	Bear market
Sep-87	Nov-87	Bear market
Jun-90	Mar-91	Bear market and recession
Jul-98	Oct-98	Bear market
Mar-00	Oct-02	Bear market and recession
Oct-07	Jun-09	Bear market and recession

Sources: NBER and Forbes Magazine

The purpose of the contest is to examine the financial performance of factor and sector investing. In line with Ehling and Ramos (2006), we run tests on the mean-variance efficiency of the market portfolio in order to investigate the ability of factor-based and sector-based efficient frontiers to beat the market. The two tests we use for this are based on distances in the mean-variance plane. First, the test proposed by Basak et al. (2002) checks whether the horizontal distance between a portfolio and its same-return counterpart efficient portfolio is significantly positive. Second, the Brière et al. (2013) test is based on the vertical distance between a given portfolio and its same-return counterpart on the efficient frontier. The two tests offer complementary views on the mean-variance attractiveness of efficient portfolios.

11.3 Descriptive Statistics

Panel A in Table 11.2 provides the figures for all ten sectors and the market. The average annualized returns reveal that two sectors outperform all the others: non-durables (12.93%) and health (12.79%). The utilities, durables, and telecom sectors are the worst performers (10.01%, 10.23%, and 10.53%, respectively). The risk levels differ substantially across sectors. Volatilities range from 13.90% (utilities) to 22.26% (tech).[5] Skewness is negative for all but three sectors (durables, energy, health). Kurtosis is higher than 3.0 (between 4.10 and 7.80). The Sharpe ratios range from 0.45 (durables) to 0.85 (non-durables).

Table 11.2 Descriptive statistics, sectors, and factors, July 1963–December 2016

Panel A: Sectors

	Non-dur	*Durable*	*Manuf*	*Energy*	*Tech*	*Telecom*	*Shops*	*Health*	*Utilities*	*Others*	*Market*
Mean (%)	1.08	0.85	0.97	1.02	0.99	0.88	1.03	1.07	0.83	0.94	0.90
Ann. mean (%)	12.93	10.23	11.59	12.21	11.84	10.53	12.31	12.79	10.01	11.28	10.83
Median (%)	1.08	0.81	1.19	0.93	0.99	1.02	0.96	1.13	0.90	1.37	1.22
Maximum (%)	18.88	42.63	17.51	24.56	20.75	21.34	25.85	29.52	18.84	20.22	16.61
Minimum (%)	−21.03	−32.63	−27.33	−18.33	−26.01	−16.22	−28.25	−20.46	−12.65	−23.60	−22.64
Std. dev. (%)	4.24	6.27	4.90	5.42	6.43	4.61	5.13	4.85	4.01	5.27	4.41
Volatility (%)	14.69	21.73	16.96	18.77	22.26	15.98	17.77	16.79	13.90	18.25	15.28
Skewness	−0.26	0.12	−0.47	0.04	−0.22	−0.20	−0.25	0.04	−0.08	−0.47	−0.50
Kurtosis	5.14	7.80	5.62	4.32	4.38	4.28	5.54	5.46	4.10	4.87	4.95
Sharpe ratio	0.85	0.45	0.66	0.63	0.51	0.63	0.67	0.74	0.69	0.60	0.68
Alpha	0.28***	−0.12	0.04	0.21	−0.04	0.09	0.12	0.24**	0.17	−0.02	0.00
Observations	642	642	642	642	642	642	642	642	642	642	642

Panel B: Factor components

	Small	*Big*	*Value*	*Growth*	*Robust profit*	*Weak profit*	*Conserv invest*	*Aggres invest*	*High mom*	*Low mom*
Mean (%)	1.19	0.93	1.27	0.88	1.14	0.90	1.20	0.89	1.36	0.69
Ann. mean (%)	14.33	11.15	15.23	10.60	13.74	10.83	14.40	10.68	16.29	8.32
Median (%)	1.63	1.26	2.00	1.00	1.33	1.30	1.47	1.25	1.81	0.60
Maximum (%)	27.12	16.65	26.00	18.00	20.26	21.21	20.21	21.08	17.49	40.13
Minimum (%)	−29.54	−21.41	−24.00	−28.00	−25.80	−27.52	−25.54	−27.77	−27.87	−24.82
Std. dev. (%)	5.80	4.34	4.99	5.47	4.89	5.61	4.92	5.61	5.29	6.24
Volatility (%)	20.09	15.02	17.30	18.93	16.95	19.43	17.04	19.43	18.33	21.61
Skewness	−0.45	−0.42	−0.47	−0.45	−0.55	−0.50	−0.51	−0.50	−0.62	0.38
Kurtosis	5.43	4.88	6.31	4.72	5.36	4.92	5.21	4.73	5.29	7.00
Sharpe ratio	0.69	0.71	0.86	0.54	0.79	0.54	0.82	0.53	0.87	0.37
Alpha	0.21*	0.04*	0.36***	−0.11	0.21***	−0.09	0.27***	−0.12*	0.40***	−0.32***
Observations	642	642	642	642	642	642	642	642	642	642

Source: Ken French's website and authors' calculation

Panel A reports the descriptive statistics of the ten sectors (non-durables, durables, manufacturing, energy, technology, telecom, shops, health, utilities) compared with the market. Panel B provides the descriptive statistics of the ten factor components (small, big, value, growth, robust profitability, weak profitability, conservative investment, aggressive investment, high momentum, low momentum). Alphas of sectors and factor components relative to the market are provided with their significance level. The sample covers the period July 1963–December 2016. ***, **, *: significant at the 1%, 5%, and 10% levels, respectively

Panel B in Table 11.2 gives the corresponding information for our ten factor components. The annualized returns range from 8.32% (low momentum) to 15.23% (value). Volatilities lie between 15.02% (big) and 21.61% (low momentum). Skewness is negative for all factor components, except low momentum. The highest absolute value of skewness (0.62) corresponds to high momentum. This is consistent with the evidence reported by Daniel and Moskowitz (2016) and Barroso and Santa-Clara (2015) to the effect that, despite attractive Sharpe ratios, momentum strategies can lead to severe losses, making them unappealing for investors sensitive to extreme risks. Kurtosis ranges between 4.72 and 7.00. The Sharpe ratios range from 0.37 (low momentum) to 0.87 (high momentum), showing a slightly higher performance dispersion than for sectors. Six of the ten factor components generate significantly positive alphas. The five long legs of the Fama and French factors (small, value, robust profit, conservative investment, and high momentum) have positive alphas since they were built for that specific purpose. More surprisingly, the "big" factor also exhibits a significantly positive alpha.

Table 11.3 reports intra-group pairwise correlations, as well as correlations with the market, for sectors (Panel A) and factor components (Panel B), respectively. The average correlation computed for factor components (0.92) is much higher than for sectors (0.65). The high average correlation tends to indicate that diversification benefits will be harder to capture with factors than with sectors. However, correlations among sectors exhibit substantial heterogeneity. High correlations (above 0.80) are found for manufacturing, shops, and the last sector ("others"), which includes finance. In contrast, the correlations between the returns of utilities and durables, and between the returns of energy and tech are particularly low (0.42 and 0.45, respectively). The manufacturing sector is highly correlated with the market (0.94). Correlations between factor components are far more homogeneous, ranging from 0.74 (between low and high momentum) to 0.99 (between growth and aggressive investment). As expected, the highest correlation with the market is found for big stocks, which have the highest capitalization, and thus the largest share of the investment universe.

Table 11.3 Correlation matrices, sectors, and factors, July 1963–December 2016

Panel A: Sectors

	Non-dur	*Durable*	*Manuf*	*Energy*	*Tech*	*Telecom*	*Shops*	*Health*	*Utilities*	*Others*	*Market*
Non-dur	1.00	0.65	0.81	0.48	0.58	0.61	0.83	0.76	0.61	0.82	0.83
Durable	0.65	1.00	0.84	0.47	0.68	0.59	0.75	0.52	0.42	0.79	0.81
Manuf	0.81	0.84	1.00	0.63	0.77	0.64	0.83	0.70	0.52	0.89	0.94
Energy	0.48	0.47	0.63	1.00	0.45	0.42	0.43	0.42	0.55	0.58	0.66
Tech	0.58	0.68	0.77	0.45	1.00	0.62	0.71	0.61	0.30	0.71	0.86
Telecom	0.61	0.59	0.64	0.42	0.62	1.00	0.63	0.53	0.50	0.67	0.75
Shops	0.83	0.75	0.83	0.43	0.71	0.63	1.00	0.67	0.46	0.83	0.86
Health	0.76	0.52	0.70	0.42	0.61	0.53	0.67	1.00	0.46	0.71	0.76
Utilities	0.61	0.42	0.52	0.55	0.30	0.50	0.46	0.46	1.00	0.56	0.58
Others	0.82	0.79	0.89	0.58	0.71	0.67	0.83	0.71	0.56	1.00	0.93

Panel B: Factor components

	Small	*Big*	*Value*	*Growth*	*Robust profit*	*Weak profit*	*Conserv invest*	*Aggres invest*	*High mom*	*Low mom*	*Market*
Small	1.00	0.86	0.93	0.95	0.94	0.96	0.96	0.95	0.93	0.88	0.89
Big	0.86	1.00	0.90	0.92	0.95	0.91	0.93	0.93	0.89	0.86	0.99
Value	0.93	0.90	1.00	0.85	0.92	0.91	0.95	0.88	0.86	0.87	0.89
Growth	0.95	0.92	0.85	1.00	0.96	0.96	0.93	0.99	0.94	0.86	0.95
Robust profit	0.94	0.95	0.92	0.96	1.00	0.92	0.95	0.97	0.94	0.88	0.96
Weak profit	0.96	0.91	0.91	0.96	0.92	1.00	0.96	0.96	0.93	0.89	0.93
Conserv invest	0.96	0.93	0.95	0.93	0.95	0.96	1.00	0.94	0.92	0.88	0.94
Aggres invest	0.95	0.93	0.88	0.99	0.97	0.96	0.94	1.00	0.94	0.88	0.96
High mom	0.93	0.89	0.86	0.94	0.94	0.93	0.92	0.94	1.00	0.74	0.92
Low mom	0.88	0.86	0.87	0.86	0.88	0.89	0.88	0.88	0.74	1.00	0.87

Source: Ken French's website and authors' calculation

Panel A reports the correlation matrix between the market and the ten sectors (non-durables, durables, manufacturing, energy, technology, telecom, shops, health, utilities). Panel B provides the correlation matrix between the market and the ten factor components (small, big, value, growth, robust profitability, weak profitability, conservative investment, aggressive investment, high momentum, low momentum). The sample covers the full period from July 1963 to December 2016

11.4 Contest

We consider six scenarios, which combine three sample periods (full sample period, crisis, non-crisis) with long-only and long-short portfolios. In each case, we determine two efficient frontiers, the first built from the ten sectors, the second from the ten factor components. Figure 11.1 shows

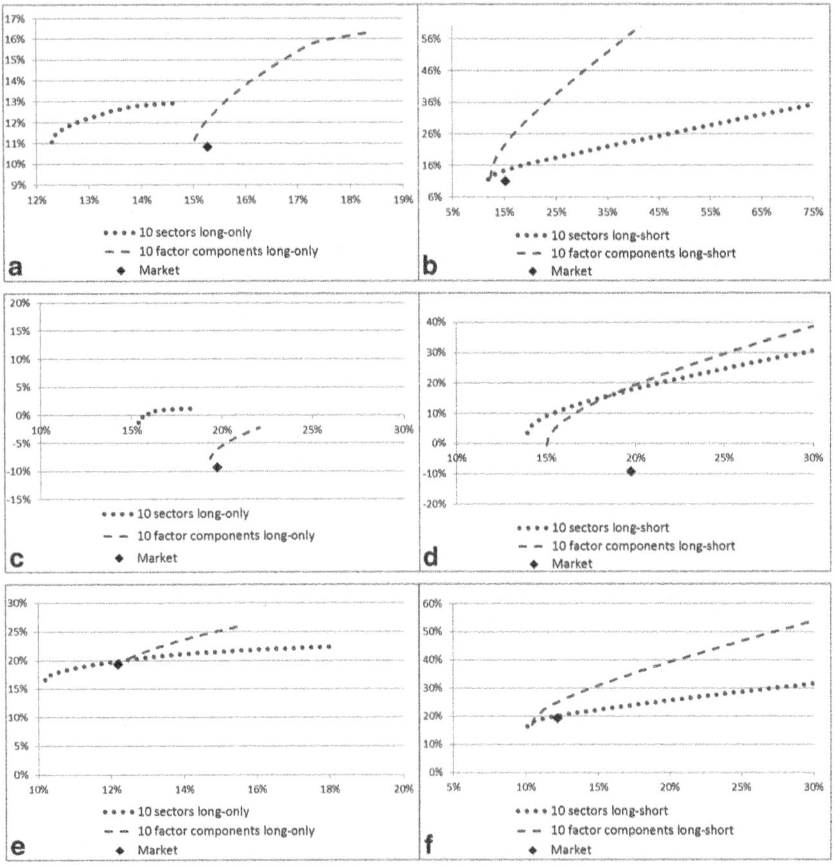

Fig. 11.1 Efficient frontiers: Sector investing and factor investing

the efficient frontiers and the market portfolio. For long-only investments, no frontier dominates any other. Figure 11.1a illustrates that the risk levels reached by sector-based portfolios are disconnected from those accessible with portfolios composed of factor components. This is because investors with high risk aversion will prefer diversified industry-based portfolios, whereas less risk-averse investors will prefer the opportunities based on factor components, which capture higher risk premia at the cost of higher levels of risk. Yet, a small portion of the factor-based frontier (expected return below 13%) is dominated by sector-based portfolios, meaning that investors holding these low-return portfolios made up of factor components are worse off than those holding sector-based portfolios. This dominance effect is stronger during crises (Fig. 11.1c), but it disappears during the non-crisis periods (Fig. 11.1e). For long-only portfolios, sector investing is a better strategy in troubled times, regardless of the investor's level of risk aversion.

The picture is different for long-short portfolios, where factor components perform much better than their sector-based competitors. For the full sample (Fig. 11.1b), factor investing beats sector investing in every respect, since its efficient frontier sits uniformly above the other one. The same evidence applies to non-crisis periods (Fig. 11.1f) except for the far-left tail of the frontiers. The situation is more balanced for the crises (Fig. 11.1d), where the two frontiers intersect, so that sector investing looks particularly attractive to investors with high risk aversion, and portfolios composed of factor components are more suitable for their more risk-tolerant counterparts. The possibility of shorting allows investors to keep positive expected returns, which contrast with both the long-only frontiers and the market index during crises.

To test whether our style-based portfolios outperform the market, we use both the Basak et al. (2002) test, which computes the horizontal distance between the market portfolio and its same-return counterpart efficient portfolio, and the Brière et al. (2013) test, which exploits the vertical distance between the market portfolio and its same-variance counterpart efficient portfolio. In the few cases where the counterpart is inexistent (see Fig. 11.1), we use its closest proxy, located on the efficient frontier either on the left for the vertical test or upwards for the horizontal test. Table 11.4 reports the results. The winning style is such that it beats the market with the greatest distance, provided that this distance is significant at the 5% level. Table 11.4 presents the test results corresponding to the graphs in Fig. 11.1. They use geometric distances between the market portfolio and the efficient frontiers.

Table 11.4 Contest between sector investing and factor investing

Style	*Sector investing*	*Factor investing*	*Winner*	*Sector investing*	*Factor investing*	*Winner*
	Beating the market on expected returns: Vertical distance			*Beating the market on volatility: Horizontal distance*		
Panel A: Long-only portfolios						
Full sample	0.0017*	0.0011***	=	0.0007***	0.0001***	Sector investing
Crisis	0.0088***	0.0027***	Sector investing	0.0013***	0.0001**	Sector investing
Non-crisis	0.0005	0.0001	=	0.0001***	0.0000	Sector investing
Panel B: Long-short portfolios						
Full sample	0.0031**	0.0102***	Factor investing	0.0008***	0.0007***	Sector investing
Crisis	0.0226***	0.0234***	Factor investing	0.0016***	0.0014***	Sector investing
Non-crisis	0.0007	0.0049***	Factor investing	0.0002***	0.0003***	Factor investing

Source: Authors' calculation

Panel A (resp. B) shows the outcomes of significance tests for the vertical (resp. horizontal) distance between the market portfolio and the efficient frontier. ***, **, *: significant at the 1%, 5%, and 10% levels, respectively. The winning style, if any, beats the market with the highest distance, provided that this distance is significant at the 5% level. There is a tie ("=") either if both styles have distances significant at the 5% level, or if none does. The absence of result ("–") means that at least one style lacks an efficient vertical/horizontal counterpart of the market portfolio

The results in Panel A (long-only portfolios) show that sector investing is the winner for all trials that are not draws. All three winners of horizontal-distance contests are sector-based. These findings confirm the visual impression from Fig. 11.1 that sector-based long-only optimal portfolios are less risky than their counterparts using factor components. Less expectedly, Panel B indicates that the same holds true for long-short portfolios in the full sample period and during crises. The result is reversed for non-crisis periods when factor investing manages to significantly mitigate market risk. When short sales are authorized, investing in factor components gives its full potential in enhancing expected returns and wins the three contests relying on the vertical distance. Overall, the winning style for long-only is sector investment and the winning style for long-short portfolios is factor investment. The left-hand side of Table 11.4 indicates that factors tend to enhance expected returns, while the right-hand side shows that sectors perform well in reducing portfolio volatility. Such a balanced overall outcome suggests that combining styles might generate attractive investment opportunities. The next section explores these innovative options.

11.5 Combination

The overwhelming success of factor investing has overshadowed other investment styles, especially from the perspective of investors who wish to benefit from diversification potential. The previous section of this chapter shows that sector investing is competitive in specific circumstances, including in the presence of long-only restrictions and high risk aversion. An additional advantage of sector investing stems from its quasi-passive structure, which is more cost-effective than factor investing (Novy-Marx and Velikov 2016). On the other hand, factor investing delivers significant risk premia and short positions help to hedge, at least partially, risks that investors wish to avoid. For all these reasons, we now explore portfolios that optimally combine sectors and factor components. The resulting efficient frontiers are presented in Fig. 11.2.

Does mixing the two styles improve on the winner of the previous contest? The answer to this question depends on the situation. Figures 11.2e and 11.2f reveal that the gain is modest, especially with respect to factor investing, in the non-crisis cases, regardless of whether short-selling is allowed. Figure 11.2c indicates that, in a long-only context, sectors alone can be sufficient to handle crises. By contrast, Fig. 11.2d suggests that combining sectors and factor components in long-short portfolios might be a smart strategy in order to prepare for financial crises and recessions. The full sample graphs deliver intermediate results. Figure 11.2a shows that the combination is especially valuable to investors with medium levels of risk aversion.

Table 11.3 shows that the optimally combined portfolios always beat the market index, both vertically (higher expected return for same volatility) and horizontally (lower volatility for same expected return) at the 1% level. In 10 out of 12 cases, the result derives from the winner's performance in Table 11.2. In the case of long-short portfolios (Panel B), the distance obtained for mixed portfolios is always strictly larger than the one computed for the previous winner. These results suggest that investors aiming to beat the market are better off with combined portfolios than

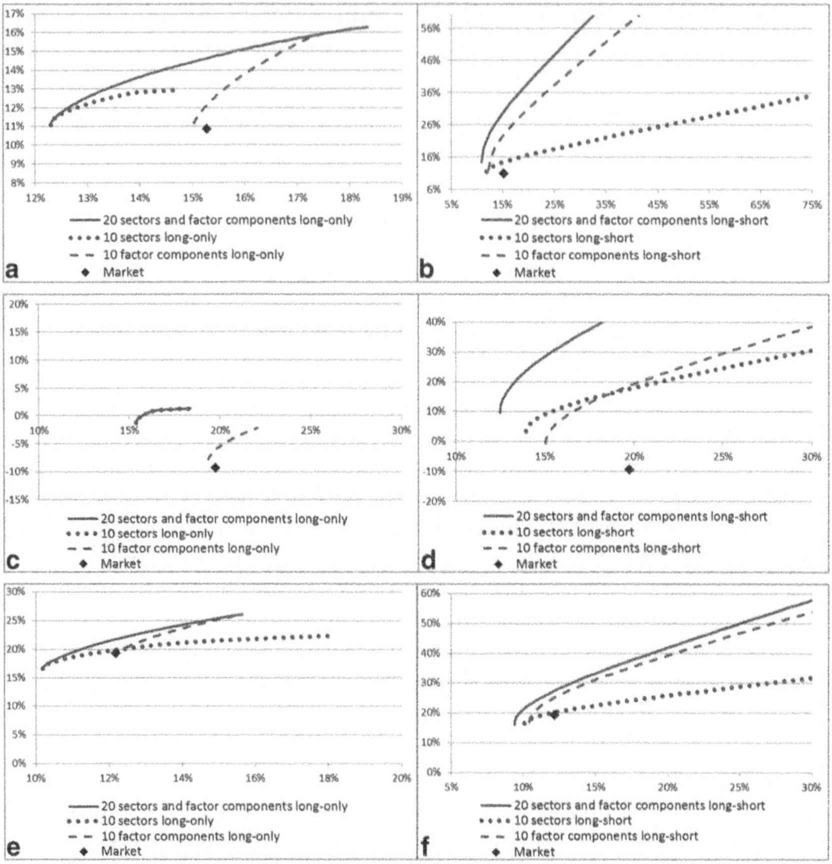

Fig. 11.2 Efficient frontiers with combinations

single-style ones. For long-only portfolios, the figures are less clear-cut. During crises, the optimally combined portfolios are made up of sectors only; factor components not only perform poorly, they fail to bring any diversification benefit. Yet, the full sample and non-crisis results suggest that combining the two styles leads to notable improvements in terms of increasing the distances from the market index.

Table 11.5 compares the test outcomes for the mixed portfolios with those of the winner of the previous contest presented in Table 11.2. First, significant scores are obtained under any circumstances, including for long-only portfolios during non-crisis periods where tests using the vertical distance show neither sector investing nor factor investing was able to beat the market on expected returns (see Table 11.4). The results from Panel B reveal that the added value from the inclusion of sectors into optimal portfolios originally made up of factor components comes from increasing the dominance scores with respect to the market expected returns. The figures suggest that the most spectacular impact takes place during crises: the vertical distance to the market expected return in crises passes from 0.0234 (or 0.28% per annum) for factor components alone to 0.0449 (or 0.59% per annum) for the "sector + factor" investing combination.

Table 11.6 presents the compositions of the "sector + factor" portfolios, which beat the market. It shows the fit between factor components and sectors. Over the full sample and the non-crisis periods, vertical long-only portfolios mainly include factor components, while horizontal long-only

Table 11.5 Combining sector investing and factor investing

Style	*Previous winner*	*Sector + factor investing*	*Previous winner*	*Sector + factor investing*
	Beating the market on expected returns: vertical distance		*Beating the market on volatility: horizontal distance*	
	Panel A: Long-only portfolios			
Full sample	=	0.0031***	0.0006***	0.0006***
Crisis	0.0088***	0.0088***	0.0012***	0.0012***
Non-crisis	=	0.0021***	0.0001***	0.0002***
	Panel B: Long-short portfolios			
Full sample	0.0102***	0.0161***	0.0007***	0.0009***
Crisis	0.0234***	0.0449***	0.0016***	0.0019***
Non-crisis	0.0048***	0.0068***	0.0003***	0.0004***

Source: Authors' calculation

Panel A (resp. B) shows the outcomes of significance tests for the vertical (resp. horizontal) distance between the market portfolio and the efficient frontier. ***, **, *: significant at the 1%, 5%, and 10% levels, respectively. "=" indicates that either both styles were significant in Table 11.4 at the 5% level, or no style was significant at that level

Table 11.6 Sector + factor portfolios beating the market

	Vertical portfolios			*Horizontal portfolios*		
	Full sample	*Crisis*	*Non-crisis*	*Full sample*	*Crisis*	*Non-crisis*
	Panel A: Long-only portfolios					
Sectors	37%	100%	45%	100%	100%	72%
Factor components	63%	0%	55%	0%	0%	28%
	Panel B: Long-short portfolios					
Sectors: Long exposure	120%	191%	93%	96%	79%	120%
Sectors: Short exposure	−209%	−373%	−86%	−73%	−172%	−31%
Factor components: Long exposure	916%	1127%	634%	614%	858%	486%
Factor components: Short exposure	−727%	−845%	−542%	−537%	−665%	−474%

Source: Authors' calculation

This table shows the compositions of the optimal portfolios, which are made up of sectors and factor components, and beat the market. The vertical portfolios beat the market with same expected return and lower volatility, while the horizontal portfolios beat the market with same volatility and higher expected returns. The table provides the results for long-only portfolios (panel A) and long-short (panel B) portfolios, and over three periods (full sample, crisis, and non-crisis). For long-short portfolios, an indication of the degree of leverage is given through the sum of positive and negative weights

factors have a heavier loading on sectors. These results are consistent with the risk reduction associated with sector investment, as opposed to the return enhancement triggered by factor components. Our results also confirm the previous finding that factor components do not help in beating the market in long-only portfolios during crisis periods, both vertically (in order to achieve higher expected returns) and horizontally (to reach lower volatility). For the long-short portfolios reported in Panel B, both the vertical and the horizontal portfolios include unrealistically high short exposures. Even so, differences emerge between the loadings of sectors and the factor components. Both the long and the short exposures of factor components are impressive, but the net exposure (long + short) is always positive. By contrast, the net exposure of sectors is positive in non-crisis periods and negative during crises. The figures in Panel B confirm that all the efficient long-short portfolios (i.e. those that permit short-selling) have long and short exposures both to sectors and to factor components. In Panel A, by contrast, 50% of the portfolios include assets of one category only (see the detailed compositions in Appendix A).

11.6 Discussion and Conclusion

From a theoretical perspective, sector investing and factor investing rely on different logics. On the one hand, industrial sectors were originally built to diversify risks across economic activities. Risk reduction stemming from diversification is a benefit that is especially needed in crisis periods when volatility spikes. On the other hand, the advantage of factor components lies in being able to earn the risk premia they were built to deliver (Brière and Szafarz 2015). Our first results confirm that both styles keep their promises and produce the expected outcomes. Regarding the factor/sector contest, our findings suggest that factor investing performs better when short-selling is authorized. By contrast, sector investing outperforms its competitor when short sales are forbidden. Overall, factor investing is riskier than sector investing as a direct consequence of the obvious: capturing risk premia primarily means taking more risks (see the volatilities reported in Table 11.2). In addition, sector investing has superior diversification potential, and factors exhibit large and positive extreme correlations (Christoffersen and Langlois 2013).

Next, guided by the hope that combining the two styles would have a positive effect on the financial performance, we mixed them and then observed the mean-variance performance of the resulting portfolios. Our results show that the gain is especially visible for long-short portfolios, where the already good performance of factor investing is enhanced by including lower-risker sectors. The benefits are higher during crisis periods, suggesting that the diversification benefits brought by sectors play their part very well when needed. This favorable outcome in troubled times, however, fails when short sales are prohibited. For long-only portfolios, factors can still enhance returns by delivering alphas with respect to the market during quiet times, but they lose their attractive properties for hedging against crises. By showing that industry-based portfolios can help asset managers reduce factor-specific risks, this chapter offers a strategy to bypass short-sale restrictions in factor investing using industry-based portfolios. This is because several industries have negative loadings on factors (Chou et al. 2012), implying that a well-chosen combination of sectors could shrink the loadings on the factors. Thus, sector-based investment strategies could help long-only investors achieve better risk-return properties for their portfolios. Further research could assess in a general setting how efficiently industry-based portfolios hedge investor against performance losses associated with short-sale restrictions.

Acknowledgments The authors thank Vafa Ahmadi, Alexander Attié, Narayan Bulusu, Eric Bouyé, Jacob Bjorheim, Tony Bulger, Joachim Coche, Melchior Dechelette, Pierre Collin-Dufresne, Arnaud Faller, Pascal Farahmand, Tom Fearnley, Nicolas Fragneau, Campbell Harvey, Antti Ilmanen, Jianjian Jin, Theo Kaitis, Yvan Lengwiler, Christian Lopez, Gabriel Petre, Bruce Phelps, Sudhir Rajkumar, Alejandro Reveiz, Francisco Rivadeneyra, Mihail Velikov, and the participants of the Sixth Joint BIS, World Bank, Bank of Canada Public Investors Conference.

Appendix

Table 11.7 Factor + sector long-only portfolios beating the market, detailed portfolio composition

	Vertical portfolios			*Horizontal portfolios*		
	Full sample	*Crisis*	*Non-crisis*	*Full sample*	*Crisis*	*Non-crisis*
			Panel A: Sectors			
Non-dur	25%	100%	5%	16%	10%	12%
Durable	0%	0%	0%	0%	0%	0%
Manuf	0%	0%	0%	0%	0%	0%
Energy	1%	0%	11%	7%	0%	12%
Tech	0%	0%	0%	0%	0%	3%
Telecom	0%	0%	8%	21%	26%	11%
Shops	0%	0%	0%	0%	0%	2%
Health	4%	0%	0%	12%	19%	1%
Utilities	7%	0%	20%	44%	45%	31%
Others	0%	0%	0%	0%	0%	0%
			Panel B: Factor components			
Small	0%	0%	0%	0%	0%	0%
Big	0%	0%	0%	0%	0%	0%
Value	17%	0%	0%	0%	0%	0%
Growth	0%	0%	0%	0%	0%	0%
Robust profit	0%	0%	0%	0%	0%	0%
Weak profit	0%	0%	0%	0%	0%	0%
Conserv invest	0%	0%	0%	0%	0%	0%
Aggres invest	0%	0%	0%	0%	0%	0%
High mom	46%	0%	55%	0%	0%	28%
Low mom	0%	0%	0%	0%	0%	0%

Table 11.8 Factor + sector long-short portfolios beating the market, detailed portfolio composition

	Vertical portfolios			*Horizontal portfolios*		
	Full sample	*Crisis*	*Non-crisis*	*Full sample*	*Crisis*	*Non-crisis*
			Panel A: Sectors			
Non-dur	3%	60%	−9%	11%	27%	2%
Durable	−37%	−72%	−18%	−11%	−14%	−10%
Manuf	−50%	−88%	−20%	−12%	−31%	−2%
Energy	−13%	−34%	4%	4%	−18%	13%
Tech	60%	76%	42%	23%	9%	33%
Telecom	9%	1%	7%	14%	15%	6%
Shops	5%	7%	9%	4%	−17%	18%
Health	43%	46%	26%	19%	21%	19%
Utilities	−9%	−5%	6%	20%	8%	27%
Others	−100%	−173%	−38%	−50%	−93%	−19%
			Panel B: Factor components			
Small	295%	274%	269%	292%	348%	264%
Big	337%	400%	255%	322%	468%	223%
Value	−58%	−52%	−63%	−61%	−108%	−40%
Growth	−269%	−281%	−185%	−67%	−129%	−62%
Robust profit	81%	54%	50%	−63%	−81%	−39%
Weak profit	−130%	−192%	−86%	−71%	−112%	−68%
Conserv invest	−19%	24%	−7%	−94%	−106%	−54%
Aggres invest	−251%	−319%	−165%	−137%	−130%	−119%
High mom	153%	224%	59%	−23%	31%	−42%
Low mom	49%	150%	−36%	−20%	12%	−50%

Notes

1. The way individual stocks are grouped into industrial sectors raises specific issues (Vermorken et al. 2010).
2. Brière and Szafarz (2017) examine intermediate situations such as the 130/30 and the case where only the market index can be shorted.
3. http://mba.tuck.dartmouth.edu/pages/faculty/ken.french/data_library.html.
4. In Brière and Szafarz (2015), we consider crises and bear periods separately.
5. In fact, t-tests fail to detect any significant differences among means, while some differences in variances are statistically significant.

References

Ang, A. (2014). *Asset management—A systematic approach to factor investing*. Oxford: Oxford University Press.

Bae, J. W., Elkhami, R., & Simutin, M. (2016). The best of both worlds: Accessing emerging economies by investing in developed markets. *SSRN Working Paper 264475*.

Barroso, P., & Santa-Clara, P. (2015). Momentum has its moments. *Journal of Financial Economics, 116*(1), 111–120.

Basak, G., Jagannathan, R., & Sun, G. (2002). A direct test for the mean-variance efficiency of a portfolio. *Journal of Economic Dynamics and Control, 26*(7–8), 1195–1215.

Brière, M., & Szafarz, A. (2015). Factor investing: Risk premia vs. diversification benefits. *SSRN Working Paper 2615703*.

Brière, M., & Szafarz, A. (2017). Factor investing: The rocky road from long-only to long-short. In E. Jurczenko (Ed.), *Factor Investing*. Elsevier, 25–45.

Brière, M., Drut, B., Mignon, V., Oosterlinck, K., & Szafarz, A. (2013). Is the market portfolio efficient? A new test of mean-variance efficiency when all assets are risky. *Finance, 34*(1), 7–41.

Carhart, M. M. (1997). On persistence in mutual fund performance. *Journal of Finance, 52*(1), 57–82.

Chou, P. H., Ho, P. H., & Ko, K. C. (2012). Do industries matter in explaining stock returns and asset-pricing anomalies? *Journal of Banking and Finance, 36*(2), 355–370.

Christoffersen, P., & Langlois, H. (2013). The joint dynamics of equity market factors. *Journal of Financial and Quantitative Analysis, 48*(5), 1371–1404.

Daniel, K. D., & Moskowitz, T. J. (2016). Momentum crashes. *Journal of Financial Economics, 122*(2), 221–224.

Ehling, P., & Ramos, S. B. (2006). Geographic versus industry diversification: Constraints matter. *Journal of Empirical Finance, 13*, 396–416.

Fama, E. F., & French, K. R. (1992). The cross-section of expected stock returns. *Journal of Finance, 47*(2), 427–465.

Fama, E. F., & French, K. R. (2015). A five-factor asset pricing model. *Journal of Financial Economics, 116*(1), 1–22.

Goetzmann, W. N., Li, L., & Rouwenhorst, K. G. (2005). Long-term global market correlations. *Journal of Business, 78*(1), 1–38.

Heston, S. L., & Rouwenhorst, K. G. (1994). Does industrial structure explain the benefits of international diversification? *Journal of Financial Economics, 36*(1), 3–27.

Lewellen, J., Nagel, S., & Shanken, J. (2010). A skeptical appraisal of asset pricing tests. *Journal of Financial Economics, 96*(2), 175–194.

Novy-Marx, R., & Velikov, M. (2016). A taxonomy of anomalies and their trading cost. *Review of Financial Studies, 29*(1), 104–147.

Sharpe, W. F. (1992). Asset allocation: Management style and performance measurement. *Journal of Portfolio Management, 18*(2), 7–19.

Vermorken, M., Szafarz, A., & Pirotte, H. (2010). Sector classification through non-Gaussian similarity. *Applied Financial Economics, 20*(11), 861–878.

PART IV

Asset Classes for Public Investors

CHAPTER 12

The Impact of Benchmark Investing by Institutional Investors on International Capital Allocations

Claudio Raddatz, Sergio L. Schmukler, and Tomás Williams

This chapter was prepared for the Proceedings of the "Sixth Bank for International Settlements/World Bank/Bank of Canada Public Investors' Conference" in Washington, DC, and draws on the background work for our paper forthcoming at the *Journal of International Economics*. We thank the World Bank Research Department, Knowledge for Change Program, Research Support Budget, and Strategic Research Program for financial support. We are grateful to Juan José Cortina, Sebastián Cubela, Julián Kozlowski, Matías Moretti, and Lucas Núñez for excellent research assistance in putting together the databases. We received very useful comments from Ghislain Martial Yanou and conference participants. The views expressed here do not necessarily represent those of the International Monetary Fund (IMF) or the World Bank. Affiliations: IMF, World Bank, Universitat Pompeu Fabra, and George Washington University. Email addresses: craddatzkiefer@imf.org; sschmukler@worldbank.org; tomaswilliams@email.gwu.edu.

C. Raddatz
International Monetary Fund (IMF), Washington, DC, USA
e-mail: craddatzkiefer@imf.org

N. Bulusu et al. (eds.), *Advances in the Practice of Public Investment Management*, https://doi.org/10.1007/978-3-319-90245-6_12

12.1 Introduction

Over the past two decades, many countries have tried to foster the development of their capital markets through the promotion of institutional investors. The expectation was that they would invest domestically and internationally, providing opportunities for retail investors to hold a diversified, well-balanced portfolio, simultaneously helping to deepen financial markets and, more generally, increase access to finance for firms and sovereigns. Moreover, institutional investors were anticipated to have long-term investment horizons, which would allow them to take advantage of long-term risk and illiquidity premiums to generate higher returns on their assets. In addition, they were expected to behave in a patient, countercyclical manner, making the most of cyclically low valuations to seek attractive investment opportunities, helping to promote financial stability.

As a result of these policies and the more general trend toward the use of capital markets, non-bank institutional investors emerged across countries and rapidly became key participants in global financial markets. In fact, the proportion of household savings channeled through these institutional investors has grown significantly in recent decades, and their assets under management are rapidly catching up with those of the banking system. Data from the Organization for Economic Co-operation and Development (OECD) show that in 2013, financial assets under management reached USD24.7 trillion for pension funds, USD26.1 trillion for insurance companies, and USD34.9 trillion for mutual funds (Fig. 12.1).

In the context of this rapid expansion, it has become important to understand how institutional investors allocate their assets and how they can affect investments in different countries. In this chapter, we focus on international mutual fund investments across countries. Whereas mutual funds are just one part of the industry, and we cannot immediately extrapolate our findings to other players, their analysis provides an illustration of

S. L. Schmukler (✉)
World Bank, Washington, DC, USA
e-mail: sschmukler@worldbank.org

T. Williams
Universitat Pompeu Fabra, Barcelona, Spain

George Washington University, Washington, DC, USA
e-mail: tomaswilliams@email.gwu.edu

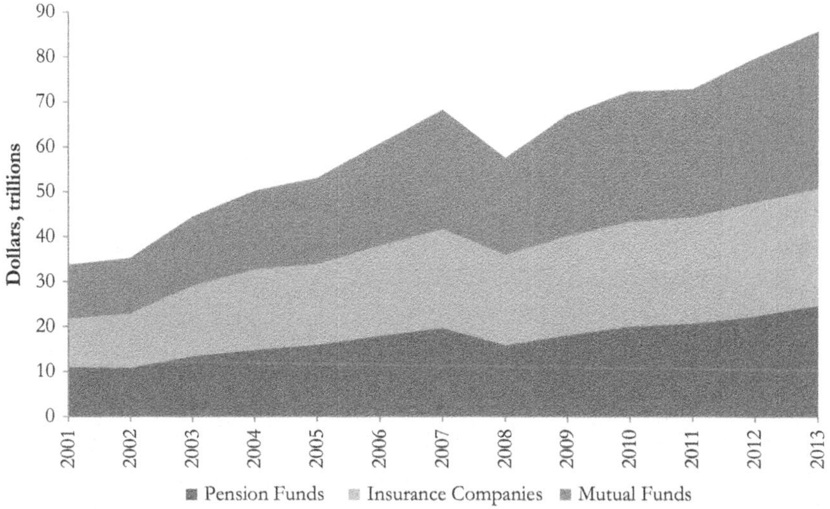

Fig. 12.1 Assets under management of non-bank institutional investors, 2001–2013

the drivers of institutional investors' behavior and the incentives they face. Also, in many countries they are the largest institutional investors. Because data for mutual funds are much more detailed than for the remaining institutional investors, it is easier to analyze the behavior of managers and their underlying investors. Furthermore, an advantage of international mutual funds in particular is that they enable us to study the effects these funds have on the international investments countries receive, as well as on the respective asset prices.

There are different types of international mutual funds, which as a group have been expanding worldwide and, by the end of 2016, had accumulated USD43.5 trillion in assets under management around the world (Investment Company Institute, ICI).[1] But one notable development in the industry (of both mutual funds and institutional investors more generally) has been the growing importance of index funds and exchange-traded funds (ETFs) that follow certain well-known benchmark indexes and are vehicles for passive investments (Fig. 12.2). These funds now account for

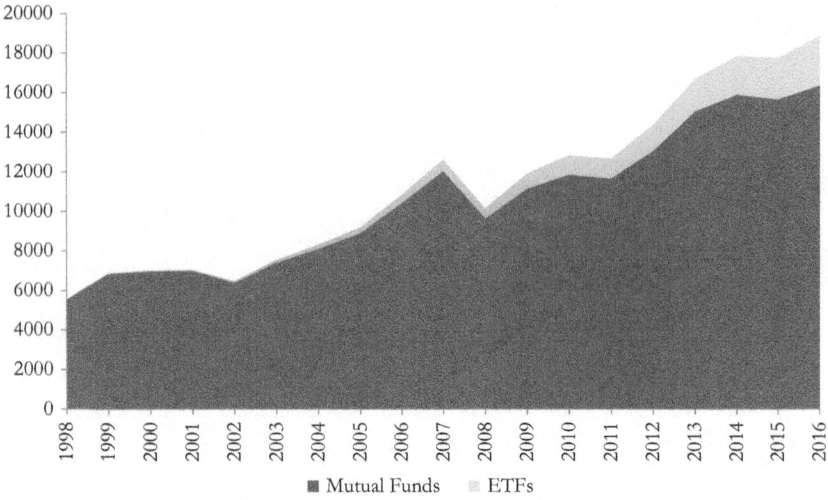

Fig. 12.2 US mutual fund assets by fund type

8.7 percent of the industry worldwide and 15.4 percent of the U.S. mutual fund industry. Moreover, this trend toward benchmark investing is likely to accentuate for three reasons. First, several studies have argued that many active funds already manage their assets as passive investors (Cremers and Petajisto 2009; Cremers et al. 2016). Second, since the global financial crisis, there have been outflows from active mutual funds that have gone to both index funds and ETFs (Fig. 12.3). Third, in a global environment of low interest rates, the low costs, higher transparency, and the simplicity of benchmark investing might further tilt investors toward this type of vehicles. Despite the growing importance of passive institutional investors, there is little evidence on how they invest across countries.

In this chapter, we illustrate how index investing can affect international capital allocations and the related capital flows across countries, extending the analysis in Raddatz et al. (2017). In particular, we focus on a factor that, so far, has been mostly absent from the literature on international investments and that we call "the benchmark effect." The benchmark effect refers to the impact that, through various channels, prominent international equity and bond market indexes (such as, the

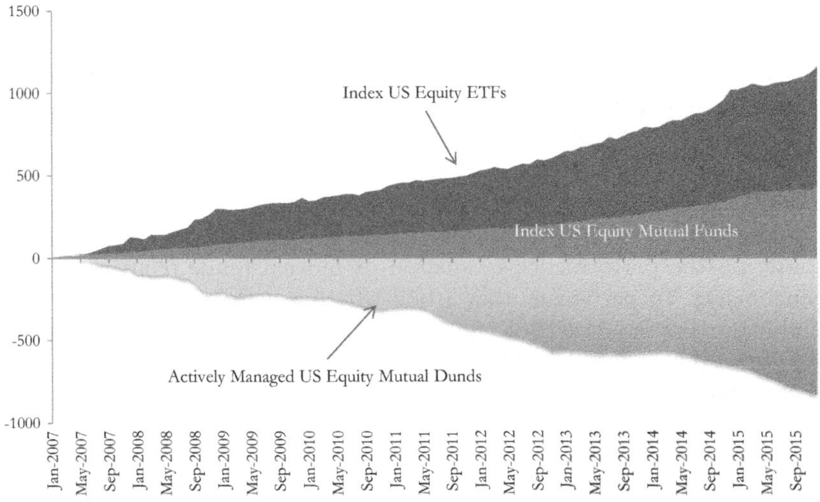

Fig. 12.3 Outflows/inflows from US equity mutual funds from ICI

MSCI Emerging Markets Index or the MSCI World Index) have on asset allocations, capital flows, and asset prices across countries.

Raddatz et al. (2017) show that large changes in benchmark indexes have effects on capital flows, asset prices, and exchange rates. In this chapter, we delve in more detail on the different channels through which benchmarks affect international capital allocations. We show how the influence of benchmarks on mutual fund asset allocations across countries impacts international capital flows. Furthermore, we describe the extent to which the use of benchmarks can generate amplification and contagion effects across countries. Building on the analysis in Raddatz et al. (2017), in this chapter, we show algebraically the presence of the different effects, describe them through various examples derived from the data, and quantify their importance.

The focus on benchmark investing is relevant to the theoretical and empirical work on country portfolios (international asset and liability positions) and capital flows. A significant part of the literature has focused on the role that macroeconomic fundamentals play in international investment decisions, but has not analyzed the behavior of institutional investors, and in particular the effects of benchmarks, on those decisions. Some examples of the many papers on the topic are Di Giovanni (2005), Kraay et al. (2005), Lane and Milesi-Ferretti (2007), Antràs and Caballero (2009), Martin and Taddei (2013), Reinhardt et al. (2013), and Gourinchas and Rey (2014).

Other papers studying the importance of benchmarks have focused primarily on the performance evaluation of mutual funds relative to their benchmarks. In particular, they study whether active management pays (Lehmann and Modest 1987; Sharpe 1992; Wermers 2000; Cremers and Petajisto 2009; Sensoy 2009; Busse et al. 2014; Cremers et al. 2016). A related literature focuses on how benchmark redefinitions affect stock returns, pricing, and liquidity (Harris and Gurel 1986; Shleifer 1986; Chen et al. 2004; Barberis et al. 2005; Greenwood 2005; Hau et al. 2010; Hau 2011; Vayanos and Woolley 2011; Faias et al. 2012; Bartram et al. 2015; Chang et al. 2015) or how the fact that managers follow benchmarks could explain the growing correlations in financial markets between emerging economies and the United States during the 2000s (Levy Yeyati and Williams 2012). But these papers do not analyze how benchmarks affect capital allocations across countries. By simultaneously documenting how benchmarks affect capital flows and country-level asset prices, in this chapter, we help to bridge these two lines of research.

12.2 Data

To conduct our study, we use data from different sources. We work with mutual fund portfolios, benchmark indexes, and fund- and country-specific information. Raddatz et al. (2017) describe in detail the data, including the specific sources we use. Because we closely follow their procedure in matching the different databases, we limit ourselves here to providing a brief summary.

Our two main sources for country portfolio allocations of international mutual funds are Emerging Portfolio Fund Research (EPFR) and Morningstar Direct (MS). Both sources include dead and live mutual funds. The data are at monthly frequency and include open-end equity and bond funds. We complement this with information on the funds' net asset value from Datastream and MS. We also compile data on the composition and returns of several major benchmark indexes directly from FTSE, J.P. Morgan, and MSCI through bilateral agreements, and indirectly through MS for indexes produced by Dow Jones, Euro Stoxx, and S&P.

Our main matched database consists of (1) country weights, w_{ict}, which are the country portfolio allocations of international mutual funds (those investing in several countries) as a percentage of total assets; (2) benchmark weights, w_{ict}^{B}, which are the value of the country's securities included in the relevant benchmarks as a percentage of the total securities included in the relevant benchmark; (3) mutual fund-specific information, such as its assets (A_{it}), returns (R_{it}), and relevant benchmarks; and (4) country-specific information, such as stock and bond market index returns, R_{ct}.[2] The sub-index i refers to funds, c to countries, t to time, and the supra-index B to benchmarks. This database covers the period from January 1996 to July 2012 and constitutes an unbalanced panel. Our database contains 2837 equity funds and 838 bond funds, including global, global emerging, and regional funds, and funds in our combined dataset capture an important part of the assets held by the industry of international funds.

12.3 Conceptual Framework

In this section, we explore the consequences of previous findings that the weight of a country's assets in a benchmark index affect the weight of that country on the portfolios of mutual funds following that index and the capital flows originating from these funds. We study the quantitative importance of various channels through which changes in benchmark weights impact country flows and how it is reflected in mutual fund flows and aggregate capital flows. By *capital flows* we mean the flows coming from the funds we analyze into the countries in which they invest and by *aggregate capital flows* those captured in the aggregate official statistics of countries. Because we do not have aggregate detailed data for all countries, we cannot always determine to what extent these mutual fund flows map into the balance of payments statistics at the country level. However, according to some estimates, the flows coming from only one of our data sources (EPFR) account for around 25 percent of total foreign portfolio investments (from all sources) at the country level (Puy 2013) and there is a significant correlation between the EPFR flows and those obtained from the balance of payments (Fratzscher 2012; Miao and Pant 2012). Our inclusion of data from Morningstar should ensure even better coverage.

Raddatz et al. (2017) study systematically how mutual fund weights respond to benchmark weights, using fund-level panel regressions, including different fixed effects that capture shocks to the fund at each point in time and preferences in the investments of each fund toward each country. More specifically, we estimate the parameters of the following specification:

$$w_{ict} = \theta_{ic} + \theta_{it} + \alpha_1 w_{ict}^{B} + \varepsilon_{ict}, \tag{12.1}$$

where w_{ict} is the weight for fund i, in country c, and at time t; w_{ict}^{B} is the respective benchmark weight that fund i follows; θ_{ic} and θ_{it} are fund-country and fund-time fixed effects. Raddatz et al. (2017) show that benchmarks have statistically and economically significant effects on mutual fund allocations and capital flows across countries. Mutual funds follow benchmarks rather closely. For example, a 1 percent increase in a country's benchmark weight results on average in a 0.7 percent increase in the weight of that country for the typical mutual fund that follows that benchmark. However, there is relevant heterogeneity across funds. Explicit indexing funds follow benchmarks almost one-for-one, generating some mechanical effects in allocations and capital flows.[3] Although the most active funds in our sample are less connected to the benchmarks, they are still significantly influenced by their behavior, with about 50 percent of their allocations explained by the benchmark effect.

In this chapter, we attempt to build on the previous results on asset allocation, to understand how they might affect international capital flows through different channels. To capture the relation between benchmark weights and capital flows, we start from the following identity:

$$F_{ict} = w_{ict} F_{it} + \tilde{A}_{it} \left(w_{ict} - w_{ict}^{BH} \right), \tag{12.2}$$

where F_{ict} is the net flow (in dollars) from fund i in country c at time t. w_{ict} is the portfolio weight the fund decides to have in that country at time t, $\tilde{A}_{it} = R_{it} A_{it-1}$ is the value of the fund's assets at the beginning of time t, and w_{ict}^{BH} is the fund's buy-and-hold weight in that country resulting from movements in total and relative returns.[4] F_{it} is the net flow (in dollars) to fund i at time t, which is equal to injections less redemptions.

The two terms in the equation above relate to the two forces driving a fund's flows to a country: net inflows and reallocations. Net inflows to countries occur as net flows to the fund (F_{it}) are allocated across countries in proportion to the fund's desired country weight at that moment (w_{ict}). We use the term "desired country weight" to refer to the weight the fund decides to have in that country considering all the possible constraints it faces. It does not mean to imply that it is the optimal weight that the fund would choose in an unconstrained scenario. For example, if the fund cannot change positions in a country to align them with its view of the country fundamentals because of cost considerations, we consider the desired outcome of this trade-off as the desired weight. Thus, this is a constrained optimal decision of the portfolio manager. The flows due to the reallocations of existing assets, $\tilde{A}_{it}\left(w_{ict}-w_{ict}^{BH}\right)$, arise from the difference between a fund's desired country weight and the buy-and-hold weight that mechanically results from the fund's previous allocation and movements in relative returns.

Equation 12.2 shows a direct connection between weights and country flows. Fund managers' decisions about country weights have a direct impact on country flows. For instance, an increase in the desired weight in a given country induces both a reallocation of existing assets to that country and more inflows to that country when the fund itself has injections.

To describe and quantify the various mechanisms through which the benchmark effect operates on flows, it is useful to normalize Eq. 12.2 by lagged fund assets (A_{it-1}), obtaining,

$$f_{ict}=\frac{F_{ict}}{A_{it-1}}=w_{ict}\left(\frac{A_{it}}{A_{it-1}}\right)-w_{ict-1}R_{ct}=w_{ict}\gamma_{it}-w_{ict-1}R_{ct},\qquad(12.3)$$

where $f_{it}=F_{it}/A_{it-1}$, $\gamma_{it}=f_{it}+R_{it}$, using $F_{it}+\tilde{A}_{it}=A_{it}$ and $w_{ict}^{BH}=w_{ict-1}R_{ct}/R_{it}$.

Starting from Eq. 12.3 along with the use of Eq. 12.1 linking w_{ict} and w_{ict}^{B}, we can derive the response of flows to changes in several variables, and the role that the link between funds and benchmarks has on these responses. The derivations below summarize the responses of country flows to shocks to benchmark weights, fund flows, own-country returns, and third-country returns, respectively. All of them assume that variables as of month $(t-1)$ are kept constant. The effects on flows are

$$\frac{\partial f_{ict}}{\partial w_{ict}^{B}} = \alpha\left(f_{it} + R_{it}\right) = \alpha\gamma_{it}, \tag{12.4}$$

$$\frac{\partial f_{ict}}{\partial f_{it}} = \alpha w_{ict}^{B} + \varepsilon_{ict}, \tag{12.5}$$

$$\frac{\partial f_{ict}}{\partial R_{ct}} = \alpha\gamma_{it}\frac{w_{ict-1}^{B}\left(1-w_{ict}^{B}\right)}{R_{it}^{B}} + w_{ict}w_{ict-1}\left(1+\frac{\partial f_{it}}{\partial R_{it}}\right) - w_{ict-1} + \gamma_{it}\frac{\partial \varepsilon_{ict}}{\partial R_{ct}}, \tag{12.6}$$

$$\frac{\partial f_{ict}}{\partial R_{\tilde{c}t}} = -\alpha\gamma_{it}\frac{w_{ict}^{B}\left(1-w_{ict-1}^{B}\right)}{R_{it}^{B}} + w_{ict}\left(1-w_{ict-1}\right)\left(1+\frac{\partial f_{it}}{\partial R_{it}}\right) + \gamma_{it}\frac{\partial \varepsilon_{ict}}{\partial R_{\tilde{c}t}}. \tag{12.7}$$

Using Eqs. 12.4, 12.5, 12.6, and 12.7, we discuss and illustrate the different effects of benchmarks on capital flows. While Eq. 12.4 directly shows the response of flows to changes in benchmark weights, the other benchmark effects on flows appear in the first terms of Eqs. 12.5, 12.6, and 12.7.[5]

Equation 12.4 captures the ***direct benchmark effect***, or the direct impact of changes in benchmark weights. The impact on flows of an exogenous change in benchmark weights (i.e., a change not driven by returns) is proportional to the gross growth in fund assets, γ_{it} or (f_{it} + R_{it}). The proportionality depends on how closely fund weights track benchmark weights, as captured by the α estimated in Raddatz et al. (2017).

Equation 12.5 shows the ***sensitivity effect*** in its first term, which captures that an increase (decrease) in a fund's inflows will increase (decrease) the fund's capital flows to a country proportionally to the country's benchmark weight. Thus, benchmark weights determine the sensitivity of country flows to fund flows. The last term in this equation corresponds to the response of the active part of a fund portfolio to the shock. The sensitivity effect shows that countries with higher weights in a benchmark are more prone to more inflows (outflows) when the funds receive injections (suffer redemptions), possibly explaining why large countries might be subject to large changes in capital flows regardless of their fundamentals.

Equation 12.6 shows the response of country flows to own-country returns. The first term measures the ***amplification effect***, according to which an increase in a country's return has a positive impact on its flows. In this case, the link to a benchmark induces inflows into (outflows from) countries experiencing positive (negative) return shocks when a fund expands. The second term captures the extent to which the increase in returns increases the value of the fund's existing assets and, if fund flows respond to returns, also its injections. The third, negative term in this expression comes from the direct effect of country returns on buy-and-hold weights and, for a given benchmark weight, reallocations.

Equation 12.7 displays the response of country flows to third-country returns. The first term shows the *contagion effect* associated with returns. This contagion effect is different from the "margin call" and other effects described in the literature, and occurs in the absence of leverage (Calvo and Mendoza 2000; Kodres and Pritsker 2002; Manconi et al. 2012; Hau and Lai 2013). This effect is qualitatively similar to that in Eq. 12.6, but in this case, the effect is negative because an increase in every other country's returns reduces a country's relative market capitalization (and thus its benchmark weight). Therefore, it brings home shocks to returns occurring in other countries that share the benchmark. This form of contagion could be benign when negative shocks to other countries bring inflows to the unaffected one (although positive shocks to other countries bring outflows to the unaffected one). However, even under negative shocks to other countries, it is possible to have outflows in the unaffected country if the effect on the second term is large enough, namely, if flows to the fund decline strongly enough in response to a shock to its returns. Notice that, when this happens and α is small, the second term in Eq. 12.7 dominates and the contagion is no longer benign.

We perform simulations to illustrate the quantitative importance of the various manifestations of the benchmark effect. We impute values to the different parameters involved in Eqs. 12.4, 12.5, 12.6, and 12.7 using the medians and interquartile ranges of the actual data.[6] Table 12.1 yields order-of-magnitude estimates for the four effects described above, where a shock entails a move from the 25th to the 75th percentile for each variable in our sample. The different manifestations of the benchmark effect result in non-trivial variations in country flows. The simulation shows that the direct benchmark effect has the highest potential to induce inflows (or outflows). For instance, a 1.5 percentage point increase in a country's benchmark weight (from 4 percent to 5.5 percent in this case) results in an inflow corresponding to approximately 30 percent of a fund's total assets allocated to that country.[7] On the other extreme, the sensitivity effect has the lowest impact (a 3.2 percent increase in response to a 4 percentage point increase in fund flows). This is reasonable because, as its name suggests, the direct benchmark effect has a direct impact on flows. An exogenous, independent

Table 12.1 Quantitative benchmark effects on capital flows

A. Calibration				
Parameters				
A			0.8	
γ_{it}			1.0	
$w_{ict}{}^{B}$			4.0	
$w_{ict-1}{}^{B}$			4.0	
R_{ct}			1.01	
$R_{it}{}^{B}$			1.01	
B. Quantitative effects				
	Shock	Value (percentage points)	Δf_{ict}	$\Delta(f_{ict}/w_{ict-1}{}^{B})$ (in %)
Direct benchmark effect	$\Delta w_{ict}{}^{B}$	1.5	1.212	30.3
Sensitivity effect	Δf_{it}	4.0	0.128	3.2
Amplification effect	ΔR_{ct}	10.0	0.307	7.7
Contagion effect	$\Delta R_{c't}$	10.0	−0.307	−7.7

This table presents the calibration of each of the effects presented in Sect. 12.5. Parameters are calibrated according to the median values in our sample. Panel A presents the calibration for each parameter and Panel B displays the quantitative benchmark effects for shocks on different variables

Source: Authors' computations

change in a country's benchmark weight induces net inflows and reallocation effects to that country in detriment of all other countries. In contrast, an increase in fund flows is shared across all countries where a fund invests; its effect is more or less proportional to the (usually small) country weights. The sizes of the amplification and contagion effects are identical in our baseline parameterization. They both lie between the direct benchmark and sensitivity effects. The reason is that these effects work indirectly through the response of benchmark weights to each of the changes. These responses depend on the initial level of returns and benchmark weights and are usually less than one for one.

The effects described in this section affect different types of funds differently. For closed-end explicit indexing funds, the country flows are different from zero only when there is a direct benchmark effect. For open-end index funds, all the channels operate because of the flows the funds receive. For non-explicit indexing funds, the total country flows depend on the level of active management and how the manager allocates the active part of the portfolio. However, the effects described above illustrate how their country flows respond to different shocks to the extent that they follow benchmark indexes.

In summary, this analysis shows that benchmarks can affect flows directly and indirectly by (1) affecting a fund's desired allocations (direct benchmark effect), (2) determining how a fund allocates funds across countries when facing inflows or outflows (sensitivity effect), and (3) mediating the relation between a country's flows and shocks to its returns (amplification effect) or to the returns of other countries that are part of the same benchmark (contagion effect). The next section provides some evidence on these various channels.

12.4 Evidence

In this section, we provide evidence on how benchmarks affect international capital flows through the different channels detailed in Sect. 12.2. We provide both case studies and systematic evidence to illustrate these different mechanisms.

The direct benchmark effect presented in Eq. 12.4 helps explain, for example, the counterintuitive outflows when Israel was upgraded from the MSCI Emerging Markets Index to the MSCI World Index. To show the effect of the exogenous change in benchmark weights, we compare the explicit indexing funds tracking these two indexes (Fig. 12.4).

The direct benchmark effect captures almost all the variations in country flows for both types of funds, which occur due to all the reallocations right at the time of the switch. To understand the total effect on country flows, it is important to consider that, at that time, Israel's weight in the MSCI Emerging Markets Index was 3.17 percent and in the MSCI World Index 0.37 percent, and the assets in the funds following these two indexes were not very different. Emerging market funds withdrew USD2 billion from Israel, while developed market funds injected USD160 million.[8]

One can also analyze the direct benchmark effect from the perspective of our conceptual framework. Using Eq. 12.4 in levels and assuming that all funds act as passive investors, we can multiply the total assets of funds following the MSCI Emerging Markets and the MSCI World Index by the change in benchmark weights. That corresponds to an outflow of USD8.2 billion from funds following the MSCI Emerging Markets and an inflow of USD329 million from funds following the MSCI World Index. These numbers are much larger than the observed flows because we

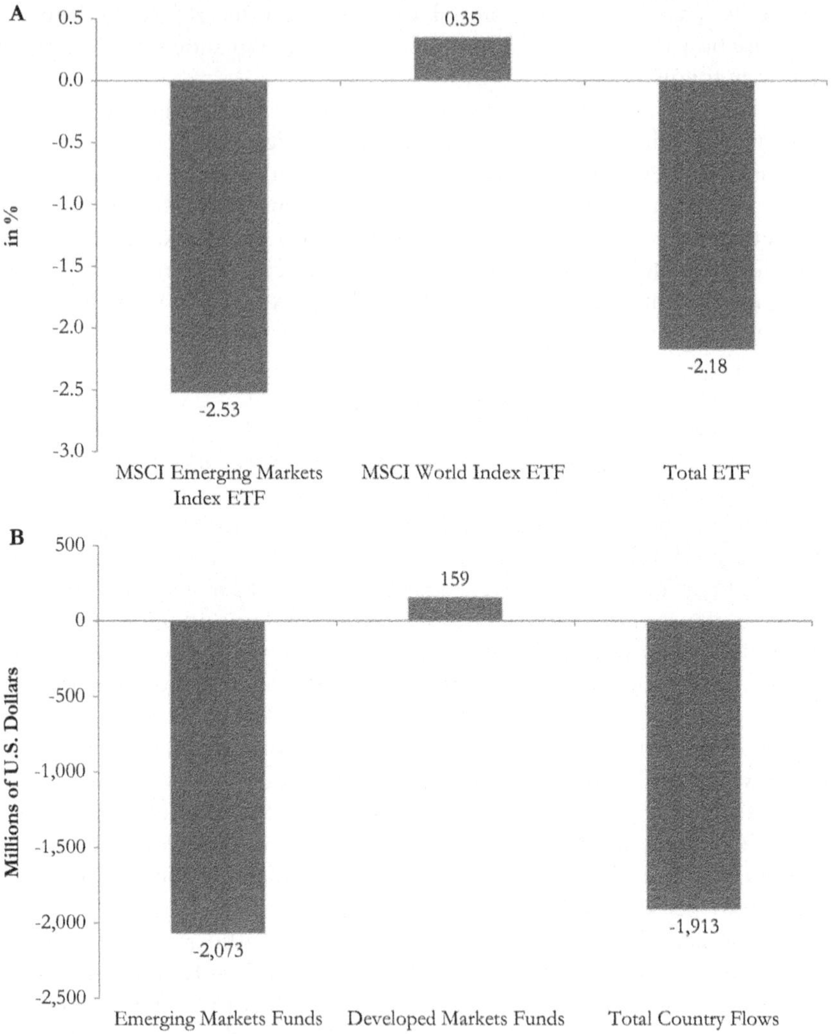

Fig. 12.4 Direct benchmark effect: The Case of Israel

assume that all funds act as passive investors. Deviations from this passive strategy would yield lower estimates. In fact, most funds are not purely passive. However, these estimates go in the direction of the observed capital flows from Israel around the month of the rebalancing.

The cases of the upgrade of Qatar and the United Arab Emirates also illustrate the impact of the direct benchmark effect on the stock market prices of these two countries as well as those of other countries in the MSCI Frontier Market Index. These two countries were upgraded from frontier to emerging market status in 2014. Because capital inflows of around USD800 million were expected for Qatar and the United Arab Emirates, there were sharp increases in prices in the MSCI stocks of these countries relative to their non-MSCI stocks (Fig. 12.5), both during the announcement date and before the effective date (when most of the buying from the emerging market funds happened). Moreover, because Qatar and the United Arab Emirates comprised around 40 percent of the MSCI Frontier Markets Index, the rest of the frontier markets were expected to have their benchmark weight increased considerably as frontier market funds reallocated away from Qatar and the United Arab Emirates. Given the size of the expected reallocations in the MSCI Frontier Markets Index, MSCI considered not removing Qatar and the United Arab Emirates from this index (even when they would still be moved to the emerging market category). In the end, it decided to move forward with the removal, but did it gradually to ameliorate the disruption in the markets (MSCI Barra 2014). The upgrade of Qatar and the United Arab Emirates not only had effects on these two countries, but also on the countries that shared the MSCI Frontier Markets Index with them. In particular, mutual fund managers tracking their performance against this index had to reallocate nearly 40 percent of their portfolio from Qatar and the United Arab Emirates to the rest of frontier markets. This portfolio reallocations generated positive capital inflows, which had positive impact on stock market prices. This episode is described in detail in Raddatz et al. (2017).

The direct benchmark effect not only affects capital flows and aggregate prices, but can also affect asset prices at the company level within a country. Argentina's downgrade by MSCI from the emerging to the frontier country category illustrates this. The event was first announced on February 20, 2009, with the effective date at the end of May 2009. Since liquidity in Argentina's stock market was not up to MSCI requirements, the company announced at the same time a change in the underlying securities. As of the effective date, the American Depositary Receipt (ADR)

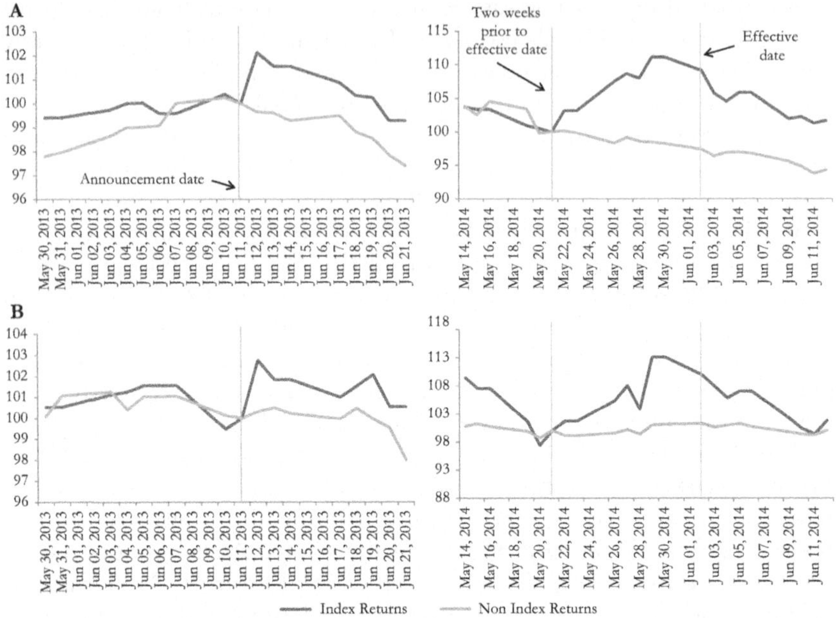

Fig. 12.5 MSCI upgrade of Qatar and the United Arab Emirates

counterparts would replace the stocks included in Argentina's index. Thus, we analyze the premium between the ADRs and the corresponding underlying stocks (Fig. 12.6). The premium fluctuated around zero before the announcement, and increased to almost 20 percent a couple of months later, even when the announcement was a downgrade. Moreover, there was a significant increase from 22 percent to 32 percent in the days previous to the effective date.

Next, we present illustrations for the sensitivity effect described in Eq. 12.5. The sensitivity effect shows that countries with higher weights in a benchmark are more prone to more inflows (outflows) when the funds receive injections (redemptions), possibly explaining why large countries

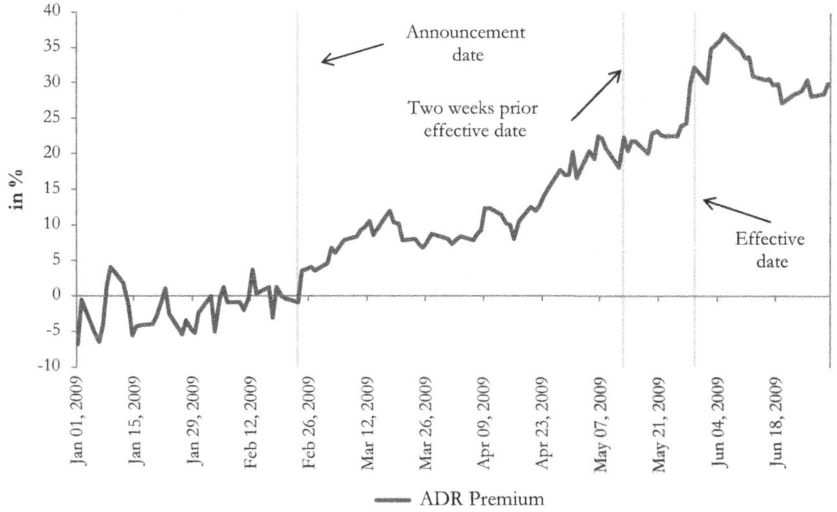

Fig. 12.6 Direct benchmark effect and asset prices: Argentina equity market

might be subject to large changes in capital flows regardless of their fundamentals. Fig. 12.7 illustrates this effect by showing the flows to Brazil and India from explicit indexing funds, tracking the MSCI Emerging Markets Index against the flows into each of these equity funds. The relation of country and fund flows is depicted by two points in time, when each country had different benchmark weights. The relation becomes steeper as each country's benchmark weight increases, as shown in Eq. 12.5.

For a more systematic analysis of the sensitivity effect, we regress country flows against benchmark weights multiplied by fund flows (Table 12.2). There is a positive and significant relation between the two variables, which monotonically decreases with the degree of active management. For example, on average across all equity funds, an injection of one dollar to a fund is associated with country flows of 0.74 dollars times the benchmark weight. Every dollar an explicit fund receives is associated with 84 cents allocated proportionally to the benchmark weight. This number declines for funds that are more active, being 0.69, 0.55, and 0.41 for closet indexing, mildly active, and truly active funds, respectively. The relation is also maintained

Table 12.2 Country flows versus benchmark flows

Explanatory variables	*Total sample*	*Degree of activism*			
		Explicit indexing	*Closet indexing*	*Mildly active*	*Truly active*
A. Equity funds					
Dependent variable: country flows					
Benchmark weight × fund flows	0.744***	0.839***	0.690***	0.547***	0.407***
	(0.028)	(0.036)	(0.014)	(0.014)	(0.017)
Fund-country fixed effects	No	No	No	No	No
Fund-time fixed effects	No	No	No	No	No
Country-time fixed effects	No	No	No	No	No
Number of observations	962,344	12,895	286,890	378,626	283,933
R-squared	0.296	0.627	0.177	0.081	0.045
Dependent variable: country flows					
Benchmark weight × fund flows	0.700***	0.794***	0.644***	0.468***	0.254***
	(0.035)	(0.043)	(0.018)	(0.018)	(0.018)
Fund-country fixed effects	Yes	Yes	Yes	Yes	Yes
Fund-time fixed effects	Yes	Yes	Yes	Yes	Yes
Country-time fixed effects	No	No	No	No	No
Number of observations	962,344	12,895	286,890	378,626	283,933
R-squared	0.410	0.700	0.299	0.192	0.214
Dependent variable: country flows					
Benchmark weight × fund flows	0.739***	0.854***	0.676***	0.532***	0.381***
	(0.031)	(0.045)	(0.013)	(0.015)	(0.016)
Fund-country fixed effects	Yes	Yes	Yes	Yes	Yes
Fund-time fixed effects	No	No	No	No	No
Country-time fixed effects	Yes	Yes	Yes	Yes	Yes
Number of observations	960,928	12,895	285,897	378,101	284,035
R-squared	0.331	0.770	0.213	0.132	0.130

B. Bond funds					
Dependent variable: country flows					
Benchmark weight × fund flows	0.634***	–	0.730***	0.610***	0.615***
	(0.036)	–	(0.036)	(0.043)	(0.082)
Fund-country fixed effects	No	–	No	No	No
Fund-time fixed effects	No	–	No	No	No
Country-time fixed effects	No	–	No	No	No
Number of observations	59,415	–	25,327	23,440	10,648
R-squared	0.066	–	0.099	0.068	0.049
Dependent variable: country flows					
Benchmark weight × fund flows	0.369***	–	0.683***	0.371***	0.120
	(0.051)	–	(0.053)	(0.065)	(0.113)
Fund-country fixed effects	Yes	–	Yes	Yes	Yes
Fund-time fixed effects	Yes	–	Yes	Yes	Yes
Country-time fixed effects	No	–	No	No	No
Number of observations	59,415	–	25,327	23,440	10,648
R-squared	0.251	–	0.236	0.236	0.274
Dependent variable: country flows					
Benchmark weight × fund flows	0.551***	–	0.748***	0.586***	0.585***
	(0.045)	–	(0.035)	(0.050)	(0.101)
Fund-country fixed effects	Yes	–	Yes	Yes	Yes
Fund-time fixed effects	No	–	No	No	No
Country-time fixed effects	Yes	–	Yes	Yes	Yes
Number of observations	59,773	–	25,327	23,440	10,648
R-squared	0.147	–	0.242	0.186	0.230

This table presents Ordinary Least Squares (OLS) regressions of country flows in billions of US dollars against benchmark weights multiplied fund flows with different sets of fixed effects. Panel A displays results for equity funds and Panel B for bond funds. Funds are divided by fund type and degree of active management. Explicit indexing bond funds are not included due to the low number of observations. Standard errors are in parentheses and clustered at the benchmark-time level. *** denote statistical significance at 10 percent, 5 percent, and 1 percent, respectively

Source: Authors' computations

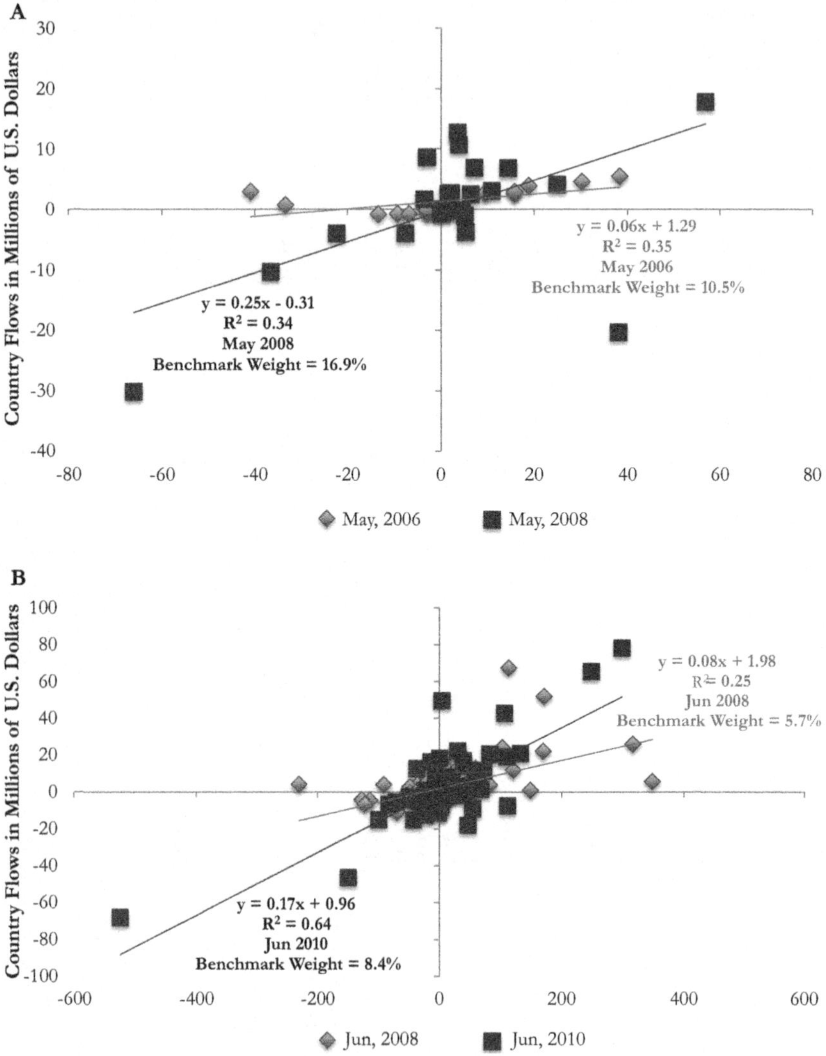

Fig. 12.7 Sensitivity effect of country flows

when we control for different sets of fixed effects. Under this estimation, a change in the benchmark weight changes the sensitivity of country flows to fund flows as indicated above.

There can also be interesting interactions between the sensitivity, amplification, and contagion effects. Notice that changes in benchmark weights (or returns) change the sensitivity of country flows to fund flows. This leads to interesting dynamic interactions between various effects. For instance, a decline in the returns of the rest of the countries sharing a benchmark with country A will induce a higher benchmark weight for country A. But the same increase in benchmark weights makes country A more vulnerable to future movements in fund flows. If in reaction to the initial shock there are large withdrawals of funds, country A would be more affected even though it was the country that performed relatively well. Namely, during good times (when funds are receiving injections), a country that does relatively well gets more country flows. But during bad times, a country that does relatively poorly (its weight decreases) is less affected by the outflows.

Some of these effects can be illustrated by the evolution of country flows to China and Russia from explicit indexing funds following the MSCI Emerging Markets Index, before the global financial crisis and during the European crisis (Fig. 12.8). Before the global financial crisis, China and Russia had similar benchmark weights and flows. However, during the global financial crisis, China did relatively well compared with Russia, which increased its benchmark weight significantly. During the peak of the European crisis, emerging market funds had net withdrawals, which translated into much larger outflows from China than from Russia (proportional to their weights). That is, China was penalized as a result of its stronger pre-crisis performance.

This outcome is the result of the interaction of the sensitivity, amplification, and contagion effects. As China performed well during the global financial crisis, its benchmark weight (amplification) became larger, while Russia's benchmark weight in the index grew but much less (contagion). Thus, the subsequent outflows by investors during the European crisis period translated into higher capital outflows for China than for Russia (sensitivity).

We also illustrate a similar case with Spain and Ireland for the explicit indexing funds tracking the MSCI Europe, Australasia, and Far East Index. Spain and Ireland received inflows during the pre-European crisis, with the former receiving four times more flows than Ireland according to its benchmark weight. Still, Ireland received around USD80 million in that period. Immediately after the crisis, Ireland did relatively worse than Spain, and the subsequent outflows were smaller in Ireland than in Spain.

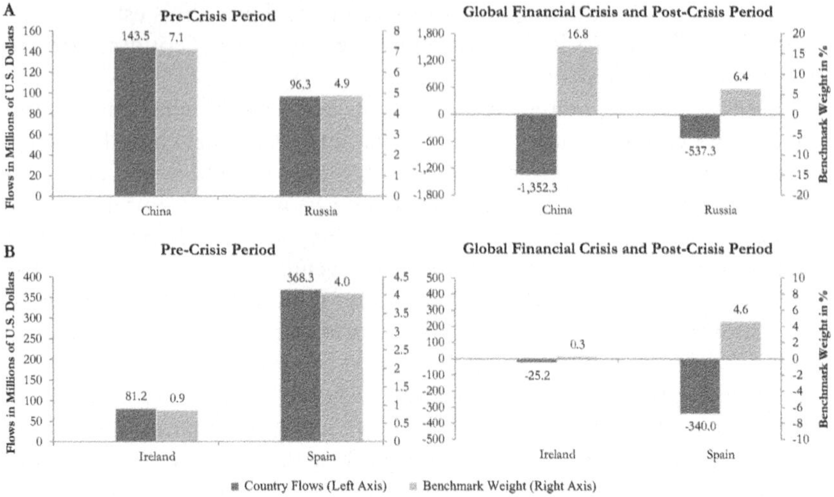

Fig. 12.8 Capital flows and benchmark weights

The various effects described above can interact and build up. A shock to a country's returns increases its benchmark weight and induces inflows through the amplification effect. If these inflows are important enough to have an impact on returns, a feedback loop might be established. Also, a current increase in benchmark weights, either through the direct benchmark effect or other channels will increase the future response of that country's flows to injections through the sensitivity effect. Moreover, with the exception of the direct benchmark effect, other effects could be present for funds that do not follow a benchmark ($\alpha = 0$) through the response of the non-benchmark component to each of the shocks. What is particular about the benchmark effect is that the manner in which benchmarks are calculated guarantees that the response of flows to an own-country shock through benchmarks is positive, and it is negative for shocks to the returns to other countries. For the non-benchmark component, the sign of these responses is indeterminate.

12.5 Conclusions

This chapter provides a detailed illustration of how benchmarks affect international capital flows through different channels that might help explain some of the findings documented in the literature, as well as sometimes counterintuitive and unexpected movements in cross-country investments. First, the reclassification of countries across benchmarks has important reallocation effects on capital flows, and is affected by the size of benchmark investors and the relative importance of countries in these benchmarks. For example, emerging countries tend to have larger weights in emerging market indexes than in developed market ones, because in the latter they share the benchmark with much larger countries. This can provide an explanation of why countries might face capital outflows when upgraded and capital inflows when downgraded. Moreover, the removal of a large country from a benchmark can have consequences in terms of capital flows to the rest of the countries in the same index. These effects might even occur without changes to the fundamentals of a country.

Second, sensitivity, amplification, and contagion effects can occur even when fundamentals or the absolute returns of a country do not warrant them. For example, during global crises, some countries might suffer the curse of being large or having done relatively well. That is, during large retrenchments, countries with larger weights will suffer more withdrawals (although in some cases their larger market capitalization might help them withstand the shock).[9] During generalized declines in asset prices, countries whose stock market indices fall less than other countries in the same benchmark will see their benchmark weight increase and, thus, will be more exposed to subsequent withdrawals by the underlying investors of the funds that follow that benchmark. During good times, when funds receive injections, countries that do relatively well will receive more inflows, witnessing an amplification of the shock that increased its relative return.

More generally, as a country becomes more relevant in a benchmark, it becomes more sensitive to shocks because injections and redemptions have stronger effects on the capital flows to this country. While this effect might be entirely driven by fundamentals (e.g., by the country growing relatively fast), it can also be driven by non-fundamental factors such as bubbles, self-fulfilling expectations, shocks to other countries sharing the same benchmark, or exogenous decisions made by the company constructing the benchmark. For example, if investors suddenly favor a country and drive its asset valuations upward, the subsequent injections that the relevant mutual funds receive will be more tilted toward this country. This, in turn, might generate more upward pressure on prices, reinforcing the effect. This positive-feedback loop increases as more funds follow benchmark indexes more closely over time, generating pro-cyclicality and possibly explaining (along with other factors) some of the widely documented momentum effect, whereby investment reallocations are related to past returns. Furthermore, the link between benchmarks and market capitalization could create a pro-cyclical bias in benchmark allocations because countries that do relatively well will tend to gain weight in a benchmark relative to the rest.

This chapter presents several new findings that point to further directions in which the research on the effects of benchmarks could likely take. First, the evidence suggests that funds worldwide are becoming less active (Cremers et al. 2016) and the number of benchmarks is increasing rapidly. Therefore, the types of mechanisms documented here are expected to grow over time.

Second, models of international asset allocations and capital flows that use macroeconomic fundamentals and other important factors might start incorporating the type of mechanisms described in this chapter.

Third, benchmarks offer several advantages for researchers. Among other things, they help compare individual portfolios against some well-known specific asset allocations, make portfolio allocations easier to evaluate, and allow for the identification of various effects.

Fourth, although benchmark effects shed light on the behavior of heterogeneous investors, the general equilibrium effects still need to be understood. For example, does the use of benchmarks as a disciplining mechanism coordinate manager decisions across institutions, generating herding, information cascades, and other systemically important effects? Given that some funds try to replicate their benchmark index almost mechanically, do other funds or sophisticated investors anticipate or compensate for their reaction? Are there wealth transfers? Or do they also follow these benchmarks? How do funds manage their active portfolio? What are the effects of benchmarks on capital market financing, the returns to retail investors, and the real economy? These and other questions will likely induce further research in this area.

NOTES

1. ICI and OECD have different coverage of mutual funds, so their estimates are not directly comparable.
2. Benchmark weights w_{ic}^{B} are fund specific because each fund chooses its benchmark. We thus denote it with sub-index *i*. The same applies to other benchmark characteristics such as benchmark returns.
3. As in Raddatz et al. (2017), we define different types of funds according to their degree of activism using the active share measure used in Cremers and Petajisto (2009). We classify funds as "explicit indexing," "closet indexing," "mildly active," and "truly active" funds. Explicit indexing funds are those that declare themselves as index funds or ETFs. We then define closet indexing funds as those that on average have an active share within two standard deviations of the active share of explicit indexing funds. Funds not belonging to the explicit indexing or closet indexing groups are classified into mildly active (truly active) if they are in the lower (upper) part of the distribution of the active share measure (using the median active share).
4. More precisely, the buy-and-hold weights are the ones that result only from the impact of the different returns obtained by the various assets that a fund had in its portfolio at the end of the previous period, in absence of any injection/redemption and any active reallocations by the fund manager.
5. The derivations take w_{ict-1} as given and use the following expressions: $w_{ict} = \alpha w_{ict}^{B} + \varepsilon_{ict}$, $R_{ict} = \sum_{c} w_{ict-1} R_{ct}$, and $R_{ict}^{B} = \sum_{c} w_{ict-1}^{B} R_{ct}$.
6. The median country depends on the specific benchmark and time period used. Therefore, different countries represent our median benchmark weight, according to the case being analyzed at that point.
7. This is an approximation because we divide Δf_{ict} by w_{ict-1}^{B}, and thus take it as a percentage of a fund's total assets in a country if it perfectly followed the benchmark.
8. Williams (2017) also uses this framework to estimate the capital inflows to Colombia around a benchmark rebalancing in the J.P. Morgan Government Bond Index and finds that the predictions from Eq. 12.4 are very close to the actual capital inflows in that episode.
9. Whether the larger market capitalization helps will depend, for instance, on whether its pre-shock increase was driven by fundamentals. If instead it was driven by stretched asset valuations, the larger ensuing withdrawals may accelerate price corrections.

References

Antràs, P., & Caballero, R. (2009). Trade and capital flows: A financial frictions perspective. *Journal of Political Economy, 117*(4), 701–744.

Barberis, N., Shleifer, A., & Wurgler, J. (2005). Comovement. *Journal of Financial Economics, 75*(2), 283–317.

Bartram, S., Griffin, J., Lim, T. H., & Ng, D. (2015). How important are foreign ownership linkages for international stock returns? *Review of Financial Studies, 28*(11), 3036–3072.

Busse, J., Goyal, A., & Wahal, S. (2014). Investing in a global world. *Review of Finance, 18*(2), 561–590.

Calvo, G., & Mendoza, E. (2000). Rational contagion and the globalization of securities markets. *Journal of International Economics, 51*(1), 79–113.

Chang, Y.-C., Hong, H., & Liskovich, I. (2015). Regression discontinuity and the price effects of stock market indexing. *Review of Financial Studies, 28*(1), 212–246.

Chen, H., Noronha, G., & Singal, V. (2004). The price response to S&P 500 index additions and deletions: Evidence of asymmetry and a new explanation. *Journal of Finance, 59*(4), 1901–1929.

Cremers, M., & Petajisto, A. (2009). How active is your fund manager? A new measure that predicts performance. *Review of Financial Studies, 22*(9), 3329–3365.

Cremers, M., Ferreira, M. A., Matos, P., & Starks, L. (2016). Indexing and active fund management: International evidence. *Journal of Financial Economics, 120*(3), 539–560.

Di Giovanni, J. (2005). What drives capital flows? The case of cross-border M&A activity and financial deepening. *Journal of International Economics, 65*(1), 127–149.

Faias, J., Ferreira, M., Matos, P., & Santa-Clara, P. (2012). Does institutional ownership matter for international stock return comovement? *Darden School of Business, mimeo.*

Fratzscher, M. (2012). Capital flows, push versus pull factors and the global financial crisis. *Journal of International Economics, 88*(2), 341–356.

Gourinchas, P., & Rey, H. (2014). External adjustment, global imbalances and valuation effects. In G. Gopinath, H. Helpman, & K. Rogoff (Eds.), *Handbook of International Economics* (Vol. 4). Amsterdam: Elsevier.

Greenwood, R. (2005). Short- and long-term demand curves for stocks: Theory and evidence on the dynamics of arbitrage. *Journal of Financial Economics, 75*(3), 607–649.

Harris, L., & Gurel, E. (1986). Price and volume effects associated with changes in the S&P 500 list: New evidence for the existence of price pressures. *Journal of Finance, 41*(4), 815–829.

Hau, H. (2011). Global versus local asset pricing: A new test of market integration. *Review of Financial Studies, 24*(12), 3891–3940.

Hau, H., & Lai, S. (2013). The role of equity funds in the financial crisis propagation. *CEPR Discussion Papers 8819.*

Hau, H., Massa, M., & Peress, J. (2010). Do demand curves for currency slope down? Evidence from the MSCI global index change. *Review of Financial Studies, 23*(4), 1681–1717.

Kodres, L., & Pritsker, M. (2002). A rational expectations model of financial contagion. *Journal of Finance, 57*(2), 769–799.

Kraay, A., Norman, L., Servén, L., & Ventura, J. (2005). Country portfolios. *Journal of the European Economic Association, 3*(4), 914–945.

Lane, P., & Milesi-Ferretti, G. M. (2007). The external wealth of nations mark II: Revised and extended estimates of foreign assets and liabilities, 1970–2004. *Journal of International Economics, 73*(2), 223–250.

Lehmann, B., & Modest, D. (1987). Mutual fund performance evaluation: A comparison of benchmarks and benchmark comparison. *Journal of Finance, 42*(2), 233–265.

Levy Yeyati, E., & Williams, T. (2012). Emerging economies in the 2000s: Real decoupling and financial recoupling. *Journal of International Money and Finance, 31*(8), 2102–2126.

Manconi, A., Massa, M., & Yasuda, A. (2012). The role of institutional investors in propagating the financial crisis of 2007–2008. *Journal of Financial Economics, 104*(3), 491–518.

Martin, A., & Taddei, F. (2013). International capital flows and credit market imperfections: A tale of two frictions. *Journal of International Economics, 89*(2), 441–452.

Miao, Y., & Pant, M. (2012). Coincident indicators of capital flows. *IMF Working Paper 12/55.*

MSCI Barra. 2014. MSCI to consult on potential changes to the methodology for the MSCI frontier markets 100 index. Press Release.

Puy, D. (2013). Institutional investors flows and the geography of contagion. *European University Institute Working Paper 2013/06.*

Raddatz, C., Schmukler, S., & Williams, T. (2017). International asset allocations and capital flows: The benchmark effect. *Journal of International Economics, 108*, 413–430.

Reinhardt, D., Ricci, L., & Tressel, T. (2013). International capital flows and development: Financial openness matters. *Journal of International Economics, 91*(2), 235–251.

Sensoy, B. (2009). Performance evaluation and self-designated benchmarks indexes in the mutual fund industry. *Journal of Financial Economics, 92*(9), 25–39.

Sharpe, W. (1992). Asset allocation: Management style and performance measurement. *Journal of Portfolio Management, 18*(2), 7–19.

Shleifer, A. (1986). Do demand curves for stocks slope down? *Journal of Finance, 41*(3), 579–590.

Vayanos, D., & Woolley, P. (2011). Fund flows and asset prices: A baseline model. *LSE FMG Discussion Paper No. 667*, Financial Markets Group.

Wermers, R. (2000). Mutual fund performance: An empirical decomposition into stock-picking talent, style, transaction costs, and expenses. *Journal of Finance, 55*(4), 1655–1695.

Williams, T. (2017). Capital inflows, sovereign debt, and bank lending: Micro-evidence from an emerging market. *Universitat Pompeu Fabra, mimeo.*

CHAPTER 13

Equity Markets Integration and Active Portfolio Management

Gabriel Petre, Olga Sulla, and Daniel Vela Barón

13.1 Introduction

This chapter analyzes portfolio diversification and active management strategies that could enhance risk-return properties of equity portfolios versus benchmarks despite the effect of international financial integration. The chapter's hypothesis is that despite the high degree of global stock market integration, local equity indices and specific industries can be

Comments from the participants of the Sixth Public Investors Conference Bank of International Settlements—World Bank—Bank of Canada are highly appreciated. The opinions and statements are the sole responsibility of the authors and do not necessarily represent those of the World Bank.

G. Petre (✉)
Pension & Endowments Department (PEN), World Bank Treasury, Washington, DC, USA
e-mail: gpetre@worldbank.org

O. Sulla • D. Vela Barón
Quantitative Solutions, Strategic Asset Allocation, and Analytics Department (QSA), World Bank Treasury, Washington, DC, USA
e-mail: osulla@worldbank.org; dvelabaron@worldbank.org

N. Bulusu et al. (eds.), *Advances in the Practice of Public Investment Management*, https://doi.org/10.1007/978-3-319-90245-6_13

identified by portfolio managers to take active positions that improve their performance versus benchmarks.

Global diversification opportunities are identified by selecting the least co-integrated equity indices in various regions and industries. The analysis indicates that there might be opportunities for improving risk-return profiles of global equity index portfolios, but further work is warranted to better understand the liquidity implications on transaction costs as well as the scalability of such strategies.

Although relevant for any active portfolio manager, the chapter seeks to provide strategies for institutional investors, particularly pension funds and sovereign wealth funds that have large exposures to global equity markets. Eighty percent of sovereign wealth funds invest in public equity, some of them exceeding 50% of the allocation of their entire portfolio, as illustrated in Figs. 13.1 and 13.2. Most of these institutions implement active portfolio management strategies, either internally or through external managers, seeking to generate returns in excess of market benchmarks. The recent surge in their total assets under management makes them major players in global equity markets (Fig. 13.3). Therefore, an analysis of equity market integration and potential returns from diversification into less integrated markets and industries is beneficial for the active strategies of these institutions.

Some of the factors behind equity market integration include (1) larger global interdependence due to increased trade and greater policy coordination across countries (Fig. 13.4); (2) increasing diversification of firms' sales and financing sources, (3) convergence in industrial composition due to emergence of large global conglomerates, (4) adjustment of institutional investors' regulations to global markets allowing to invest across border; (5) cross-listing regulations permitting companies to directly raise funds or borrow abroad (Fig. 13.5); and (6) emergence of regional stock exchanges like Euronext; Eastern Caribbean ECSE, BRVM, and BVMAC in Africa; ASEAN in East Asia; and MILA in Latin America, harmonizing corporate governance and listing procedures and supporting the trend of integration.

This chapter emphasizes integration at both country level and industry level and studies its implications for portfolio diversification strategies. Research on global integration at the industry level is important due to increasing economic integration as well as industrial developments. Some of the industries may be driven more by local factors, while others by global ones. The latter affects the behavior of the industry indices in terms of their co-movements globally.

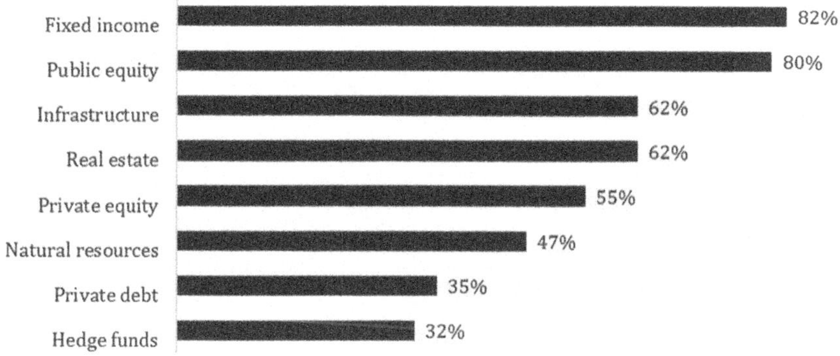

Fig. 13.1 Portion of sovereign wealth funds investing in each asset class

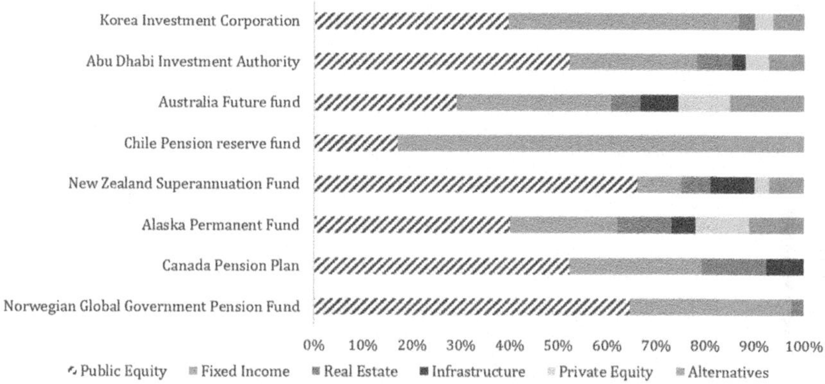

Fig. 13.2 Asset allocation of selected institutional investors, percentage of total portfolio

Co-integration tests are the tool used to identify potential diversification opportunities, in order to select the least co-integrated stock markets within various geographical regions and the least co-integrated industries within the global industries. The stock market indices identified as the

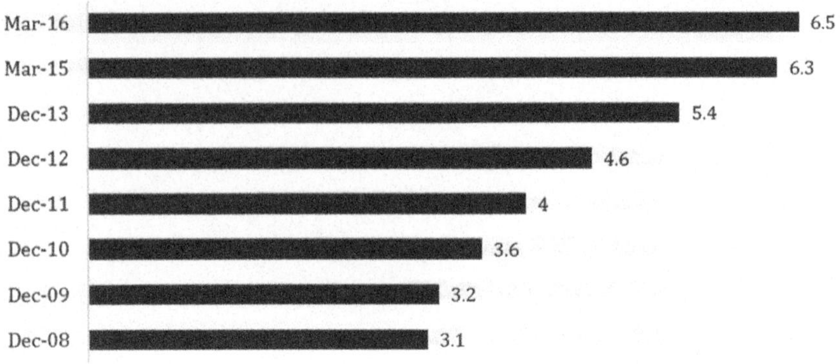

Fig. 13.3 Sovereign wealth funds' assets under management, USD trillion

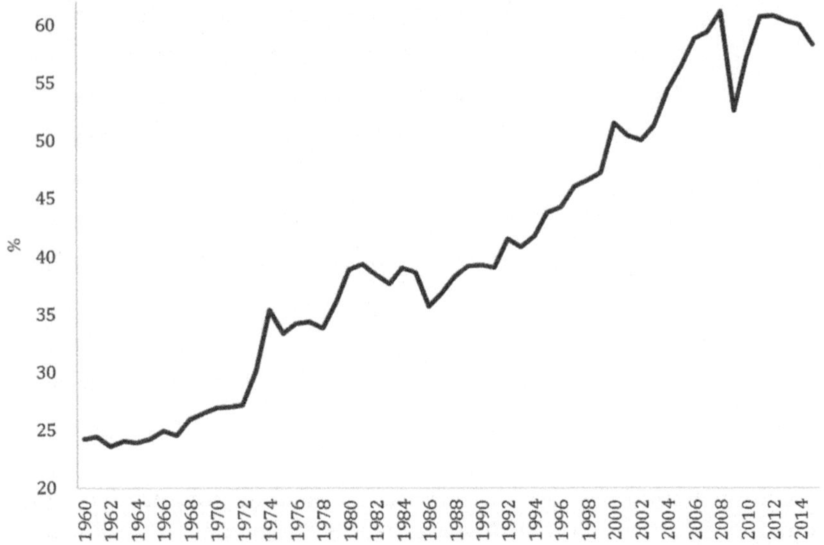

Fig. 13.4 World trade as a percentage of GDP

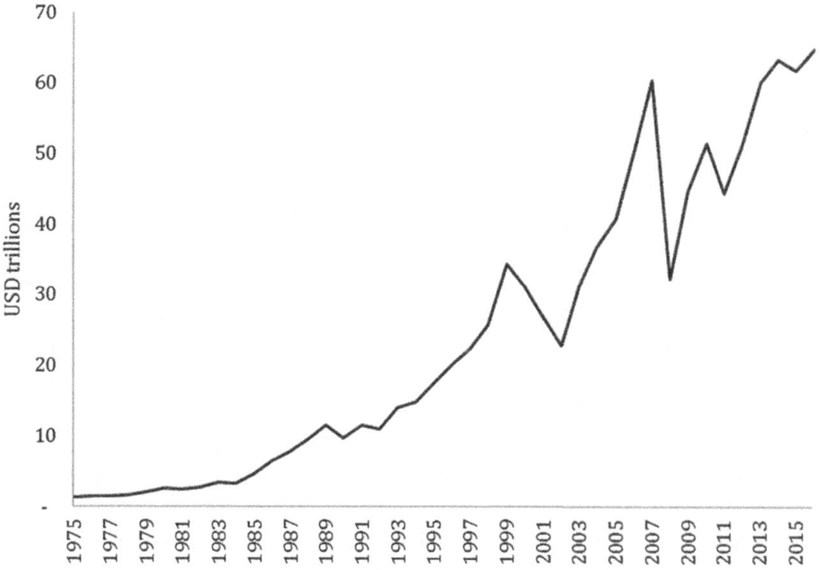

Fig. 13.5 Market capitalization of globally listed companies

least co-integrated are then analyzed under an active management strategy, where their weight in an original benchmark MSCI (developed, emerging, or industry) is increased with various scenarios, and a risk-return analysis is conducted.

Seven sections are included in this chapter. Following this introduction, the next section reviews the literature that analyzes stock market integration both at country and industry levels. The third section provides an overview of the hypothesis and the methodology used to identify the diversification opportunities by selecting stock market indices by country and industry. The fourth section reviews the data used for the analysis. The fifth section describes the results of the co-integration analysis for the examined regions and shows the back-test performance of portfolios applying active strategies that consider the diversification opportunities. The subsequent section expands the analysis to industry data. Finally, the seventh section concludes with the results of the analysis and suggests further research.

13.2 Literature Review

This section reviews papers focused on examining stock market integration in developed and emerging countries, using either bivariate or multivariate co-integration techniques.

Financial and econometric literature encompasses various co-integration analyses of equity markets among different regions. Neaime (2015) examines the co-integration among the stock markets of countries in the Middle East and North Africa (MENA) region with some of the biggest stock markets in the world. The author finds that Turkey, Egypt, and Morocco are highly linked to the US, UK, and French markets. Jordan is found to be linked in a smaller degree and the countries of the Gulf Cooperation Council (GCC, composed of Bahrain, Oman, Qatar, Kuwait, Saudi Arabia, and the United Arab Emirates) are shown to be segmented from the main stock markets in the world, mainly because of their traditional restrictions on participation of non-GCC investors.

Likewise, Paramati et al. (2013) test the co-integration between Australia and 18 frontier markets in 5 different regions and find that Australian investors have diversification opportunities in these 18 markets as the co-integration test indicates no long-term relationship. These two papers perform a Johansen co-integration test, which is a linear test that does not consider structural breaks. In other papers, described below, both assumptions are shown to produce biased results in favor of the null hypothesis of no co-integration.

Lim et al. (2003) study the Association of Southeast Asian Nations (ASEAN) countries' stock markets (Indonesia, Malaysia, Philippines, Singapore, and Thailand) from 1998 to 2002. Their analysis concludes that there is a collective factor which drives the five markets together in the long run, mainly as a result of their trade and investment agreements. In this paper, the authors conduct Bierens's test, which, in contrast to other co-integration tests (Johansen, Engle-Granger, and Gregory-Hansen) is non-linear.

Syriopoulos (2011) tests the co-integration between the stock markets of Balkan countries (Romania, Bulgaria, Croatia, Turkey, Cyprus, and Greece) and the stock markets of the United States and Germany. The author finds co-integration among them by performing an eight-dimensional vector error correction model. The most significant relationship he finds is between Germany and Greece, while Romania and Turkey are found to be integrated to a lesser extent with the US and German stock markets.

Beyer et al. (2009) studied the co-integration among inflation and nominal interest rates in 15 markets. This paper shows the importance of considering structural breaks, as nine economies are found to lack a long-term relationship when testing for co-integration without considering the breaks, but the conclusion changes once the structural breaks are considered with a Carrion-i-Silvestre and Sansó test.

Furthermore, Aggarwal, Lucey, and Muckley (2010) studied the dynamic integration between European stock markets by performing three different tests: (1) dynamic robust eigenvalue analyses, (2) a Kalman filter approach, and (3) a recursive co-integration technique proposed by Hansen and Johansen. The authors find that the co-integration in the stock markets of the continent has increased throughout the tested sample.

Some of these papers also perform a Granger causality test to further explain the dynamics of the long-term relationships among the stock markets in the regions. Such is the case of Neaime (2015) with the MENA region, Syriopoulos (2011) in the Balkan region, and Paramati et al. (2013) with Australia and 18 frontier markets.

Brooks and Del Negro (2004) find that industry effects have gone from less than half as important as country effects in the mid-1990s to almost twice as important in early 2000s, in the technology, media, and telecom (TMT) industries.

Finally, Bekaert, Hodrick, and Zhang (2009) examine if the degree of stock market integration varies across industries by comparing the variance explained by global factors relative to the total explained variance. They find that the least integrated industry is mining, followed by oil and gas. Although these are industries affected by global commodity prices, they are also more likely to be regulated by local authorities. Furthermore, they find that the most integrated industries were machinery and construction. Overall, the differences in the degree of integration among different industries are less marked than the differences between countries, reflecting the fact that industry portfolios represent well-diversified portfolios across countries.

13.3 Hypothesis and Methodology

Depending on their level of co-integration, the equity market indices that are not co-integrated with the rest can offer profitable opportunities to international investors, both at the country and industry levels. This chapter aims to identify if idiosyncratic factors which provide diversification opportunities for investors remain despite the current high levels of stock market integration. The presence of common trends between developing and mature equity markets or among the developing markets themselves may indicate limited portfolio gains from diversification. This is because common factors limit the amount of independent variation.

While simple correlation measures the linear synchronicity of the changes between two time series, co-integration measures the long-term convergence of the levels of the time series and whether the residual between them is stationary (absent a trend). Although the co-integrated time series levels can show some unstable periods, they should exhibit a mean-reverting spread. Thus, co-integration measures the long-run equilibrium relationship among two-time series, where each of them exhibits a non-stationary trend. Two non-stationary ($I(1)$) time series are co-integrated if the residual of some linear combination between them is stationary.

To test for co-integration, usually the Engle-Granger two-step test is performed. As introduced in Engle and Granger (1987), one-time series (y_t) is regressed with a series of independent variables ($x_{1,t}$, $x_{2,t}$, …, $x_{n,t}$). The residuals of the linear combination ($u_t = y_t - \beta X_t$), estimated with ordinary least squares, are then tested for a unit root, with either the Augmented Dickey Fuller (ADF) test (see Fuller 1976) or the Phillips-Perron test. If the residuals are stationary, there is co-integration among the time series and hence a long-run equilibrium relationship between them. The linear combination of the time series is usually called the co-integrated relation, with the coefficients of the regression (β_1, β_2, …, β_n) representing the co-integration vector. In the Engle-Granger co-integration test, the residual of a linear combination of two non-stationary and co-integrated time series must be stationary.

In this chapter, the Gregory-Hansen (GH) test was used (see Gregory and Hansen 1996) to test for co-integration (instead of the Engle-Granger test or the Johansen[1] test), given that equity indices could possibly exhibit structural breaks, for example, during the global financial crisis. Gregory and Hansen include three alternative models: (1) level, (2) level shift with trend, and (3) regime shift, by providing additional statistics with their corresponding critical values and allow controlling for those structural breaks.

Therefore, the analysis to identify the least co-integrated indices both by country and industry consists of two main econometric tests: the ADF unit-root test to establish non-stationary of the stock market indices and the Gregory-Hansen co-integration test with structural breaks to identify the least co-integrated indices by country and industry. If the ADF unit-root tests show that the time series imply an $I(1)$ process, then a GH test can be performed. In the GH test, the null hypothesis of no co-integration with structural breaks is tested against the alternative of co-integration with structural breaks.

Following the co-integration analysis conducted per the methodology described above, the stock market indices exhibiting the least co-integrated characteristics are given greater weights in portfolios than they have in the benchmark MSCI index portfolios. Three portfolio analysis scenarios are conducted: (1) invest an additional 2% in each one of the least co-integrated country stock market index, (2) invest an additional 3% in each of the least co-integrated country stock market index, and (3) invest a total of the maximum between 5% of the index in the least co-integrated stock market country index and the amount allowed by its market capitalization. The last scenario considers possible liquidity constraints that can be found in the market, as the investment is subject to the availability of the asset in the market. If its market capitalization relative to the total market capitalization of all the other countries in the index is below 5%, then the investment is limit to that cap.

13.4 Data

Two separate data sets were created—one for the country analysis and the second for the industry analysis.

For the country analysis, 68 countries were selected and divided into 11 different regions: (1) Eastern Asia—Emerging, (2) Southern Asia, (3) Eastern Asia—Developed, (4) Latin America and the Caribbean, (5) North America, (6) Middle East, (7) Africa, (8) Eastern Europe, (9) Western Europe, (10) Southern Europe, and (11) Northern Europe. The MSCI data in dollar terms was used for each country. Monthly data were collected from 1969; however, the analysis was conducted from the date of the most recent available information of all the countries within the regions with data for no less than ten years.

For the industry analysis, the data was divided between developed and emerging markets, and MSCI monthly data was used from June of 2008. The analysis was conducted in US dollar terms rather than on local currency indices in order to allow co-integration tests on a series of the same properties and neutralize the exchange rate effect. The industries considered were (1) consumer discretionary, (2) consumer staples, (3) energy, (4) financial, (5) health care, (6) industrials, (7) information technology, (8) materials, (9) telecommunication services, and (10) utilities.

13.5 Results by Country

13.5.1 Co-integration Tests

The results of co-integration test on stock market indices globally are demonstrated in Table 13.2 preceded by ADF test on each one of the indices to establish their lack of stationarity (Table 13.1). The Gregory-Hansen co-integration tests with structural breaks show that stock market indices globally exhibit high co-integration overall; however, some countries are less co-integrated within their own regions. Countries were identified as the least co-integrated if the test indicates that the co-integration with most of the other countries within its region is not significant. Given that the null hypothesis of the GH test is no co-integration, if the country has high p-values with some of its peers, then it is identified as belonging to the set of the least co-integrated countries in the region. This chapter identifies the following as the least co-integrated stock market indices: Philippines, New Zealand, Jordan, Nigeria, Austria, Denmark, and the Netherlands.

More specifically, within the stock market indices of the emerging countries of Eastern Asia, the one of the Philippines is the least co-integrated, as it seems not to be co-integrated with either Malaysia or Indonesia's stock market indices. New Zealand's stock market index is the least co-integrated country in the developed countries of Eastern Asia and Oceania. Narayan and Smyth (2005) arrive at a similar conclusion; they suggest that New Zealand is only co-integrated with the United States, but is not co-integrated with other G7 economies. The stock market indices of the three countries clustered as Southern Asia are highly co-integrated. Jordan seems to have the least co-integrated stock market index in the Middle East, as it does not have a significant statistical relationship with some of the biggest stock markets in the region, including Morocco, Egypt, and Israel. This reinforces the conclusion in Neaime (2015), since he describes Jordan as a country linked to a smaller degree with other countries in the Middle East. Nigeria's stock market is the least

Table 13.1 Augmented Dickey Fuller test

Country	*p-value*	*Country*	*p-value*	*Country*	*p-value*	*Country*	*p-value*
China	0.15	Trinidad and Tobago	0.92	Czech Republic	0.57	Belgium	0.84
India	0.97	United Arab Emirates	0.21	Hungary	0.69	Denmark	1.00
Malaysia	0.83	South Africa	1.00	Croatia	0.47	Norway	0.71
Thailand	0.61	Israel	0.68	Romania	0.64	Portugal	0.48
Indonesia	0.98	Qatar	0.45	Ukraine	0.16	Finland	0.43
Philippines	0.93	Kuwait	0.32	Lithuania	0.57	Austria	0.47
Pakistan	0.84	Morocco	0.71	Bosnia and Herzegovina	0.29	Ireland	0.50
Vietnam	0.40	Nigeria	0.59	Estonia	0.61	Greece	0.23
Sri Lanka	0.83	Egypt	0.82	Serbia	0.19	Japan	0.51
Kazakhstan	0.37	Kenya	0.97	United Kingdom	0.86	Hong Kong	0.80
Brazil	0.44	Jordan	0.43	France	0.77	Korea	0.88
Mexico	0.74	Bahrain	0.09*	Germany	0.79	Australia	0.90
Chile	0.60	Tunisia	0.85	Switzerland	0.87	Taiwan	0.62
Colombia	0.57	Mauritius	0.90	Sweden	0.87	Singapore	0.63
Argentina	0.49	Lebanon	0.46	Netherlands	0.84	New Zealand	0.81
Peru	0.68	Russia	0.41	Spain	0.63	United States	0.98
Jamaica	0.97	Poland	0.52	Italy	0.48	Canada	0.93

The test is conducted with all the available data for each country. *Indicates significance at the 10% level.
Source: Authors' calculations

co-integrated in Africa. In Western Europe, Austria and the Netherlands' stock market indices are the least co-integrated, while Denmark seems to have the least co-integrated stock market index in Northern Europe. These results follow Worthington and Higgs (2007), as they identify the Netherlands as the least influential market in Europe through a Granger causality test, and together with Denmark are described as two of the less integrated markets in Europe. In Eastern Europe, all the indices are highly co-integrated, only the ones of Hungary and the Czech Republic do not have a strong co-integration relationship between them, but co-integration is significant with other countries' indices of the region. Finally, the countries of Latin America and the Caribbean and the countries of North

Table 13.2 Gregory-Hansen co-integration test with structural breaks (p-value) among different regions

Latin America and the Caribbean

		Independent variables							
		Brazil	Mexico	Chile	Colombia	Argentina	Peru	Jamaica	Trinidad and Tobago
Dependent variables	Brazil	–	0.00**	0.00**	0.00**	0.03**	0.00**	0.00**	0.00**
	Mexico	0.00**	–	0.07*	0.12	0.03**	0.00**	0.00**	0.01**
	Chile	0.00**	0.02**	–	0.00**	0.02**	0.00**	0.00**	0.01**
	Colombia	0.00**	0.01**	0.00**	–	0.00**	0.00**	0.02**	0.01**
	Argentina	0.06*	0.01**	0.03**	0.03**	–	0.00**	0.01**	0.01**
	Peru	0.00**	0.01**	0.00**	0.03**	0.02**	–	0.00**	0.01**
	Jamaica	0.01**	0.00**	0.00**	0.00**	0.08*	0.00**	–	0.00**
	Trinidad and Tobago	0.00**	0.00**	0.02**	0.01**	0.01**	0.01**	0.00**	–

Eastern Asia—Emerging

		Independent variables					
		China	Malaysia	Thailand	Indonesia	Philippines	Vietnam
Dependent variables	China	–	0.00**	0.02**	0.01**	0.00**	0.00**
	Malaysia	0.00**	–	0.00**	0.01**	0.09*	0.00**
	Thailand	0.01**	0.00**	–	0.02**	0.02**	0.00**
	Indonesia	0.00**	0.00**	0.01**	–	0.10	0.00**
	Philippines	0.00**	0.01**	0.00**	0.01**	–	0.00**
	Vietnam	0.01**	0.01**	0.01**	0.02**	0.04**	–

Eastern Asia—Developed and Oceania

		Independent variables						
		Japan	Hong Kong	Korea	Australia	Taiwan	Singapore	New Zealand
Dependent variables	Japan	–	0.06*	0.00**	0.02**	0.00**	0.02**	0.02**
	Hong Kong	0.01**	–	0.00**	0.00**	0.00**	0.00**	0.10
	Korea	0.03**	0.00**	–	0.02**	0.00**	0.01**	0.02**
	Australia	0.01**	0.00**	0.00**	–	0.00**	0.00**	0.08*
	Taiwan	0.00**	0.04**	0.00**	0.01**	–	0.01**	0.00**
	Singapore	0.02**	0.01**	0.01**	0.00**	0.00**	–	0.03**
	New Zealand	0.06*	0.05*	0.00**	0.07*	0.00**	0.03**	–

Africa

		Independent variables			
		South Africa	Nigeria	Kenya	Mauritius
Dependent variables	South Africa	–	0.11	0.00**	0.00**
	Nigeria	0.16	–	0.01**	0.00**
	Kenya	0.00**	0.06*	–	0.00**
	Mauritius	0.03**	0.00**	0.00**	–

(*continued*)

Table 13.2 (continued)

Northern Europe

		Independent variables							
		Lithuania	Estonia	UK	Sweden	Denmark	Norway	Finland	Ireland
Dependent variables	Lithuania	–	0.04**	0.00**	0.00**	0.01**	0.00**	0.00**	0.00**
	Estonia	0.03**	–	0.00**	0.04**	0.05**	0.00**	0.08*	0.00**
	UK	0.00**	0.00**	–	0.01**	0.39	0.00**	0.02**	0.00**
	Sweden	0.00**	0.01**	0.00**	–	0.27	0.01**	0.01**	0.00**
	Denmark	0.00**	0.08*	0.03**	0.00**	–	0.12	0.04**	0.00**
	Norway	0.00**	0.00**	0.00**	0.06*	0.65	–	0.04**	0.00**
	Finland	0.00**	0.06*	0.01**	0.02**	0.08*	0.00**	–	0.01**
	Ireland	0.00**	0.00**	0.00**	0.00**	0.06*	0.00**	0.01**	–

Middle East

		Independent variables									
		UAE	Israel	Qatar	Kuwait	Morocco	Egypt	Jordan	Bahrain	Tunisia	Lebanon
Dependent variables	UAE	–	0.04**	0.00**	0.01**	0.00**	0.01**	0.01**	0.00**	0.00**	0.00**
	Israel	0.11	–	0.04**	0.00**	0.02**	0.01**	0.11	0.00**	0.00**	0.00**
	Qatar	0.01**	0.03**	–	0.01**	0.02**	0.07*	0.01**	0.00**	0.00**	0.00**
	Kuwait	0.06*	0.02**	0.02**	–	0.01**	0.00**	0.01**	0.00**	0.00**	0.00**
	Morocco	0.01**	0.01**	0.05*	0.00**	–	0.02**	0.25	0.00**	0.00**	0.01**
	Egypt	0.00**	0.01**	0.02**	0.02**	0.02**	–	0.11	0.00**	0.00**	0.00**
	Jordan	0.01**	0.01**	0.02**	0.01**	0.05*	0.01**	–	0.00**	0.00**	0.00**
	Bahrain	0.02**	0.01**	0.03**	0.00**	0.00**	0.01**	0.00**	–	0.00**	0.00**
	Tunisia	0.00**	0.00**	0.01**	0.00**	0.00**	0.00**	0.00**	0.00**	–	0.00**
	Lebanon	0.05*	0.00**	0.03**	0.01**	0.02**	0.00**	0.01**	0.00**	0.00**	–

North America

		Independent variables	
		United States	Canada
Dependent variables	United States	–	0.01**
	Canada	0.08*	–

Southern Europe

		Independent variables						
		Croatia	Bosnia and Herzegovina	Serbia	Spain	Italy	Portugal	Greece
Dependent variables	Croatia	–	0.12	0.00**	0.04**	0.02**	0.00**	0.01**
	Bosnia and Herzegovina	0.02**	–	0.01**	0.00**	0.00**	0.02**	0.02**
	Serbia	0.02**	0.01**	–	0.12	0.08*	0.01**	0.00**
	Spain	0.04**	0.00**	0.00**	–	0.00**	0.06*	0.04**
	Italy	0.01**	0.00**	0.00**	0.00**	–	0.02**	0.06*
	Portugal	0.00**	0.04**	0.00**	0.02**	0.02**	–	0.00**
	Greece	0.02**	0.03**	0.00**	0.01**	0.01**	0.00**	–

Eastern Europe

		Independent variables					
		Russia	Poland	Czech Rep.	Hungary	Romania	Ukraine
Dependent variables	Russia	–	0.00**	0.00**	0.02**	0.01**	0.02**
	Poland	0.00**	–	0.01**	0.05*	0.00**	0.00**
	Czech Rep.	0.00**	0.00**	–	0.10*	0.05*	0.00**

(*continued*)

Table 13.2 (continued)

Eastern Europe

	Hungary	0.03**	0.03**	0.25	–	0.00**	0.02**
	Romania	0.00**	0.00**	0.02**	0.00**	–	0.00**
	Ukraine	0.00**	0.00**	0.00**	0.02**	0.00**	–

Western Europe

		Independent variables					
		France	Germany	Switzerland	Netherlands	Belgium	Austria
Dependent variables	France	–	0.03**	0.02**	0.23	0.05*	0.49
	Germany	0.06*	–	0.00**	0.00**	0.00**	0.48
	Switzerland	0.05*	0.00**	–	0.00**	0.02**	0.22
	Netherlands	0.08*	0.00**	0.00**	–	0.13	0.45
	Belgium	0.01**	0.00**	0.00**	0.15	–	0.42
	Austria	0.13	0.07*	0.02**	0.13	0.30	–

Southern Asia

		Independent variables		
		India	Pakistan	Sri Lanka
Dependent variables	India	–	0.00**	0.00**
	Pakistan	0.00**	–	0.00**
	Sri Lanka	0.01**	0.00**	–

The test is conducted with all the available data for each country

The null hypothesis for the Gregory-Hansen test is no co-integration

Source: Authors' calculations

*Indicate significance at the 10% level, **Indicate significance at the 5% level

Table 13.3 Correlation among selected regions

Eastern Asia-Emerging

	China	Malaysia	Thailand	Indonesia	Philippines	Vietnam
China	1	0.61	0.65	0.61	0.55	0.44
Malaysia	0.61	1	0.63	0.66	0.58	0.30
Thailand	0.65	0.63	1	0.74	0.66	0.41
Indonesia	0.61	0.66	0.74	1	0.68	0.42
Philippines	0.55	0.58	0.66	0.68	1	0.43
Vietnam	0.44	0.30	0.41	0.42	0.43	1

Middle East

	UAE	Israel	Qatar	Kuwait	Morocco	Egypt	Jordan	Bahrain	Tunisia
UAE	1	0.42	0.71	0.58	0.26	0.56	0.42	0.57	0.17
Israel	0.42	1	0.32	0.26	0.23	0.45	0.32	0.20	(0.00)
Qatar	0.71	0.32	1	0.54	0.10	0.56	0.48	0.48	0.16
Kuwait	0.58	0.26	0.54	1	0.21	0.38	0.18	0.55	0.12
Morocco	0.26	0.23	0.10	0.21	1	0.34	0.08	0.17	0.12
Egypt	0.56	0.45	0.56	0.38	0.34	1	0.31	0.37	0.18
Jordan	0.42	0.32	0.48	0.18	0.08	0.31	1	0.27	0.07
Bahrain	0.57	0.20	0.48	0.55	0.17	0.37	0.27	1	0.15
Tunisia	0.17	(0.00)	0.16	0.12	0.12	0.18	0.07	0.15	1

Africa

	South Africa	Nigeria	Kenya	Mauritius
South Africa	1	0.23	0.43	0.43
Nigeria	0.23	1	0.21	0.23
Kenya	0.43	0.21	1	0.55
Mauritius	0.43	0.23	0.55	1

Source: Authors' calculations

America are highly co-integrated when the statistical test is performed considering the structural breaks.

Under a short-term measure, such as the Pearson correlation[2] of the time series returns, results can differ as shown in Table 13.3. The least co-integrated countries are not necessarily the ones with the lowest correlation. In the case of the emerging countries in Eastern Asia, Vietnam has the lowest correlation. The same is the case for Tunisia in Africa. However, Nigeria is the country with the lowest correlations in Africa. Co-integration entails a mean reversion dynamic within a long-term horizon, in shorter horizons time series returns can be correlated or uncorrelated.

13.5.2 Portfolio Analysis

Following the identification of the least co-integrated stock market indices, a portfolio analysis is conducted by actively overweighting the least co-integrated stock market indices versus the benchmark. This analysis is done from 2006 to 2015 to review the impact of performing active management with the selected countries. Thus, the historical indices of MSCI-developed countries and MSCI-emerging countries are overweighed with the least co-integrated countries' equity indices. As shown in Fig. 13.6, the weights of the actual indices are reduced proportionally to add an additional percentage of the least co-integrated countries. The allocation for the Philippines in the actual MSCI index is around 1%, and for Jordan, the allocation is below 0.2%. In this chapter, Nigeria is also included in this index of the emerging markets, although this country is considered a frontier market by MSCI. For the developed countries, the Netherlands is the least integrated country with the highest allocation in the actual MSCI index, with an assigned percentage between 2% and 3%. Denmark has an allocation between 1% and 2%, while the actual allocation for New Zealand and Austria is below 1%. Three long-term overweighting strategies are analyzed, as mentioned in section three.

Notably, all three portfolio scenarios show better performance than the benchmark actual index for both emerging and developed market indices and in both an absolute and relative basis. Table 13.4 shows the absolute returns for the three scenarios when an additional portion is added for the

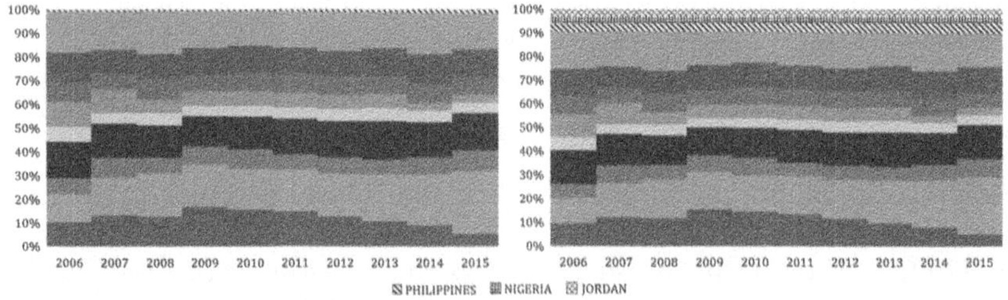

Fig. 13.6 Actual MSCI emerging market index versus overweighed MSCI emerging market with additional 3% in non-integrated countries

Table 13.4 Absolute return analysis for developed market index

	Actual	*Invest additional 2%*	*Invest additional 3%*	*Invest max (5% in total, market size cap)*
Annual returns	−1.51%	−1.35%	−1.28%	−1.10%
Annual standard deviation	18.72%	18.35%	18.18%	18.34%
Risk adjusted returns	−0.08	−0.07	−0.07	−0.06
Maximum drawdown	58.16%	58.12%	58.10%	57.78%
1st percentile	−14.24%	−14.36%	−14.42%	−14.28%
5th percentile	-9.60%	-9.45%	-9.51%	-9.43%

Source: Authors' calculations

least co-integrated stock market indices in the developed market index. The risk-adjusted returns increase for the three scenarios as the four countries that are added improve both the risk and return characteristics of the index.

The best improvement is shown by the alternative that allows a maximum investment of 5% or the amount allowed by its market capitalization, where the risk-adjusted returns increase from −8.09% to −6.00%. In the case of the emerging market index (see Table 13.5), the risk-adjusted returns improve for all the three scenarios, the last scenario being the one that shows the best results. The tables also show that the tail risk decreases in the emerging market index for all scenarios and the maximum drawdown is lower in both indices for all the scenarios.

Moreover, Table 13.6 presents the results on a relative basis (alternative scenario vs the actual index) for the developed market index. All the scenarios present a positive information ratio, the maximum is the option that caps the investment on the market capitalization as it limits the volatility of the liquidity premium from illiquid markets like the ones of New Zealand and Austria. This scenario also has a smaller tail than the scenario where an additional investment of 3% is included for all the least co-integrated economies.

Additionally, Table 13.7 presents the relative return analysis for the emerging market index. Again, all the scenarios show a positive information ratio, the highest being the option that caps the investment according to its market capitalization. Nonetheless this option has the highest volatility as a bigger portion of non-traditional investments is included.

Table 13.5 Absolute return analysis for emerging market index

	Actual	*Invest additional 2%*	*Invest additional 3%*	*Invest max (5% in total, market size cap)*
Annual returns	−0.08%	0.03%	0.09%	0.39%
Annual standard deviation	23.64%	22.83%	22.44%	22.60%
Risk-adjusted returns	−0.00	0.00	0.00	0.01
Maximum drawdown	62.67%	61.75%	61.30%	61.57%
1st percentile	−17.24%	−16.61%	−16.29%	−16.12%
5th percentile	−9.39%	−9.17%	−9.07%	−9.33%

Source: Authors' calculations

Table 13.6 Relative return analysis for developed market index

	Invest additional 2%	*Invest additional 3%*	*Invest max (5% in total, market size cap)*
Excess return	0.16%	0.24%	0.41%
Tracking error	0.81%	1.22%	0.89%
Information ratio	0.20	0.19	0.47
Maximum drawdown	2.11%	3.16%	1.64%
1st percentile	−0.57%	−0.85%	−0.59%
5th percentile	−0.32%	−0.49%	−0.33%

Source: Authors' calculations

Table 13.7 Relative return analysis for emerging market index

	Invest additional 2%	*Invest additional 3%*	*Invest max (5% in total, market size cap)*
Excess return	0.12%	0.17%	0.47%
Tracking error	1.17%	1.76%	2.00%
Information ratio	0.10	0.10	0.24
Maximum drawdown	4.14%	6.15%	4.87%
1st percentile	−0.70%	−1.05%	−1.35%
5th percentile	−0.52%	−0.78%	−0.90%

Source: Authors' calculations

Overall the results of the country analysis suggest that identifying and overweighting least co-integrated stock market indices can improve portfolio performance significantly both in relative and absolute terms under an active investment strategy. Both the returns and the risk measures showed an improvement; however, most of the improvement comes as a result of higher returns in the least co-integrated countries. It is important to consider that this can be a result of an embedded liquidity premium, which may also imply additional transaction costs.

13.6 Results by Industries

13.6.1 Co-integration Tests

Applying similar methodology, the chapter next analyzes the degree of integration among various global industrial stock market indices, identifies the least co-integrated ones, and performs portfolio analysis by applying active management strategies and overweighting those industries versus MSCI benchmark portfolios. As shown in Table 13.8, all the historical time series of the stock market indices by industry follow a $I(1)$ process; this allows the Gregory-Hansen co-integration test to be executed. Table 13.9 shows the results of the GH test with structural breaks for the stock market indices by industry in developed countries, with all of them being significantly co-integrated. Only the interaction between industrials

Table 13.8 Augmented Dickey Fuller test for industries

Industry in DM	*p-value*	*Industry in EM*	*p-value*
Energy	0.32	Energy	0.10
Materials	0.33	Materials	0.18
Industrials	0.81	Industrials	0.28
Cons Disc	0.88	Cons Disc	0.82
Cons Staples	0.96	Cons Staples	0.85
Health Care	0.95	Health Care	0.92
Financials	0.44	Financials	0.61
IT	0.70	IT	0.98
Telecom	0.81	Telecom	0.42
Utilities	0.24	Utilities	0.45

Source: Authors' calculations

Table 13.9 Gregory-Hansen co-integration test with structural breaks (*p*-value) among industries in developed countries

		Independent variables									
		Energy	*Materials*	*Industrials*	*Cons Disc*	*Cons Staples*	*Health Care*	*Financials*	*IT*	*Telecom*	*Utilities*
Dependent variables	Energy	–	0.03**	0.00**	0.00**	0.00**	0.00**	0.00**	0.00**	0.00**	0.00**
	Materials	0.03**	–	0.01**	0.00**	0.05**	0.01**	0.00**	0.01**	0.00**	0.00**
	Industrials	0.00**	0.00**	–	0.00**	0.00**	0.01**	0.00**	0.00**	0.01**	0.00**
	Cons Disc	0.00**	0.00**	0.00**	–	0.02**	0.00**	0.00**	0.00**	0.00**	0.00**
	Cons Staples	0.00**	0.00**	0.00**	0.01**	–	0.02**	0.00**	0.00**	0.00**	0.00**
	Health Care	0.00**	0.00**	0.01**	0.00**	0.03**	–	0.00**	0.00**	0.00**	0.00**
	Financials	0.01**	0.01**	0.01**	0.00**	0.00**	0.00**	–	0.01**	0.01**	0.00**
	IT	0.00**	0.00**	0.02**	0.00**	0.00**	0.00**	0.01**	–	0.02**	0.00**
	Telecom	0.00**	0.00**	0.02**	0.00**	0.12	0.00**	0.00**	0.00**	–	0.00**
	Utilities	0.10*	0.03**	0.10	0.02**	0.04**	0.01**	0.01**	0.09*	0.01**	–

The null hypothesis for the Gregory-Hansen test is no co-integration

Source: Authors' calculations

*Indicate significance at the 10% level, **Indicate significance at the 5% level

Table 13.10 Gregory-Hansen co-integration test with structural breaks (p-value) among industries in emerging countries

		Independent variables									
		Energy	*Materials*	*Industrials*	*Cons Disc*	*Cons Staples*	*Health Care*	*Financials*	*IT*	*Telecom*	*Utilities*
Dependent variables	Energy	–	0.00**	0.01**	0.00**	0.01**	0.02**	0.00**	0.13	0.02**	0.00**
	Materials	0.00**	–	0.04**	0.01**	0.00**	0.01**	0.00**	0.08*	0.02**	0.00**
	Industrials	0.00**	0.04**	–	0.00**	0.00**	0.00**	0.00**	0.17	0.00**	0.00**
	Cons Disc	0.00**	0.00**	0.00**	–	0.06*	0.01**	0.00**	0.30	0.00**	0.00**
	Cons Staples	0.00**	0.00**	0.00**	0.05*	–	0.00**	0.00**	0.31	0.00**	0.00**
	Health Care	0.00**	0.00**	0.00**	0.01**	0.03**	–	0.00**	0.20	0.00**	0.00**
	Financials	0.00**	0.00**	0.00**	0.00**	0.00**	0.00**	–	0.07*	0.05**	0.01**
	IT	0.00**	0.00**	0.00**	0.02**	0.08*	0.18	0.00**	–	0.00**	0.00**
	Telecom	0.00**	0.03**	0.00**	0.00**	0.00**	0.00**	0.03**	0.01**	–	0.00**
	Utilities	0.00**	0.00**	0.01**	0.01**	0.01**	0.01**	0.04**	0.19	0.00**	–

The null hypothesis for the Gregory-Hansen test is no co-integration

Source: Authors' calculations

*Indicate significance at the 10% level, **Indicate significance at the 5% level

Table 13.11 Absolute return analysis for emerging market index with industries

	Actual	*Invest additional 2%*	*Invest additional 3%*
Annual returns	0.17%	0.31%	0.38%
Annual standard deviation	23.32%	23.26%	23.24%
Risk-adjusted returns	0.71%	1.32%	1.62%
Maximum drawdown	57.75%	57.65%	57.59%
1st percentile	−17.28%	−17.25%	−17.23%
5th percentile	−8.99%	−9.00%	−9.00%

Source: Authors' calculation

Table 13.12 Relative return analysis for emerging market index with industries

	Invest additional 2%	*Invest additional 3%*
Excess return	0.14%	0.24%
Tracking error	0.23%	0.35%
Information ratio	0.61	0.69
Maximum drawdown	0.42%	0.28%
1st percentile	−0.13%	−0.20%
5th percentile	−0.09%	−0.13%

Source: Authors' calculations

and utilities, and consumer staples and telecommunications appear to be not co-integrated, when those are estimated as the independent variables respectively. Nevertheless, even these industries are co-integrated with all the others in the pool. Therefore, no diversification opportunities seem to be identified at the industry level for developed countries using the proposed methodology.

However, when the same analysis is performed for the stock market indices by industry in emerging countries, the information technology (IT) sector exhibits little co-integration with all other industries (except for telecom), signaling a possible diversification opportunity (Table 13.10).

13.6.2 Portfolio Analysis

The portfolio analysis overweighting the IT sector in emerging market is conducted next, and shows a portfolio performance improvement on the risk-return frontier. As shown in the absolute basis analysis in Table 13.11, the risk-adjusted returns improve significantly and the tails remain invariant once the IT sector is overweight with an additional 2% and 3%.[3] Table 13.12 presents the results on a relative basis against the benchmark, both scenarios show a positive information ratio.

Overall, industry-level analysis shows that information technology sector in the emerging market category can present opportunities for diversification and additional portfolio gains in terms of risk return through active management versus a benchmark investment in the MSCI index.

13.7 Conclusion

The analysis in this chapter demonstrates potential opportunities for diversification and clear risk-adjusted return benefits in overweighting equity indices relative to the MSCI benchmarks in countries and industries found to be least co-integrated with the rest. Further in-depth research is needed to assess the factors behind the co-integration of global equity markets, including macro-economic, regulatory, and industry analysis. A deeper factor analysis would allow investors to forecast co-integration patterns and identify diversification opportunities going forward in a systematic way, given the overall financial integration trend.

In this chapter, the emerging countries' equity indices identified are the Philippines, Jordan, and Nigeria, which improved the portfolio risk-adjusted returns when included as an active portfolio strategy under three different scenarios. Among developed countries, New Zealand, Austria, the Netherlands, and Denmark stock market indices were identified as being least co-integrated. The returns of the historical MSCI benchmark were also enhanced when adding active strategies that consider these countries. Further research is needed to assess the likelihood of it being sustained going forward by identifying how the market and regulatory factors have shifted and impacted the observed idiosyncratic trend.

When the analysis is done by industry rather than by country, the diversification opportunities decrease, particularly in the developed markets, as the larger and the more co-integrated economies have a greater participation in each industry. For emerging markets, however, the analysis here indicates that the information technology sector can provide diversification opportunities. This industry enhances the MSCI benchmark risk-adjusted returns once its allocation in the index increases with active management strategies. This sector is mainly comprised of Asian companies in China, Taiwan, South Korea, Indonesia, and India. An individual GH test for these countries[4] in this sector shows that India is not co-integrated with South Korea nor with the United States. Additionally, a Granger causality test shows that the IT sector in South Korea and India has no effect on bigger industries like China's or Taiwan's. The sub-sectors that most of these companies belong to are internet software, semiconductors, technology hardware, electronic components, and IT consulting.

Finally, the fact that most of the regions or industries (except for the ones above) were found to be co-integrated does not mean that the potential of active management strategies is absent in the short run. Through strategies like pair trading, portfolio managers can identify if the short-term trend deviates from the long-term trend and consequently adjust their positions assessing the time when the two trends will converge again.

Notes

1. The Johansen co-integration test examines the co-integration relationship up to the rank of the time series. The test can be executed either with the trace or with eigenvalue. The test follows a sequence up to the first non-rejection of the null hypothesis, which will be the estimate of the number of co-integration relationships among the group of time series.
2. Correlations are estimated with monthly data from August 2008 to August 2016.
3. The scenario with the maximum between 5% and the total market capitalization is not considered in this case, since the emerging market index already invests more than 5% in the sector.
4. Data is not available for smaller industries, such as the one of the Philippines and Indonesia.

References

Aggarwal, R., Lucey, B., & Muckley, C. (2010). Dynamics of equity market integration in Europe: Impact of political economy events. *Journal of Common Market Studies, 48*(3), 641–660.

Bekaert, G., Hodrick, R. J., & Zhang, X. (2009). International stock return comovements. *Journal of Finance, 64*(6), 2591–2626.

Beyer, A., Haug, A., & Dewald, W. (2009). Structural breaks, cointegration and the Fisher Effect. *European Central Bank Working Paper Series, No. 1013.*

Brooks, R., & Del Negro, M. (2004). The rise in comovement across national stock markets: Market integration or IT bubble? *Journal of Empirical Finance, 11*(5), 659–680.

Engle, R., & Granger, C. (1987). Co-integration and error correction: Representation, estimation and testing. *Econometrica, 55*(2), 251–276.

Fuller, W. A. (1976). *Introduction to statistical time series.* New York: John Wiley and Sons.

Gregory, A. W., & Hansen, B. E. (1996). Tests for co-integration in models with regime and trend shifts. *Oxford Bulletin of Economics and Statistics, 58*(3), 555–560.

Lim, K., Lee, H., & Liew, K. (2003). International diversification benefits in ASEAN stock markets: A revisit. *Economics Working Paper*, University Putra, Malaysia.

Narayan, P. K., & Smyth, R. (2005). Cointegration of stock markets between New Zealand, Australia and the G7 economies: Searching for common trends under structural change. *Australian Economic Papers, 44*(3), 231–247.

Neaime, S. (2015). Portfolio diversification and financial integration of MENA stock markets. In J. Olmsted (Ed.), *Money and finance in the Middle East: Missed opportunities or future prospects?* Bingley: Emerald Group Publishing.

Paramati, S., Gupta, R., & Tandon, K. (2013). Dynamic analysis of time-varying correlations and co-integration relationship between Australia and frontier equity markets. *International Journal of Business and Emerging Markets, 8*(2), 121–145.

Syriopoulos, T. (2011). Financial integration and portfolio investments to emerging Balkan equity markets. *Journal of Multinational Financial Management, 21*(1), 40–54.

Worthington, A. C., & Higgs, H. (2007). Assessing financial integration in European Union equity markets, 1990–2006: Panel unit root and multivariate cointegration and causality evidence. *University of Wollongong, School of Accounting and Finance Working Paper Series No. 07/10.*

CHAPTER 14

Government Bond Clienteles and Yields

Jianjian Jin, Francisco Rivadeneyra, and Jesús Sierra

14.1 Introduction

Bond clienteles—investors with preferences for bonds with particular characteristics—have been suggested as a potential explanation for several episodes in fixed-income markets. During those episodes, price changes cannot be easily reconciled with standard frictionless asset pricing theories, but are more easily understood from the perspective of supply and demand shifts. For example, Greenwood and Vayanos (2010) argue that the

Jianjian Jin and Francisco Rivadeneyra are with the Bank of Canada, jjin@bankofcanada.ca and riva@bankofcanada.ca. Jesús Sierra is with the Canada Deposit Insurance Corporation, jsjimenez@cdic.ca. The opinions reflected here are of the authors and do not necessarily reflect the ones of the Bank of Canada or the Canada Deposit Insurance Corporation. We thank participants of the 6th BIS/WB/BoC Public Investors Conference and the Bank of Canada 2017 Fellowship Exchange for their comments. All errors remain our own.

J. Jin • F. Rivadeneyra (✉)
Bank of Canada, Ottawa, ON, Canada
e-mail: jjin@bankofcanada.ca; riva@bankofcanada.ca

J. Sierra
Canada Deposit Insurance Corporation, Ottawa, ON, Canada
e-mail: jsjimenez@cdic.ca

N. Bulusu et al. (eds.), *Advances in the Practice of Public Investment Management*, https://doi.org/10.1007/978-3-319-90245-6_14

decrease in long-term real yields observed in the UK during 2004–2005 can be explained by a regulation-induced increase in the demand for inflation-linked long-term bonds by UK pension funds, following the introduction of the Pensions Act of 2004.[1] Similarly, Krishnamurthy and Vissing-Jorgensen (2012) find evidence of the existence of a clientele for long-term safe US Treasury assets. Finally, using a dataset of sovereign bond investor holdings from 2000 to 2011, Andritzky (2012) finds that increased non-resident institutional investor holdings is associated with lower and more volatile government bond yields.

For most of these studies, a clientele is defined as a relatively homogeneous investor group and is usually based on geographic location and legal entity types. Examples of these clienteles are domestic and foreign private investors, or domestic and foreign public sector funds (like foreign reserve managers or sovereign wealth funds). The implicit assumption is that such classification is adequate to summarize their key portfolio characteristics such as holding horizon, turnover rate and risk exposures. That assumption, however, is violated in practice. For example, among mutual funds, there are some that are subject to strict directives to closely replicate a bond index, while others have greater freedom for active management. One of the key contributions of this chapter is that we refine the classification of clienteles. We believe our classification can better identify the relationship between clienteles and asset prices.

In this chapter, we study this relationship in the context of the Canadian government bond market. There are two reasons for choosing Canada for our study. First, for most of the past decade, Canada witnessed a significant change in the investor base for its sovereign bond market. Foreign official investors significantly increased their holdings of Canadian dollar-denominated assets after the global financial crisis in 2008–2009 and the European debt crisis in 2010–2012, while foreign private investors reduced their holdings by a similar measure. The Canadian sovereign market therefore offers an ideal test bed for studying the relationship between holdings by type of investor clientele and bond prices. Second, compared to the aggregate clientele holding data utilized by Andritzky (2012), we have much more granular holding data at the bond and individual investor level.

Our dataset includes a range of domestic and international institutional investors. In this study, we focus on two specific types of investors: Canadian mutual funds and foreign official investors (foreign reserve managers, sovereign wealth funds, etc.). These represent two of the most active groups of investors in the Government of Canada (GoC) market (especially in the short- to medium-duration sectors) and their holding data are available at a much more granular level than those of other groups. We then classify mutual funds into an index fund group and non-index (or active) fund group, and foreign official investors into those with a "strict mandate," and those with a "non-strict mandate," according to how closely they follow an investment mandate of targeting a given duration in their Canadian dollar-denominated portfolio.

Using fixed-effect panel regressions, we study the contemporaneous relationship between yield changes and bond flows by investor group. We run separate tests for short-duration (defined as bonds with duration from 1.5 years to 5.5 years), medium-duration (defined as bonds with duration from 5.6 years to 9.5 years) and long-duration bonds (with 9.6 years and longer). We also look specifically into bonds with age of more than 6 months and bonds with a coupon level higher than 5%.

We identify significant heterogeneity in the fund flow—bond yield interaction across different maturity sectors and different investor clienteles. In the short-duration sector, there is a significant negative contemporaneous relationship between strict-mandate foreign official investor trading (mostly buying in the sample period) and bond yields, while Canadian active mutual funds' bond holding changes are positively related to yield changes. In the medium-duration sector, changes in the holdings of Canadian index funds are negatively associated with yield changes, while changes in the holdings by strict-mandate foreign official investors are positively linked with changes in the yield. In the long-duration sector, we find that bond flows of both Canadian mutual funds and foreign official investors are negatively related with bond yields.

It is usually difficult to provide an interpretation of the contemporaneous relationship between bond flows and bond prices changes. In the case of negative correlation between bond flows and yields, the causality can go either way. Borrowing the terminology of Andritzky (2012), it can either be that specific investors "push" the yield to a low level, or it can be that expectations of low and stable yields "pull" investors to a particular bond sector. Our key finding is that there is non-negligible heterogeneity in the effect of bond clientele flows and bond prices.

Out study contributes to both the academic and policy-oriented research on fixed-income clientele effects. We provide empirical context to the Vayanos and Villa (2009) preferred-habitat explanation of the term structure of yields. Many studies focus on the long-term bond sector, where pension or life insurance funds have inelastic demand. Further, there might be strong effects when central bank or government reduces the available supply of long-term government bonds (the Quantitative Easing channel). Our results show that clientele-bond interaction can happen in various sectors along the yield curve, presumably due to the imperfect substitutability between bonds to fulfill investor's mandates and objectives. This clientele-yield relationship is clear in the short-term sector (duration less or equal to 5.5 years) for a subset of foreign official investors, while in the medium-term sector (duration less than 9.5 years), it is most evident for the domestic index mutual funds.

Our study also provides empirical evidence to help evaluate the impact of foreign demand for government bonds (Sierra 2014). While an increased foreign investor base lowers the issuance cost of government debt, a change in the investor composition could also result in episodes of rapid capital flight. Debt managers, therefore, can use our results to understand the effects on bond yields when foreign capital flows out of their bond market.

The remainder of the chapter is organized as follows. In Sect. 14.2 we present the data and empirical methodology. In Sect. 14.3, we discuss the panel regressions results of short-, medium- and long-duration bucket. We conclude in Sect. 14.4.

14.2 Data and Methodology

14.2.1 GoC Bond Description

GoC bonds refer to marketable coupon fixed-income securities issued by the Government of Canada with maturity at issue of two years or more. With an outstanding amount of 420 billion Canadian dollars (as of March 2013), they constitute the largest liability of the Government of Canada. GoC bonds are often the most actively traded fixed-income securities in the Canadian fixed-income markets and are essential to implementing monetary policy and ensuring financial market stability (Bulusu and Gungor 2018). In this study, GoC bond pricing and outstanding amount information are collected from Bloomberg and Bank of Canada debt management data, respectively.

To provide an overview of the clienteles of GoC bonds, in addition to the foreign official and domestic mutual funds, we present aggregate bond-holdings statistics from 2004 to 2013. Table 14.1 illustrates the distribution of GoC bond holdings in each year of our sample based on

Table 14.1 Distribution of holdings of Government of Canada marketable bonds among domestic and international investors

	Total (bn)	*Life Ins. and pension (%)*	*Banks (%)*	*Fin. Inst. (%)*	*BoC (%)*	*Other Canadian (%)*	*Foreign (%)*
3/31/2004	258.4	23.2	15.5	19.6	9.3	16.5	15.9
3/31/2005	244.3	22.9	14	21.2	10.1	17.7	14.1
3/31/2006	237.3	22.1	14.6	21.9	10.9	17.2	13.3
3/31/2007	231.4	22.0	15.0	23.0	10.7	15.3	14.0
3/31/2008	224.4	24.0	12.0	22.0	11.4	16.6	14.0
3/31/2009	263.5	22.0	14.0	19.0	10.9	20.1	14.0
3/31/2010	333.3	23.0	18.5	17.1	9.1	15.8	16.5
3/31/2011	378.7	24.8	14.1	14.5	9.1	16.3	21.2
3/31/2012	406.8	23.3	13.8	12.1	11.0	14.8	25.0
3/31/2013	425.4	23.0	14.0	12.0	13.4	7.6	30.0

Source: Statistics Canada, Debt management report of Government of Canada 2004–2013

Statistics Canada data.[2] Between 2004 and 2013, the total outstanding amount of GoC bonds grew from 260 billion to 425 billion dollars. Some investors, such as Canadian life insurance funds, pension funds and domestic commercial banks, hold a stable share of the total outstanding amount. The Bank of Canada also holds a stable share of GoC bonds over time.

Other groups of investors, however, display interesting trends. In particular, during the sample period, the domestic financial institutional investors (mutual funds, property insurance funds, etc.) displayed a decreasing trend in holding GoC bonds, while foreign investors added more GoC bonds to their portfolios since the crisis. In March 2004, the domestic financial institutions held 20% of GoC bonds, while foreign investors held 16%. Domestic investors' holdings fell to 12% in 2013, while foreign investors increased their share of total ownership of GoC bonds to 30%. Interestingly, the undisclosed domestic investors (hedge funds, corporate treasury, etc.) also reduced their shares in a similar fashion to mutual fund investors, from 16.5% in 2004 to 7.6% in 2013.

In order to paint a more granular picture of GoC holdings, we collect bond-level holding data of multiple investors from multiple sources. Our main dataset is the proprietary data starting in the early 2000s of the security-level holdings of foreign official investors that use the Bank of Canada as their custodial bank for Canadian-denominated fixed-income assets. These are mainly central bank reserve managers, but also include some development banks and international institutions. Furthermore, we obtain a dataset of Canadian fixed-income mutual funds from Morningstar from 2004 to 2013. Finally, the Lipper eMAXX dataset provides the holdings of a subset of US insurance funds, US and non-US foreign mutual fund holdings of GoC bonds from 2007 to 2013.

Figure 14.1 plots the quarterly GoC bond holdings as a percentage of outstanding by all sample investor types in our dataset. Consistent with Table 14.1, there have been two divergent trends in GoC holding. On the one hand, foreign official investors steadily increased their GoC positions since 2011. On the other hand, mutual fund investors, domestic or foreign consistently trimmed their holdings in GoC bonds since 2009–2010. Furthermore, foreign, non-US mutual funds were quite active in GoC bond markets in 2007–2009, while US mutual funds were mostly active in the period of 2010–2012.

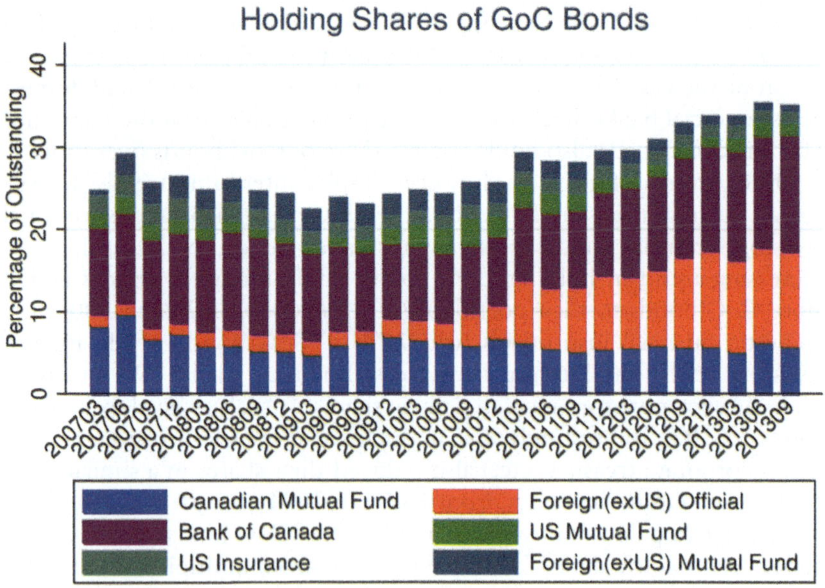

Fig. 14.1 Quarterly GoC holdings as the share of the total outstanding by domestic and international investors

What exactly caused these trends is still an open question. The trend is certainly affected by the combination of several factors such as the low interest environment domestically and globally, the 2008–2009 great financial crisis and European sovereign debt crisis, the US debt ceiling deadlock and rising commodity (especially energy) prices during the sample period. The high credit rating of Canada may also have helped GoC bonds gain popularity among foreign investors (for more detailed discussion, see Feunou et al. 2015).

The data we collect are in fact of a subset of the GoC clientele. Table 14.2 reports the percentage of total outstanding of bonds held by our sample investors, which is the same as what is shown in Fig. 14.1 (we ignored the Bank of Canada due to the full coverage of this data). On the domestic (Canadian) side, our data mainly covers the fixed-income mutual funds, which represents the largest group of domestic investors in the GoC market. On the foreign side, we cover official investors, US insurance funds and US and non-US mutual funds. Our coverage generally increases over the years, from roughly 40% to slightly more than 50% for each type of investors. The relatively stable coverage allows us to study the behavior of each type of investors. One of the key assumptions in our study is that investors in our sample are not systematically different from investors not included in our sample in terms of GoC bond holding behavior.

For a more detailed study of the clientele behavior and their association with GoC bond yields, we focus on Canadian mutual funds and foreign official investors. There are two reasons to do so. First, they represent the most active resident and non-resident investors in our sample. Second, the

Table 14.2 Percentage of outstanding of bonds held by Canadian and international investors

	CAN mutual	*US mutual*	*US insurance*	*Foreign official*	*Foreign mutual*	*Foreign total*
3/31/2007	9.3	1.9	2.2	1.3	0.2	5.6
3/31/2008	8.4	1.6	2.3	1.8	3.2	8.8
3/31/2009	6.5	1.1	1.8	1.6	3.2	7.7
3/31/2010	8.1	2.9	1.6	2.3	2.4	9.2
3/31/2011	7.8	2.8	1.7	7.5	2.2	14.2
3/31/2012	7.1	1.4	1.7	8.6	1.2	12.8
3/31/2013	6.4	1.9	1.5	11.2	0.9	15.5

Source: Bank of Canada, Morningstar, Thomson Reuters eMAXX

data available for these two investors are at monthly frequency and date back to 2004, which gives us a longer time sample than other groups of investors of potential interest.

Table 14.3 reports the summary statistics of the end-of-year GoC holdings by foreign official investors and Canadian fixed-income mutual funds. Like previous results, both our sample and the holdings of these investors grew significantly after the great financial crisis of 2008–2009.[3] Overall, the GoC portfolio is about 2% of the foreign official investors' total asset under management (AUM), consistent with the IMF surveys. For Canadian fixed-income mutual funds, their holdings of GoC securities moved significantly over time. The year-on-year change was between 20% and 30%. This could reflect that mutual funds dynamically allocate their funds to GoC portfolio as the macro environment changes.

Table 14.3 Summary statistics of the GoC bond holdings of foreign official investors and Canadian mutual funds

Year	*N obs*	*Median*	*Mean*	*Max*	*Mean AUM*
Foreign official investor (CAD, billion)					
2004	4	0.2	0.3	0.9	41.0
2005	7	0.1	0.3	1.6	60.0
2006	5	0.3	0.6	1.9	82.7
2007	6	0.2	0.4	1.4	86.3
2008	5	1.1	1.0	1.6	112.2
2009	7	0.7	0.9	1.9	139.0
2010	8	1.1	1.8	6.8	177.9
2011	12	1.5	3.0	15.9[a]	187.2
2012	13	1.8	3.7	17.7	185.5
2013[b]	13	1.8	3.8	19.0	196.0
Canadian mutual fund (CAD, billions)					
2004	186	0.02	0.10	1.42	0.42
2005	208	0.02	0.11	1.44	0.48
2006	215	0.02	0.10	1.20	0.51
2007	223	0.02	0.08	0.99	0.52
2008	231	0.02	0.05	0.81	0.48
2009	236	0.02	0.10	1.49	0.61
2010	241	0.02	0.11	1.63	0.70
2011	266	0.02	0.09	1.37	0.73
2012	273	0.03	0.09	1.40	0.84
2013	209	0.02	0.08	0.87	0.71

Source: Bank of Canada, Morningstar, Thomson Reuters eMAXX

[a]The large jump in the maximum holding is due to the incorporation of some large foreign official investors into the sample

[b]Foreign official investor holding data only available until Sep. 2013

14.2.2 *Investor Classification*

The conventional approach to classifying investors is based on their legal type and geographic domicile. In our case, for example, it can be either foreign (non-Canadian) official investors (mostly foreign central bank reserves) or domestic (Canadian) mutual funds.

Since we believe that existing classification schemes ignore within-group heterogeneity that matters for their effect on bond yields, we take advantage of the granularity of our data to further classify our sample of investors into types based on their self-claimed objective (for mutual funds) or actual trading behavior (for foreign official investors). For Canadian fixed-income mutual funds, we label funds that claim to closely track a public fixed-income index as "index" funds whose main mandates are replicating a given benchmark while minimizing costs and tracking errors. The rest of the fixed-income funds are considered as active investing funds whose main mandate is to outperform a benchmark and attract fund flows. Among foreign official investors, we would not be able to find an explicit benchmark for their GoC portfolio (although the outstanding-weighted index may be a good proxy). We therefore identify a few foreign official investors that follow a "strict mandate" by actively managing the portfolio duration and exposures to certain sectors in their portfolio held in custody at the Bank of Canada. The rest of the foreign official investors in our sample are classified as "non-strict" mandate investors; they trade relatively more infrequently and allow the duration of their portfolio to vary considerably more than the first group.[4] In the remainder of the chapter, we use the terms "foreign official investor" and "foreign central bank" interchangeably.

14.2.3 *Portfolio Duration Characteristics*

Figure 14.2 reports the par-value-weighted duration of the GoC portfolio held by Canadian mutual funds (solid line) and their index and non-index sub groups (dotted and dashed lines). For comparison, we plot the outstanding-weighted index (dash dot line) and the Canadian overnight repo interest rate (long dash line). As can be seen, the portfolio duration varies over time and ranges from four to eight years. The duration of mutual fund holdings was below that of the duration of the outstanding-weighted index before 2006–2007 and higher afterwards, possibly as a result of investments in longer-dated securities driven by the need to boost returns in a low (or declining) interest rate environment. There is also a

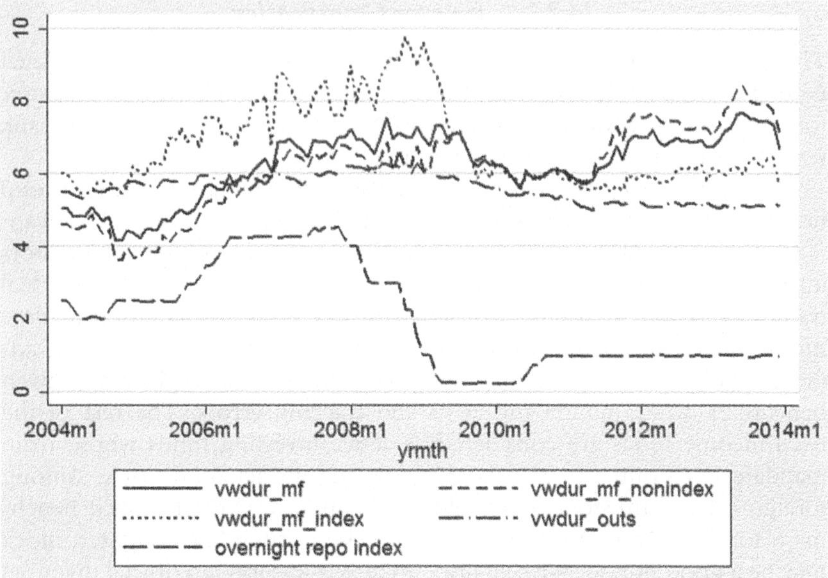

Fig. 14.2 Average portfolio duration of Canadian fixed-income mutual funds. The units of the Y-axis are years

significant difference in duration preference between index funds and non-index funds: index funds held a significantly higher proportion of long-term bonds before 2009 but since 2010, non-index funds significantly increased the duration exposure of their GoC portfolio, possibly due to the "reach-for-yield" effect discussed previously.

Figure 14.3 reports the distribution of duration profiles among index-like domestic mutual funds. As clearly shown, there is a relatively high dispersion in portfolio duration for the domestic mutual funds: the difference in duration between the top 5 percentile and bottom 5 percentile is about 15 years. There also seems to be a positive skew in the distribution of duration of Canadian fixed-income mutual funds, perhaps driven by large index mutual fund portfolios, which typically contain a significant number of long-maturity bonds.

Figure 14.4 reports the value-weighted duration profile of foreign official investors. As can be seen, the average duration of foreign official investors is significantly below that of the outstanding-weighted index. In the early period of our sample, active investors maintained a portfolio with a much higher duration than passive investors. However, that rela-

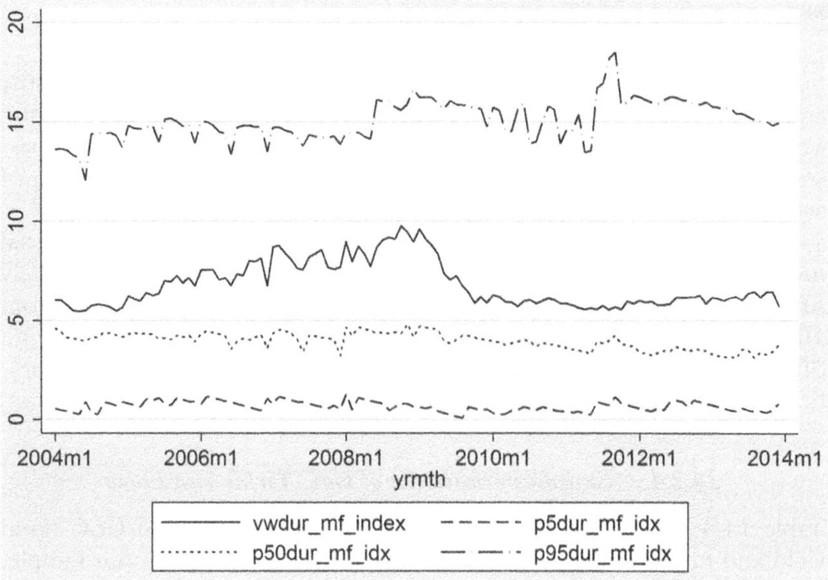

Fig. 14.3 Distribution of portfolio duration of Canadian fixed-income mutual funds. The units of the Y-axis are years

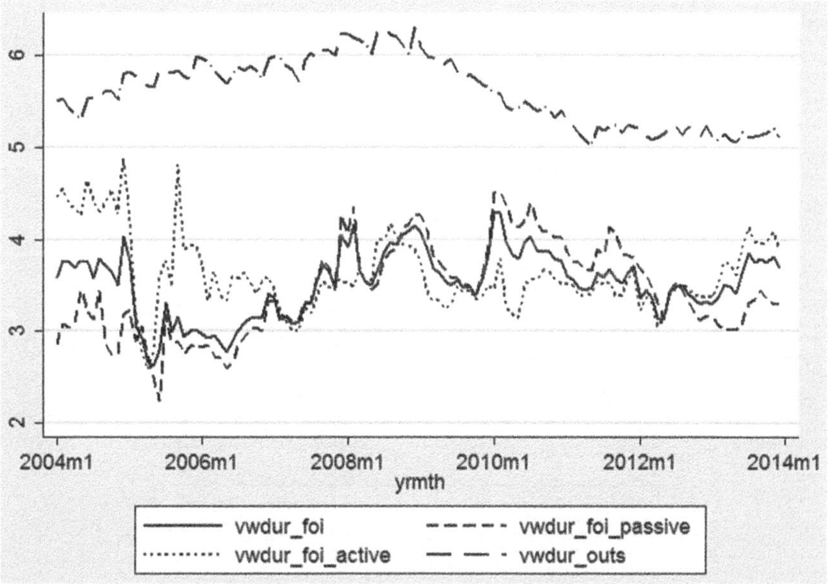

Fig. 14.4 Portfolio duration of foreign official investors. The units of the Y-axis are years

tionship simply reversed since the financial crisis until late 2012. Over the latter period, the demand for short-term bonds was much higher among active official investors than passive investors. In much of the 2013, passive investors' duration reverts to being significantly less than that of active investors.

Figure 14.5 reports the distribution of the duration of foreign official investors. Since our sample size for foreign official investors is relatively small, we can only plot the duration of the top 10 percentile and bottom 10 percentile over time. The median and mean of the duration of foreign official investors are quite close, suggesting that the distribution of duration among foreign official investors is generally symmetric.

14.2.4 *Summary Statistics of GoC Yields and Flows*

Table 14.4 reports the summary statistics of the changes in GoC bond yield and fund holdings over the previous month changes in our sample. The yield changes (first row) are the pooled average over each bond and month from 2004 to 2013. The level factor of yields (second row) is

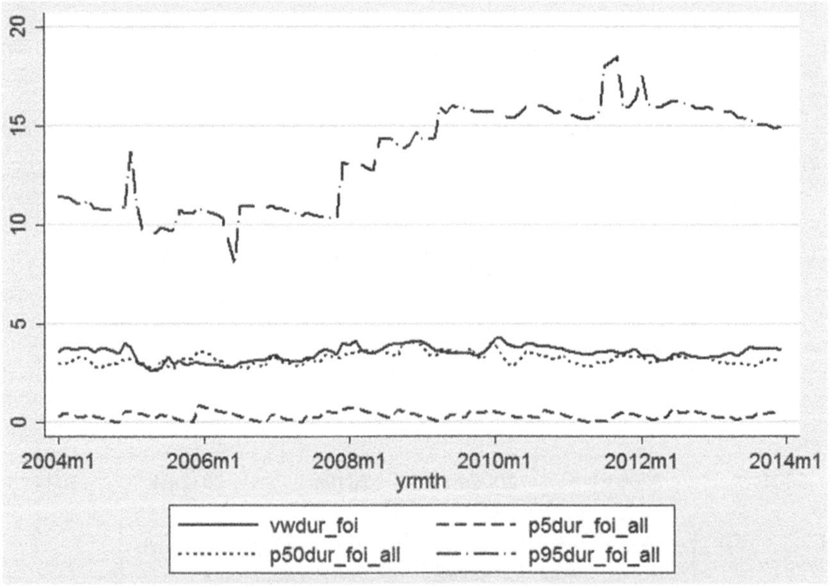

Fig. 14.5 Duration profile of foreign official investors. The units of the Y-axis are years

Table 14.4 Summary statistics of yield changes and bond flows

Variable	*Mean*	*S.D.*	*Min*	*p5*	*p50*	*p95*	*Max*
dym	−0.024	0.189	−0.906	−0.336	−0.013	0.290	0.559
dlevel	−0.013	0.156	−0.702	−0.269	0.020	0.221	0.324
dslope	−0.009	0.229	−0.770	−0.340	−0.010	0.390	1.060
dmf flow	0.000	0.021	−0.232	−0.031	0.000	0.031	0.218
dmf flow index	0.000	0.009	−0.114	−0.012	0.000	0.011	0.114
dmf flow non-index	0.000	0.019	−0.232	−0.026	0.000	0.028	0.222
FOI flow	0.001	0.014	−0.116	−0.014	0.000	0.022	0.133
FOI flow mandate	0.001	0.012	−0.132	−0.011	0.000	0.016	0.127
FOI flow non-mandate	0.001	0.006	−0.062	−0.005	0.000	0.008	0.081

The first three rows of this table contain the changes in yields (dym), the level (dlevel) and slope (dslope) factors of the term structure. Fourth to sixth rows contain the domestic mutual fund (dmf) flows in aggregate and by subgroups. Seventh to ninth rows report the flows of foreign central banks (FOI) in aggregate and by subgroups

Source: Bank of Canada, Morningstar

defined as the average of all GoC yields for a given month. Similarly, the month-to-month changes in the slope factor are reported (third row) where the slope is defined as the difference in yields between ten- and two-year benchmark yields. The flows of a particular bond are computed as the net holding changes of that bond for a particular type of investor divided by the outstanding amount issued of the bond.

The first three rows suggest that over the sample period, both the average yield and the slope of the GoC bonds have significantly decreased. The average month-to-month yield change is 2.4 basis points (bps) and its standard deviation is 18 bps. The cross-sectional distribution statistics also show that the yield changes are significantly negatively skewed, which is consistent with the fact that the period covers the great financial crisis in 2007–2008 and the European debt crisis from 2010 to 2012, when interest rates were lowered to almost zero in a short amount of time.

The fourth to sixth rows report the summary statistics for holding changes by Canadian mutual funds (dmf). The seventh to ninth rows report the summary statistics of the holding changes by foreign official investors (FOI) and the subtypes.[5] Overall, the average flows into the GoC bonds from domestic mutual funds are almost zero and are not significant skewed. However, compared to foreign official investors, the flow into the GoC securities from non-index Canadian mutual funds is much more variable. For example, in our sample, non-index mutual funds have sold as much as 23% or purchased as much as 22% for some bonds over a month. In contrast, flows into a particular bond by foreign official investors or index funds are no more than 13% of the outstanding. For the total sample, the average monthly holding change for foreign official investors is 0.14% of the total outstanding amount issued in the bond. The holding changes are also significantly skewed upward, as indicated by the mean being much larger than the median.

14.2.5 *Empirical Test Methodology*

We adopt a panel regression model to investigate the relationship between clientele holding changes and yield changes:

$$\Delta y_t^i = \alpha^i + \delta_\tau + \beta' f_t^i + \gamma' x_t + \varepsilon_t^i \tag{14.1}$$

where Δy_t^i is the monthly yield change of bond i in month t; $f_t^i = \left(f_{i,t}^{FOI}, f_{i,t}^{DMF}\right)'$ or $\left(f_{i,t}^{FOI,mandate}, f_{i,t}^{FOI,nomandate}, f_{i,t}^{DMF,index}, f_{i,t}^{DMF,nonidx}\right)'$ is the vector of normalized flows into bond i at time t by GoC investors; $x_t = (\Delta l_t, \Delta s_t)'$ represents the control variable vector and includes the monthly changes in the level and slope of the GoC zero-coupon term structure; α^i captures bond fixed effects; δ_τ are year effects; and ε_t^i is the idiosyncratic bond error.

Our main interest is in the coefficient β, with the null hypothesis being that they are statistically non-significant, that is, after controlling for the shape change of the yield curve, the flows into a particular bond should not be contemporaneously related to the change of the yield of that bond. The standard errors are calculated in the cluster-robust way.

The reason for including bond fixed effects is as follows: each bond has its own characteristics that may be persistent enough so that the change of the yield can be auto-correlated. For example, a bond can be popular among investors during its period as a benchmark (like on-the-run Treasury bonds). Since benchmark status is deterministic and can be quite persistent, for example, it lasts for a couple of years in the case of long-maturity bonds, the bond-fixed effect could capture the changes in yield curve that are the result of such persistent characteristics. Then it becomes gradually less popular and difficult to trade (loss of benchmark status and held mostly by passive investors). The benchmark status is deterministic and can last for a couple of years in the case of originally long-maturity bonds.

14.3 Empirical Results

For comparison, we start with the regression without the different clienteles of GoC investors we identify. Table 14.5 reports the results of the fixed-effect panel regression when considering only the aggregate bond flows from official investors and mutual fund investors. Overall, even after considering bond flows from different investor types, we fail to spot any statistically significant contemporaneous relationship between holding changes and yield changes. This result may not be too surprising given that the full sample potentially masks effects from bond characteristics (duration, age, coupon level) and investors characteristics (active or passive investors). Next we report the results for each duration sector.

At any point in the sample, we classify bonds into three sectors: bonds with duration between 1.5 and 5.5 years, 5.5 and 9.5 years, and over 9.5 years, respectively, as being in the short-duration, medium-duration and long-duration sectors. Recall these are not necessarily the original nor the remaining maturities of the bonds; therefore, they require some justification.

Table 14.5 Panel regression for the full sample of investor and duration groups

	dym
dmf_flow	0.124 (1.35)
FOI_flow	0.063 (0.65)
dlevel	1.015 (33.74)**
dslope	0.185 (8.52)**
N_Clust	85
N	3226
Time fixed effects	Yes
Cusip fixed effects	Yes

This table presents the results of fixed-effects panel regressions of normalized flows on yields. The dependent variable "dym" is the monthly change in yields. The explanatory variables "dmf_flow" and "FOI_flow" are the percentage flows, by domestic mutual funds and foreign official institutions, respectively. The flow variables are changes in the par value of holdings (by investor type) normalized by total outstanding stock of the bond. The variables "dlevel" and "dslope" are the changes in the level and slope factors and are included as controls. The data are at a monthly frequency from 01/2004 to 12/2013. The regressions include year and bond fixed effects. One, two and three stars denote statistical significance of the coefficient at the 10%, 5% and 1% levels, respectively

Source: Authors' calculations

First, on the short side, we chose the 1.5-year duration cutoff to distinguish between bond and money market investors. Typically, money market investors invest in Treasury bills issued originally as discount instruments of less than 1-year maturity but sometimes might mix older bonds with up to remaining maturity of 18 months. Second, the cutoff between the short- and medium-duration sectors was selected so that this sector includes all the original two- and five-year benchmark bonds. Some GoC bonds, on occasion, have been issued as a benchmark and then become a new one in a shorter maturity as they roll down.

The label "short-duration" is not intended to convey the message that this is a low amount of duration risk; it just indicates that the duration risk is the lowest of the three segments in our sample. This segment of the bond market is in fact the most active in terms of trading volume (Bulusu and Gungor 2018) and encompasses a broad spectrum of bond investors. Given that it includes the aforementioned benchmarks, it is used by repo traders, for futures contracts and cash transactions alike. The cutoff between medium- and long-duration sectors was chosen to exclude all the originally issued 10-year benchmarks from the medium-term sector. In other words, all 10-year benchmarks are in the long-duration sector. Finally, although the Government of Canada has issued 50-year bonds recently, the upper bound is innocuous as in our sample all bonds have less than 30 years' duration. We perform some robustness checks on cutoff choices at the end of this section.

14.3.1 Short-Duration Bond Sector

Table 14.6 reports the results when we only consider bonds with short duration, defined as the bonds with duration between 1.5 and 5.5 years. Column 1 reports the regression results when we consider only Canadian mutual fund and foreign official investor in the aggregate. Columns 2 and 3 report the results when we consider each the clienteles within each group of investor types (index vs. non-index for mutual funds, active vs. passive for foreign official investors). Column 3 focuses on bonds with age equal to or larger than 6 months.

When investors are considered in the aggregate, we find that bond flows from Canadian mutual funds are positively correlated with yields, suggesting that mutual funds as a group provide liquidity to the bond market. On the other hand, bond flows from foreign official investors are negatively correlated with yields, suggesting that foreign official investors in aggregate are liquidity demanders when trading GoC bonds. The coefficient is

Table 14.6 Panel regression for the short-duration (1.5- to 5.5-year) bond sector

	(1)	(2)	(3)
			Seasoned (>0.5 years)
dmf_flow	0.321 (3.51)***		
FOI_flow	−0.262 (2.37)**		
dmf_flow_index		−0.120 (0.83)	−0.048 (0.35)
dmf_flow_nonindex		0.484 (3.92)***	0.626 (4.69)***
FOI_flow_mandate		−0.397 (2.42)**	−0.414 (2.11)**
FOI_flow_nomandate		−0.062 (0.32)	−0.013 (0.06)
N_Clust	65	64	63
N	1442	1424	1267
Time fixed effects	Yes	Yes	Yes
Bond fixed effects	Yes	Yes	Yes

This table presents the results of fixed-effects panel regressions of normalized flows on yield changes in the short-duration sector. The dependent variable is the monthly change in yields. In column (1), the explanatory variables "dmf_flow" and "FOI_flow" are the percentage flows, by domestic mutual funds and foreign official institutions, respectively. The flow variables are changes in the par value of holdings (by investor type) normalized by total outstanding stock of the bond. In columns (2) and (3), "dmf_flow_index" and "dmf_flow_nonindex" are the percentage flows by index (or passive) and active (or non-index) funds, respectively. In addition, also in columns (2) and (3), "FOI_flow_mandate" and "FOI_flow_nomandate" refer to the flows by strict-mandate and non-strict-mandate foreign official institutions, respectively. In all regressions the change in the level and slope factors are included as controls. Coefficients are not reported for the controls. Data are at monthly frequency from 01/2004 to 12/2013. The regressions include year and bond fixed effects. One, two and three stars denote statistical significance of the coefficient at the 10%, 5% and 1% levels, respectively

Source: Authors calculations

both statistically and economically significant. For example, a one standard deviation increase in holding by foreign official investors is associated with about 26 bps drop in the short-duration bond yield.

When investor subtypes are considered, we find that the positive relationship between yield changes and bond flows for Canadian mutual fund is mostly contributed by active mutual funds, while active foreign official investors are the ones whose holding changes are linked with yield changes. This result is consistent with the anecdotal story that since the great financial crisis and the European debt crisis, the Canadian dollar-denominated asset has become an emerging preferred designation for foreign official reserve funds (Pomorski et al. 2014). Since short-term bonds constitute a significant part of their portfolio, foreign official investors' demand for short-term bonds is therefore relatively inelastic. These investors are likely to be liquidity takers in the GoC market. On the other hand, our results show that the active Canadian fixed-income mutual funds generally reduce their holdings of short-duration bonds when the yield decreases and increase when the yield increases. In the aggregate, active Canadian fixed-income funds appear to be a contrarian or carry-oriented investor in the short bond sector during the sample period. Finally, we find the association between mutual fund holding changes and yield changes is significantly stronger for bonds 6 months old or more, which is consistent with the institutional setup in Canada as newly issued bonds typically become liquid, heavily traded benchmark bonds after a few months of issuance.

14.3.2 *Medium-Duration Bond Sector*

Table 14.7 reports the regression results for the medium-duration bond sector. As in the previous table, column 1 records the result when mutual funds and foreign official investors are considered in the aggregate and the

Table 14.7 Panel regression for the medium-duration (5.6 and 9.5-year) sector

	(1)	*(2)*	*(3)*
	All	*All*	*Age (>0.5 years)*
dmf_flow	−0.172 (2.05)*		
FOI_flow	0.643 (5.16)***		
dmf_flow_index		−1.114 (2.62)**	−1.118 (2.88)**
dmf_flow_nonindex		−0.075 (0.66)	−0.134 (1.31)
FOI_flow_mandate		0.622 (4.81)***	0.616 (4.85)***
FOI_flow_nomandate		0.736 (1.42)	0.819 (1.50)
N_Clust	17	17	16
N	558	534	509
Time fixed effects	Yes	Yes	Yes
Bond fixed effects	Yes	Yes	Yes

This table presents the results of fixed-effects panel regressions of normalized flows on yield changes in the medium-duration sector. The dependent variables are monthly changes in yields. In column (1), the explanatory variables "dmf_flow" and "FOI_flow" are the percentage flows, by domestic mutual funds and foreign official institutions, respectively. The flow variables are changes in the par value of holdings (by investor type) normalized by total outstanding stock of the bond. In columns (2) and (3), "dmf_flow_index" and "dmf_flow_nonindex" are the percentage flows by index (or passive) and active (or non-index) funds, respectively. In addition, also in columns (2) and (3), "FOI_flow_mandate" and "FOI_flow_nomandate" refer to the flows by strict-mandate and non-strict-mandate foreign official institutions, respectively. In all regressions, the change in the level and slope factors are included as controls. Coefficients are not reported for the controls. The sample period is 01/2004 to 12/2013. The regressions include year and CUSIP fixed effects. One, two and three stars denote statistical significance of the coefficient at the 10, 5 or 1% levels, respectively (i.e., *$p < 0.1$; **$p < 0.05$; ***$p < 0.01$)

Source: Authors calculations

other columns consider the subcategories. In column 1, the pattern of effects is the reverse of what is found in the case of the short-duration sector. Bond flows from domestic mutual funds are negatively correlated with yields changes, suggesting that they are market liquidity demanders. On the other hand, bond flows from foreign official investors are generally positively correlated with yield changes, suggesting that they provide liquidity to the market by acting as contrarian investors.

Columns 2 and 3 report regression results when the different clienteles for each investor type are considered. We find that the negative correlation between bond flows and yield changes is mostly contributed by index funds. Although the research on index fund behavior is beyond the scope of this chapter, we interpret our finding to be consistent with the hypothesis that index mutual funds generally tend to sell medium-duration bonds that have lost benchmark status or when the time-to-maturity has decreased below a certain threshold. At the same time, index funds will purchase newly issued medium-duration bonds or bonds that have just acquired their benchmark status. Although index funds put significant effort into controlling effects from rebalancing, our regression results suggest that in aggregate they might be paying market impact costs.

On the other hand, the positive association between foreign official investors' holding changes and yield changes is contributed by the active foreign official investors. Although we describe them as investors with a strict mandate, this result suggests that the active foreign official investors behave somewhat opportunistically trading medium-duration bonds. Finally, we find that whether the bond is older than 6 months does not materially impact the regression results.

14.3.3 Long-Duration Bond Sector

Table 14.8 reports the regression results for the long-duration bond sector. As in the previous tables, column 1 records the result when mutual funds and foreign official investors are considered in the aggregate and the other columns consider the subcategories. Bond flows from both domestic funds and foreign official investors are negatively correlated with yields changes, suggesting that they are liquidity demanders or appear to cause a price impact.

Again, column 2 reports the regression results when clienteles of investor subtypes are considered. We find that the negative correlation between bond flows and yield changes is mostly contributed by non-index funds, and in close to the same magnitude that the index funds but in the medium-duration sector.

Table 14.8 Panel regression for the long-duration (9.6- and 30-year) bond sector

	(1)	*(2)*	*(3)*
			Coupon > 5%
dmf_flow	−0.978 (2.72)**		
FOI_flow	−0.601 (2.12)*		
dmf_flow_index		−0.372 (0.27)	−0.173 (0.09)
dmf_flow_nonindex		−1.045 (2.59)**	−1.527 (5.05)***
FOI_flow_mandate		−0.613 (2.31)**	−0.621 (2.88)**
FOI_flow_nomandate		−0.670 (0.39)	−1.451 (0.71)
N_Clust	10	10	7
N	428	428	340
Time fixed effects	Yes	Yes	Yes
Bond fixed effects	Yes	Yes	Yes

This table presents the results of fixed-effects panel regressions of normalized flows on yield changes in the long-duration sector. The dependent variables are monthly changes in yields. In column (1), the explanatory variables "dmf_flow" and "FOI_flow" are the percentage flows, by domestic mutual funds and foreign official institutions, respectively. The flow variables are changes in the par value of holdings (by investor type) normalized by total outstanding stock of the bond. In columns (2) and (3), "dmf_flow_index" and "dmf_flow_nonindex" are the percentage flows by index (or passive) and active (or non-index) funds, respectively. In addition, also in columns (2) and (3), "FOI_flow_mandate" and "FOI_flow_nomandate" refer to the flows by strict-mandate and non-strict-mandate foreign official institutions, respectively. In all regressions the change in the level and slope factors are included as controls. Coefficients are not reported for the controls. The sample period is 01/2004 to 12/2013. The regressions include year and CUSIP fixed effects. One, two and three stars denote statistical significance of the coefficient at the 10, 5 or 1% levels, respectively (i.e., $^*p < 0.1$; $^{**}p < 0.05$; $^{***}p < 0.01$)

Source: Authors calculations

In the case of the subtypes of foreign official institutions, the negative association between foreign official investors' holding changes and the yield changes is largely due to the flow of active foreign official investors. Contrary to the medium-duration sector, this result suggests that due to their mandate in this sector, their behavior is associated with a price impact. These findings are reinforced by an additional regression with the subtypes for the subset of bonds with original coupons larger than 5%. Given the sample, this selection in effect chooses the older bonds that were issued when interest rates were higher.

14.3.4 Robustness Checks

We perform additional robustness tests to gauge the sensitivity of our results to the duration cutoff points. Specifically, for each duration group (short, medium, long), we re-ran the regressions by perturbing the upper and lower cutoff points by +1 or −1 year. For example, for the medium-duration segment, since it is originally defined as those bonds with duration between 5.6 and 9.5 years, we re-estimated the coefficients for the following alternative duration intervals: 4.6–9.5, 6.6–9.5, 5.6–8.5 and 5.6–10.5 years. A similar logic applies for bonds of short and long duration.

For the short-duration segment, we find that the changes in the cutoff points only alter the main findings for the case of foreign official institutions and only in one case: specifically, we found that flows from strict-mandate official investors are not significant when we consider the 2.5–5.5-year duration group, while flows from index mutual funds now appear to be significantly negatively related to yield changes. Importantly, for all other combinations, flows from non-index (or active) mutual funds are always found to be significantly positively related to yield changes, while flows from strict-mandate official investors in otherwise all other cases are still found to be significantly negatively related to yield changes, as in the baseline case.

For the medium-duration segment, we find that the changes in cutoff points never alter the conclusions obtained from the baseline case: flows from index mutual funds are significantly negatively related to yield changes, while flows from strict-mandate official investors are positively related to yield changes.

For the long-duration segment, like the case of short-duration bonds, we find that the changes in cutoff points only alter the main findings for the case of foreign official institutions: flows for non-mandate official institutions become significantly positively related to yields in the 8.6–30-year duration segment. However, the significantly negative relationship between non-index (or active) mutual fund flows and yield changes found in the baseline results remains significant throughout the different changes considered, as is the significantly negative relationship between strict-mandate official investor flows and yields in all other cases considered. We conclude from these tests that the main findings in our baseline regressions are in general robust to alternative definitions of the duration groups.

14.4 Conclusion and Future Work

The great financial crisis and the European debt crisis made Canadian dollar-denominated assets attractive to many foreign reserves managers. In this chapter, we study the empirical relationship between flows into Government of Canada sovereign bonds by different institutional investors and their yield changes. Our unique dataset allows us to study the effects of bond-level holding changes by two different groups of investors: Canadian fixed-income mutual funds and foreign official investors.

We find that the empirical relationship between flows and yield changes depends both on the type of investor and the characteristics of the bond being purchased. For short-duration bonds, we find that non-index mutual fund flows are positively related to yield changes (i.e., negatively related to price increases), while strict-mandate foreign official institution flows are negatively related to yield changes. These effects suggest that mutual funds' role in this segment is to provide liquidity (by buying the bond when its price has gone down or, alternatively, demanding a price concession to accommodate a trade), while official institutions' demands cause price pressure, pushing down its yield. For medium-duration bonds, index fund flows are negatively related to yields, while strict-mandate official investor flows are positively related to yields; index fund flows appear to be causing price impact, while official investor's flows resemble either liquidity providers or momentum traders that chase bonds whose yields have increased. Finally, for long-duration bonds, we find that both strict-mandate foreign official institution and non-index funds appear to cause price impact, as both types of flows are negatively related to yields.

One caveat to our analysis is that, although we explain our findings in terms of a causal relationship between flows and yields, the contemporaneous relationship between holding changes and yields that we estimate is not necessarily indicative of a causal relationship, although in our regressions we control for other factors that might cause changes in yields. Future work could explore valid instruments for changes in demand or a natural experiment that could allow for a direct causal interpretation of regression coefficients.

Notes

1. Since the Act introduced penalties for funds considered to be underfunded, it provided strong incentives to hold the asset whose changes in value were most correlated with the present value of pension liabilities, namely, long-term real bonds.
2. http://www5.statcan.gc.ca/cansim/a26?lang=eng&id=3780121.
3. Since our sample changes over time, some of the increase in GoC holdings is due to a certain investor moving the safekeeping of their GoC portfolio to the Bank of Canada, even if the portfolio may have already been purchased before the date when it is incorporated in the sample. Therefore, our analysis focuses on changes of holdings instead of the level of the holdings.

4. Due to confidentiality restrictions, we are not able to reveal more details on the trading behavior of the custody clients of the Bank of Canada we used to classify our investors.
5. Due to the sample coverage difference, the sample period for all foreign official investors is longer than both active and passive foreign official investors.

References

Andritzky, J. (2012). Government bonds and their investors: What are the facts and do they matter. *IMF Working Paper No. 12-158.*

Bulusu, N., & Gungor, S. (2018). Government of Canada securities in the cash, repo and securities lending markets. *Bank of Canada Staff Discussion Paper No. 2018-4.*

Feunou, B., Fontaine, J.-S., Kyeong, J., & Sierra, J. (2015). Foreign flows and their effects on government of Canada yields. *Bank of Canada Staff Analytical Note No. 2015-1.*

Greenwood, R., & Vayanos, D. (2010). Price pressure in the government bond market. *American Economic Review, 100*(2), 585–590.

Krishnamurthy, A., & Vissing-Jorgensen, A. (2012). The aggregate demand for treasury debt. *Journal of Political Economy, 120*(2), 233–267.

Pomorski, L., Rivadeneyra, F., & Wolfe, E. (2014). The Canadian dollar as reserve currency. *Bank of Canada Review, 2014*(Spring), 1–11.

Sierra, J. (2014). International capital flows and bond risk premia. *Quarterly Journal of Finance, 4*(1), 1–36.

Vayanos, D., & Villa, J.-L. (2009). A preferred-habitat model of the term structure of interest rates. *NBER Working Paper No. 15487.*

Index[1]

[1] Note: Page numbers followed by 'n' refer to notes.

N. Bulusu et al. (eds.), *Advances in the Practice of Public Investment Management*, https://doi.org/10.1007/978-3-319-90245-6

The manufacturer's authorised representative in the EU is Springer
Nature Customer Service Centre GmbH, Europaplatz 3, 69115 Heidelberg,
Germany. If you have any concerns regarding our products, please
contact ProductSafety@springernature.com

Printed and bound by CPI Group (UK) Ltd, Croydon, CR0 4YY
30/09/2026
02225235-0004